New Realism and Contemporary Philosophy

Also Available from Bloomsbury

Metanoia: A Speculative Ontology of Language, Thinking, and the Brain,
Armen Avanessian and Anke Hennig
Romanticism and Speculative Realism, ed. by Chris Washington and
Anne C. McCarthy
Lacanian Realism: Political and Clinical Psychoanalysis, Duane Rousselle
Genealogies of Speculation: Materialism and Subjectivity since Structuralism,
ed. by Suhail Malik and Armen Avanessian

New Realism and Contemporary Philosophy

Edited by Gregor Kroupa and Jure Simoniti

BLOOMSBURY ACADEMIC
LONDON • NEW YORK • OXFORD • NEW DELHI • SYDNEY

BLOOMSBURY ACADEMIC
Bloomsbury Publishing Plc
50 Bedford Square, London, WC1B 3DP, UK
1385 Broadway, New York, NY 10018, USA
29 Earlsfort Terrace, Dublin 2, Ireland

BLOOMSBURY, BLOOMSBURY ACADEMIC and the Diana logo are trademarks of
Bloomsbury Publishing Plc

First published in Great Britain 2020
This paperback edition published in 2022

Copyright © Gregor Kroupa and Jure Simoniti, 2020

Gregor Kroupa and Jure Simoniti have asserted their right under the Copyright, Designs
and Patents Act, 1988, to be identified as Editors of this work.

For legal purposes the Acknowledgements on p. ix constitute an extension
of this copyright page.

Cover design by Charlotte Daniels
Cover image: Die Toteninsel (*The Island of the Dead*) by Arnold Böcklin (1883)
(© Peter Horree / Alamy)

This work is published open access subject to a Creative Commons
Attribution-NonCommercial-NoDerivatives 3.0 licence (CC BY-NC-ND 3.0,
https://creativecommons.org/licenses/by-nc-nd/3.0/). You may re-use, distribute,
and reproduce this work in any medium for non-commercial purposes, provided
you give attribution to the copyright holder and the publisher and provide
a link to the Creative Commons licence.

Bloomsbury Publishing Plc does not have any control over, or responsibility for, any
third-party websites referred to or in this book. All internet addresses given in this book
were correct at the time of going to press. The author and publisher regret any
inconvenience caused if addresses have changed or sites have ceased to exist, but can
accept no responsibility for any such changes.

A catalogue record for this book is available from the British Library.

Library of Congress Cataloging-in-Publication Data

Names: Kroupa, Gregor, editor. | Simoniti, Jure, 1977- editor.
Title: New realism and contemporary philosophy / edited by Gregor Kroupa and Jure Simoniti.
Description: London; New York: Bloomsbury Academic, 2020. |
Includes bibliographical references and index. | Summary: "In the field of contemporary continental
ontology, Speculative realist thinkers are now grappling with the genealogy of their ideas in the
history of modern philosophy. The Speculative Realism movement prompted a debate,
criticizing the predominant postmodernist orientation in philosophy, which located its origins in
Kantian "correlationism" which supposedly ended the period of early modern naive realist
metaphysics by showing that the mind and the outside world can only ever be understood as
correlates. The debate over a new kind of realism has attracted many supporters and critics. In order to
refocus its specific interpretation of modern philosophy in general and of the Kantian gesture in
particular, this volume brings together major authors working on contemporary ontology and historians
of ideas. It underlines and illustrates the fact that contemporary continental philosophy is
rediscovering its past in original ways by productively re-interpreting some of the key concepts
of modern philosophy. The perspectives and accounts of the key concepts of the history of philosophy
are different in the views of individual contributors, and sometimes radically so, yet the discussion between
contemporary realists and their critics shows that the real battleground of new ideas lies not in developing the
philosophical motifs of the end of the 20th century, but rather in rethinking the milestones of
modern philosophy"– Provided by publisher.

Identifiers: LCCN 2020009667 (print) | LCCN 2020009668 (ebook) | ISBN 9781350101777 (hardback) |
ISBN 9781350101760 (ebook) | ISBN 9781350101784 (epub)
Subjects: LCSH: Realism.
Classification: LCC B835 .N495 2020 (print) | LCC B835 (ebook) | DDC 149/.2–dc23
LC record available at https://lccn.loc.gov/2020009667
LC ebook record available at https://lccn.loc.gov/2020009668'

ISBN: HB: 978-1-3501-0177-7
PB: 978-1-3503-3627-8
ePDF: 978-1-3501-0176-0
eBook: 978-1-3501-0178-4

Typeset by RefineCatch Limited, Bungay, Suffolk

To find out more about our authors and books visit www.bloomsbury.com
and sign up for our newsletters.

Contents

Preface *Gregor Kroupa and Jure Simoniti*		vi
Acknowledgments		ix
1	"Philosophical Snuff": The Speculative Story of the Mind *Miran Božovič*	1
2	Leibniz's Linguistic Realism *Gregor Kroupa*	19
3	Desert Islands and the Origins of Antirealism *Jure Simoniti*	41
4	To Make Truth: Ontology, Epistemology, Technology *Maurizio Ferraris*	73
5	The Real Scandal *Lee Braver*	85
6	Realism with a Straight Face: A Response to Leonard Lawlor *Graham Harman*	99
7	A Return to the Pre-critical? On Meillassoux's Speculative Realism and a More General Problem *Zdravko Kobe*	113
8	Meta-transcendentalism and Error-First Ontology: The Cases of Gilbert Simondon and Catherine Malabou *Adrian Johnston*	145
9	On the Essence and Existence of So-called "Fictional Objects" *Markus Gabriel*	179
10	Klein Bottle: *Le tube de caption*, or, the Subject's Snout *Slavoj Žižek*	195
Notes on contributors		211
Index		213

Preface

"Realism" is undoubtedly *the* watchword of twenty-first century continental philosophy. It seems as if, suddenly, everyone calls herself a realist. Moreover, one might get the impression that the entire heterogeneous field of contemporary realism—in which the adjectives "new" and "speculative" combine well with both "realism" and "materialism"—is approaching the phase of maturity.

At the outset, each doctrine tends to be preoccupied with implementing one preparatory, methodological "basic" procedure. The invention that put speculative realism on the map was the insight into the necessity of thinking being outside any correlation with thought; consequently, the first operation to be performed was the subtraction of the human perspective from the order of being. Thus, Quentin Meillassoux's aim was to establish the possibility of making claims about the time prior to the advent of humanity, a position he proposed to found upon the mathematical absolute. In Graham Harman's object-oriented ontology, the human relation to the world was methodically leveled down to being only one of the many possible relations between objects. Iain Hamilton Grant, in his transcendental naturalism, advocated a reduction of mental, social, and cultural phenomena to the more fundamental level of the pure productivity of nature preceding all human and individual forms. Furthermore, Ray Brassier argued for the strict exclusion of every possible human sense from the world by posing the "transcendental extinction" of humanity as a necessary condition of thought. In short, the procedures of speculative realists came across as eliminativist and subtractive, indeed, quite literally so in the cases of Brassier and Meillassoux, creating the appearance of a somewhat flattened, leveled representation of being. In this sense, one could speak of a "reductive phase" of the movement.

However, after the first stage of aspiring to overcome the mental constraints and inhibitions of the past, there usually follows a second, "productive" phase. Just as Descartes, after bringing the aberrations of doubt to the point of certainty and defining the principles of knowledge of clear and distinct ideas, had to venture into the open terrain of physical ontology, the contemporary realists too are becoming increasingly engaged in proposing more positive, applied, hands-on, determinate, and substantial programs of disclosing reality in its anti-humanist dimensions.

This volume discusses a range of topics that have proved stimulating since 2007, when the inaugural speculative realism conference took place in London. It builds upon the fact that the early phase of the movement succeeded in winning back the right for philosophy to engage with a range of questions that had been deemed unworthy of serious contemporary thought. However, this has often led to misunderstandings and simplistic readings of its treatment of the correlation and the transcendental, to the point that it was sometimes suggested that any critique of transcendentalism must inevitably fall back into dogmatism. The contributions in this volume, in addition to exhibiting some very original approaches to reality, recognize the necessity to resume the original premises of speculative realism, both apologetically and critically.

Graham Harman thus provides a clearly written account of the reasons why contemporary realism does not simply amount to a return to pre-critical realism; along with it, his chapter provides a summary of the notable differences between his own object-oriented ontology and Meillassoux's project of speculative materialism. On the other hand, Zdravko Kobe offers an in-depth critique of the main premises of Meillassoux's project and argues that the relations between the so-called ancestral, correlationist, and speculative theses are incompatible.

The contributions of Gregor Kroupa and Miran Božovič build on the topics inspired by Meillassoux while deliberately placing them in the context of pre-critical philosophy. Kroupa outlines the opposition between linguistic realism and determinism in the history of modern philosophy; on this basis, he portrays Leibniz as someone who uniquely combines both approaches in the framework of a non-subjective idealist ontology that is very different from the one criticized by contemporary realists. In the same vein, Božovič reverses the de-humanizing perspective of contemporary realism. Instead of pursuing the narrative of ancestrality and extinction, in which the earth is contemplated without human minds, he makes recourse to the thought experiments and the literary imagination of early-modern spiritualism in order to explore the pre-Kantian visions of human minds existing beyond this earth. By contrast, Jure Simoniti endeavors to track down the origins of Western antirealism and, for this purpose, examines the relation between the emergence of a surplus-truth and the subsequent disclosure of an inhuman, non-conceptual reality. Simoniti argues for a strict separation of the regime of *truth* from the regime of *reality*, the two philosophical concepts that benefit from their newly acquired dignity in contemporary realism.

Another take on the issue of truth and reality is then presented by Maurizio Ferraris and, to some extent, Markus Gabriel, the two advocates of new realism. Ferraris proposes the concept of "mesotruth" as mediating between ontology and epistemology, and argues that it only emerges from reality as a product of technology, i.e., a set of practical, sometimes pre-conceptual actions and skills. Gabriel, on the other hand, further develops his distinction between existing and fictional entities and explains that interpretations of works of art rely on so-called meta-fictional objects (fictional characters, musical scores, etc.), which require imagination or aesthetic experience to be completed. Gabriel then makes a case for realism of fictional entities by providing them with his fields-of-sense ontology in which objects are bundles of truths belonging to a specific domain.

In his chapter, Lee Braver takes a different stance toward realism. He sees the point of contact between reality and the subject not in terms of truth or intelligibility, both being comprised within a transcendental framework, but rather in experience. It is precisely the experiences of failure to know the world, ones that baffle us and unsettle our lives, that witness the disclosure of reality beyond the constraints of intelligible forms. For Adrian Johnston, however, transcendentality is not to be viewed as incompatible with realism. On the contrary, he argues, there is nothing inherently idealist in transcendentality that would prohibit the move beyond subjectivity. In this sense, Johnston's "critical-dialectical naturalism" starts from the point of spontaneous subjectivity and, on this basis, dialectically retrogresses toward an ontology of pre-subjective nature which, in turn, serves as the foundation of every epistemology. Finally, Slavoj Žižek maintains that only the excess of the Real, the place of inscription of the subject, can make the incomplete whole of reality consistent; using a number of examples, including the Klein bottle, the Real is shown to be the stain, the gap, the torsion within reality itself.

When all is said and done, it is this element of excess that represents a common feature that unites many of the otherwise diverse thinkers both of this volume and of contemporary realism in general. After the first swing of speculative realism left us with nothing but an image of a dull, indiscriminate, flatly unmanned outside world, now, in an attempt to elaborate and justify a more viable and robust realist stance, a quest to define *the point of surplus* over the mere subsistence of reality has begun. Many contributions are on track to catch in the act a transcendent factor, an irruption, an emergent product, i.e., an entity not simply derivable from the sensual, given aspects of our quotidian world. Žižek insists on the Real as the subjective condition of a consistent reality establishing itself in the first place; Harman maintains the irreducibility of the excessive "thing-in-itself" to any relation between the objects of reality; Ferraris professes the concept of "mesotruth" as emerging from reality by way of technology; Braver pins great hopes on the possibility of intellectually transcendent experiences; and Simoniti poses the surplus-truth as an indispensable condition of realism. It seems as if, for some of the contributors, an excessive element is needed from where any kind of methodology of disclosing the world can be applied at all, thereby enabling a new outlook on reality, one no longer constrained by the twentieth-century totalitarianism of phenomenological perspectives, hermeneutic interpretations, language games, metaphorical and metonymical transfers, and common sense. And there is probably no reason not to name this surplus simply "truth."

Gregor Kroupa and Jure Simoniti
Ljubljana, February 2020

Acknowledgments

The editors wish to thank the Slovenian Research Agency for the financial support. This book could not have been published in open access form without the generous funding of the research project "Language and Science: the Possibility of Realism in Modern Philosophy" (no. J6-7364) conducted at the University of Ljubljana, Faculty of Arts.

1

"Philosophical Snuff": The Speculative Story of the Mind[1]

Miran Božovič

With speculative realism, a certain argumentative strategy, which became outmoded with Kant's transcendental turn, seems to have been reinstated in philosophy: namely, the strategy of thought experiment, which transfers the philosopher (and his reader) to another world, i.e., in either the past or future state of this planet or even to a different celestial body altogether. It is there, in the purity of a new, contrived, sometimes entirely fictional setting, that the authentic scene of truth can finally be thoroughly and unconditionally enacted. Along these lines, the opening move of the entire movement of speculative realism consisted in Meillassoux devising a case of an "arche-fossil" *not* being gazed upon by the "ancestral witness" in the times preceding the emergence of the human race.[2] Brassier, similarly, but inversely, invents the doctrine of "transcendental extinction," picturing a world devoid of humans as the ultimate test of the scope and purview of what reality is really about.[3] But it is perhaps little known that the great philosophers before Kant resorted to similar scenarios of envisaging completely novel locations and environments, in which they hoped the bounds of their terrestrial, everyday existence would be magically circumvented.[4]

In this sense, a thought experiment always seems to express, in the most concise manner possible, what the confines of the mentality of a respective era actually amount to. Accordingly, since in the twenty-first century the fundamental limitation not to be trespassed is that of the human's "correlation" to the world, it is *a world without man* which is most commonly fantasized about. By contrast, the imagination of the seventeenth and eighteenth centuries appears to have been constrained by an entirely different set of limitations that needed to be overcome. At that time, the great "prison of thought" was not guarded by consciousness and language, as in the twentieth century, but predominantly by our own earthly corporeality. It thus became some sort of ultimate philosophical fantasy of the spiritualist, idealist age extending from Descartes to Berkeley to imagine the human mind no longer weighted down by the fleshly impediments of its burdensome body. Suddenly, the mind was envisioned as being able to travel anywhere in the universe, to communicate with other minds directly, fully, and instantaneously, to surpass the limits of human mortality, and to develop and accumulate knowledge *ad infinitum*.

Thus, while today's realists ruminate on the possibilities of standing face-to-face with non-human reality, the pre-Kantian idealists dreamt about exceeding the bodily boundaries between souls, thus enabling the mind to gain direct, intimate access to the minds of others. The popular philosophical reverie was not a world without man, i.e., the material substance without the supplement of the mind, but rather *man without body* and, correspondingly, even an entire world liberated from the shackles of corporeal reality.

The intention of this chapter is therefore to present some cases of this "speculative life" of the mind in seventeenth- and early eighteenth-century philosophy, the aim of which was to transcend the inhibitions imposed on our thinking by the carnal constraints of human existence.

I Descartes among the Lapp shamans

In the last chapter of his *Essay concerning Human Understanding,* John Locke famously says that "the scene of ideas that makes one man's thoughts cannot be laid open to the immediate view of another,"[5] and that, therefore, for us to be able to communicate our thoughts to others or preserve them for our own future use, signs of ideas are also necessary. It is not hard to imagine that, for centuries, philosophers were intrigued by the idea of one's thoughts being directly accessible to another, that is, without one's wishing in any way to communicate them to the other. It is perhaps because it appears to be so improbable and implausible that this idea is found mostly in the works in the genre of speculative or even fictional history of philosophy. The thinker most often associated with the notion of the ability to read the thoughts of others is Descartes, which is hardly surprising, given the privileged status of thought in his metaphysical theory as the principal attribute of mental substance.

One such work of speculative philosophical historiography is a slim booklet by Pierre-Daniel Huet, *Nouveaux mémoires pour servir à l'histoire du cartésianisme,* originally published in 1692 under the pseudonym M. G. de L'A. It is a highly satirical piece of writing focused on a traveler with a bent for Cartesian philosophy who has heard rumors on his travels that in Lapland there is a stranger teaching Cartesian philosophy with such authority and confidence that Descartes could not have done it better himself. Since Descartes had officially been dead for several years by then, the traveler decides to visit Lapland to investigate the rumors on the spot, and it transpires that the learned stranger is none other than Descartes himself, who did not really die in February 1650, but only feigned his death. In what follows, Descartes recounts for the benefit of the inquisitive visitor—through a dialogue with Pierre Chanut, French ambassador to Sweden, in whose house in Stockholm Descartes staged his own death—the series of events which brought him to Lapland. Disappointed by the lack of understanding of his teachings, by the ridicule and contempt with which his metaphysical theory was received—to give just one example, the medicine Descartes's valet brings him one day from the pharmacist is wrapped in paper which Descartes recognizes with horror as a page torn out of his *Meditations*[6]—he decides to withdraw to the extreme north, to Lapland, where he expects to find a much more receptive and appreciative audience for his metaphysical theories. He hopes to find peace and solitude there, and to be able to devote himself to contemplation and the study of nature. At the time, Lapland was obviously considered a mysterious but pure and pristine land, far from the traps of civilization. Descartes says he has always felt a strong inclination for the countries of the far north. As well as the natural phenomena such as "long summer days without night" and "long winter nights without day," the Northern Lights, termed *aurora borealis* by his contemporary Pierre Gassendi, and so forth, Descartes says he is also attracted by various supernatural phenomena, such as the ghosts which frequently appear there, demons in the form of a fly, magic cords containing a number of knots the untying of which produces wind, and so on. What most intrigues him, however, are "the astonishing effects of ... magic drums" of the Lapp shamans. By studying all these phenomena, he hopes to gain an insight into "where the natural ends and the supernatural begins" (36–7).

Descartes's retreat to the far north does not necessarily entail severing all ties with the people in the rest of the world, in particular his old friends and disciples. In maintaining these ties Descartes relies on "a great secret" (41) passed on to him by the Rosicrucians, who, he says, "know how to render themselves invisible at will," who are able "to prolong their illness-free life up to four or five hundred years," and, more importantly, who "know the thoughts of other people" (47). Although, as a rule, Descartes does not flaunt these exceptional powers—such behavior is forbidden by the strict rules of the Brotherhood of the Rosicrucians, of which he was allegedly a member—nevertheless, from time to time, he does perform a clever trick or two for the benefit of his closest friends: thus, he says, he has more than once surprised Father Mersenne by repeating before him "not only everything he [i.e., Father Mersenne] had said and done in my absence, but also everything he had thought" (50). Descartes is not going to misuse these powers, which enable him to penetrate "without the ring of Gyges and without the helmet of Pluto" into "the deepest secrets of actions of men, and not only of their actions, but also of their thoughts" (51). He is going to use them exclusively to advance and promote his own philosophy. Since the Lapps have the power to transport themselves wherever they wish by means of their magic drums, he will send them to Paris, Leyden or Utrecht to inquire about the state of the Cartesian sect; and if the need arises, he will transport himself there, too, and make himself known to his "wise friends and faithful disciples" and "give them advice and instructions necessary for the propagation of my sect and the extirpation of Peripateticism" (53–4). That is, he will advise his disciples as to the best course of defense to adopt in their verbal duels with Peripatetic adversaries and "provide them with captious distinctions, equivocal terms, and ambiguous expressions capable of holding back the shrewdest dialecticians"; he will "fortify them against all kinds of objections, and when they will find themselves caught in a flagrant contradiction ... [he] will encourage them ... to boldly save themselves by resorting to some specious argument" (54). For him to be able "to boast as long a list of commentators as Aristotle had," he "will not have to wait for as many centuries as Aristotle did," Descartes observes, and goes on to add that "one can accomplish quite a bit in five hundred years of life" (54–5).

The satire ends with Descartes's feigned death and burial in Stockholm, in which "a log wrapped in clothes" was buried instead of the metaphysician. Meanwhile, Descartes, who has hidden himself in the attic, is straining his ears in the hopes of catching what the mourners have to say about him but, regrettably, he is too far away to hear anything.

"Although he had not had this pleasure, he nevertheless had another, no less rare one of witnessing his own funeral" (71), adds Huet. Shortly afterwards, an unnamed Peripatetic visits the grave—one wonders if the mysterious visitor was not perhaps Huet himself, who visited Descartes's grave in 1652[7]—who, to his horror, notices that the inscription on the tombstone of the great "restorer of truth" does not correspond to the truth. While the inscription reads "sub hoc lapide," the tombstone itself is made of wood and only "painted to resemble stone."[8] And to make matters even worse, it was Descartes himself who composed the inscription for the tombstone during his (feigned) terminal illness. Thereupon, the Peripatetic "furtively and maliciously" crosses out the word "lapide" and adds, in charcoal, the word "ligneo" (72)—and thereby restores the truth of things.

One of the more interesting ramifications of this satire, which is definitely not its author's best work, is that the success of Cartesian philosophy and the ensuing decline of the Peripatetic philosophy were in no small degree helped by Descartes's subsequent, that is, "posthumous" interventions in developments on the philosophical stage, made possible by his exceptional powers, first and foremost, by his uncanny ability to read the thoughts of others. It was Descartes's knowing the thoughts of others that gave his disciples an important, perhaps even decisive, advantage over their Peripatetic adversaries and enabled the Cartesians to emerge victorious in verbal combats with the Peripatetics. What people witnessing such an exchange mistakenly took to be a series of well-reasoned arguments on the part of Descartes's disciple and his effective, convincing, refutations of the Peripatetic's objections and counter-arguments was, in reality, nothing other than a charade. In fact, it was Descartes, who—having made himself invisible and transported himself, with the help of magic drums, from Lapland to, say, Paris—was surreptitiously literally putting words in his disciple's mouth. And these words may well have appeared carefully weighed, measured and to the point, since Descartes, owing to his ability to read his interlocutor's thoughts, knew in advance what the latter was going to say. If Descartes had not had these exceptional powers, which he owed to the Rosicrucians, and had he not, at the same time, relied on the help of Lapp shamans, the history of philosophy could well have taken an entirely different course and, in the long run, Peripatetic philosophy could, conceivably, have overshadowed or even superseded Cartesian philosophy.

Although, on the surface, the work openly ridicules Descartes—despite his exceptional powers, all he was able to come up with to help his disciples were "equivocal terms," "ambiguous expressions," "specious arguments," and so on, which could merely confuse their Peripatetic adversaries—it is, on a deeper level, actually much more than just a straightforward satire. Coming from the pen of one of the main opponents and critics of Cartesian philosophy of the period, the work could alternatively be read as a kind of mourning for the former domination of Aristotelian philosophy and a rationalization of the growing influence of Cartesian philosophy: in the context of Huet's work, seventeenth-century Aristotelian philosophers have justly felt tricked and deceived, since their failure in verbal duels with the Cartesians was due, in no small part, to the unfair advantage of the latter. The battle between the two schools for domination of the philosophical stage could be said to have been equal only if the Peripatetic philosophers, too, had been helped, in the midst of their discussions with

Cartesians, by Aristotle himself—just as their Cartesian adversaries were helped by Descartes himself—that is, only if Aristotle, having made himself invisible and being able to read the thoughts of others, had secretly whispered the answers to his disciples and indicated to them a possible line of defense against their Cartesian critics. Only this would make the duel fair and equal, since the two great masters themselves would get to face one another and cross swords through their disciples; only the one victorious in such a duel could really be said to have deservedly won.

II Aristotle the reader of Descartes

On the last page of his last work, *Éléments de physiologie,* Denis Diderot says that "it is a rather common fantasy among the living to imagine themselves dead, standing beside their own corpse, and following their own funeral."[9] A man standing next to his own corpse, Diderot goes on to add, reminds him of "a swimmer in the water looking back at his clothes, which he has left lying on the shore."[10] In Huet's *Nouveaux mémoires,* the fantasy of witnessing one's own funeral is only half-realized. In Huet, Descartes, having merely staged his own death, observes a mock funeral procession burying a log wrapped in his clothes, while the mourners, on whom he is surreptitiously eavesdropping, are tricked into believing that it is Descartes himself who is being buried. What was merely a charade in Huet, actually does take place in Brigitte Hermann's 1996 novel *Histoire de mon esprit ou le roman de la vie de René Descartes.* This beautifully written novel consists entirely of a first-person narrative, in which Descartes recounts in detail what he himself apparently called "the story of my mind."[11] The very last sentence of this voluminous novel reads: "And while they, all in tears, carried me towards the other world ..., my soul, filled with joy, finally liberated itself from my body and freely set out on the path of discovery of Truth."[12] In this sentence we hear the voice of Descartes, who is clearly observing, and commenting on, the burial of his own dead body. Even this one sentence alone would make reading the nearly 500 preceding pages worthwhile. The moment we read this sentence, everything changes; everything we have read up to that point takes on, in retrospect, an ominous and uncanny quality. In that moment, we come to realize that, all along, we have been listening to the voice of someone who has apparently crossed the divide between life and death, that is, a voice coming from beyond the grave. What Descartes has been narrating all this time from the afterlife, is essentially an account of his earthly life or this-worldly existence, that is, the story of his embodied mind. The death of the body, however, does not mean an end to the story of a mind that is "really distinct" from the body. Obviously, the story of Descartes's mind continues even after its separation from the body. Moreover, as the mind's embodied state is only a minor part of its overall existence, the story of embodied mind is merely a passing episode in its total life history, the greater part of which is formed by the story of its disembodied, "separate" existence.

Precisely such a story, that is, a story of Descartes's disembodied mind, can be found in the novel to which we now turn, namely *Voiage du Monde de Descartes* by the French Jesuit historian Gabriel Daniel, published in Paris in 1690. This delightfully imaginative novel depicts an encounter, in which the Cartesians, at the end of the seventeenth century, come face to face with Aristotle himself. It is a special merit of this novel that it shows how vertiginously complex, rich and multi-layered stories of disembodied minds can be in comparison with their earthly, embodied lives. Just how famous this novel must have been at the time can perhaps best be seen in the fact that it was translated into English soon after its original appearance and, in the next few years, also into Latin, Italian, and so forth. Before the end of the seventeenth century, Pierre Bayle writes about it with great admiration and quotes extensively from it in remark G of his *Dictionary* article "Rorarius."[13] Despite the notoriety it enjoyed at the turn of the seventeenth century, the novel later gradually fell into oblivion. It is an extraordinary piece of writing, whose genre could perhaps best be characterized as phi-fi, that is, as philosophical fiction: the author takes as his premise the Cartesian notion of the "real distinction" between mind and body and works through some of its more colorful and intriguing ramifications, such as space travel and the implicit need for a complete revision and rewriting of the history of philosophy—in the light of the novel's premise, the history of philosophy as we know it retrospectively turns out to be incomplete, if not plain wrong.

Before exploring these ramifications in more detail, let us first take a brief look at the main plot device of Father Daniel's novel. In the novel, Descartes is said to have penetrated into "the most curious Secret in the World," that is, the secret not only of "the Union of the Soul and Body," but also "that of separating, and re-uniting them when he pleas'd."[14] That is, he knew how to make his soul leave his body and return to it. As a mind or a "thinking thing," he was able to separate himself from the body or the "extended thing," to which he was joined for the duration of his earthly existence and return to it at will. As a mind, he separated himself from the body by taking "Tobacco-Snuff," which he got from an Amsterdam merchant, who had brought it from an island close to China (21). Since the pure tobacco was too strong for his taste, Descartes added "a certain Herb" to it. As Descartes believed, it was this herb "dried to Powder" that caused his soul to separate itself from the body (22). Descartes passed on some of the magic herb to one of his disciples but was unwilling to disclose its name or reveal the place where it grew (21). Apparently, it was Descartes's beloved pastime to take a pinch of snuff every now and then and, as a "separate Soul," fly around the world with great speed—"three or four thousand Leagues" per minute (20)—instructing himself in "the greatest Curiosities in Nature" (22). Immediately upon his return from such a trip, Descartes would reenter his body which, in the meantime, had been lying motionless on his bed awaiting his return. By pure coincidence, some people came to see Descartes just when he was on one of his excursions and found his inert body in bed. Unable to awaken him, that is, to bring his temporarily soulless body back to life, they assumed that Descartes had died and they buried him. Since there was now no body for him to inhabit upon his return, Descartes decided to quit this world for good and travel to the outskirts of the universe, where he still lives forty years after his supposed death. As it transpires, he has settled in "the Third Heaven," where he is busy constructing a world of his own which will run on principles laid out in his "posthumously" published treatise on cosmology *The World*.

The story of the novel is rather simple. It centers around a young man, an avid reader and student of philosophy, "determin'd to dive to the bottom of Descartes's

Philosophy" (7), who is going to visit Descartes, where he has been invited by "an old Cartesian" and "the Spirit of Father Mersenne," two of the "very few" to know the truth about his supposed death. The purpose of the visit is to witness the trial run of the world mechanism Descartes is planning to perform "before he puts the Design of his World in Execution" (37-8). The "old Cartesian," apparently as close an associate and confidant of Descartes as Father Mersenne, is also familiar with his master's secret of separating the soul from body. He is said to be in possession of a "great Quantity" of Descartes's mixture of the Chinese tobacco and the mysterious herb, by means of which he has already visited Descartes "six or seven" times in his exile on the outskirts of the universe, bringing him news from our world. Having taken Descartes's snuff, they set out for the third heaven. As it happens, on their journey through the universe, the Cartesian space travelers run into various illustrious thinkers—Socrates, Plato, and Aristotle among others—all of whom obviously also knew the secret of separating the soul from the body. As "separate Souls," these thinkers live on the Moon, where, as the space travelers are pleased to learn, they continue to work on the projects conceived while they were still living in "the lower World," that is, on the Earth. Just as Descartes is constructing his own world in the third heaven, so Plato too is ruling his own "Republick" on the Moon, that is, a state which he has established according to the principles laid out in his dialogue of the same name, the *Republic*, while Aristotle is running a philosophy school on the Moon, the new Lyceum, which he has founded and where, at the end of the seventeenth century, that is, more than 2,000 years after his supposed death, he still teaches philosophy (75), and so forth.

The following two conversations our space travelers have on their way through the heavens—one with Socrates and the other with Aristotle—neatly capture the spirit of the novel. Upon learning that the visitors are from Earth, where he is wrongly believed to be dead, Socrates recounts what actually happened in Athens in that distant year of 399 BCE. "The Soul of a Philosopher, such as I am," explains Socrates, "staid not to be dismissed from the World by the Decree of a Faction of Corrupt Judges, and the Clamours of a Multitude" (71); instead, what really happened was that upon arrest, Socrates immediately quit his body and instructed his "Familiar Spirit," that is, his *daimon*, to move in there in his place and put up a bold front until the very end, which the *daimon* did admirably well (71-2). This means that the one who listened to his death sentence with the utmost composure and self-possession, the one who calmly and courageously faced death, the one who, in short, acted as a true philosopher to the very end, was not really Socrates, but his *daimon*. Consequently, the fame and admiration Socrates has enjoyed for long centuries after his presumed death is, at least in part, undeserved, while his heroic, "philosophical death" which earned him a high place in western culture and in the personal pantheon of many later philosophers is nothing more than a myth.[15] Moreover, his reputation of being an honorable and courageous man is at least somewhat tarnished, as he avoided death through a cowardly deception, that is, by sending someone else, his *daimon*, to die in his place.

What our travelers hear from Socrates would already entail considerable revisions in the history of philosophy. At least some of Plato's dialogues of the early and middle period, such as *Apology*, *Crito*, and *Phaedo*, which all rank among his undisputed masterpieces, would very probably lose their place in Plato's canon and therefore also in the history of philosophy, since the dramatic, fateful event they all deal with, actually happened in a radically different way. As a result, these dialogues could no longer be considered as authentic, faithful, depictions of events. Would not the ruse Socrates performed at the (supposed) end of his life, also cast doubt on some of his previous actions—having once mistakenly believed that the sage who willingly drank the cup of hemlock in jail was Socrates himself, while, in fact, it was someone else, the *daimon*, who just came to inhabit Socrates' body, how are we to know that this had not also been the case on some previous occasion? For example, what if the one who had fought bravely as a hoplite in three military campaigns was not really Socrates, but the *daimon* in his body, whom Socrates had sent to fight in his place? This would mean that his reputation as a fearless warrior, too, was a result of deception. Furthermore, how would Plato react were he to realize that in some central dialogues of the early and middle period he had actually fallen victim to Socrates' deception? Moreover, in the eyes of the young Plato, Socrates' death was a turning point that profoundly influenced his decision to pursue a career in philosophy—how would he react if he knew that his own unquestionably brilliant career in philosophy was founded on a lie or deception on the part of his teacher? Not much is said about all this in the novel, although by the end of the seventeenth century, Plato could be reasonably expected to be aware of the true course of events surrounding the supposed end of Socrates' life, especially given that "'tis more than probable" that Socrates has taken up his abode "in his belov'd Disciple Plato's Commonwealth" (75), that is, in Plato's new republic on the Moon.

What the Cartesian space travelers learn in their conversation with Aristotle would entail even more radical and far-reaching revisions of the history of philosophy. As already noted, on the Moon, Aristotle is running his Lyceum where he apparently still teaches philosophy. The really interesting question, which, regrettably, the book does not address, would be: what is Aristotle's own philosophical theory like at the end of the seventeenth century, that is, with 2,000 years of growth and development behind it? While the thinkers on Earth are not even aware of the existence of the vibrant philosophical life on the Moon, the Aristotle that the space travelers encounter, on the other hand, is well acquainted with Cartesian philosophy. He says at one point, "I have seen [Descartes's] Books and pity 'em" (76). He has studied in great detail the *Meditations*, the *Discourse on Method*, and the *Principles of Philosophy, Part One*. Over several pages, he gives an authoritative interpretation of all these works and presents an especially strong critique of *Meditations* (76–85). At times, it even seems as though Aristotle is openly flaunting his knowledge of Descartes's metaphysical theory before the visiting "Gentlemen Cartesians." Obviously, Aristotle on the Moon closely follows the evolution of philosophical thought on Earth; that is, for 2,000 years he has been reading and studying the works of thinkers who have entered—and left—the philosophical stage on Earth after his supposed death and withdrawal to the Moon.[16] Descartes, on the other hand, when the travelers finally meet him face to face in the third heaven, admits to being largely ignorant of the developments taking place in philosophy on Earth in the forty years following his supposed death. For example, all Descartes knows about the state of Cartesian philosophy in "the lower World" is that it still has many followers, as well as many adversaries (176), but he has never heard of Malebranche, who is considered as one of the greatest Cartesians at the time on Earth

(196). This, explains Descartes, is in part because ever since he quit his body at the moment of his supposed death, he has been experiencing an "Indifference and Disregard ... for the Sentiments of Men" (176). Aristotle's lectures on the history of philosophy at his new Lyceum on the Moon must surely be utterly unique and precious, since they are given by a speaker who has been a living contemporary of Plotinus, St. Augustine, and St. Thomas Aquinas, as well as of Giordano Bruno, Galileo, and Descartes. Thus, to listen to his lectures on the history of philosophy would no doubt be to learn about the topic from a most knowledgeable source. But even more interesting would be to listen to Aristotle lecturing on his own philosophy: the philosophical theory Aristotle is developing in the seventeenth century on the Moon must be something entirely other than the one taught by him in the fourth century BCE at the Lyceum in Athens, since Aristotle on the Moon is no doubt familiar with all the objections to his philosophy raised over the centuries, and has, by the end of the seventeenth century, most likely resolved them and incorporated his replies to those objections into his new philosophical theory. Incidentally, in the new Lyceum on the Moon, there is a painting, recently completed, showing Aristotle as he receives "a Thunderbolt" from the hand of Minerva, to wipe out "all the Chieftains of the New Sects of Philosophy," among whom the travelers easily recognize Descartes, Gassendi, and so forth (108).[17] Aristotle, speaking about his own philosophy from the perspective of its 2,000 years of development, would undoubtedly make an incomparably more interesting interlocutor—and complex and multi-layered thinker—than Descartes, whom we encounter in the heavens a mere forty years after his presumed death putting his ideas, outlined in *The World*, into practice, and who, by his own admission, no longer bothers to read philosophy.

Another interesting implication of the novel would run as follows: we are told in the novel that the majority of the "separate Souls" wandering through space are those of philosophers, presumably because it is among the philosophers that "the Secret of separating the Soul and Body" was common knowledge (30–1; 46). This means that the founders of several philosophical schools that have flourished and declined on Earth over the centuries are still alive somewhere in space, mostly on the Moon, but their disciples on Earth, who came after them, for the most part do not know this. Thus, on Earth, it is generally believed that all thinkers from Socrates to Descartes are dead. It may, perhaps, be safely assumed that no small number of these "Philosophical Souls" are still keenly interested in philosophy and that, like Aristotle—but unlike Descartes—they, too, closely follow each other's work, all the while revising and amending their original philosophical systems in the light of criticism from each other or in view of new and inspiring ideas found in later, sometimes even centuries younger, thinkers. In light of the latest developments in the heavens, even Descartes's *The World* would seem to be in need of revision, although it can, on the Lunar time scale, still be considered a relatively recent work in the 1690s. In the original, "lower World" version of the book, Descartes famously presents the making of the "new world" as "a fable."[18] Once having completed the construction of his own world in the third heaven, however, he would most probably proceed to modify the text to reflect this fact. Written as a first-hand report describing the process of the new world's coming into being, the book would now perhaps read somewhat like the Book of Genesis. If there were inhabitants in the newly constructed world, they might well consider Descartes's *The World* as the Bible of their world, and Descartes himself as God. Let us try to picture what the history of philosophical ideas might be like in the universe of Father Daniel's novel: it is not just that, high in the heavens, representatives of various philosophical schools—most of whom could not even have met on Earth, since the schools to which they belonged are divided by centuries—would meet and exchange ideas, as for example, Duns Scotus, in the novel, comes to visit Aristotle and notices several volumes of Descartes's works (126) whereupon, perhaps, as one can easily imagine, a lively discussion ensues, in which the two interlocutors jointly criticize, say, Descartes's account of the Eucharist. It is also that, in the heavens, all these schools are still active and, what is more, they are presumably still being led by their original founders or, more precisely, their souls. On Earth, some of these schools have ceased to exist and been replaced by new ones, while some others continue to exist. In the heavens, on the other hand, all philosophical schools exist concurrently, one beside the other; it is just that some are older— sometimes even centuries older—than others, depending on the time of their first appearance on the philosophical stage. Since, with the exception of rare Cartesians, members of those schools that continue to exist on Earth after the apparent death of their founder do not know that their masters are still alive and continuing their philosophical pursuits in the heavens, most often on the Moon, there is an obvious need for a new genre of philosophical historiography, that is, at least for a history of the Lunar philosophy, as an other-worldly follow-up to its earthly history. Of the history of philosophy on Earth, this much may perhaps safely be said: that it is but a pale and meager shadow of the immensely rich and burgeoning philosophical activity taking place across the Moon. By the end of the seventeenth century, many of the "Philosophical Souls" have spent a far longer time on the Moon than they had previously on Earth. Duns Scotus, for example, when the Cartesians run into him, has been on the Moon, roughly, nine times longer than he had been on Earth. If these thinkers were anywhere near as productive on the Moon as they had been during their earthly lives, the number of their "posthumous" works, as one could surmise, would have vastly surpassed the total of their writings on Earth.

Just how radically other the Lunar philosophical canon must be, can perhaps best be seen if one considers the separate souls' extraordinary cognitive powers. Let us first take a brief look at the way the separate souls of the Cartesian space travelers communicate with one another and with the souls they meet on their way through space. Since they have no bodies to express their thoughts and ideas by speaking or writing, the souls communicate with one another "in Language Spiritual" (29), that is, by a sort of "immediate Communication of ... Thoughts" (40). However, this does not mean that one soul can in any way know the thoughts of another without the latter's consent or even against its will. The immediacy of communication of thoughts merely means that it takes place without the medium of a body. On the one hand, a body or "extended thing" has the power of speech, and makes spoken communication possible, but, on the other hand, it significantly limits the communication, since a tongue is able to pronounce "but one Syllable at a Time" (67). Speaking of apparently lengthy conversations between the separate souls, the narrator of the novel, addressing the readers, says that however much space the conversations between the separate souls may seem to have taken up on paper, in reality "they lasted but one single instant" (67). This is because a single "Spiritual Word" in which one soul communicates to another expresses more than "a thousand pronounced or written" words can convey to those who hear or read them (67). One of the space travelers—the one who took Descartes's snuff for the first time—observes that his transient out-of-body experience has taught him many novel things he will be able to put to good use when trying to explain, in the book he is writing, the way angels, as pure spiritual substances free from all matter, communicate between themselves (67). Given the spectacular expressiveness of the "Spiritual Words," the separate souls' intellectual cognitive powers must be truly exceptional to be able to take in and process such a great quantity of information at a time. In conversation with one of his disciples, Descartes likens his snuff-induced state of separation from the body to a "Trance," saying that in both these states "there is no use of the Senses; one can neither See, nor Hear, nor Feel the Impression of External Objects" (17). Yet, unlike the soul in trance, a separate soul has "Perceptions of itself" and is therefore aware of "the Cessation of its Organical Functions" (17). It is in this state of separation from the body that his soul acquired "a World of Immaterial or purely Spiritual Notices"; and the soul acquired this vast amount of spiritual knowledge, Descartes continues, "in an abundantly more perfect and lively manner" than in the embodied state in which its attention is constantly interrupted by the appearances of imagination (17). And by way of conclusion he adds: "More discoveries of Truth could be made thus in one Minute, than in ten years by the ordinary means" (17). The implication here is not that the growing impact of Cartesian philosophy and the gradual decline of Aristotelian influence in the second half of the seventeenth century is a result of Descartes's use of the substance capable of separating his soul from the body and thereby greatly enhancing its cognitive powers. As Descartes himself discovers with surprise, the secret of separating the soul from body—that is, "the Secret, of which he took himself to be the first Inventer" (31)—has been known to most of his rivals and predecessors in philosophy, including Aristotle, all of whom should therefore, in principle, be able to develop equally effective cognitive abilities. Rather, what is implied is how very intense, rich in content, and fruitful must be the life of philosophical ideas on the Moon, and how utterly complex and wildly ramified the interactions among the separate "Philosophical Souls," in comparison to those taking place between their embodied equivalents on Earth.

III "Two Selves in the same brain"

A brilliant spin-off of Father Daniel's notion of separation of soul from body by taking snuff can be found in two of the essays George Berkeley wrote for the *Guardian*. In the wonderfully clever essay No. 35 of April 21, 1713, Berkeley, writing under the assumed name of Ulysses Cosmopolita, claims to have come into possession of Descartes's obviously already notorious mixture of tobacco and the mysterious herb—or "philosophical snuff,"[19] as it is happily termed in the essay—which he says was given him by the nephew of "the author of *The Voyage to the World of Descartes*" (185), which he had apparently read and most likely enjoyed. The effect of the snuff, that is, the separation of soul from body, is exploited by Berkeley, a philosopher of ideas for whom everything exists in the mind, in a different, more innovative way. After taking the snuff and leaving his body behind, Berkeley does not simply fly around in the sky visiting far-away places. Having separated itself from its body, Berkeley's soul, rather, enters another body, which, however, it does not animate. That is, Berkeley's soul comes to inhabit another body while the latter is still being animated by its own soul—and Berkeley's soul comes to inhabit this body surreptitiously, that is, without its soul taking any notice of it.

In the essay, the Berkeley character is presented as being extremely curious and inquisitive—that is, eager to acquire knowledge in arts and sciences. And it is primarily to satisfy his intellectual curiosity that he travels the world. Eventually, his travels bring him to France, where he meets Father Daniel's nephew, who, upon learning of his thirst for knowledge, presents him with "a small box of snuff," saying that he knows "no readier way to furnish and adorn a mind with knowledge in the arts and sciences than that same snuff rightly applied" (185). The nephew then goes on to explain to Berkeley the working of the snuff in detail, saying that the soul, having separated itself from its body, is "at liberty to transport herself with a thought wherever she pleases" (186). The separate soul can, among other things, also enter the brain, or more specifically, the pineal gland, i.e., the seat of the soul, according to Descartes, of another person, suggests the nephew. By literally entering another person's mind and observing the thoughts as they occur to that person, Berkeley's separate soul should be able to gain direct, intimate, and as it were, inside, knowledge of the ideas in that person's mind. Moreover, this privileged insight into the mind of another would instruct Berkeley's soul "in a much less time than the usual methods" (186). In the rest of the essay, Berkeley recounts how he spent time in the brains of philosophers, mathematicians, and statesmen, as well as in those of poets, beaux, and even ladies, and outlines the knowledge he acquired while there. Thus, for example, on one occasion, he followed the labyrinthine process of conceiving of a theorem in the mind of a mathematician, while on another occasion, he witnessed the ideas as they were taking shape in the mind of a philosopher. And he was able to do so, he adds, "without any fatigue or wasting of my own spirits" (186).

Shortly afterwards, Berkeley devotes an entire essay, No. 39 of April 25, 1713, to his stay in the pineal gland of one of his main adversaries, the materialist philosopher and radical freethinker Anthony Collins, where he actually observes the process of his thinking out his next book, *A Discourse of Free-Thinking,* which was published that same year and which Berkeley, obviously, strongly disliked. Berkeley ends this essay on a delightful note, remarking maliciously that the utter confusion which reigned among ideas in Collins's mind is reflected in the printed book itself, where the representatives of those ideas are "drawn up in the same confused order upon paper" (190).

Berkeley's account of his soul's stay in Collins's pineal gland (and in those of mathematicians, politicians, poets, and so on) brings to mind the words the Genevan naturalist Charles Bonnet used, later in the century, in presenting a rare case of the fusion of the brains of two fresh-water polyps into a single brain: what we have here, writes Bonnet in his *Considérations sur les corps organisés*, are "two Selves in the same brain."[20] However, there is an important difference between Bonnet's two-selved polyp and Berkeley's temporarily two-souled philosopher (or mathematician, politician, poet, and so on). Berkeley appears to have some kind of direct conscious access to the thoughts and experiences of the persons whose pineal gland he enters. Describing his awareness of his hosts' current thoughts and experiences, Berkeley at one point says he was "conscious of the sublime ideas and comprehensive views of a philosopher"; at another point he was "present when a battel or a storm raged, or a glittering palace rose in [poet's] imagination," and at yet another, he observed "the tender images in the mind of a young lady" (186), and so forth. Meanwhile, Berkeley's hosts remained unaware of his presence within themselves, as Berkeley is either unable or unwilling to influence their thoughts and experiences. While Berkeley is clearly aware of his hosts' thoughts and experiences, most probably at precisely the time they are having them, none of the two Selves lodged in Bonnet's polyp's brain has any access to the experiences of the other. As Bonnet writes, "it does not seem that the two Selves could have the same sensation in the same indivisible instant of time";[21] that is, some sensations are had by one Self and some by the other. Bonnet's polyp, with its two Selves taking turns in manifesting themselves and controlling their single body, and presumably unaware of each other, could perhaps be considered a case of the so-called alternating personality, *avant la lettre*. Even though only multi-headed polyps, "hydras," were categorized by Bonnet as "composite persons,"[22] there could be little doubt that he would also have classified their single-headed, two-selved variety among them.

IV Philosophy of the "glorified body"

Father Daniel depicts in great detail the mind after its separation from the body at death. In his novel, the mind in the afterlife apparently persists in its disembodied state for centuries. As we have seen, when the Cartesians run into Socrates, Plato, and Aristotle on the Moon, the three sages have been without a body for more than two thousand years already. On the other hand, there are also accounts of the post-mortem fate of the mind, in which the mind immediately after the death of its former, earthly body, unites itself with a new body in the afterlife. A rare story of an embodied mind in the afterlife can be found in Simon Tyssot de Patot's 1720 novel *La Vie, les avantures et le Voyage de Groenland du Révérend Père Cordelier Pierre de Mésange*. In his travels, the titular hero of the novel, Pierre de Mésange, finds himself in Greenland, where he spends some time in two of its cities, constructed underground because of the polar weather conditions. Here he hears a story about a certain Raoul, who claimed that he had come back from the afterlife.[23] Raoul, however, has not actually resurrected from the dead, since it was not after death that he found himself in the afterlife; rather, he got there, by accident, while still alive. One day while hunting in the woods, he lost his way and fell into a precipice where there was a crack in the rock apparently leading to the afterlife. Like the earthly cities, in Greenland, the paradise, too, is located underground. While strolling through the paradise, accompanied by a guide who is "an accomplished philosopher" (1: 171), Raoul notices several odd details. For example, the bodies of the inhabitants of paradise are of human shape, yet much shorter, just about "two feet" (1: 150) tall. But even odder, they all look exactly alike and cannot be distinguished one from another, not even by sex. In their appearance, they remind Raoul of "slightly deformed children" (1: 152). Even odder still: although in paradise everything is in abundance, its inhabitants do not seem to know how to enjoy all these goods. For example, even though trees bear great quantities of delicious-looking fruit throughout the year, nobody eats them; all they seem to do is observe and contemplate them. The people of paradise, as the guide quickly explains to the visibly bewildered visitor, enjoy things in a different way—not by eating or drinking them, but by "seeing them, considering them, and admiring in them the works of Providence" (1: 163). In paradise, then, pleasures are merely aesthetic and intellectual, whereas sensual ones are apparently unknown. But not only do the people of paradise neither eat nor drink, they never sleep, as the visitor is puzzled to notice. In the afterlife, sleep is considered a punishment for sins committed in the previous life. That is, the sinners serve out their sentence by simply sleeping for a certain time, the duration of which is proportionate to the gravity of the sin committed (1: 178–9). Having served their sentence, they integrate themselves in the paradisiac community and never sleep again. A deep sleep may not seem much of a punishment, except perhaps in a world of purely aesthetic and intellectual pleasures that require wakefulness and constant attention.

In its post-mortem fate, as portrayed by Raoul, the soul immediately after the death of its "sensual," earthly body comes to inhabit a new, "glorified body." As the guide describes the experience of his own death to the inquisitive visitor, "there is no interval of time between the mind's separation from the sensual body and its joining to a glorified body"; he, at least, did not notice that his "soul has been without a body a single moment" (1: 156). The absence of biological needs such as hunger and thirst is reflected in the physiology of their new, "glorified" bodies. As we read in Tyssot's earlier novel, *Voyages et avantures de Jacques Massé,* bodies in the afterlife are mere empty, hollow shells, devoid of those inner parts which, in their earthly condition, serve the intake and digestion of food and its excretion.[24] The bodies of the people of paradise have no fingernails, no teeth, no alimentary canal and no digestive organs, because they are not necessary for their physiological functioning and survival in the afterlife. In both of Tyssot's novels, the description of the state of the bodies in the afterlife is given by someone who has seen the "glorified" bodies with his own eyes, that is, by someone who has actually witnessed the resurrection of bodies from the dead. Incidentally, in the afterlife, the absence of the sensations of hunger, thirst, and fatigue apparently does not depend exclusively on the "glorified" bodies' physiology, since Raoul, too, who came to paradise in his "mortal," "heavy and carnal" body, during the whole time he spent there felt "neither hunger nor thirst nor sleepiness" (1: 169).

Upon entering the afterlife and joining themselves to new bodies, as Raoul learns, the souls are almost entirely without knowledge. The only thing they seem to remember, "although in a rather confused way," is that in their previous lives they were humans and the place in Greenland where they come from; but beyond that, they know nothing (1: 169). Their originary ignorance is explained by the guide as follows: whatever knowledge they possessed in their previous life has vanished without trace in the afterlife, as "the brain itself and the entire body [*toute la machine*], of which it was but a part, perished" (1: 157). In the afterlife, they have "another body, which is a true blank tablet," onto which the "images of things" that present themselves to them in paradise will imprint themselves (1: 157). That is, all their knowledge must be acquired anew after they arrive in the afterlife. The people of paradise must have been very efficacious in acquiring new knowledge. For example, on his stroll through paradise, Raoul is amazed to see, among other things, an intricate water fountain device that is a unique and concrete example of a perpetual motion machine (1: 173). While touring the so-called "Laboratory of the world," he learns to his astonishment that the people of paradise are in possession of "the true philosopher's stone" (1: 178). Further on, he sees a square table upon which sits an imperial crown of a perfectly circular shape; as the guide explains, the area of this table is equal to that of the inner circular opening of the crown, which is to say that the people of paradise have successfully solved the problem of squaring the circle (1: 182), and so forth. Unfortunately, Raoul is not sufficiently interested in mathematics and the sciences to further inquire about the details of the solutions to these problems, which still remain unsolved in our world after his return from the afterlife. Even though Raoul brings back no specific knowledge from the afterlife, the mere news of the existence of the future life causes a great stir among the people of Greenland, who begin taking their own lives in great numbers, in the hope of reaching the paradise in the shortest way possible (1: 185).

The people of paradise had amassed this vast and magnificent knowledge not in spite of, but at least in part because of, their being embodied. For Tyssot, knowledge—both on earth and in the afterlife—apparently requires a material substrate in which to subsist. As already noted, the people of Greenland lost all their knowledge together with their earthly bodies at death. Similarly, after death, a new body and a new brain are needed for the new knowledge, that is, the new "images of things" to imprint themselves onto. Unlike the earthly, "sensual" body, which is "heavy and corruptible" (1: 172), their new, "glorified" body is "small, light, [and] composed of porous and delicate parts" (1: 153). While their "glorified" body puts them in a position "to walk, swim and fly with equal facility" (1: 153) it is apparently still material. In Tyssot, it is their "glorified" body that makes it possible for the souls of the dead Greenlanders to confidentially exchange ideas between themselves and even to read the thoughts of others. The guide demonstrates that it is through their "glorified" bodies that the souls of the dead are able to read the thoughts of others by showing Raoul that he knows his innermost secret thoughts. Having explained that their "glorified" bodies, although small and deformed, are entirely suited for the enjoyment of "pleasures of eternal beatitude" (1: 153), the guide mildly reproaches Raoul for his having previously taken the people of paradise to be of a rather "small size and badly built" (1: 154). When Raoul defends himself by claiming that he never said any such thing, the guide begins his reply by saying that it may well be that the visitor did not say any such thing, and then adds: "but you've had the thought [*mais vous en avez eu la pensée*]; I was holding your hand at the time, and I noticed this through the beating of your pulse" (1: 154). It is here, in what is perhaps the most sublime moment of Tyssot's novel, that it turns out that it is the materiality of the "glorified" body that makes it possible for its soul to read the thoughts of others—the inhabitants of paradise read the thoughts of others by literally feeling them with their fingers. While it may well be true, as Locke believed, that "the scene of ideas that makes one man's thoughts cannot be laid open to the immediate view of another," it can, Tyssot would argue, nevertheless be exposed at least to the latter's sense of touch.

Notes

1. The research included in this chapter was funded by the Slovenian Research Agency (ARRS) under the research project "Language and Science: The Possibility of Realism in Modern Philosophy" (J6-7364).
2. See Quentin Meillassoux, *After Finitude: An Essay on the Necesssity of Contingency*, trans. Ray Brassier (London: Continuum, 2008), 10ff.
3. See Ray Brassier, *Nihil Unbound: Enlightenment and Extinction* (London: Palgrave Macmillan, 2007), ch. 7, 205–39.
4. It is an interesting issue as to why the form of the thought experiment proliferated precisely in the era extending between Descartes and Hume, perhaps the most famous being Locke's thought experiments of one consciousness being transferred from one body to another (as in the case of the soul of a prince entering the body of a cobbler, whose soul has already departed) or two consciousnesses sharing one body (as in the case of the waking and sleeping Socrates). Hans Jonas, in his somewhat dated "philosophy of life," defined the transition from pre-modern "animist" monism to modern dualism as a separation of the spheres of spirit and matter, a move that opens an entirely new space of rearranging the two: "From the hard-won observation that there can be matter without spirit, dualism inferred the unobserved reverse that spirit can also be without matter" (Hans Jonas, *The Phenomenon of Life: Toward a Philosophical Biology* [Evanston, IL: Northwestern University Press, 2001], 16). Accordingly, with and after Descartes, the mind was suddenly forced to renegotiate its place in the world. Something along these lines was argued by Charles Taylor in his theory of the "disengaged" modern subject (see Charles Taylor, *Sources of the Self: The Making of the Modern Identity* [Cambridge, MA: Harvard University Press, 1989]), where he convincingly demonstrates that in Plato or Aristotle the order of things still embodied an ontic logos, whereas with Descartes ideas were no longer located in the world but in the subject's mind, thus exhibiting all kinds of symptoms of their newly developed independence (see ibid., 186–8). In brief, after the pre-modern innocence of ideas being incarnated in reality had been lost, early modern philosophy seems to have been driven by an effort to realign the two orders; one need only consider Spinoza's parallelism, Leibniz's monadology or Berkeley's immaterialism. Thus, a number of, nowadays bizarre, "thought experiments" of the era are but a consequence of ideas being haunted by the threat of having forfeited their once natural conjunction with the material world. And so the mind finds itself in perpetual search of its rightful body, a union which can no longer be taken for granted. With Kant, the peculiar phenomenon of the specific early modern thought experiments vanishes from philosophy once again; famous is his skeptic, non-sprituralist attack on Swedenborg in *Dreams of a Spirit-Seer*. Or, as Jure Simoniti contends in *The Untruth of Reality*, "these thought experiments could not pose as a Kantian touchstone of truth" (Jure Simoniti, *The Untruth of Reality: The Unacknowledged Realism of Modern Philosophy* [Lanham, MD: Lexington Books, 2016], 30). Simoniti claims that Kant performs another momentous shift in the relation between the ideal and the real, so that now concepts and ideas are elevated to the level of "conditions of possibility," and no longer strive to be immediately pinned down to this or that thing. Since, for instance, the Kantian mind only "accompanies" the representations of its senses, it can, on the one hand, never experience the purely spiritual, disembodied Cartesian self-evidence, but on the other, it can be more or less sure of its body.
5. John Locke, *An Essay concerning Human Understanding*, ed. A. C. Fraser, 2 vols. (New York: Dover, 1959), 2: 462.

6   Pierre-Daniel Huet, *Nouveaux mémoires pour servir à l'histoire du cartésianisme* (n.p. 1692), 26. Subsequent references to this work will be given in brackets in the body of the text.
7   See Huet, *Memoirs of the Life of Peter Daniel Huet, Bishop of Avranches*, trans. John Aiken, 2 vols. (London: Longman, 1810), 1: 154.
8   Ibid.
9   Denis Diderot, *Éléments de physiologie*, in *Œuvres*, ed. Laurent Versini, 5 vols. (Paris: Robert Laffont, 1994-7), 1: 1317.
10 Ibid.
11 See Guez de Balzac to Descartes, March 30, 1628, in *Œuvres de Descartes*, ed. Charles Adam and Paul Tannery, rev. edn, 12 vols. (Paris: Vrin/CNRS, 1964-76), 1: 570.
12 Brigitte Hermann, *Histoire de mon esprit ou le roman de la vie de René Descartes* (Paris: Bartillat, 1996), 460.
13 Pierre Bayle, *Dictionnaire historique et critique*, 5th edn, 4 vols. (Amsterdam, Leiden, The Hague, Utrecht: P. Brunel et al., 1740), 4: 81b-82a.
14 Gabriel Daniel, *A Voyage to the World of Cartesius*, trans. T. Taylor, 2nd edn (London: Thomas Bennet, 1694), 9. Subsequent references to this work will be given in brackets in the body of the text.
15 For more on the dramatic impact of Socrates' death on western culture, see Emily Wilson, *The Death of Socrates: Hero, Villain, Chatterbox, Saint* (Cambridge, MA: Harvard University Press, 2007).
16 The extraordinary complexity of Daniel's character of Aristotle becomes apparent if we briefly recall the Aristotle portrayed by Jonathan Swift in his *Gulliver's Travels* (1726). When, during his visit to Glubbdubdrib, Gulliver calls Aristotle's spirit up from the dead and has two of Aristotle's main opponents and critics, Descartes and Gassendi, both also called up from the dead, present their "Systems" to Aristotle, the latter first openly acknowledges "his own Mistakes in Natural Philosophy" but then goes on to add that, by that time, Descartes's vortex theory and Gassendi's atomist natural philosophy have themselves been disproved, and predicts that the same fate also awaits the then new and widely accepted Newtonian cosmology (see Jonathan Swift, *Gulliver's Travels*, ed. Claude Rawson [Oxford: Oxford University Press, 2005], 184-85). While most of what Swift's Aristotle has to say may well be true, it was hardly worth summoning him from the dead merely for that reason.
17 In Swift's satire *The Battle of the Books* (1704), where the quarrel of the ancients and the moderns is depicted as an armed conflict, Aristotle does, in fact, although inadvertently, kill Descartes: Aristotle's arrow misses Francis Bacon, for whom it was intended, and strikes "the valiant bowman" Descartes, fatally wounding him (see Swift, "The Battle of the Books," in *Major Works*, ed. Angus Ross and David Woolley [Oxford: Oxford University Press, 2003], 14).
18 Descartes, *The World*, in *The Philosophical Writings of Descartes*, trans. John Cottingham, Robert Stoothoff, Dugald Murdoch, and Anthony Kenny, 3 vols. (Cambridge: Cambridge University Press, 1985-91), 1: 90.
19 George Berkeley, *The Works of George Berkeley, Bishop of Cloyne*, ed. A. A. Luce and T. E. Jessop, 9 vols. (Edinburgh: Thomas Nelson, 1948-57), 7: 187. Subsequent references to this work will be given in brackets in the body of the text.
20 Charles Bonnet, *Considérations sur les corps organisés*, 2 vols. (Amsterdam: Marc-Michel Rey, 1762), 2: 86.
21 Ibid.
22 Ibid., 2: 83.

23 For the episode, see Simon Tyssot de Patot, *La Vie, les avantures et le Voyage de Groenland du Révérend Père Cordelier Pierre de Mésange,* 2 vols. (Amsterdam: Etienne Roger, 1720), 1: 142–97. Subsequent references to this work will be given in brackets in the body of the text.
24 See Simon Tyssot de Patot, *Voyages et avantures de Jacques Massé* (Bourdeaux: Jacques L'Aveugle, 1710), 15.

2

Leibniz's Linguistic Realism[1]

Gregor Kroupa

In the opening chapter of his exceptionally influential book *After Finitude*,[2] Quentin Meillassoux gives us his now well-known diagnosis of what has come to be understood—at least in contemporary realist circles—as the main trait of the majority of post-Kantian philosophy: so-called correlationism, that is, the view that being cannot be known in itself, but only as a correlate of the thinking subject. Meillassoux offers a compact and lucid reading of this idea, which has been as conceptually all-encompassing, particularly since the second half of the twentieth century, as it has become widespread. His view consists in the interpretation that philosophy since Kant has rejected the possibility of a transparent cognitive relation to reality as dogmatic metaphysics and embraced the reflection of correlation as the only kind of knowledge that avoided such traps of early modern *naïveté*. One of the implications of identifying Kant as the progenitor of correlationism is that the history of philosophy turns out to be divided according to the lines of its approaches to reality: on the one side, pre-critical naïve realism, instantiated particularly by early modern rationalism in which the philosophy of substance dominates, and on the other, post-Kantian transcendental philosophy, which was given a new impetus by Husserl and his followers. In the twentieth century, the correlationist approach then took many new forms, according to which reality and truth were always already given to us as colored by particular transcendental spheres, each with their own *a priori* (power, discourse, economic relations, gender, etc.), yet the two chief "media" of correlation remained *consciousness* and *language*, developed by advocates of phenomenology and analytic philosophy, respectively.[3]

In the present chapter, I shall discuss the connection between the two correlations in the context of the history of European philosophy. While it is true that the so-called linguistic turn is commonly associated with developments in Anglophone philosophy (as embodied, for example, in the famous collection that Richard Rorty prepared in 1967[4]) in which the philosophy of language acquired the status of "first philosophy," I am certainly not the first to point out that a similar turn towards language had also happened on the European continent much earlier. This fact has been little discussed in realist circles, as the debate has focused largely on both challenging and transforming transcendentalism and the ensuing promise of a new ontology. Therefore, I would first like to present a basic differentiation between "realist" and "antirealist" approaches to language in the history of modern philosophy, which relies heavily on the way epistemological issues are handled. I will then try to situate Leibniz's linguistic thought in this context in order to show that his strategy for avoiding the danger of relativism and keeping a strong realist position in his epistemology and semiotics is only possible through a version of strong Platonist idealism, which, in his view, saves our direct access to truth and reality from the hopeless subjectiveness of ideas. In order to facilitate the mind in its contact with things themselves, Leibniz then outlines his idea of a *real* or *universal characteristic* in which signs or words become the aid of knowledge, rather than an obstacle to it, or a mere external tool of communication.

I Linguistic realism and determinism

Some historians of the philosophy of language have suggested a division that is perhaps less clear-cut, but still in a way analogous to the split between realist dogmatic metaphysics and antirealist transcendental philosophy.[5] This division, however, does not run along the same lines, as the major turning point here is not Kant, but some of his critics and contemporaries.

According to this interpretation, the German philosophy of language culminating in Wilhelm von Humboldt's so-called "principle of linguistic relativity" is contrasted with its "naïve" predecessor, namely a certain assumption that words find their meanings in independently formed ideas, rather than in linguistic use. The latter view was widely held in the seventeenth-century tradition of universal grammar, as represented by the Port-Royal *Grammar* and *Logic*, and also in the rare but revealing passages about language in Descartes's writings, but particularly in Book III of Locke's *Essay concerning Human Understanding*. According to this doctrine, articulated sounds are arbitrary signs of pre-linguistic thoughts, and human beings have the capacity of language because they are endowed with reason (Descartes, Port-Royal) or a certain species-specific semiotic capability (Locke). The belief that language is conditioned by human consciousness was sufficient to imply that it is something external to mental contents and processes, that it is merely instrumental to them and has no constitutive role in them.[6] That is not to say that language was deemed unproblematic and could not influence thought. Locke, especially, made a long analysis of the perils of communication, which, according to him, often leads the mind into error for reasons ranging from the inherent "imperfection of words" to deliberate "abuse of words" giving rise to "*learned Gibberish*" of Scholasticism.[7] But the challenges that language imposed on thought did not follow from some intrinsic linguistic nature of our ideas in virtue of which language would constitute the unsurpassable horizon of our minds; rather, the reasons for the so-called *cheat of words* lay in an improper understanding of the mechanism of signification. Thus, since the mental and linguistic domains were understood to be essentially separate, and true statements consisted in their correct connections, problems with language were deemed manageable if only the speakers stated clearly the meanings of their words, that is, if they specified the precise collections of simple ideas they associated with particular verbal sounds.

In the eighteenth century, this view of the mind's principal autonomy from language was progressively abandoned, to the point where historians speak of a genuine "linguistic turn," which had been completed by the time of Humboldt's *The Diversity of Human Language-Structure and its Influence on the Mental Development of Mankind* (first published posthumously in 1836). Exactly who originated the new approach is somewhat debated, however, as are the lines of influence between its main figures. Christina Lafont,[8] for example, has stressed the importance of Johann Georg Hamann's *Metakritik* (1784) of Kant's *Critique of Pure Reason* in which Hamann pointed out "the genealogical priority of language" over the faculty of thought and argued that "the entire faculty of thought [is] founded on language."[9] Michael Forster has recently argued, however, that it was actually Herder who had influenced Hamann, and that the crucial points of Humboldt's philosophy of language were all put forward by Herder.[10] On the other hand, Hans Aarsleff emphasized in the late 1970s the influence of the then-neglected philosophy of Condillac and the circle of *Idéologues* on both Herder's and Humboldt's linguistic theories, and he downplayed the importance of a direct influence of Herder on Humboldt.[11] Scholarly differences aside, all these historical accounts nevertheless agree that a paradigm shift in the way the relationship between language and thought was understood had been completed in German hermeneutic philosophy, a shift that was perhaps as radical as the one separating early modern realist metaphysics from transcendental philosophy.

Forster nicely summarizes the traits of this new linguistic philosophy when he lists the four views that Humboldt shared with Herder:

1. "that thought is essentially dependent on and bounded by language";
2. "that concepts or meanings are constituted—not by referents, Platonic forms, mental 'ideas,' or whatnot, but—by word-usages";
3. "that mankind exhibits deep linguistic and conceptual-intellectual diversities, especially between historical periods and cultures," and consequently;
4. that "the investigation of the varying characters of people's modes of thought and conceptualization should primarily take the form of an investigation of the varying characters of their languages."[12]

This new take on the relationship between thought and language has sometimes been labeled "linguistic idealism"[13] (a term I shall refrain from using in the following to avoid confusion with another kind of idealism I shall discuss in connection with Leibniz). It is no exaggeration to portray such views as a genuine "linguistic turn" vis-à-vis the linguistic theories of the preceding century. Moreover, they openly target every philosophy, such as Descartes's or Kant's, which does not elevate language into a kind of gateway to epistemology. It has been argued that this shift from the unity of reason toward the plurality of languages amounts to nothing less than a "*detranscendentalization* of reason"[14] in favor of language, the ramifications of which can be traced in the theories of such different intellectual pedigrees as the linguistics of Saussure, the philosophy of late Heidegger, Gadamer or late Wittgenstein. It seems that the notion of the incommensurability of language games, which has been so popular in recent decades, is fundamentally a descendant of Humboldtian linguistic philosophy, much like phenomenology is nowadays often understood to be an offshoot of Kantian transcendentalism.

The history of modern linguistic philosophy thus indicates two main outlooks. What I shall call the "linguistic realism"[15] of the rational grammarians and Locke (but the basic doctrine goes back to Aristotle's *De interpretatione*[16]), refers primarily to the relation of language to the mind, not of language to the world. In line with the doctrine of pre-linguistic thoughts, truth is still primarily burdened with the correspondence between ideas and things, and it is deemed adequately expressible in language, on two conditions: *first*, that the thinking subject has previously done her cognitive work properly, and *second*, that the utterances of the speaking subject are backed up by sufficiently well-defined ideas involved in them, i.e., that no words are used blindly. But if the first challenge which the seventeenth-century philosophy saw in language was to avoid, as Locke described it, "the using of Words, without clear and distinct *Ideas*; or, which is worse, signs without any thing signified,"[17] then the second was how to guard the precise thoughts of one's mind against the fluidity of intersubjective semantics of which the speaking subject is not the master. In other words, language, if used carelessly, enables one *to speak without thinking*, whereas the most pure cognitive ideal was rather *to think without speaking*. Because of the unfortunate impracticability of telepathy of pure ideas, language was regarded as an imperfect tool for their communication; however, the connection between the two spheres was by no means seen as necessary, as nothing essentially prevented reasoning from happening without words. "Linguistic realism" thus refers to the claim that the relation between thought and language *is not a correlation*, since language does not necessarily interfere with our conception of reality. Berkeley nicely sums up the early modern belief that reality is accessible beyond language: "We need only draw the curtain of words to behold the fairest tree of knowledge, whose fruit is excellent, and within the reach of our hand."[18]

"Linguistic determinism," represented by the above-mentioned German philosophy, on the other hand, *does* assume a correlation between language and consciousness. Whereas the Kantian *cognitive* correlation consists in not being able to know the thing-in-itself without turning it into for-us (as it is forever in a correlation in which the world is given to *me* and this givenness is implied in every thought about the world), *linguistic* correlation means that, similarly, our ideas are not simply "there" for us as pure thoughts without their being (always already) mediated by some linguistic structure. In other words, if the Kantian correlation concerns the world trapped inside consciousness, then the linguistic turn in the German tradition can be understood as a further twist to the Kantian revolution: not only is the world of things only ever a correlate of thought, but even our thoughts themselves are only ever cast in linguistic mold, since no thought is formed without linguistic means. As Humboldt put it, "[t]hought and language are ... one and inseparable from each other. But the former is also intrinsically bound to the necessity of entering into a union with the verbal sound; thought cannot otherwise achieve clarity, nor the idea become a concept."[19] It is precisely this idea that Humboldt probably learned from Condillac, who was one of the first to break with the doctrine of pre-linguistic thoughts, having maintained that reflection was effectively enabled by language.[20]

The "detranscendentalization of reason" mentioned above thus should be understood as adding the language–consciousness correlate to the consciousness–world correlate in which transcendentality is effectively doubled. In the light of the developments of various forms of linguistic determinism in the twentieth century, it is clear that this approach is essentially antirealist and takes us even further away from the thing-in-itself, as it not only drives a wedge between reality and the thinking subject, but additionally alienates his thought through a pre-given symbolic system. Moreover, once the diversity of languages is brought into the picture, the path to different degrees of relativism is opened,[21] as neither the views about the world-disclosing nature of language nor about the limits of one's language corresponding to the limits of one's world and the like have any ambition to step outside of our linguistic practices and "draw the curtain of words." If knowledge and thought are linguistically determined, if thought unspoiled by historically conditioned language is even impossible, the question as to where thought should take its resources for the old-fashioned campaign against *the cheat of words* seems like an epitome of early modern naïve metaphysics.

Leibniz occupies a peculiar place in this historical picture. Although he subscribed to a version of linguistic realism, contending that "ideas do not depend upon names,"[22] he also insisted, before Condillac, that all reasoning was conducted in signs of some kind. In the variety of early modern linguistic theories, the two claims are seldom found together, because they seem incompatible at first. *Either* one admits the doctrine of pre-linguistic thoughts which are formed independently, and the sole purpose of language is then to be the external medium of their communication, however imperfect and imprecise, *or* thoughts are always already shaped by the grammatical and semantic systems of one's language, and then reasoning or a sequence of these thoughts is always verbalized, even if only cursorily and within the confines of one's mind. Leibniz, however, seems to adopt the premise of the former approach and the consequence of the latter: ideas and their connections are essentially free of the semantic and syntactic determinations of a particular language, since the concepts in our minds are governed by the laws of logic alone, and yet the process of connecting them into reasoning, even if they are not communicated, can never happen without language or at least some kind of symbolic expression—for Leibniz, the cognitive process is necessarily a semiotic operation.

I shall first explore Leibniz's account of the relationship between words, ideas and things in his critique of Locke's epistemology to account for the general "linguistic ontology" which relates to any symbolic system, including natural language, and then turn to his plan for *characteristica universalis* (CU). It is in his CU project, in the connection between his logic and semiotics (theory of expression) that Leibniz's views on the matter are best explored, rather than in his speculations about the origin of peoples based on what he considered etymological evidence, which he had delved into since the late 1680s.[23]

II Leibnizian linguistic ontology

Locke's treatise on language in Book III of the *Essay* claims a place in the history of linguistic thought because it attempted to put an end to what he considered careless formulations found in writings about language, which used "ideas" and "things" interchangeably when discussing what words actually referred to. Locke's central premise is that "*Words in their primary or immediate Signification, stand for nothing, but the Ideas in the Mind of him that uses them*, how imperfectly soever, or carelessly those *Ideas* are collected from the Things, which they are supposed to represent."[24] Words represent the ideas and knowledge a particular speaker has about a thing, as the speaker can only hope that the words uttered will evoke the same ideas in the listener. However, for Locke, the common mistake among philosophers had been not only that they often took the identity of words to imply identity of meaning, but, more importantly, that "*Men ... often suppose their Words to stand also for the reality of Things.*"[25] This nicely captures a standard linguistic ontology implicit in Cartesian writings as well, which puts words, ideas and things in a linear fashion, whereby an idea of a thing is formed from perceptions and abstractions, and a "Word is made arbitrarily the Mark of such an Idea."[26] There is thus no way in which words would indicate things themselves or their essences directly without the mediation of private ideas. It is clear from the outset that Leibniz's linguistic ontology redistributes the ideas–words–things relations differently: words do not refer to things only by mediation of ideas concealed in one's mind, because they can refer to anything. Leibniz completely disregards Locke's separation of language and reality in the *New Essays*, emphasizing that "words indicate the things as well as the ideas."[27]

The premises of this view can be traced in one of the most vocal disagreements between Leibniz's Theophilus and Locke's Philaletes in the *New Essays*. Leibniz never approved of the Lockean *new way of ideas*; in fact, he even accuses Locke of speaking incongruously when he chooses to refer to ideas as if they were merely private psychological entities secluded in our minds. Despite the fact that Leibniz occasionally does adjust to Locke's usage of the word in the *New Essays* to keep the flow of the conversation (as he seems to do in the above quote), he often stresses that 'idea' should not be "confounded with the image,"[28] for ideas are not our "actual thoughts."[29] The primary dispute between Leibniz and Locke is thus perhaps not the notorious question of whether or not ideas are innate, but first and foremost their ontological status: Leibniz takes them to be wholly objective models of reality residing in God's intellect, logical blueprints according to which he chooses to create;[30] they are present in our minds only as potential demonstrative knowledge about the thing in question. In *Quid sit idea* (1677?), he maintains that "we are said to have an idea of a thing even if we do not think of it, if only, on a given occasion, we can think of it."[31] It is in this sense that he states in the *New Essays* that ideas are not the content of our consciousness, our thoughts, but rather "the very form or possibility of those thoughts."[32] Thus, when Philaletes claims that the absurdities arising in reasoning about eternity are due to the fact that any idea of eternity is insufficient, "however great a duration someone represents to himself," Theophilus clearly distinguishes between ideas as objects of knowledge and mental images as objects of imagination: "There reigns here that same confusion of the image with the idea. We have a 'comprehensive', i.e., accurate, idea of eternity, since we have the definition of it, although we have no image of it at all."[33] Consequently, ideas are innate insofar as they are in our minds as possibilities, forms of knowledge, and not as items of consciousness; they represent essences (genera and species of things), which we can laboriously unfold with our fragmentary concepts, aided by perception and logical reasoning:

That the ideas of things are in us means therefore nothing but that God, the creator alike of the things and of the mind, has impressed a power of thinking upon the mind so that it can by its own operations derive what corresponds perfectly to the nature of things. Although, therefore, the idea of a circle is not similar to the circle, truths can be derived from it which would be confirmed beyond doubt by investigating a real circle.[34]

Hence, the ideas of genera and species of all "things" (such as gold, parricide, circle, eternity, redness, etc.) are complete concepts representing their natures or essences, which, like the complete concepts of individual substances in God's intellect, *contain the same amount of information as things themselves*. Of course, the difference between the ideas of individual and eternal essences is that the latter involve different degrees of generality, which makes the series of steps required for their complete analysis finite, even if our knowledge about them, our notions, often remain imprecise, partial, distorted, or simply false.

This is, of course, not merely an issue of terminology in which Leibniz would simply reserve the term 'idea' for a different entity than Locke. The critical point here is that Leibniz develops his epistemology based on rational concepts belonging to the objective domain of logical relations rather than on the intricate psychology of mental representations and their associations. For this reason, he cannot accept the necessary consequence of Locke's linguistic ontology in which the meanings of terms like 'gold' or 'parricide' consist in particular collections of simple ideas, which are the results of one's sensory inspection of gold objects, or one's own understanding of what constitutes the killing of a parent. For Locke, all words refer exclusively to subjective ideas; he only distinguishes the ways in which different kinds of abstract ideas are formed in the mind: whereas ideas of substances do have some external model with which they accord, ideas of "mixed modes" like 'parricide' are purely "*the Workmanship of the Understanding*."[35] The essences of things, the various genera and species of beings we designate using words with general meanings, are thus only abstract ideas in individual minds attached to a word, or, as Locke calls them (to Leibniz's horror), only *nominal essences*,[36] since, in the case of substances, the *real* essences responsible for the collections of our sensory ideas are unknown to us, and in the case of mixed modes, the distinction between real and nominal is superfluous for the reason that mixed modes are not "real"—their nominal essence (e.g., what one understands under the word 'parricide') perfectly matches their real essence (what parricide really is), which is "the workmanship" of anyone's understanding. For Leibniz, on the other hand, "essence is fundamentally nothing but the possibility of the thing under consideration"[37] and is thus always real and never merely "nominal." If there is a clear-cut example of classic realism in the early modern period, it is found here: what ultimately constitutes the essences of genera and species is not the fact that a perceived resemblance between many things is labeled by a word with a general meaning, but that "this resemblance is a reality"[38] in things themselves. This is as valid for mixed modes and relations as it is for substances and simple ideas, because no essence, insofar as it is the possibility of the thing, depends on our will—a combination of ideas either is or is not correct. Parricide, in short, has no less of an objective essence than gold, because this essence depends neither on the way one chooses to understand it nor on the name one chooses to attach to it.[39]

Leibniz's epistemology thus relies on his essentialist ontology. If anything is real as long as it is an essence and essence is nothing but the *possibility* of the thing, then whatever idea can be shown to be non-contradictory represents something real, which means that it exists in God's intellect (to which I shall return a bit later) independently of the knowing subject. Our more or less comprehensive knowledge of things, however, is distinguished on the background of what, unlike essences, *does* allow for the distinction between real and nominal, that is, definitions, for "although a thing has only one essence, this can be expressed by several definitions."[40] This distinction had been very important for Leibniz's epistemology at least since the late 1670s: a *nominal definition* of a thing is descriptive; the concepts involved in it have not yet been fully resolved to form an idea in the proper sense, because this type of definition merely lists a series of qualities which allow us to recognize the thing and distinguish it from others (Leibniz's example is the knowledge an assayer has of gold).[41] *Real defintion*, on the other hand, is analytical in that it shows the thing as possible (and thus the essence of the thing as real) by demonstrating the non-contradiction in its constitutive terms or concepts. Now, Leibniz distinguished between several kinds of real definitions, but what they all have in common is precisely that they all establish the *possibility* of the thing. In the case of substances, for example, this includes "definitions involving the generation of a thing, or if this is impossible, at least its constitution, that is, a method by which the thing appears to be producible or at least possible";[42] however, the most perfect a priori real definitions (those pertaining to mathematics, but also to metaphysics) are the ones "which resolve the thing into simple primitive notions understood in themselves."[43] In this way, for the Leibnizian subject to know a thing by its real definition is to uncover the secrets of its eternal essence, regardless of whether the thing was actually produced or created. A real definition thus represents cognitive access to reality itself, not just to a collection of ideas that is merely corroborated by experience. The whole business of science and knowledge is then to transform nominal definitions into real ones, or, to elevate fragmentary concepts about things into ideas mirroring their essences.

To return now to the question of language, it seems that Locke made a quasi-transcendental step that Leibniz is trying to reverse when he says that "words indicate things as well as ideas." Since ideas in the Leibnizian sense are not our private mental entities, but assume an objective reality as soon as they prove to be non-contradictory, and because our conceptions lose their purely subjective character as soon as they make contact with the domain of logical possibility, words can refer to these possibilities directly just as well as to ideas in Locke's sense. According to Leibniz, terms like 'gold' or 'parricide' refer not to our representation of a substance with a particular color, weight, fusibility etc., or to our own interpretations of moral acts, but to the eternal essence of that substance or that act itself, just as the term 'circle' refers to an essence about which eternal truths can be demonstrated, which makes the target of linguistic reference independent of any person's knowledge about it. As Jaap Maat has nicely explained, the advantage of the Leibnizian approach is that it allows for the progress of knowledge about the thing without the need to update the reference of the word every time this occurs. It shows that *meaning* (our nominal definition of the thing) *does not determine reference*, as meaning is provisional and does not yet take into account potential new knowledge.⁴⁴ We use words *as if they refer to everything that is true about the things,* even if a significant portion of these truths remain unknown to us; therefore, if our knowledge about gold is refined as a consequence of a particular experiment, we are adding to our knowledge about the very thing we have been referring to as 'gold' all along.

III Language as calculus

It was necessary to establish this contrast between what I designate here as the linguistic ontologies of Leibniz and Locke to fully understand the idealist framework within which Leibniz's project of CU is built. For it is impossible to even fantasize about such an endeavor within a philosophy that makes essences or things themselves either completely inaccessible to, or a product of, either mind or language. By contrast, a strong tenet of a parallelism, even isomorphism, between concepts and reality had been a leading motif of Leibniz's writings ever since his first published work *De arte combinatoria* (1666) in which he says that just as things have real parts insofar as they *exist*, so they have conceptual parts insofar as they can be *thought*.⁴⁵ A striking example of this appears in the *New Essays*, where, in the debate about simple ideas, Leibniz claims that the idea of green only appears to be simple, since it must be, like the color green itself, composed of ideas of blue and yellow and can thus be analyzed into its constituent parts, notwithstanding the fact that even after this analysis is performed with the help of an experiment, the perception of green (our "sensory idea of green") will remain confused and thus appear simple.⁴⁶ So, if a thing is composed in reality, it must be composed conceptually, too.

However, the parallelism between the ideal and the real alone is not enough to satisfy the requirements of CU. What Leibniz needs to establish is that the symbols of a language (words, characters, numbers etc.) themselves mirror reality, for only thus can reasoning become a mechanical process of symbolic operation wherein reasoning is truly determined and guided by signs alone. When he was considering Hobbes's claim—as shocking as it sounded to his ears—that all truths are arbitrary for the simple reason that arguments rely on definitions of words which are themselves settled arbitrarily, he came up with an answer which tries to establish some accord between the domains of language and things. If language was to convey truth, then it was necessary for the system of signs to be expressive, i.e., that there was something common in the two domains. In the theory of expression that he first developed in *Dialogus* (1677), he holds that the arbitrariness of language, or the fact that words are not made to resemble the things to which they refer, by no means precludes a certain isomorphism between them. Every expression is founded on something which serves as the foundation of their correspondence, indeed as the foundation of *truth*, even if they are very dissimilar: "For although characters are arbitrary, their use and connection have something which is not arbitrary, namely a definite analogy between characters and things, and the relations which different characters expressing the same thing have to each other."⁴⁷ While Leibniz admits that similarity between signs and things—as a drawn circle is a sign of an ideal one and a map is a sign of an area—would make the words of natural languages all the more useful and expressive, it is enough that there be a formal analogy between them, "a kind of complex mutual relation [*situs*] or order which fits the things; if not in the single words at least in their combination and inflection, although it is even better if found in the single words themselves."[48] Thanks to this formal analogy, truths can be uttered in different languages, just as calculations can be made in different systems of arithmetic notation, since truth does not depend on what is arbitrary, but on what is invariable in the symbols, i.e., "the very connection and arrangement of characters."[49]

Now, even if this general analogy between words and their referents is granted, the problem with natural languages remains in the fact that they do not allow for a calculus, since the truth of an uttered or written proposition is not apparent *from its very form*.[50] Any symbolic system thus can express truths, but the reasoning behind them is wholly dependent on the cognitive and rational powers of knowing subjects. The usefulness of symbols is measured by their expressivity, and the latter in turn by the quantity of relations that the symbols convey. For this reason, mathematical symbols, which can be blindly trusted, relieve the subject of the constant need for intuition, and provide what he calls *filum meditandi*:

> The more precision the characters have, that is, the more relations of the things they exhibit, the more useful they are. And when they exhibit all the relations of the things among themselves, in the way the arithmetical characters used by me do, then *there is nothing in the thing which cannot be grasped through the characters*.[51]

This kind of maximum expressivity of characters is precisely the final piece of the puzzle that Leibniz needs to establish to at least theoretically satisfy the ambitions of CU. As he says in *La vraie méthode*, the quintessential but neglected benefit of mathematical calculation is the fact that it is performed by operating the symbols alone. A system of notation such as algebra is thus much more than just a neutral tool for representing quantitative relations; it enables us to check the correctness of a calculation merely on the level of symbols, and thus needs no external verification. According to Leibniz, this was the principal reason for the regrettable fact that the mathematical method had been only partially implemented in other sciences and was wholly absent from metaphysics and morals: it consists not only in a deductive procedure, but also in the fact that mathematical symbols fully relieve the mind of the burden of reflecting upon the quantities themselves. In virtue of this, such symbols enable one to perform an easily available experiment, a test "not made on a thing itself, but on the characters which we have substituted in place of the thing,"[52] so one can fully trust the operations of semiotic substitutions, transpositions or transformations without needing to perpetually attend to the "semantic" values of the symbols.

This last point is the principal requirement Leibniz had envisaged for his CU—the so-called "blind thought," the mechanical operation of carefully invented characters according to rules, which guarantees that the truth about any subject matter whatsoever as it were effortlessly unfolds on a piece of paper. If we said earlier that the early modern ideal was, *first*, to think without speaking, and *second*, to avoid the questionable use of language in which people seemed to speak without thinking, then Leibniz adopts the contrary approach: (1) He never stops reminding us that "all human reasoning is performed by means of certain signs or characters" and that it is indeed "neither possible nor desirable that the things themselves or even the ideas of them be always distinctly observed by the mind," since no geometrician, arithmetician or jurist would ever reach the end of their proof, calculation, or legal consideration if they were to recall each time the definitions or "modes of construction" of a hyperbolae, "the values of all the marks or ciphers" or mentally examine the essential conditions of a particular "action, exception or benefits of a law."[53] (2) For this reason, Leibniz wants to devise a universal symbolism so "expressive" that the symbols alone dispose of the need for thought (other than the observance of the formal rules of transposition of characters) in complex and winding reasonings. Blind thought, which amounts to trusting that the signs of a language are backed up by clear and distinct notions and definitions, does indeed have negative consequences when we wish to reason in natural languages (and Leibniz gives many examples of such cases in metaphysics),[54] but it becomes an asset of artificial philosophical language, which is thereby designed as a kind of semiotic truth-machine. In other words, if "ideas do not depend on names," this "defect" is to be rectified in CU: reasoning would be made fully dependent on characters by way of making characters dependable, which is Leibniz's way of combining very strong linguistic realism with linguistic determinism.

In order to fully grasp the linguistic realism of CU, we must keep in mind that it is founded on Leibniz's theory of double expression: just as ideas may express things perfectly, so signs can be made to express ideas perfectly and, by the same token, things themselves, for expression is not a relation between the signifier and the signified, but between the logical and real composition. The basic scheme of Leibniz's plan to unlock the power of science is then founded on his combinatorial logic, according to which a complex concept is a particular combination of simpler concepts in conformity with intentional logic, which observes his principle that the concept of the predicate is included in the concept of the subject (predicate-in-notion). Thus, every term or concept can be analyzed into its simpler constituents, the ultimate goal being, of course, the reduction to "simple primitive notions understood in themselves."[55] However, Leibniz wrestled with the status of primitive concepts, and he grew increasingly skeptical through the years about whether they were at all within our reach. While in *De arte combinatoria*, where the idea of CU first appeared, he was still convinced that a limited number of intelligible highest genera or categories existed, which, when combined in various ways, make up the whole world, he had settled on the claim since the 1670s that it is perhaps not within human power to resolve everything *a priori* "to the first possibles or to irreducible concepts, or (what is the same thing) to the absolute attributes of God themselves or the first causes and the final end of things."[56] Accordingly, Leibniz claimed that we must at least reduce the multitude of things "to a few, whose possibility can either be supposed and postulated, or proved by experience,"[57] and then show how everything is made of their combinations, just as it is possible to analyze curves as products of combining straight lines and circles in geometry, and just as in jurisprudence a particular legal case consists in a combination of actions, promises, sales etc., which are understood to compose it as its "parts."[58]

In a further step, a catalogue of such primitive or provisionally primitive notions (categories of highest genera) would amount to "an alphabet of human thoughts,"[59] while their organization, the display of their natural order, would form an encyclopedia unlike any other, i.e., not a simple collection of facts, but rationally ordered hierarchies of concepts which would reflect the composition of complex units. Now, to devise a universal language, one only needs to find suitable characters for the primitive (or provisionally primitive) notions, since the composition of complex characters will follow the composition of complex concepts and the different domains of the things–ideas–language triangle will thus be harmonized:

> As a matter of fact, when thinking about these matters a long time ago, it was already clear to me that all human thoughts may be resolved into very few primitive notions; and that, if characters are assigned to them, it will then be possible to form characters for the derived notions, from which it will always be possible to extract all their conditions [*essentialia requisita*], as well as the primitive notions they contain, and—let me say explicitly—their definitions or values, and, therefore, the properties which may be deduced from the definitions as well. Once this is assured, anyone who would use this sort of character in reasoning or writing, would either never make a mistake, or his mistakes would always be easily detectable by himself as well as by others. Moreover, he would, as far as possible, discover the truth from the given, and if in some cases the available data were not sufficient for discovering that which is sought, he would still see which experiments or observations are necessary in order, at least, to be able to approach the truth, as far as possible from the data, either by approximations or by the determination of a higher degree of probability. In this system of characters, sophisms and paralogisms would be nothing more than what errors of calculation are in Arithmetic, or solecisms and barbarisms in language.[60]

The crucial element of Leibniz's idea of CU is thus not simply that we should devise a symbolic system that would simply mirror our thoughts adequately, unequivocally or unambiguously. Moreover, it is a language where the semantics of its terms are determined by the logical syntax of the predicate-in-notion principle. To know the true "meaning" of a character amounts to an explanation of the true nature of the thing itself and, consequently, its relations to other things. As Leibniz puts it in a letter to Tschirnhaus, "the analysis of concepts thus corresponds exactly to the analysis of a character,"[61] from which it follows that the definition of a certain concept is performed by substituting for a complex character simpler ones that are involved in it, much like the product 35 can be equivalently expressed, defined or substituted by combining its "primitive notions," the primes 7 and 5. Moreover, any proposition or truth expressed in subject–predicate form—and according to Leibniz, *all* truths can be expressed in this way—is a combination of two terms in a composite term, which makes demonstration and definition the two sides of the same coin: a demonstration of a truth is a chain of definitions of the concepts involved, but also, as we have seen, a real definition is nothing short of a demonstration of the possibility of the thing in question—it proves that the complex concept is not contradictory. It is symbolic or blind thought supported by characters carrying their own definitions that precisely helps our reasoning in transforming nominal definitions into real ones,[62] and Leibniz does not shy away from saying that new knowledge obtained from such definitions and demonstrations which only consist in substitution of characters is explained by "what Plato called 'reminiscence'."[63]

On the basis of a scheme so conceived, Leibniz frequently made very ambitious claims about CU, such as that it would enable truths to be grasped "as if pictured on paper with the aid of a machine,"[64] that reasoning would become no more difficult than speaking, and truths could be expressed in this language even without knowing, since the characters themselves will reveal them to us, or that this language is like a telescope for the mind, a *filum meditandi* leading us "into the interior of things" themselves, etc.[65] Furthermore, in one of the most famous rhetorical exaggerations with which Leibniz frequently described the benefits of CU, he promises that once this language is invented and adopted, the verbal disputes not only of scientists, but also of metaphysicians, lawyers and moralists would disappear, for whenever two scholars disagreed on a matter, they would resolve their controversy "by simply taking a pen, so that it will suffice for two debaters (leaving aside issues of agreement about words) to say to each other: let us calculate!"[66]

IV Conclusions

There are, of course, also many hitherto unmentioned issues, problems and inconsistencies in Leibniz's *characteristica* project, particularly surrounding the application of its rigid aprioristic design to empirical sciences. He merely outlines some ideas about how new findings from experiments would have been incorporated into the system of characters or how it would have been possible to use the characters for judging not only truth but also probability in moral or political matters. Further, his claim that one could start with merely provisional characters of simple terms before finding "true" ones is far from clear, given the fact that his design essentially calls for a bottom-up approach. Moreover, nothing has been said about his attempt to find the expression of logical relations in significantly reduced and simplified Latin grammar; and finally, we find a fair amount of hesitation about the very typographic appearance of the characters, as Leibniz originally proposed a kind of pictographic script in *De arte combinatoria*, then settled on using prime numbers and letters in his various sketches of logical calculi, only to return to his original idea in the *New Essays*. I have deliberately ignored these issues. My intention was to situate his linguistic thought in general, and universal characteristic in particular, into the general scheme of the relationship between words (or characters), ideas (or concepts) and things (or essences). I shall now add some concluding remarks about the Leibnizian doctrine regarding the loosening of the divide between linguistic realism and determinism, the widening of the scope of reality as a consequence of his Platonism, and about his ontological approach to philosophy, which seems to benefit the cause of realism even today.

(a) The conceptual character of language

If we play linguistic realism against determinism, there is a consequence on each side to be avoided. In the linguistic realism typical of the early modern era, it is the fact that language and meaning are treated only after the theory of knowledge has already been established, as it merely adds to it a non-essential layer demanded by the need to account for communication. On the side of linguistic determinism, it takes some effort to resist its relativist consequences once the view of language as imposing a particular worldview is combined with empirical study of linguistic diversity. Of course, the version of linguistic determinism Leibniz was facing was considerably less nuanced than the one developed in the time after Humboldt. But whereas he did not have to deal with the transcendentalist premises of linguistic relativity, he did have to address the concerns about relativism, particularly as they were raised by Hobbes's above-mentioned arbitrariness thesis.

Leibniz's engagement with these issues can be summed up in three steps. *First*, against the realists, he recognizes the necessity of language for cognition, since constant non-symbolized pure intuition would be epistemologically too burdensome. *Second*, against Hobbes, he denies that this dependency on language would lead into relativism and establishes a definite analogy between relations among the items of any language and relations among things, which leads to his theory of expression. And *third*, he devises a plan for a symbolic system expressing all the known conceptual relations between things and their parts (and allowing for the later inclusion of hitherto unknown relations). So, after disposing with the particular consequences of both linguistic realism and determinism, the proposed system of characters also decisively embraces their most productive characteristics. On the one hand, such universal language is *realist* in that it does not lock the mind into a *particular* worldview imposed by a *particular* language, nor does it distort its access to reality; in fact, it provides an external aid to the mind to penetrate being, for the composition of characters wholly reflects the essential composition of things themselves. On the other hand, it is also *determinist*, as these characters do not allow one to perform any operations that are not permitted by its logical syntax. The skeptical claim that language is the unsurpassable horizon of thought is thereby given an optimistic reversal: if the system of symbols is sufficiently expressive, then this horizon matches reality itself, just as algebraic notation allows for perfect expressions of all possible quantitative relations, including theorems that have not yet been discovered. We see that Leibniz utilizes linguistic determinism normatively, rather than descriptively: it is not a positive theory of natural language, but a criterion to be observed in designing the ideal future language. CU *must* be devised in such a way that the written characters themselves completely determine the correct way to reason. The early modern wedge between the domains of signs and ideas is thus removed; however, unlike the positions resulting from the Humboldtian linguistic turn, it does not result in, as Lafont describes it, "the immanent linguistic character of concepts,"[67] but rather in *the immanent conceptual character of CU*.

(b) Idealism and realism

Before we dismiss Leibniz's placing of eternal ideas in God's intellect as metaphysical dogmatism of the worst kind, we must point out that the status of the divine is somewhat debatable here. Whereas Leibniz certainly cannot escape such accusations in his doctrine of the best possible world, the "inclining" though not "necessitating" reasons God had for creating it and a plethora of other claims in his metaphysics and theodicy, I think that the role of the divine in his epistemology and logic is surprisingly lightweight. Unlike in Berkeley's "hypostatization" of the correlation in God's mind, as Meillassoux puts it,[68] where God continuously perceives all ideas to ensure that the world does not cease to exist behind our backs, and unlike in the case of Descartes's God, who not only warrants the truth of clear and distinct ideas, but also determines which truths are to be necessary, in Leibniz's idealism, the placing of ideas in God's mind seems to be motivated by his wish to give ontological grounding to logic itself, but without the metaphysical commitments. The reason for this is that the intelligible domain is regulated by the predicate-in-notion principle of combinatorial logic, non-contradiction, the doctrine of compossibility, etc., over which God has no power whatsoever. Nowhere does Leibniz *justify* ideas by cloistering them in God's mind; he rather labels the domain of ideas with divine character as a *consequence* of the infinity of such a domain. Strictly speaking, something is not a possibility because God contemplates it; rather, because there are infinite possibilities, God must contemplate them all. If the human intellect is too limited to know all truths, particularly to perform infinite analyses of contingent truths, it is simply not conceivable for Leibniz that unthought truths would thus exist nowhere. The divine intellect is then a convenient place for the infinite realm of possibilities with objective validity, the existence of which any logic must permit in one way or another, but the totality of which we cannot possess due to our finitude. In other words, insofar as he equates the realm of eternal ideas with the divine intellect, the latter is just Leibniz's way of expressing the absolute validity of logic and its principles, to which God is equally subject.

That the realm of the divine intellect is used as a synonym for logic itself can be observed in various passing comments Leibniz makes when dealing with epistemological matters, in which he frequently invokes theistic vocabulary to convey his conviction that something must be valid in itself even if there is no human mind to confirm that validity. In such instances, a higher intelligence presents itself as a means of ontologizing logic rather than the principle or source of logic. Thus, when he wishes to convince one of his correspondents that it is *impossible* to explain perception by way of Aristotelian forms, Leibniz rhetorically amplifies this by saying that even an angel "will accomplish nothing by chattering about forms and faculties."[69] Similarly, when he wants to establish that everything happens due to causes which are *intelligible* even if the causes remain permanently unknown to us, Leibniz translates this into a claim that we would understand such causes "if some angel wished to reveal them to us."[70] Also, to say that the reality of relations and modes depends on "a supreme intelligence" is just another way of saying that "the ideas of them are *real* just so long as the modes are *possible*,"[71] which means that "a divine idea" is perfectly synonymous with "real possibility,"[72] and so on. *Reality, possibility, impossibility,* and *intelligibility* need some ontological grounding outside the human mind, which shows that the divine *intelligence*—but not divine grace, goodness, omnipotence, etc.—is precisely coextensive with the infinite domain of the combinatory logic of concepts, and that, in this limited respect, Leibniz's theistic phrasing acts merely as a rhetorical device to convey the universality of logic. So, whereas genuinely metaphysical reasons exist for God's creating of this individual substance or another, in Leibniz's epistemology, the guardianship of God and the angels over ideas appears to be a secondary maneuver serving merely as a tool to desubjectivize them, whereby he establishes a version of Platonist idealism.

Thus, we must carefully distinguish the idealism in Leibniz's writings about logic and language from the more widely established "idealism" of his metaphysics of monads, which is a doctrine of *reality as existence*, and thus requires the principle of sufficient reason in addition to the principle of non-contradiction. One of the often-neglected aspects of Leibniz's CU, however, is the fact that it was never intended as a tool for describing existing individual objects or singular events, but rather as a scientific language expressing primarily truths about the genera and species of things. For Leibniz, general terms come before individual ones in the natural order of ideas, "they have a wider spread over individuals with which they agree, carry a lighter load of ideas or essences; they were very often the easiest to form, and are the most useful,"[73] whereas the knowledge of individuals, as is well known, is burdened with infinity and is therefore in the domain of divine, rather than scientific, knowledge. Hence, for Leibniz's wider project of General Science, of which the universal characteristic is a tool, possibilities, which include all non-contradictory concepts and categories insofar as they are the building blocks of the intelligible world, belong to the domain of reality no less than existing things precisely because it is the business of science to extract the general and universal, i.e., possible features from existing individual things. The point of Leibnizian idealism is thus neither to exchange the existing physical reality for lofty heights nor to convert the worldly into the ideal, but *to widen the scope of the real* from the existing and individual to the possible and universal in which the reality (but not the existence) of the individual ultimately consists. For not only are existing things, insofar as they were chosen by God to make up the best possible world, only a subset of possible things; more importantly, they are all instances of certain genera and species, which are not individual, and the scientific knowledge of them therefore consists in what is possible and ideal in them. The reality to be known and designated by CU *is essentially ideal*, for it is through the essential and eternal that the existing and individual is known and designated by science.

On this account, Leibniz's realism appears to be twofold: he is, of course, a pre-critical realist in the sense that, for him, the access to in-itself is granted, but he is also a realist in the sense of no lesser philosophical pedigree than anti-nominalism or Platonist idealism. Leibniz's insistence that essences are *real* whenever ideas of them are demonstrated as *possible* makes the whole framework of his epistemological theory decisively Platonist:[74] ideas *qua* possibilities *represent reality in the most literal sense*. Thus, notwithstanding the limited reach of human knowledge, for Leibniz there had never been a radical gap between the subject and what Meillassoux calls "the great outdoors."[75] The notions of the mind, even if fragmentary or false, are woven into the fabric of ideal reality with the help of perception and logic; they must be ordered into logically coherent ideas in which the human mind thereby always already participates. In this perspective, the doctrine of innate ideas serves as an epistemological supplement to Leibniz's preconceived idealist ontology. Hence, the two meanings of 'realism' mentioned above are connected: if Leibniz believes that things themselves are accessible to knowledge, it is only because the conceptual relations explaining their essences are real and not imposed on them by the mind. The basic Leibnizian view is thus that cognitive labor consists in navigating the maze of pre-existing potential knowledge rather than in bridging the gap between thought and being with adequation. The former was the trademark of the Platonist ontological vein in philosophy, which had been receding in Leibniz's time, whereas the latter has been more at home in the epistemological tradition ever since Aristotle.

(c) Philosophies of consciousness, philosophies of being

When scouting for allies and foes of realism in the history of philosophy, this distinction between philosophies of consciousness and philosophies of being should perhaps be kept in mind even more than the historical divide between Kantian transcendentalism and pre-critical dogmatism. One's chances of reaching the in-itself are greatly influenced by whether one decides to approach the issue of what there is through the gateway of epistemology or ontology. Descartes is perhaps the most typical example of the former approach, since, strictly speaking, it is epistemology rather than metaphysics that is the real Cartesian *prima philosophia*. Similarly, Locke, Hume, Kant, and Husserl all belong to this tradition, regardless of whether their philosophical endeavors end up as realist or not. However, one can hardly overestimate the importance of the fact that for Leibniz (and even more explicitly for Spinoza), the point of departure is very different: the question is not how to reach ontological statements from the mind, the *esse* from the *cogito*, but how to account for the mind, among other things, within the pre-given structure of reality. Rather than questioning the possibility of true knowledge of things by way of scrutinizing the subtleties and inner workings of our mental sphere, Leibniz harmonizes the issues of being, knowledge, and language within the pre-given ontological framework.[76] As his debate with Locke clearly shows, the *existence* of desubjectivized ideas and eternal essences is given and need not be proven per se; it is their *nature* that has to be laboriously explored and demonstrated. So, unlike Locke or Descartes, Leibniz does not start philosophizing from introspection to then demonstrate the existence of the external world, other minds and the workings of language; rather, he starts with ontological commitments, and accounts for cognition as he proceeds. The method of doubt, for example, is thus entirely alien to this vein of philosophy, according to which objectivity is not to be secured within consciousness or from consciousness—it is out there, and within us, waiting to be uncovered in the infinite complexities of logically nested concepts. In short, for philosophies of being, reality is never treated as *the great outdoors*, because our minds are always already navigating across it.

As this division is as old as philosophy itself, it also seems to run through the present debate about realism. Meillassoux, for example, acknowledges the strength of correlationism, but tries to overcome its limitations by absolutizing them, by "put[ting] back into the thing itself what we mistakenly took to be an incapacity in thought."[77] He accepts the epistemological game of correlationism and seeks the absolute within the implications of its commitments. However, object-oriented ontology, particularly in Graham Harman's iteration, rejects the transcendental perspective altogether and starts with a flattened ontology in which the cognitive relation between the mind and objects is reduced to a mere instance of relations between any objects whatsoever. While Harman admits that human cognition is significant, at least in its being far more complicated than most other relations, it is nevertheless not *ontologically* special or so radically different from any other object–object relation as to deserve the status of the original meta-relation from which every philosophy should depart.[78] The difference between Meillassoux and Harman is therefore not a difference of conclusion, but a difference of the original premise. Harman does not derive his ontology of withdrawn objects from the fact that they elude our knowledge, nor does he ground their unity in the categories of cognition; he prioritizes objects, inexhaustible by the relations between them, and *then* attributes the status of such a relation to cognition. Now, even if Harman would advocate neither transcendental nor transcendent realism of the Platonist kind, what he nonetheless shares with Leibniz is that they both prefer to ground their epistemologies in their ontologies (unlike Descartes, Locke, or Meillassoux, who take the opposite route). Moreover, just as for Harman, the point is not "that all objects are equally real, but that they are equally *objects*,"[79] which includes sailboats, atoms, the Dutch East India Company as well as pixies, nymphs, utopias, and even square circles, so in the Leibnizian universe indeed *not everything exists, but everything is equally an essence insofar as it is a possibility*, including number, parricide, gold and redness—granted, with the exception of square circles and other contradictory notions. I would argue that the necessary condition of this particular similarity is the fact that they both share the ontology-first approach to philosophy.

The break between philosophies that favor introspection as a starting point and which must then deal with the "scandal" they impose on themselves, and philosophies that attack being directly, appears to be more fundamental than the historical turning point at which dogmatic metaphysics is superseded by transcendental philosophy. It has also been decisive in the history of the philosophy of language. The doctrine of pre-linguistic thoughts and instrumental views of language can be found in the epistemologically oriented philosophies of language between Aristotle and Kant, and they are, of course, burdened with bridging yet another gap between language and mind. Leibniz, as we have seen, avoids this by being a much stronger linguistic realist than Locke, who, despite having kept the primacy of ideas over words untouched, nevertheless completely excluded things themselves from all semiotic relations. For, just as in the Kantian transcendental philosophy the truth of a scientific statement is decided based on the verifiability of that statement within the scientific community, and not in correspondence with thing in itself, so, too, in Locke's linguistic philosophy the meaning of a word in communication is determined by an agreement between the complex ideas of individuals using a particular word and not by the essence of a particular substance or mode. By contrast, Leibniz believes that our knowledge and our semiotic systems, be it natural language, CU or algebra, are simply harmonized expressions of a pre-given ontological structure.

Notes

1   The research included in this paper was funded by the Slovenian Research Agency (ARRS) under the research project "Language and Science: The Possibility of Realism in Modern Philosophy" (J6-7364).

2   Cf. Quentin Meillassoux, *After Finitude: An Essay on the Necessity of Contingency*, trans. Ray Brassier (London: Continuum, 2006).
3   Cf. ibid., 6.
4   Richard Rorty, ed., *The Linguistic Turn: Essays in Philosophical Method* (Chicago: University of Chicago Press, 1967).
5   See, e.g., Cristina Lafont, *The Linguistic Turn in Hermeneutic Philosophy*, trans. José Medina (Cambridge, MA and London: MIT Press, 1999) ix–xviii, 3; Michael N. Forster, *After Herder: Philosophy of Language in the German Tradition* (Oxford and New York: Oxford University Press, 2010), 1–5, 249. For the Cartesian theory of language, see Ulrich Ricken, *Linguistics, Anthropology and Philosophy in the French Enlightenment: Language Theory and Ideology*, trans. Robert E. Norton (London and New York: Routledge, 1994), 9–11, 27–32.
6   As I shall make Locke an example of this view, a cautionary remark is in order. Michael Losonsky attributes the first "linguistic turn" in modern philosophy to Locke, because he was the first to recognize the important role of language in epistemology (see Michael Losonsky, *Linguistic Turns in Modern Philosophy* [Cambridge and New York: Cambridge University Press, 2006], 10–12). I do not dispute this importance. But whereas in the drafts of the *Essay* Locke indeed made claims which seem to ascribe to language a role above and beyond communication and recording of one's thoughts, the textual evidence in the *Essay* is less convincing. It is true that Book III shows an important shift away from the theories of rational grammar, and although Locke's sensualist epistemology could thus not avoid stating the close connection between ideas and words, this connection nevertheless remains decisively weaker compared to the later German tradition, or even Condillac, since language and thought in principle remain separable.
7   John Locke, *An Essay concernig Human Understanding*, ed. Peter H. Nidditch (Oxford: Oxford University Press, 1975), 475, 490, 495 (III.ix–x, III.x.9). Here and hereafter, the italics are Locke's.
8   Cf. Lafont, *The Linguistic Turn in Hermeneutic Philosophy*, 5–7.
9   Johann Georg Hamann, *Writings on Philosophy and Language*, trans. Kenneth Haynes (Cambridge: Cambridge University Press, 2007), 211.
10 Cf. Forster, *After Herder*, 3, 9, 17, 56–7.
11 Cf. Hans Aarsleff, *From Locke to Saussure: Essays on the Study of Language and Intellectual History* (Minneapolis: University of Minnesota Press, 1985), 14–15, 335–55. Forster criticizes this interpretation as "provocative but rather eccentric" (Forster, *After Herder*, 79n).
12 Michael N. Forster, *German Philosophy of Language: From Schlegel to Hegel and Beyond* (Oxford: Oxford University Press, 2011), 88–9.
13 Cf. Lafont, *The Linguistic Turn in Hermeneutic Philosophy*, xiv; Lia Formigari, *Signs, Science, and Politics: Philosophies of Language in Europe, 1700–1830* (Amsterdam: John Benjamins, 1993), 169. The phrase has also been widely used in analytic philosophy of language.
14 Lafont, *The Linguistic Turn in Hermeneutic Philosophy*, 3; cf. also Forster, *German Philosophy of Language*, 92.
15 This has also been called the "nomenclaturist perspective" on language. See Roy Harris, *Language, Saussure and Wittgenstein: How to Play Games with Words* (London and New York: Routledge, 1988), 27.
16 Cf. Aristotle, *De interpretatione*, I (16a).
17 Locke, *Essay*, 490 (III.x.2).

18 George Berkeley, "A Treatise concerning the Principles of Human Knowledge," in *Philosophical Writings*, ed. Desmond M. Clarke (Cambridge: Cambridge University Press, 2008), 82 (Introduction, §24).
19 Wilhelm Freiherr von Humboldt, *On Language: The Diversity of Human Language-Structure and Its Influence on the Mental Development of Mankind*, trans. Peter Heath (Cambridge and New York: Cambridge University Press, 1988), 54–5.
20 It must be noted, however, that this opposition of linguistic realism and determinism also has its limits, of course. Not only is it perhaps a little sketchy in its depiction of the thinkers associated with both views, but the story of the philosophy of language since the seventeenth century could also be (and has been) told through a set of different oppositions. For an alternative interpretation which portrays the history of modern philosophy of language as a battle between enlightenment empiricists and German idealists, see Lia Formigari's *Signs, Science, and Politics* (169–89). Interestingly, the prism of this duality depicts Locke and Condillac as advocates of the constitutive role of language for thinking and portrays the German tradition as having freed the mind of such empirical constraints. Formigari puts Humboldt in the same camp as Kant because of his emphasis on the *Sprachformen* and the transcendental place of language (not *empirical* language, but its ideal essence). It is beyond the scope of this article to deal with these interpretations critically; however, it must be said that the alternative divisions always stem from the original question asked. Formigari is mainly interested in the opposition between contingency and the necessity of knowledge, whereas the present division (shared by Forster and Lafont) concerns only the character of language–consciousness relation. In this sense Locke is closer to Descartes, and it is in this respect that Condillac, otherwise a Lockean phenomenalist, most significantly departs from his master.
21 However, as Losonsky (whom I follow on the terminology of "linguistic determinism" instead of "idealism" here) correctly points out, linguistic determinism should not be understood to necessarily lead to relativism, i.e., the incommensurability of different natural languages, and therefore, ways of thinking. There is no clear evidence of outright relativism in Condillac or even Humboldt. But while the connection between the two is not necessary, it was certainly frequently assumed in the twentieth century, often implicitly. Cf. Losonsky, *Linguistic Turns in Modern Philosophy*, 81.
22 Georg Wilhelm Leibniz, *New Essays on Human Understanding*, trans. Peter Remnant and Jonathan Bennett (Cambridge: Cambridge University Press, 1996), 214.
23 See G. W. Leibniz and Hiob Ludolf, *Leibniz and Ludolf on Things Linguistic: Excerpts from Their Correspondence (1688–1703)*, trans. John T. Waterman (Berkeley and Los Angeles: University of California Press, 1978).
24 Locke, *Essay*, 405 (III.ii.2).
25 Ibid., 407 (III.ii.5).
26 Ibid., 405 (III.ii.1).
27 Leibniz, *New Essays*, 287.
28 Ibid., 261.
29 Ibid., 301.
30 Cf. ibid., 296.
31 G. W. Leibniz, "What Is an Idea?" in *Philosophical Papers and Letters*, ed. Leroy E. Loemker (Dordrecht: Kluwer, 1975), 207. Hereafter, citations from this edition shall be abbreviated as L followed by the page number.
32 Leibniz, *New Essays*, 301.
33 Ibid., 262.
34 Leibniz, "What Is an Idea?" L 208.

35 Locke, *Essay*, 416 (III.iii.14).
36 Cf. ibid., 417–18 (III.iii.15–17).
37 Leibniz, *New Essays*, 293.
38 Ibid., 292.
39 Cf. ibid., *New Essays*, 292.
40 Ibid., 294.
41 Cf. Leibniz, "Meditations on Knowledge, Truth, and Ideas," L 292.
42 Leibniz, "On Universal Synthesis and Analysis, or the Art of Discovery and Judgment," L 230. A further advantage in the case of substances is that we know that they exist by experience, and therefore we know that the idea of gold is non-contradictory, even if we do not know precisely all its constitutive concepts and have thus not established its possibility *a priori* through proper real definitions. See Leibniz, "Of an Organum or Ars Magna of Thinking," in *Philosophical Writings*, ed. G. H. R. Parkinson (London and Melbourne: Dent, 1973), 4; *New Essays*, 293–4.
43 Leibniz, "On Universal Synthesis and Analysis," L 231.
44 Cf. Jaap Maat, *Philosophical Languages in the Seventeenth Century: Dalgarno, Wilkins, Leibniz* (Dordrecht: Kluwer, 2004), 345.
45 Cf. Leibniz, "Dissertation on the Art of Combinations," L 80.
46 Cf. Leibniz, *New Essays*, 120, 297, 403.
47 Leibniz, "Dialogue," L 184.
48 Ibid.
49 Ibid.
50 Cf. Leibniz, "Thought, Signs and the Foundation of Logic," translated in Marcelo Dascal, *Leibniz. Language, Signs and Thought: A Collection of Essays* (Amsterdam: John Benjamins, 1987), 182.
51 Leibniz, "A Geometric Characteristic," in *Leibniz. Language, Signs and Thought*, 167 (emphasis mine).
52 Leibniz, "Preface to the General Science" ["La vraie méthode"], in *Selections*, ed. Philip P. Wiener (New York: Charles Scribner's Sons, 1951), 14.
53 Leibniz, "Thought, Signs and the Foundation of Logic," 181.
54 Cf. Leibniz, *New Essays*, 185–6. It is on these grounds that he criticizes Descartes's ontological proof. See "Meditations on Knowledge, Truth, and Ideas," L 291–2.
55 Leibniz, "On Universal Synthesis and Analysis," L 231.
56 Leibniz, "Meditations on Knowledge, Truth, and Ideas," L 293.
57 Leibniz, "Of an Organum or Ars Magna of Thinking," 3.
58 Leibniz, "Dissertation on the Art of Combinations," L 82.
59 Leibniz, "On the General Characteristic," L 222; see also "On Universal Synthesis and Analysis," L 229.
60 Leibniz, "Thought, Signs and the Foundation of Logic," 182.
61 Leibniz, "Letter to Walter von Tschirnhaus," May, 1678, L 193.
62 On this point, see Stefano Gensini, "'Filum Meditandi': Semiotics and Scientific Knowledge in the Thought of G. W. Leibniz," *Histoire Épistémologie Langage* 14, no. 2 (1992): 116.
63 Leibniz, "On the Demonstration of Primary Propositions," in *Leibniz. Language, Signs and Thought*, 149.
64 Leibniz, "Letter to Henry Oldenburg," December 28, 1675, L 166.
65 Leibniz, "Letter to Walter von Tschirnhaus," May 1678, L 193; see also "Letter to Duke Johann Friedrich von Hannover," fall 1679, L 261–2 and dozens of other papers and letters.

66 Leibniz, "Synopsis of a Book whose Title Will Be: Foundations and Examples of a New General Science...," in *The Art of Controversies*, ed. Marcelo Dascal (Dordrecht: Springer, 2008), 217.
67 Lafont, *The Linguistic Turn in Hermeneutic Philosophy*, 17.
68 Meillassoux, *After Finitude*, 11.
69 Leibniz, "Letter to Hermann Conring," March 19, 1678, L 189.
70 Leibniz, "On a Method of Arriving at a True Analysis of Bodies and the Causes on Natural Things," L 173.
71 Leibniz, *New Essays*, 265.
72 Ibid., 268.
73 Ibid., 275.
74 For more on the Leibniz's Platonist epistemology, see Christia Mercer, "The Platonism at the Core of Leibniz's Philosophy," in *Platonism at the Origins of Modernity: Studies on Platonism and Early Modern Philosophy*, ed. Douglas Hedley and Sarah Hutton (Dordrecht: Springer, 2008), 228–30.
75 Meillassoux, *After Finitude*, 7.
76 This was emphasized particularly by Michel Serres in his *Le système de Leibniz et ses modèles mathématiques*, vol. 2 (Paris: Presses universitaires de France, 1968), 537–47.
77 Meillassoux, *After Finitude*, 53.
78 Cf. Graham Harman, *The Quadruple Object* (Winchester and Washington: Zero Books, 2011), 6; *Prince of Networks: Bruno Latour and Metaphysics* (Melbourne: re.press, 2007), 212.
79 Harman, *The Quadruple Object*, 5.

3

Desert Islands and the Origins of Antirealism[1]

Jure Simoniti

Western philosophy from Kant onward seems particularly inclined to indulge in two contradictory, yet complementary narratives on the relation between man and the world.

On the one hand, the world is being constantly recalibrated so as to fit into the mind of the modern subject.[2] Kant's epistemological constraint of "the conditions of the *possibility of experience*" being "at the same time conditions of the *possibility of the objects of experience*"[3] developed subsequently into a veritable program of practical appropriation of the world, resulting in an increasingly exhaustive interpenetration between the subject and the object. Fichte, to give only one of the many possible examples from his work, instructs us that "[t]he world must become to me what my body is."[4] Hegel defines reason as "the certainty of consciousness that it is all reality."[5] Marx puts it in economic terms: "As the earth is [man's] original larder, so too it is his original tool house."[6] In Nietzsche, "*there simply is no true world*"[7] beyond the perspective illusions of the will to power. Heidegger laments that "the farthest corner of the globe has been conquered technologically and can be exploited economically."[8] And the entire French structuralism is haunted by the discomforting feeling of being imprisoned within the structure of finite possibilities that lack any outside. Lévi-Strauss even deplores "that our world has suddenly found itself to be too small for the people who live in it."[9]

On the other hand, the very same man who incorporated the world so successfully begins drifting toward the most infinitesimal margins of an inhuman universe and pale there in his cosmic insignificance. He is, as Nietzsche notably put it, rolling from the center toward x. In Kant, the starry heavens annihilate "my importance as an *animal creature*" (*KpV* 289–90).[10] Schopenhauer places us "on one of those numberless spheres freely floating in boundless space, without knowing whence or whither."[11] Nietzsche locates our planet "[i]n some remote corner of the universe, flickering in the light of the countless solar systems into which it had been poured."[12] And Heidegger compares the earth to a "tiny grain of sand."[13] Lévi-Strauss pointedly notes: "The world began without the human race and it will end without it."[14]

It is a case of a disruptive development of man enclosing the world into his mind, while simultaneously perceiving himself as the world's most minute and trivial eventuality.[15] In this sense, the usual diagnosis that, with Kant, we have delved into the realm of antirealism and have not recovered from it since, falls short to an extent, as it fails to take into account the fact that post-Kantian philosophy never shied away from acknowledging the planetary smallness of man. A certain "normative antirealism," which puts the entire reality in the hands of man, and a certain "existential realism," which constantly shoves man towards the state of creatural negligibility, seem to go hand in hand, hardly aware of the contradiction that they nevertheless unfold. For the purpose of exploring new possibilities of realism, this chapter will thus venture a step behind the constitutive tension between the epistemic centrality and the cosmic marginality of the modern subject.

In short, the post-Kantian self-awareness seems to be torn apart by two peculiarly divergent "myths": first, the myth of absolute interiority, which leaves nothing outside the remit of man, and second, the myth of absolute exteriority, against the vastness of which the vanishing human can no longer claim having any inside. In searching for the cause of this impasse, one of the unobtrusive, unrecognized philosophical phantasms could perchance come to our aid. It is a phantasm of the subject beholding a "virginal object" in the midst of an already occupied world, an object that has fallen out of the totalizing matrices of man's theoretical and practical prerogative. The marginal texts, poetic accounts, unintended anecdotes, and passing metaphors of the great philosophers from Fichte to Marx, Nietzsche, Heidegger, and Deleuze sometimes put the philosophical subject in a specific context; they place him on an island in the sea, a deserted, coral, oceanic island, still unspoiled and untrodden by the terrestrial appetites of the human race.

The island in its uncontaminated quality serves as a representative of the "absolute Outside" of human jurisdiction. And the question is, what might be the conditions for this object to manifest itself before the eyes of the modern subject? What is it that the subject must put in the balance, so that he can finally witness an object so flagrantly exhibiting its inhumanity? As we will see, this irreducible object will only disclose itself to a certain kind of subject, one of *creative excess* over the mere subjective mediation of objectivity. Philosophy after Kant has often been reproached for positing an "object relation" in which congruity with the subject is presupposed, enforced, taken for granted, and without a surplus or remainder. But against this "conventional" background, a new, extravagant relation between the two extremes will establish itself: a novel kind of subject, who transcends the constraints of this world, will find himself in an unexpected equilibrium with a unique kind of object, one utterly resistant to subjective appropriation. And it is this new "truth form," extending between the *subject-surplus* and the *object-residue*, that will hopefully shed new light upon the common, totalizing truth form as a (projected, anticipated, asymptotic, or always already attained) correspondence with reality.

The goal of this chapter is thus to gain some insight into the origins of Western antirealism. As we hope to demonstrate, the reason for post-Kantian antirealism might not lie in the fact that the subject fails to surpass the limits of correlation, being somehow naturally unfit to egress from his "hermeneutic bubble," from the realm of his consciousness and language. It could well turn out that, instead, he is unable to come to terms with him being condemned to produce his own truth, one which is spontaneous, groundless, unforeseeable, and absolute. What he cannot face is not reality-in-itself but *truth-in-itself*, i.e., truth which discloses reality as it is, but of which reality has no need, and to which it provides no sufficient reason. Seen from this perspective, man will sooner believe in reality belonging to him, even in it being created by him, than endure the gaze into the excessive novelty of truth, which, from the point of view of reality, is entirely superfluous. Therefore, the alleged humanization of reality might well be a mere consequence, a masque, of the prior incapability of withstanding the "essentially non-derivable quality" of truth, which became imperative after Kant's invention of the spontaneity of reason. In a nutshell, examining the source of post-Kantian antirealism, we will rather shift the emphasis to the hitherto overlooked *anti-verism* of Western thought.

I Fichte's desert island

In one of the notorious scenes of the history of philosophy, Kant's moral subject raises his eyes to the night sky. At the precise moment of experiencing his innermost truth, the moral law, his gaze opens to the regions of being thus far unknown:

> Two things fill the mind with ever new and increasing admiration and reverence, the more often and more steadily one reflects on them: *the starry heavens above me and the moral law within me.*
>
> KpV 289

Within the Kantian scope, both entities, freedom and the unexplored world, standing here face to face with each other, represent a certain excess; and it is this balance of excesses that needs to be brought to light. Freedom is a breach of the otherwise universally valid causality. Along the same lines, the thought of the world being infinitely larger than me seems to violate the fact that everything I perceive, have perceived, or will ever perceive is a synthetic product of my own original creativity, "the spontaneity of concepts" and its faculty to generate representations. Thus, on the one hand, Kantianism looks at first sight like a clear-cut case of "antirealism." On the other hand, what Kant here superimposes upon this ordinary, antirealist relation, is an entirely new, unprecedented "scene of truth." While the forms of understanding must always be "filled out" with the content of the senses, now, in practical philosophy, the subject is granted the privilege of experiencing his own "absolute spontaneity," whose ace in the hole is precisely its being relieved of the telluric burden of receptivity. By hearing the voice of the moral law, by becoming free, he reaches a state of self-determination, without thereby having to synthesize any empirical, sensual object. And it is at this very point that an abyss opens above his head, a celestial void that his theoretical and practical efforts will most likely never be able to traverse and fill. The feelings of "admiration," "respect," and "sublimity" (*KpV* 290) that the starry heavens inspire in him perhaps bear testimony to the unfolding of something older and greater than the human subject. But what exactly is the lever that provides a glimpse into this pre-subjective realm of being?

With morality, Kant introduces a schism into the subject. It is the moral law that "reveals to me a life independent of animality and even of the whole sensible world . . ., a determination not restricted to the conditions and boundaries of this life but reaching into the infinite." (*KpV* 289–90). Man is no longer merely a finite subject of knowledge, but also an infinite subject of freedom. In turn, however, an unexpected deflation is set in motion. Instead of arrogantly elevating his creatural uniqueness into a divine being, the moral, sensually autonomous subject rather looks up into the sky, which "annihilates, as it were, my importance as an *animal creature*" (*KpV* 289–90). Ontogenetically, man advances from being a theoretical and empirical subject to a moral and free one; beginning as a finite creature, he becomes infinite. Yet phylogenetically, he regresses from bearing the name of "man" to calling himself an "animal."

What interests us here is the new counterbalance that inverts the values of the old, antirealist correlation. Kant's theoretical program of comprehensive knowledge of the world, placing the subject in the center of the universe and reproducing the forms of his understanding throughout its expanse, was frequently deemed to be an act of anthropomorphism. In practical philosophy, however, the subject becomes conscious of the moral law within him, while simultaneously attending, and even relishing, an unanticipated revelation of a de-anthropomorphized universe. The subject of cognition first constitutes the world, but when he, for good measure, realizes his own moral freedom as well, he is suddenly allowed to contemplate a sky that no longer reflects his figure back to him.[16] Ironically, he must become "more than man," in order to behold a "world without man" for the first time. It is from this configuration that the function of the moral law can be deduced: the law, the experience of absolute spontaneity, seems to be the only momentum powerful enough to make man briefly suspend the quintessential Kantian compulsion to synthesize experience, stare into the sky impassively, and recognize in the distant stars, not evidence of his epistemological activity, but a pervasive image of material diminishment, cosmic devaluation, and existential annihilation of his being.

Thus, the moral law and the obscurity of space achieve a taut equilibrium: freedom guarantees an exception from empirical causality, while the sky exemplifies an untraveled horizon, a world as yet unmapped. Two irreducible relations stand opposite to each other. As a reference point, there is the "antirealist" relation of the entire world being embedded in the mind of the subject. But against it, the "realist" relation is silhouetted, one in which the true "otherness of the world" unwittingly reveals itself to a free, excessive, self-sustaining subject. It is a juxtaposition of two correlations:

Spontaneity of Understanding – Receptivity of the Senses
Moral Law – Starry Heavens

This double balance may well represent the matrix that will help us understand all the other appearances of "nonhuman objects" in the philosophy to follow.

Our first case is Fichte. In his work, he sporadically made use of the metaphor of the desert island as signifying a not-yet-occupied world. However, in his short treatise *A Contribution to the Rectification of the Public's Judgment of the French Revolution*, the reference to *die wüste Insel* is somewhat more conspicuous.

Fichte embodies the post-Kantian stance at its purest, centering his entire ontology around the spontaneous, autonomous, self-positing, originally practical, and consequently relentless absolute subject, who invents being, modifies matter, and has the right to take possession of everything on which he can impress his form.

Nevertheless, this hyperbolic idealism of the I soon reaches a most prosaic empirical limit. Even though reality, the not-I, is posited within the I alone, the I experiences a shortage of the given world. The great subject of the *a priori* practical infinity must face the *a posteriori* finitude of the meager planet on which he was born.

It is this discontent over an unduly cultivated world, this imbalance between the new work mania of the modern man and the earth being too small for his endeavors, that sets the tone to the essay on French Revolution:

> While some take all our clothes, the others expel us to the air; for the earth and the sea have already been occupied, and the pope, by divine law, has given away even the lands that are yet to be discovered.[17]

Or:

> Our powers are thus evolved; we want to take possession of something, we look around, and everything has its owner except air and light; for the simple reason that they cannot assume a foreign form. We can travel around the earth without finding anything to which we could apply our right to appropriation, which extends only to all raw matter. Raw matter is almost non-existent.[18]

Upon this undividedly conquered globe, the desert island can merely provide a ground for the re-enactment of the property right being established:

> Imagine a number of people arriving with agricultural equipment and drought cattle to a desert, uncultivated island. Everyone carves with his plow in the earth, where he wishes; where he stands, no one else can stand. Everyone ploughs over what he can, and whoever reclaimed the greatest part until the evening, will legally possess the greatest part. — Now, the entire island is ploughed over. Whoever overslept the day, will possess nothing, and this by law.[19]

Still, it is not the last mention of the island motif. A few pages later, Fichte strikes a different chord. He draws his famous diagram of four interlinking circles, each of which encompasses its respective area of legal legitimacy. The smallest is the "domain of civil contract," which is embraced by the "domain of contracts in general," which is a part of the "domain of natural law," while all three are included in the largest "domain of conscience." According to Fichte, one has every right to resign any obligation of the first three domains. One is permitted to secede from the state, annul all contracts, and, in fact, disavow the natural law. But one can never escape one's conscience, for its voice can be heard everywhere, even on a desert island:

> The domain of conscience encompasses all and the domain of civil contract the smallest part. Everyone must be allowed to withdraw from the center to the periphery, even to step out of the domain of natural law, if one prefers to live on a desert island; but it is impossible to exit the domain of conscience if one is not an animal.[20]

The least that can be derived from these sparse indications is that Fichte distinguishes two types of desert islands. Whereas the island in its first mention merely repeats the experiment of man's right to appropriate land, it now becomes a space of retreat from the very world of property and endless cultivation.[21] Moreover, within the discursive setting of this argument, something else transpires: without the possibility of complete withdrawal from the realm of social ties, conscience would perhaps remain deprived of the most important metaphor of its absolute demand. If it is possible to pass over from the inside of an occupied land to the outskirts of an unoccupied world without thereby silencing one's conscience, then the desert island assumes an additional, metaphorically charged role. It seems also to represent the place that allows conscience to speak in its most undisturbed clarity. To put it in another way, the sole reason why the "second" desert island resists appropriation, thus undercutting the basic claim of Fichte's philosophy, is because it lets only one voice be heard, that of conscience itself.

The key point of the "metaphorical reading" is that in order not to vanish under the possessive grasp of the practical subject, this small patch of land must be maintained by a different kind of subjectivity. The primary relation of Fichte's philosophy is that of the objectivity of land surrendering to the form of the subject, letting itself be conquered, belabored, *verichlicht*, "turned into the I." As Fichte says, "*We* are *our* property: I say, and assume thereby something twofold in us, a proprietor and a property."[22] However, our discursive analysis of symptoms detected a surfeit on each side of this confined and self-evident equation, an excess irreducible to the I's exhaustive preemption of the world. On the subjective side, conscience speaks up, while on the objective side, a desert island is mentioned, serving as a limiting condition of the audibility of that inner voice. But if there is a relation here at all, what sustains it? What does the surplus of conscience over the usual practical I consist in, so that it can stand face to face with this categorically anti-Fichtean object of absolute otherness?

Conscience is not an altogether other self, but rather the pure, self-referential form of the I folding back upon itself. While the Fichtean I is still caught in the object-relation to a not-I, conscience embodies more fully his own ideal of not having anything outside himself. As an unequivocally "inner" voice, it is the origin of the moral law that lies "in our self, as it would be without any experience."[23] Whereas Fichte's I is primarily a proprietor whose function is to exclude others from the use of things of which he himself has taken hold, conscience, by contrast, surpasses the shackles of objectivity and teaches a life beyond any personal gain, thereby displacing the kernel of the subject from his "practical" center. After all, conscience commands us to do what anyone else should do in our place. Paradoxically, thus, the function of this innermost instinct of Fichte's rather egocentric subjectivity is to reveal to the subject his own intrinsic substitutability. It is this "irreducibly other subject" in the heart of the I who can finally indulge in referring to a desert island without letting it evaporate in the frenzy of his own possessive desire; he is perhaps even capable of living on a land that is never to be owned.

In summary, Fichte performed a certain redoubling at both sides of the equation. The very treatise that defines the subject as a laborer and proprietor whose ambition is to snatch away things from others, simultaneously specifies him as a conscience that, following its own inner voice, always already speaks on behalf of any other subject.

And the very treatise that first made the desert island into a laboratory of the process of appropriation then elevates it into a place of retreat from the compulsion of working, forming, and occupying the world. The Fichtean subject is split into his primary practical and secondary ethical nature.[24] And the Fichtean object is also split into the already conquered land and the desert island eluding this claim. It is in this situation that both excessive elements receive their poignant figurative charge. The reference to the desert island must be placed against the backdrop of Fichte's own admonition that the land of this world is already settled and distributed. And conscience must be contrasted with the subject's innate drive toward incessant labor and progress. To put it simply, the island is a metaphor for something that resists becoming a part of this world, and conscience is a metaphor for something speaking from the other world.[25] In this pronouncedly "secular" philosophy, they thus announce a new symmetry that serves as some kind of phantasmatic inversion of the fundamental Fichtean operation. One could speak of two relations, the first being that of appropriation and totalization, the second that of an equilibrium of extremes and de-totalization:

I – not-I
Conscience – Desert Island

What must be stressed, however, is that we could allow ourselves to write out this double correlation of still vague symptoms only in light of the subsequent appearances of desert islands in the philosophical literature. There, as remains to be seen, the logic behind it will become more solid and definite.

II Nietzsche's happy isles

After Fichte, it became a veritable contest among the philosophers of who would find a more compelling conceptual frame and a starker imagery for the subject's thoroughgoing "acculturation" and downright permeation of the object. Hegel and Marx were never weary of repeating that there is no world left outside the human endeavor to usurp and subdue it.

No one despised the oceanic feelings at the sight of the spectacle of nature as much as Hegel. In a private discussion with Heinrich Heine, he called the stars "a luminous leprosy in the sky." When he visited the Swiss Alps, the *locus classicus* of the Kantian sublime, he could not help but describe in his travel diary the tedium, monotony, and ugliness of these still pristine mountainous regions. His hike in the Bernese Alps in the summer of 1796 is considered by some as one of the great intellectual experiences in his philosophical biography. For it is there that this absolute idealist suddenly stood face to face with a piece of nature that refused to hold a mirror up to him, a glacier that persisted in the midst of the ploughed, planted, and harvested land. Its only purpose seems to have been to facilitate, by way of contrast, "a new form of seeing":

> Today we saw those glaciers [the glaciers of Grindelwald] at only half an hour of distance, and the sight is of no further interest. One could name it a new form

of seeing, which, however, does not engage the spirit, except that it may occur to it that, in the most extreme heat of the summer, it finds itself so close to the ice masses, which, even at a depth where cherries, nuts, and grain mellow, can only be melted inconsiderably.[26]

Confronted with this inhuman prospect, Hegel utters his famous judgement *Es ist so*:

> Neither the eye nor the imagination will in these formless masses find a spot to rest upon, to find occupation or reason to play with.... The sight of these eternally dead masses gave nothing to me but a monotonous and horribly dull notion: *it is so.*[27]

In the same vein, Marx considers nature to be a mere organ of man's right to achieve complete mastery over the world. The sensible reality is an overall product of society, industry, and history and the objects not bearing the stamp of man can only be stumbled upon anecdotally. Nonetheless, Marx's reference to the "coral island" in *The German Ideology* is particularly interesting, for it spells out the hidden relation between the subject's unrelenting incorporation of objectivity and the revelation of the ontological "priority of external nature":

> So much is this activity, this unceasing sensuous labour and creation, this production, the basis of the whole sensuous world as it now exists, that, were it interrupted only for a year, Feuerbach would not only find an enormous change in the natural world, but would very soon find that the whole world of men and his own perceptive faculty, nay his own existence, were missing. Of course, in all this the priority of external nature remains unassailed ... For that matter, nature, the nature that preceded human history, is not by any means the nature in which Feuerbach lives, it is nature which today no longer exists anywhere (except perhaps on a few Australian coral-islands of recent origin) and which, therefore, does not exist for Feuerbach.[28]

In Marx's universe, nature is nowhere to be seen under the vestiges of man's labor. Only under very specific conditions does its temporal antecedence shine through. At some point, the labor process reflects upon itself and becomes aware of its automatism, its self-created impetus, its emergent *causa sui*. And it is not until the subject discovers in himself a momentum of spontaneity, an element not simply derivable from nature, that it can afford to regard nature, once his mere object, as *older than himself*. The thing that now symbolizes this "priority of nature" is the island emerging from the sea, out of nothingness, as it were. Perhaps a double relation upon Fichte's matrix could be written out:

Labor – Nature
Unceasing Creation – Coral Island

Nevertheless, the structure of four elements is, at the moment, a weak coincidence of symptoms at best. Only in Nietzsche will the philosophical exploitations of desert islands get more substantial. When Zarathustra sets out to find solitude on the happy isles, it is this "residual object" which seems to offer the only possible ground for the Nietzschean "emergent subject" to stand upon.

Not only does Nietzsche fit perfectly in the tradition of the post-Kantian, i.e., Fichtean, Hegelian, Marxist total interpenetration of the subject and the object, but he intensifies this process to its utmost possibilities. In the polycentric world of the will to power, man is no longer merely Fichte's proprietor conquering new land or Marx's laborer acquiring means for living. Instead, he, being himself an "aristocracy of cells," infiltrates and impregnates things to the point of depriving them of their depth, their qualities, unity, and number. Facing the omnipotence of the will, the world ceases to exist. For the ultimate purpose of the will's overpowering is not only to take hold of everything under the Platonic Sun, but to incorporate the Sun as well. Such might be the meaning of the concluding lines of *Thus Spoke Zarathustra*, where the hero, after having projected nothing but his own self upon the walls of the cave, emerges from it as the light of the eternal noon:

> This is *my* morning, *my* day is beginning: *up now, up, you great noon!"*—
> Thus spoke Zarathustra and he left his cave, glowing and strong, like a morning sun that emerges from dark mountains.[29]

As we have vaguely observed so far, to the fall of the boundary between the subject and the object philosophy tends to react by introducing an additional distinction into each of the two poles. On the one side, some kind of "double subjectivation" is performed, and on the other side, some kind of "double objectivation." And Nietzsche carries out these two operations more forcefully and coherently than before. A certain dialectics within the subject is a recurring motive of post-Kantian philosophy: the subject of understanding stands against the subject of reason, the theoretical against the practical subject, the natural consciousness against the spirit, the capitalist against the proletariat. But it was Nietzsche who brought the logic of two subjects to the extreme of genetic differentiation, not shying away from the starkest of rhetorical effects. He opposed the heroes to the people, the master race to the slave race, Zarathustra to the crowd, the *Übermensch* to the *Untermensch*. This being the case, the object-correlate assumed two antagonistic, if concomitant, aspects as well. In Nietzsche, reality is always already absorbed by the will of the subject; everything exists in his inside, and there is no outside to the infinite process of his overpowering. Concurrently, the world discloses itself as a plain Outside with no inside, an indifferent universe, incapable of even acknowledging the existence of humanity. Thus, at one end of the spectrum, the subject liberates himself from his human origins and becomes a being of self-transcendence; at the other end, it is the object that abandons its correlation with the subject and becomes an utterly inhuman macrocosm.

Both dimensions, that is, of the world inhabiting the overwhelming inside of man and simultaneously representing his most grandiose outside, are so self-evidently synchronous that they need not be broken apart. What is more, this tension lies at the very core of the Nietzschean truth-form:

> The most extreme form of nihilism would be the view that *every* belief, every considering-something-true, is necessarily false because there simply is no *true*

> *world.* Thus: a *perspectival appearance* whose origin lies in us (in so far as we continually *need* a narrower, abbreviated, simplified world).
> —That it is the measure of strength to what extent we can admit to ourselves, without perishing, the merely *apparent* character, the necessity of lies.[30]

One might observe a certain ambiguity at play here. If there is no true world, any truth cannot but be true, since there is nothing real to belie it. Compared to what, then, could it be false? But it is. And this is so because of the specific Nietzschean abeyance, according to which the world can never falsify any of our truths, while simultaneously making them all look like illusions. Thus, for a belief to be false within a world which is itself a falsity, reality must assume two modes. On the one hand, it is *a priori* untrue, having automatically been curtailed and engulfed by our will to power. However, being caught within this circle of perfect auto-verification, one could never know of the world's untruth. Therefore, on the other hand, our "false" beliefs must additionally be measured against something nevertheless real, something factual beyond the grasp of illusions, because otherwise they could not be false. In more concrete terms, this means that, with Nietzsche, the limited, self-contained environment of our mendacious lives is indeed regularly collated with the harsh and cold facticity of the Outside.[31] Regarding the "epistemological" relation between truth and reality, the existence of "brute facts" is now shifted from the immediate things of our daily endeavors to the more large-scale prospects of universal disillusionment. While, for instance, the table here is undoubtedly a "false" projection of our simplifying self-preservation drive, and while we are the rightful usurpers of our proximate surroundings, this practical self-confidence will hardly extend to the realm of the stars above our heads, whose unintended virtue is to make us feel cosmologically null and inconsequential. And even though we might have once swallowed the sun, we will be no less dead by the end of our lives. It is for this reason that our only chance at eternity lies in the momentary radiance of the "great noon," in the creation of a truth which may outshine the facts but will never look away from them.

In other words, the double modality of reality must be echoed in truth having two modes as well. The one mode believes to be grounded in the facts of the world and lays claim to its own verifiability; it is a "false" truth, so to speak, one that requires critique. Once we recognize the falsity of every possible *Fürwahrhalten*, the concept of "truth" should become altogether obsolete. Nietzsche does sometimes sentence it to death:

> The world with which we are concerned is false, i.e., is not a fact but a fable and approximation on the basis of a meager sum of observations; it is "in flux," as something in a state of becoming, as a falsehood always changing but never getting near the truth: for—there is no "truth."[32]

And yet, he never lets go of the "regulative idea" peculiar to the semantics of "truth," reserving its name precisely for this final insight into the falsity of every holding-to-be-true. Hence, he repeatedly refers to another truth, one that is noble, grand, conscientious, almost ethical:

We have to wring the truth out of ourselves every step of the way, we have to give up almost everything that our heart, our love, our trust relied on. It requires greatness of soul: the service of truth is the hardest service.[33]

This, then, would be the second mode of truth, the "true" truth. Its aspiration is not to believe that the facts can be approached, mirrored, and expressed, but to abide them, face them with indifference, and stay alive. In a way, the highest truth is not the one corresponding to reality, but rather the one withstanding the fact that reality is itself untrue. For this reason, truth oscillates between two opposing, albeit correlative valences:

"How much truth can a spirit *endure,* how much truth does a spirit *dare*?"—*this* became for me the real standard of value.[34]

What man must dare is to create his own truth, for there is nothing outside of him that could falsify it. And what he is compelled to endure is that reality has no desire whatsoever for his truth and will also never verify it. In this way, the Nietzschean subject is constantly swaying between his unbridled creativity and his cosmically purposeless createdness. However, what looks like a contradiction turns out to be a careful proportion of *daring in order to be able to endure*. Only a truth unfolding in the medium of invention, artistic production, and spontaneity, a truth averse to approximating to the facts, will afford to look them in the eye without needing to turn away. Nietzsche's philosophy is nothing but an immense lesson that the bigger an "inside" world one creates, the more of the "outside" world one will manage to survive. And this is the frame within which Zarathustra's journey to the happy isles might finally be addressed.

While the modern subject's goal is to gain absolute possession of the world, Zarathustra's agenda is of a different sort. He looks for a place to give birth to the overman, and he finds it on an island. It is a singular setting where both the subject and the object are of a most distinct kind. What, then, defines the inner structure of the subject who sets foot on an island in the middle of the sea? The crucial quality of Zarathustra is that he himself is not a "subject in full," but only serves as a placeholder for the future incarnation of the *Übermensch*. As such, he is what we call an "essentially secondary subject." For what distinguishes the overman from man is that the first is never fully embodied. He represents a mere ideal point upon which every "temporary subject" stands for his substitutability by his own successor. And Zarathustra is precisely this transitional subject. Nietzsche consistently depicts him as defying any form of social identity, as appearing more like a woman than a man, more like a child than an adult, more like a replicate than an original. He describes him as pregnant, incomplete, and transitory, as "going to my children and returning from them; for the sake of his children Zarathustra must complete himself."[35] He is, so to speak, a uterus of an incorporeal ideal:

In order for the creator himself to be the child who is newly born, he must also want to be the birth-giver and the pain of giving birth.

> Indeed, through a hundred souls I went my way and through a hundred cradles and pangs of birth.[36]

What Nietzsche seems to aim at with these exuberant allegories is to distil a kind of "emergent subject of processual self-reference." The original design of the Nietzschean subject is already projective, dynamic, and endlessly increasing his power. But now this impetus of subjectivity is creamed off and enclosed into a circuit of both automatism and self-transcendence. After all, it is Nietzsche's regular maneuver to lift man off the ground and hold him in mid-air, thus flaunting his excessive, self-gratifying drive. Let us not forget that one of the great identification figures of Zarathustra is a tightrope walker whose performance he witnesses at the beginning of his adventure, sees him falling from the rope, comforts him in his last dying moments, and buries his body. Later, he even defines mankind as "a rope fastened between animal and overman—a rope over an abyss."[37]

However, our interest here lies exclusively in the object-correlate of this abysmal being with no land below his feet, who, in his rootlessness, nevertheless yearns for some kind of support. But what might be the proper ground for the groundless subject? The soil for him to set foot on can no longer be the world already consumed by the osmosis of the will to power. Only a piece of land resisting this overbearing ambition will do the trick; hence, an island.

In one of the nine *Dionysos-Dithyrambs,* titled "The Beacon," *Das Feuerzeichen,* Zarathustra finds his "seventh solitude," his homeland, precisely there:

> Why did Zarathustra flee from animal and man?
> Why did he suddenly desert all firm land?
> Six solitudes he knows already —,
> but the sea itself was not lonely enough for him,
> the island let him rise—at the top of the mountain he became a flame,
> toward a *seventh* solitude
> he casts, searching, a hook over his head.
>
> Lost mariners! Remains of old stars!
> You, seas of the future! Unexplored sky!
> Toward all the lonely I cast my hook...[38]

Upon a "lonely island" Zarathustra lights fire signals to fish for other lonely souls. Within the bounds of a new land, humanity thus stratifies into a peculiar kind of intersubjectivity, a vaporous community of equals, one no longer determined by the differential social roles of ancestors and progeny, adults and children, superiors and inferiors, men and women.

This line of thought is then taken up and developed in the main, prose text. Zarathustra reaches the happy isles, and what he finds there is no longer the battlefield of countless counteracting wills to power, but an eminently different kind of society:

> Like a shout and a jubilation I want to journey over broad seas until I find the blessed isles where my friends dwell —

And my enemies among them! How I love everyone now, with whom I may simply speak! Even my enemies belong to my bliss.[39]

His friends live together with his enemies; on an island even the fiercest of the social antagonisms are abolished. Nietzsche thus imagines some kind of undifferentiated partnership, united in a collective effort:

> Could you *create* a god? —Then be silent about any gods! But you could well create the overman.
> Not you yourselves perhaps, my brothers! But you could recreate yourselves into fathers and forefathers of the overman: and this shall be your best creating![40]

In brief, the only purpose of this unearthly insular existence is to produce a unique subject, the overman. And, reciprocally, the only land suitable for the birth of this new god is an island.

To come to the point, all the leitmotifs are there, but laid out more evidently than in Fichte or Marx. In view of the fact that the entire drama of absolute creation is set on an island, Nietzsche seems to elaborate, albeit unconsciously, a complex twofold equilibrium. Against the backdrop of man's sweeping assimilation of the world he places a symmetry of extremes, that between the object of the inhuman earth and the subject merely maintaining an empty space for the emergence of a superhuman entity. It is once again an instance of a double correlation:

Will to Power – Untrue World
Zarathustra (Übermensch) – Happy Isles

III Heidegger's island of Delos

Our goal is to trace out a certain unidentified relation between the subject and the object, the rationale of which is still lacking and cannot be accounted for by either epistemological, practical, pragmatic, social, or linguistic theories. Heidegger is the first in our line of cases who dared to explicate the link of the island appearing solely for the eyes of an essentially different, surplus dimension of truth. For the Greek island of Delos only discloses itself to the higher illumination of *Aletheia*.

In the basic scope of his ontology, Heidegger is yet another advocate of the thorough subjective saturation of the object. His analyses of worldhood and thinghood in *Being and Time* offer arguably the most monumental account of a rounded, suffused, holistic world, a "totality of involvements," at the center of which a demiurgic *Dasein* imbues every single thing with its adequate meaning. As shown by his famous example of the broken hammer, a thing must be malfunctioning or absent from its usual place to step out of its original "inconspicuousness" and become noticeable in the first place. In *Sojourns*, however, one of his lesser works, he witnesses the revelation of the Greek island of Delos, which does not need to be defective to display its immutable and inscrutable presence.

Heidegger recounts his journey across the Mediterranean. From a too old, too civilized, too "touristy" Venice, a mere "object of historiography,"[41] he, in an "effort to return to the origin,"[42] sets off for Greece by ship. In anticipation, he stylizes this country as an autonomous object that speaks out of itself:

> Can Greece still speak what is proper to it and claim us, as listeners to its language, we, the people of an age whose world is throughout pervaded by the force and artificiality of the ramifications of the enframing (*Ge-Stell*)?[43]

It looks as though the world has already been totalized. What remains is a search for the almost magical objects that have somehow managed to hide from the hegemony of the *Ge-Stell*. At first, Heidegger is subject to a series of disappointments. Ithaca is too Byzantine, Olympia too American, and Rhodes even too Asian; the essence of Greek existence eludes him. Then the ship drops anchor before Delos:

> [T]he island was barely inhabited and its vegetation scarce.... In comparison with everything else we have seen up to now in our journey, the island looked on first sight deserted and abandoned, in such a way, though, that it couldn't have been the result of mere decline. At once it laid a claim totally unique that we had nowhere felt before up to that point. Through every thing a veiled great beginning (*Anfangs*) was expressed that once was.
> Δῆλος is the name of the island: the manifest, the visible, the one that gathers every thing in its open, every thing to which she offers shelter through her appearing she gathers in *one* present.[44]

A pure presence shines through, one untouched by the shifts and deferrals of mainland. The subject and the object enter a new relationship. While a damaging industry dominates the world on the continent, here *Aletheia* comes to the fore. Two irreducible truth procedures stand against each other:

> What for us today is called world is the inestimable entanglement of a technological apparatus of information that confronted the unscathed φύσις and took her place, while the function of the world became accessible and tractable only by calculation.
> It is only seldom then and after long preparation that we can succeed in looking at the presence of that which had once received form and measure from the field of Ἀλήθεια.[45]

In our cases so far, the matrix of redoubling both the subject and the object has not been written out as plainly and straightforwardly as it is here. While the calculative subject of the continent transforms nature into his own product, the adventurous subject of truth witnesses the sudden manifestation of the object in its sheer *Gegenwart* and *Anwesenheit*. After all, the only reason why Heidegger set out on this journey was to flee from the "technological scientifically-industrialized world," ordained by the laborious, diligent, guileful modern man. The two truth procedures are strictly differentiated. In the first, the subject intends the object and aligns it with himself.

However, according to Heidegger, this assumed and pursued correspondence presupposes another logic, that of truth unfolding as an interplay between concealment and unconcealment. In this second, more original, inclination of truth, man is no longer the self-assured master of truth. He does not have the *Wahrheitsgeschehen* at his command but can only hope that truth might render itself to him, unexpectedly and fatefully. Heidegger devises truth as event, *Ereignis*, precisely for the purpose of depriving man of his disposition over the veridical agenda. It is now truth that appeals and summons man, while he merely answers to its call. One could perhaps observe some structural similarities between Fichte's conscience, Nietzsche's overman, and Heidegger's *Aletheia*: they all seem to evoke a higher dimension of subjectivization, a de-centerment of subjectivity, an afflatus that is irreducible to a mere mastery of things. And here, hidden in one of Heidegger's minor writings, the objective correlate of this subjective transcendence is precisely an island.

Thus, the relation between the subject-surplus, which frees itself from the form of the *Ge-Stell* as the technological enframing of the world, and the object-residue, which resists assuming any kind of practical, pragmatic, social meaning, is explicated. Again, two correlations can be juxtaposed:

Truth as Ge-Stell – Continent
Truth as Aletheia – Island of Delos

IV Deleuze's oceanic islands

The melancholy over an already occupied, overly humanized world reached its peak in French structuralism. The basic structuralist operation was to draw the lines of an ontological field "with no outside," hence, a field of totality which, admittedly, tends to be defined more and more negatively. In the heyday of the movement, Lévi-Strauss declared: "The principle of all or nothing . . . is also an expression of a property of what exists: either everything, or nothing, makes sense."[46] In the aftermath, there was hardly a structuralist who would not argue for his own version of this methodological totality. Foucault stated: "Power is everywhere; not because it embraces everything, but because it comes from everywhere."[47] Derrida put it in a famous adage: "There is nothing outside of the text."[48] And Barthes posed the question, "Everything, then, can be myth?" and answered, "Yes, I believe this, for the universe is infinitely fertile in suggestions."[49] Never had the boundaries of closed and finite structures exerted a more restrictive grip, so it comes as no surprise that an object escaping the grasp of discourse became one of the recurring phantasms of the era. Jean-Claude Milner called this search for the pure *physei* beyond *thesei* "the holy grail of structuralism."

Tristes tropiques, perhaps the most popular text of the entire movement, is nothing but a monumental testimony to the deplorable anthropogenic disenchantment of the world. Lévi-Strauss paints in somber colors the last corners of the planet being contaminated by the obscene traces of man, by concrete, poverty, and litter. It is a world where traveling, exploring, and having an adventure have become impossible. In response, however, his travelogue nurtures a specific pathos of undrawn maps and unpopulated landscapes. On one occasion, he describes the "entirely virgin landscape" in South America, which "is so monotonous as to deprive its wildness of all meaning. It does not so much defy us as return a blank stare: almost it abolishes itself as we look at it."[50] And in the celebrated, somewhat awkward last sentence of the book, he implores us, "during the brief intervals in which humanity can bear to interrupt its hive-like labors," to

> grasp the essence of what our species has been and still is, beyond thought and beneath society: an essence that may be vouchsafed to us in a mineral more beautiful than any work of Man; in the scent, more subtly evolved than our books, that lingers in the heart of a lily; or in the wink of an eye, heavy with patience, serenity, and mutual forgiveness, that sometimes, through an involuntary understanding, one can exchange with a cat.[51]

On a similar note, Barthes, in his *Mythologies*, first tries to convince us that no such thing as nature exists, that Nature itself is historical, that there is nothing outside the calculable social constraints of myths and significations. And yet he cannot but indulge in reveries of adventures, foreign places, open horizons, unnamable experiences. At some point, he regrets that wooden toys for children have gone out of fashion, since wood "is a familiar and poetic substance, which does not sever the child from close contact with the tree, the table, the floor. . . . Wood makes essential objects, objects for all time."[52]

Lastly, even Lacan, albeit more cynically, presents his own phantasy of a world without man. In *Seminar II* he says: "Suppose all men to have disappeared from the world."[53] He asks us to imagine that all living creatures have vanished, and there were only waterfalls and springs, thunder and lightning left. What would remain of reality if we were to subtract consciousness from it? Would there still be images in the world? There would be, he claims, since

> at the high point of civilization we have attained, which far surpasses our illusions about consciousness, we have manufactured instruments which, without in any way being audacious, we can imagine to be sufficiently complicated to develop films themselves, put them away into little boxes, and store them in the fridge. Despite all living beings having disappeared, the camera can nonetheless record the image of the mountain in the lake, or that of the Café de Flore crumbling away in total solitude.[54]

What Lacan evokes here in his own way is precisely our double correlation. While the consciousness of a speaking being sits in the Café de Flore, the "secondary subject" of the camera, which, as Lacan insists, is "made only with words,"[55] captures the image of the Café de Flore in a state of decay.

But it was possibly Deleuze whose phantasms of the absolute Outside went farthest. He elevated the desert island into a genuine object of philosophy. The insular experiences of post-Kantian philosophers are usually less interested in cultivating unknown land than in witnessing its power of resistance. And Deleuze made no secret of his disdain for Daniel Defoe. His anti-Robinsonian resentment found its expression in two short visions, in the posthumously published paper from the 1950s titled *Causes et raisons des îles désertes*, conceivably the most ebullient philosophical text on the subject, and in "Michel Tournier and the World without Others," a supplement to *The Logic of Sense*, where the relation between the "secondary subjectivity" and the outside of the world comes to light even more elaborately.

In *Causes et raisons*, Deleuze begins with the well-known geographical distinction between continental islands, i.e., those that are accidental, derived, born of the disarticulation and fracture of the mainland, and oceanic, originary, essential islands, some of which "emerge from underwater eruptions, bringing to the light of day a movement from the lowest depths."[56] It is this other, oceanic, type that represents the object-correlate of the new Deleuzean subject, one who does not cognize, measure, farm, and name the islands, but dreams them, yearns for them, and then creates them.

In this regard, the desert island enjoys a contradictory ontological status, for only the subject who first invented it can subsequently face its pre-human facticity. Although Deleuze unequivocally asserts, "Islands are either from before or for after humankind,"[57] they still, paradoxically, require an artistic, literary, and creative excess on the part of the human being to be able to claim true independence from humanity:

> In certain conditions which attach them to the very movement of things, humans do not put an end to desertedness, they make it sacred. Those people who come to the island indeed occupy and populate it; but in reality, were they sufficiently separate, sufficiently creative, they would give the island only a dynamic image of itself, a consciousness of the movement which produced the island, such that through them the island would in the end become conscious of itself as deserted and unpeopled.[58]

It is as if solitary islands lured human beings, because it is only through them that they could make their own solitude explicit. No matter how cryptic Deleuze's writing is, one thing seems obvious: the relationship between the human being and the island can no longer be constituted by the operations of mediation, appropriation, and totalization. Instead, it is an instance of a singular symmetry between the emancipated extremes, seeing that man repeats by himself what the inhuman island has accomplished long ago:

> While it is true that the movement of humans toward and on the island takes up the movement of the island prior to humankind, *some* people can occupy the island—it is still deserted, all the more so, provided they are sufficiently, that is, absolutely separate, and provided they are sufficient, absolute creators.[59]

The new correlates standing opposite each other are creativity and facticity. It is a relation where both sides are so thoroughly disengaged from one another that they form an unexpected equipoise. The human subject can never incorporate the inhuman island; he can only coincide with it. To find words for this new subject-object relation, Deleuze must engage with a different sort of semantics, that of dreams, literature, art, amnesia, and the divine:

The island would be only the dream of humans, and humans, the pure consciousness of the island.... To that question so dear to the old explorers—'which creatures live on deserted islands?'—one could only answer: human beings live there already, but uncommon humans, they are absolutely separate, absolute creators, in short, an Idea of humanity, a prototype, a man who would almost be a god, a woman who would be a goddess, a great Amnesiac, a pure Artist, a consciousness of Earth and Ocean, an enormous hurricane, a beautiful witch, a statue from the Easter Islands.[60]

The new man resides in the domain of the magical, timeless, divine, statuesque. More importantly, he is no longer the traditional centric subject with a particular personal identity, but rather an amnesiac, a "prototype of the collective soul."[61] And his authentic medium is a truth relation that transcends the bond of the subject actualizing himself in the object. Instead, it is an entirely imaginary accord between the creation of ideality and the disclosure of reality: "The unity of the deserted island and its inhabitant is thus not actual, only imaginary, like the idea of looking behind the curtain when one is not behind it."[62]

These puzzling, overblown, but nonetheless refined balances are perhaps more accurately dealt with and disentangled in "Michel Tournier and the World without Others." The essay's main topic is literally the nature of the object-relation in the case of the subject falling out of the social structure. What does an island represent in the eyes of a castaway? What is the object-correlate of a man who has remained alone? In Deleuze's view, it is solely within an established and functioning field of intersubjectivity that the world can be settled with deep, sharp, contrasting things. The gaze of another subject is vital for the world to assume the form of totality:

> As for the objects behind my back, I sense them coming together and forming a world, precisely because they are visible to, and are seen by, Others.[63]

Along these lines, the narrative of Tournier's novel *Friday, or, The Other Island* shows Robinson initially still embodying the inertia of intersubjectivity and extending, by aid of clocks and timetables, his mastery over things from the continent to this tropical reef. However, Robinson's fundamental experience is that, when others are missing from the structure of the world, the things gradually become inhuman: "[W]e discover then wickedness which is no longer that of man."[64] And soon he realizes that his own subjection to the savagery of nature is the only authentic object-relation. Deleuze here almost repeats the *Causes et raisons*:

> Consciousness ceases to be a light cast upon objects in order to become a pure phosphorescence of things in themselves. Robinson is but the consciousness of the island, but the consciousness of the island is the consciousness the island has of itself—it is the island in itself. We understand thus the paradox of the deserted isle: the one who is shipwrecked, if he is alone, if he has lost the structure-Other, disturbs nothing of the desert isle; rather, he consecrates it.[65]

Once the intersubjective "economic" totalization of the world has been left behind, the thing-in-itself shines through. In Tournier's novel, this in-itself assumes the form of the island being redoubled and becoming the fiery, etheric version of itself. And the emergence of the "other island"[66] is only possible under the premise of the subject himself becoming two. Robinson is thus duplicated into himself and Friday, so that it is ultimately Friday who gives the book its title and is its actual hero:

> He alone is able to guide and complete the metamorphosis that Robinson began and to reveal to him its sense and its aim.... It is Friday who destroys the economic and moral order that Robinson had established on the island....
>
> What is essential, however, is that Friday does not function at all like a rediscovered Other. It is too late for that, the structure has disappeared. Sometimes he functions as a bizarre object, sometimes as a strange accomplice. Robinson sometimes treats him as a slave ... Sometimes he treats him almost like an object or an animal, sometimes as if Friday were a "beyond" with respect to himself, a "beyond" Friday, his own double or image. Sometimes he treats him as if he were falling short of the Other, sometimes as if he were transcending the other.[67]

What we call "secondary subjectivity," is expounded here both obscurely and most remarkably, almost meticulously. Friday introduces a higher, emergent, ideal dimension of subjectivity. His precarious social status, or lack thereof, implicates that his function is merely to stand for the essential substitutability of Robinson; he is, in a way, what the *Übermensch* was to Zarathustra. Although Robinson at first enslaves him and tries to educate him, he then grants him freedom, begins to treat him as a brother, and even regards himself as his pupil. It is an affiliation beyond the hierarchies of continental intersubjectivity. Only through Friday does Robinson reach his final, "sunny," "blazing" phase, in which the island can finally be experienced as a thing-in-itself.[68]

In short, the very same logic pervades both of Deleuze's accounts. The ultimate epiphany of the island is only possible against the backdrop of juxtaposing the double objectivation, which distinguishes between the continent and the island, with the double subjectivation, in which the moralizing proprietor exchanges his identity with that of a dreamer, and Robinson with the playful savage Friday. Deleuze's hermetic texts can thus be read as a precise confirmation of the matrix of two correlations:

Waking Human – Continent
Dreamer – Desert Island

V Conclusion

It was certainly not the intention of this chapter to succumb to the metaphorical tricks of Fichte, Nietzsche, Heidegger, or Deleuze. Instead, the island was throughout envisaged as a mere token of the truth relation that philosophy was still incapable of conceptualizing. After all, this kind of "philosophical poetry" is itself one of the great syndromes of philosophy and, as such, requires elucidation. When reasoning tends to become vague and self-indulgent in its figurative inspirations, it may well have reached a limit and is short of a new paradigm to account for its doing. In philosophy, even pretentiousness should not be underestimated, as it usually hints at the opening of new logical spaces, the theory of which must first be invented. Let us then try to think the "desert island" as a *suppressed logical function* and determine the conditions of its possibility. Our attempt of "de-sublimation" of this geographical entity will be explicated as a series of seven theses.

1. *The desert island is a symptom of the already conquered and occupied world.* As the case study has shown beyond much doubt, the allusions to and exploitations of the image of the (desert) island in the philosophical literature stand, by way of contrast, for an overpopulated and entirely distributed earth. In Fichte and Marx the island epitomizes an exception to the already appropriated and belabored surface of the planet; in Nietzsche it represents a refuge from the profanity of the crowded lands; in Heidegger a retreat from the calculating civilization; and in Deleuze an alternative to the economy of the continent. Thus, it is a phantasy object that is strictly negative to the totalizing pretense of the optimist subject of world-occupation. In its essential negativity, its function is to question the very form with which the subject holds the entire world captive. To put it more simply, if the island is an antipode of the totalized world, then its outward, apostate existence indicates a certain quandary of the idea of inwardness as something total and whole. Therefore, in order to understand the role of the island as a violation of a certain basic claim of modernity, one must first shed light on the origins of the operation of totalization.

2. *The subjective excess is a symptom of the original spontaneity of the modern man.* The cases from Fichte to Deleuze have displayed a similar structure, in which the correlate of the island was some form of "subjectivity in excess," as it were. At the other side of the "absolute Outside" of the island, the "absolute Inside" of the subject was put in the balance. In the vein of Kant upgrading his theoretical subject with the "transcendentally free" agent, the post-Kantians also tended to supplement the initial, secular subject with a self-possessed or even self-referential, almost sacred version of himself: the proprietor with conscience, labor with unceasing creation, man with the overman, the *Ge-Stell* with the *Ereignis* of *Aletheia*, Robinson with Friday, etc. But what is the reason for the outburst of this subjective overflow, this self-congratulatory closure?

It seems that, at this stage of modernity, there occurred a crucial shift in the way *truth* had to legitimize its place in the world. The traces of the subject having to actively construct his knowledge might go back as far as Descartes.[69] But, before Kant, the truth-form was still defined by the invariant, parallel correspondence between the order of ideas and the order of things. Thus, reality was cut at the joints of the ideas being directly embodied in modi and monads, or the ideas originated by being immediately reproduced from perceptions. On this ground, the subject in Descartes, Malebranche, Spinoza, Leibniz, Locke, or Berkeley, could aspire to the ultimate adequacy between the idea in his mind and the thing of the outside world; it was a relation enacted by God himself. However, toward the end of the early-modern era, most notably with Hume, the basic form of truth as immediate correspondence was still there, but the boundaries of things and processes began relinquishing their lawful, substantial contours. Along with the slow farewell of God, the world could no longer maintain the ability to supply the subject with consistent forms, those of substance, cause, effect, etc., that bestow discriminate qualities to things, states, and events. On the grounds of this disintegrating world of late empiricism, Kant's revolution consisted in the insight that the subject is the only impetus left to impress his binding and necessary concepts upon reality.

This shift of the root of all logical forms from (God-created) universal correspondences to the inside of the subject has a very definite terminological name in Kant; it is called "spontaneity," the capacity of producing concepts. Pre-Kantian subjects were, to put it in simplified terms, still "theoretical," i.e., they strived to be in tune with the universe, and perhaps exhibited the tendency to become self-transparent, punctual, static, and, to an extent, passive. The Cartesian subject was a self-evidence, Leibniz's was a monad, Locke's was a *tabula rasa*, Hume's was a theatre of the mind. With Kant, however, an originally spontaneous, performative, "thetical" energy inhabits and constitutes the form of subjectivity. And with this shift *a new concept of truth* begins to evolve and establish itself, one that surpasses the frame of the simple *adaequatio rei*. Truth henceforth assumes the function of surplus over the given world. It ceases to unfold within the medium of discriminate, determinate, progressively infinitesimal consonances in the manner of Malebranche's occasionalist interventions of God, Spinoza's parallelisms of ideas and things, Leibniz's pre-established harmony between the two, or Berkeley's divine gaze on immaterial phenomena, where to every part of reality an ideal "quantum" of truth always already corresponds. Instead, the impulse of truth now surfaces unpredictably, almost miraculously, thus completely altering its ontological status: *truth is no longer derivable from reality but can only emerge within it*. Accordingly, the Fichtean I posits himself and persists only by virtue of this act; in Hegel, truth is not a "minted coin" and does not exist before it is made; in Nietzsche, truth is an illusion, projected upon the world; in Heidegger, truth is not expressed in the proposition but in the "locus of proposition," i.e., in *Dasein*'s concern, while in his later period, the concept of "truth" assumes increasingly fateful, self-justifying, and erratic traits; the structuralist universe is made entirely of *thesei* as opposed to *physei*, so that, for instance in Deleuze, "sense"[70] no longer poses as an origin, a principle, but rather as an emergent, surface effect of nonsensical components. And with this, the age of immoderateness seems to commence. The early-modern subject of Descartes or Locke already showed some cracks in his alignment with the natural *telos*, and consequently had to generate his knowledge, construct his character, and uplift his mastery over things, although he did it in moderation and only sought for his rightful place in the order of being. After Kant, however, there is emphatically no order and no place left, and the subject feels entitled to take over the world.

In short, it is no exaggeration to speak of the *essentially spontaneous character of truth* in modernity. This new form of truth, on the one hand, still aspires to be filled out with reality, which is why it condemns the subject to the hard labor of constantly vanquishing the world.[71] But, on the other hand, it also provokes experiences where the spontaneity *celebrates itself*, so to speak, in the intermittent episodes of pure excess that no longer abide by the totalizing form. Along with the renegade object of the "desert island," it is therefore this "subjectivity in excess" that might unveil the true reasons behind the seemingly natural and self-explanatory operation of totalization.

3. *Spontaneity is a mark of the modern man having lost the certitude of predestination.* There is a historical context to Kant's invention of spontaneity. Already at the outset of

the modern age a certain paradox comes forth: at the very moment when science began considering man to be cosmically infinitesimal, Descartes urged us to *nous rendre comme maistres & possesseurs de la Nature*, "make ourselves, as it were, lords and masters of nature."[72] Nonetheless, before Kant, there was still a God who knew how and where to place the subject into the world, so that he could mirror it in the parallel, adequate, pre-established manner. By contrast, the post-Kantian subject is becoming painfully aware that he is not the bearer of any creatural necessity. Epistemologically, no preprogrammed correspondence between his inner and his outer world can be vouchsafed, and ontologically, no predetermined "natural place" subsists that he must assume. He may crop up anywhere, or, what is more, he might not appear at all. It is the very essence of Fichte's subject that he is not deducible from any fact of the world, as he stands and falls with the act of his own self-positing; he is not a *Tatsache* but a *Tathandlung*. Therefore, it is a somewhat overlooked, but central and constitutional quality of the Fichtean I that he could well not have occurred. This non-derivable *causa sui* sets the criteria for the subjects to come: Hegel's spirit, Marx's laborer, Nietzsche's will, Heidegger's *Dasein* (as well as, to a degree, the poststructuralist "processual concepts" of drive, event, power, and sense) are all entities that justify their emergence and prove their existence solely by virtue of their own activity.

4. *The practical totalization of the world is the "fallacious" medium of the theoretical spontaneity of the modern subject.* From Fichte's I onward, the subject exercises his right to "actively," and somewhat strenuously, incorporate his outside. Fichte's *Verichlichung* and, more narrowly defined, his property, Marx's labor and production, Nietzsche's power and overpowering, Heidegger's care and, negatively, technique, seem to be impulses designed to absorb all absolute otherness; even Deleuze's concepts of univocal ontology are forms of imperative immanence, of a certain vitalist pervasion of being.

The most critical circumstance of the origin of this "practical totalization" is the fact that, in the historical perspective, the world was progressively incapable of delivering the form of truth and shifted this mandate onto man. At the end of the pre-Kantian era, reality forfeited its claim to exhibit constant and lawful regularities, thus forcing the subject to invent his own logical forms and impress them onto his outside. It is in this shift that the once orderly body of the world became a diffuse and formless reality, seemingly offering itself *in toto* to the subject as the only remaining source of truth. This means, of course, that the modern prerogative to take possession of everything does precisely *not* ensue from the world "belonging" to man originally, from its being innately well-rounded or even somehow pre-packaged for his appropriation, but rather from man's gradual realization that reality is lacking any evidently discriminative, conceptual, logical, that is, human form. The origins of the operation of totalization lie ultimately in the fact that man is never *a subject of equal value* standing face to face with his "co-present" object, but is himself merely a marginal, contingent, negligible product of an infinitely larger objectivity.[73] In other words, the presumed *Zusammengehörigkeit* of man and the world is definitely not an expression of them being in any way equiprimordial. Rather, the first impulse of man's mastery over the world lies in the fact that the world could not predict the late and accidental advent of man, his appearance against all odds. It is therefore not the case that reality has "always already" been within the subject, his mind, his spirit, his language, his culture. Quite the opposite, the universe has so little need and regard for the subject that, when he nevertheless enters the stage, he somehow lets himself get carried away into mistaking the fact that the world has no desire to "embody" his conceptual truth for his pretense that it will offer no resistance to being overpowered by him.[74]

Our main thesis is thus that the "verificational shift" from the theoretical to the practical disposition towards the world is one of the central fallacies of the modern condition. Its reasons could be reconstructed as follows. The modern subject is "an essentially unwanted child," a cosmic orphan, so to speak, and it is against the backdrop of him losing his firm place in the order of being that he is compelled to self-invention, practical agency, and creation. As Kant realized, (pure) concepts cannot be derived or replicated from the given world, but must be *presupposed transcendentally*, which will later increasingly mean: be *created idealiter*. These concepts justified by spontaneity—extending from Kant's categories all the way to Heidegger's meaning and sense or any of the structuralist *thesei*—can no longer be verified in a traditional way; they refuse having any "incarnated" representatives among the things or facts of the world.[75] Needless to say, as empirically non-verifiable, they are also never to be directly falsified by the given world. And now comes the crucial turn. The essential *theoretical non-falsifiability* of the conditions of any truth in modernity is (arguably by a mistake in reasoning) transposed into the domain of their *practical auto-verifiability*. There is nothing about Fichte's positing, Marx's labor, Nietzsche's will, Heidegger's care (or Deleuze's sense, for that matter) that the outside world could in any way "prove wrong" or rebut. And since the spontaneous energy of "truth" thus assumes the form of an ideal surplus, it can only lay claim to being true by *making itself true* by the sweat of its brow. To put it differently, after Kant, the concepts become aware that they have no ground beneath their feet, so they start filling the void at their core, the lack of any metaphysical guarantee, with their practical impetus. Or else, they misconstrue their being condemned to spontaneity as an entitlement to seize everything there is. And the subject as their vehicle, the cosmically degraded man, is promoted into a global master.

Nevertheless, this "practical fallacy" manifests a certain innate "unhappiness" of the antirealist stance, thereby betraying that it is, indeed, a falsehood. Here, the now popular diagnosis of "correlationism" can be called into question. The common name for what we call "totalization of reality" is either "antirealism" or, in recent times, "correlationism," both serving as near-synonyms for the continental philosophy of Kant and after. The form of "correlation" is usually defined in absolute terms: since we only ever have access to the correlation between thinking and being, our thought is eternally caught within its own *a priori* unsurpassable horizon. But if the bubble of the subject's correlation to the world is as perfect as presumed, then he should be an entity of great happiness and gratification, for he could never take cognizance of anything that could enter it and falsify his beliefs. If the post-Kantian universe is so dense and impermeable, if the antirealist subject is structurally unfit to catch sight of anything "absolutely outside" of him, what, then, remains to make him feel bad about his alleged inadequacy? Inadequacy with regard to what? How could an antirealist even know that he is one?

The mistake in postulating antirealism as a *factum brutum* of modern subjectivity is that it fails to reconstruct its genesis and recognize that it is, in fact, a *myth* of the modern condition. The form of correlation seems to have two concurrent aspects: first, the "happy" premise of correspondence, in which the entire object is posited within the subject; second, the "unhappy" effort of totalization, for in order to sustain its framework, the modern subject is convicted to some sort of coarse optimism and pragmatic megalomania. What some present-day realists neglect in their critique is all the hard work that correlation requires. Antirealism is not a given; it is not a theoretical but a practical endeavor, and one must toil incessantly to maintain it.[76] This raises a few questions. Why does the post-Kantian subject give the appearance of being a master sentenced to compulsory labor? Why does his seemingly inborn might not give him the right to idleness? Thus, in order to break the closure of correlation, the reasons of this *discontent of antirealism* should be unveiled.

5. *Antirealism is the mask of anti-verism*. While in the philosophy before Kant truth was still running in parallel with reality, with Kant, its emergence began to diverge from the given world. Kant is most often reprehended for having us plunged into the purgatory of antirealism, but there is another, overlooked, side to this reproach: he also made us enter the heavens of spontaneity of truth, its non-derivability, thus delineating the necessary surplus of the ideal over the real. However, this eruptive excess of truth prompted its first restriction, i.e., the Kantian prohibition of metaphysics, the banishment of pure idealities to the realm of dialectical agnosticism. The fact that the new truth was self-appointed, so to speak, was deemed scandalous enough to have its wings cut off by quickly bringing it back to the arms of reality. Kant's spontaneity of the concepts requires to be filled out with the receptivity of the senses, or else it remains "empty." And it is in the wake of this *re-realization of the ideal* that the post-Kantian subject is bound to get his hands dirty. Fichte's I is thus doomed to ceaselessly cultivate the not-I, Marx's laborer to exploit the earth, Nietzsche's will to overpower, *Dasein* to engage in its environment of ready-to-hand equipment; even Deleuze's virtuality must constantly be actualized. Hence, instead of accusing all these philosophers of antirealism *tout court*, one should rather try to define the reasons as to why they felt obliged to *restrain* the surplus of truth by insistently bringing it down to the ground of the senses, the land, the soil, the power, the tools, the everyday life, the singularities. Why must a genuine invention in the theoretical field be so resolutely practically neutralized? For it is this *suppression of spontaneity* that, in our view, represents the cardinal sin of having to aspire to own the world; it therefore stands at the beginning of the "discontent of antirealism."

To illustrate this point, let us recall Napoleon, who, for want of any ancestral legitimation of his claim to dominance, was supposedly driven to infinitely expand his territories, thus engaging in ever-new wars that ultimately led to his decline. Similarly, the only way the modern subject can blindfold himself from the fact that he is a usurper, an uninvited guest to the world, an intruder, is to compensate for this loss of a predestined "natural place" by holding together truth and reality at least at the grandest possible scale, i.e., within the range of totality. The frame of totalization alone can still allow man to cling to the illusion of a "natural" congruence between him and the world.[77] In short, the compulsion of the modern subject to unremittingly gain knowledge, appropriate, overpower, and invest with meaning does not so much touch upon the nature of reality as betray a certain *elementary uneasiness in the relation he has with his own truth.* It is thus not the case that reality, by its very nature, "fits" into the correlation with man's thought. Rather, this total and transcendental "theoretical correlation" is to be construed as a "practical illusion" of the subject who is unwilling to face up to his own emergent truth, its pure ideality, the stain of his cosmic vagrancy.

In this sense, antirealism is not some transhistorical anthropological constant of presuming the world as one's own, but a historical product of the subject becoming aware of the "extorted" spontaneity of truth, fallaciously interpreting it as something that aims at a deferred, but ultimately full correspondence with reality, and therefore feeling authorized to perpetually wrap his hands around it. As such, the doctrine of antirealism is merely the secondary manifestation of the more primary *impulse of anti-idealism*; it is the result of needing to offset one's own surplus of truth. This is ultimately how an antirealist *knows* of his antirealism, a stance barred from the outset by dissatisfaction. For he himself has devised the frame of totality as a pool deep and large enough in which to drown the transgressions of truth, and must now graft all days to preserve the illusion of the ideal overlapping with the real at least in its consummate, either eternally postponed or mournfully accomplished horizons.

In sum, antirealism may prove to be an effect of a certain unresolved tension in the relation between truth and reality in modern times. While its origin lies in the impulse of truth diverging from the given reality, it only manifests itself by suppressing its origin, obfuscating this divergence, and letting truth reconcile with reality in the practical dimension. Instead of defining antirealism as some sort of "primitive" of the human condition, we have rather interpreted it as a mere mask of the *authentic anti-verism* of modern man, who, after God had abdicated the throne, could at first not carry the weight of being the sole author of truth, and hoped to scatter and obliterate its ideal impulses across the totality of the world. In contrast to this fallacy, we believe that a concept of "truth" is now needed which will dare to look into the eyes of its own surplus, withstand its ideality, abstain from "realizing" it, and leave the world as it is: a reality in its untruth.

6. *The desert island as a "reality without ideality" serves to bring to light the subject as an "ideality without reality."* Perhaps the most beautiful corroboration for the claim that post-Kantian philosophy is not just one of explicit antirealism, but, before that and more fundamentally, one of disavowed and repressed anti-verism, lies in the two ultimate phantasms of these totalizing philosophies: first, in the inevitable experiences of the transcendence of truth, its subjective excess; second, in the scarce apparitions of the absolute outside of reality, its objective residue. We have seen how the paradox of reality being both narrower than the subject and infinitely larger than him develops its symptoms. Between the osmosis of inwardness and the entropy of outwardness, an utterly a-subjective object, an island, appears here and there before the gaze of man. However, the crucial point is the relation of this object to the subjective pole of the balance. In the cases discussed above, it has never been the purpose of the "island" to represent forthrightly "reality-in-itself"; there was nothing intrinsically profound and interesting about the barren matter of the small land in the sea. Its function was rather to make, by way of contrast, the "truth-in-itself" visible for the first time, i.e., to specify a certain unsolicited character of "truth" on the part of the subject, and let it be seen as

what it is: a mere idea hanging in the air. Insofar as there exists a part of the world whose absolute resistance demonstrates that it is not ideally predetermined, the ideal correlate itself must renounce the pretense of its total underpinning in reality and reconcile itself with its surplus status. The island, as the ground upon which no human foot has ever been set, represents the correlate of a man whose feet do not extend all the way to the ground. It is on precisely this account that, in Nietzsche and Deleuze, the isles are populated with such arcane and ethereal creatures. It is a soil whereupon only creatures with no heavy feet can tread; Deleuze keeps repeating that the inhabitants of the island do not abolish its desertedness. For the rare islanders, barely touching the island trails, are not "realized ideas," but rather ideas with no need for realization. The island is not the material, the body, the property of conscience, the *Übermensch*, *Aletheia*, or Friday, but a physical symbol of their *irreducible ideality*. The relation between the subject-correlate and the object-correlate is thus altogether negative; it is a coincidence of emancipated extremes. In its defiant apparition, the island merely exhibits the fact that the subject has brought something to the world to which the world can offer no material support.

7. *Only truth in its irreducibility to reality can become an organ of realism.* These scattered, unsystematic accounts on desert islands gave us at least a glimpse into the original ideal surplus of truth, suppressed under the form of the totalization of reality. They finally illuminate the emergent and excessive quality of truth, which no longer projects itself onto the world, conquers, and circumscribes it, but opens a horizon that reaches beyond the boundaries of totalization. The most valuable lesson desert islands can teach us is that the cause of realism can never be promoted by simply delving into reality frontally and immediately. There is no head-on way to the revelation of reality in itself; rather, its "veridical" counterpart, the emergent production of truth, must be taken into account. Nonetheless, these metaphors and anecdotes indicate only obscure notions of truth and reality, manifesting itself by way of two displacements. First, the idea of truth not having sufficient reason in reality is dislocated into the domain of another, suspended, postponed, and idealized subject. As we have seen, the ultimate subject of truth has always been "disjointed," assuming the form of the voice from the other world, a future collective, an ideal, a fateful event, a dream. Second, the idea of an independent world—ultimately, the idea of a universe older and larger than us—was neutralized by having to put on the mask of a small desert island. The equilibrium of excessive subjects and residual objects is still caught within the frame of antirealist totalization, since it only deals with intuitive balances of its symptomatic remainders. Hence, to surpass the limitations of totalization entirely, the displacement of objects into islands and subjects into ideals must be undone. Instead of aerial creatures almost floating over the ground of desert islands, a new relation of truth to reality could be conceived. It is our contention that the moment truth recognizes its irreducible spontaneity and absolute surplus, it will no longer pose as a practical imperative to seize the world, but will be able to think the world beyond the subjective constraints of totalization, thus disclosing reality in its realism. In other words, the true goal of realism might be to develop the concept of "truth" spoken out in the here and now, and the concept of "reality" is no longer obliged to hide itself behind the image of a desert island.[78]

Notes

1 The research included in this chapter was funded by the Slovenian Research Agency (ARRS) under the research project "Language and Science: The Possibility of Realism in Modern Philosophy" (J6-7364).
2 Since this chapter is an implicit critique of Western anthropomorphism, we can afford to treat the modern subject, the "man," as male: we will recount "his" story. As will be shown, however, his "surplus-form" is sometimes female, as, for instance, with Heidegger's *Aletheia*, Deleuze's goddess and beautiful witch, and, metaphorically, even Nietzsche's Zarathustra, insofar as he is "pregnant" with the future overman.
3 Immanuel Kant, *Critique of Pure Reason*, trans. and ed. Paul Guyer and Allen W. Wood (Cambridge: Cambridge University Press, 1998), 283, (A 158/B 197).
4 Johann Gottlob Fichte, *The System of Ethics: According to the Principles of Wissenschaftlehre*, trans. Daniel Breazeale and Günter Zöller (Cambridge: Cambridge University Press, 2005), 217.
5 G. W. F. Hegel, *Phenomenology of Spirit*, trans. A. V. Miller (Oxford: Oxford University Press, 1977), 140.
6 Karl Marx, *Capital: A Critique of Political Economy*, trans. Ben Fowkes, vol. 1 (Middlesex: Penguin Books, 1982), 285.
7 Friedrich Nietzsche, *Writings from the Late Notebooks*, trans. Kate Surge (Cambridge: Cambridge University Press, 2003) 148; *Kritische Studienaugabe*, ed. Giorgio Colli and Massimo Montinari, 15 vols. (Berlin: de Gruyter, 1988), 12: 9 (41). Hereafter cited as KSA.
8 Martin Heidegger, *Introduction to Metaphysics*, trans. Gregory Fried and Richard Polt (New Haven: Yale University Press, 2000), 40.
9 Claude Lévi-Strauss, *Tristes Tropiques*, trans. John Russell (New York: Criterion Books, 1961), 23–24.
10 Immanuel Kant, "Critique of Practical Reason," in *Practical Philosophy*, trans. Mary J. Gregor (Cambridge: Cambridge University Press, 1996), (hereafter cited as *KpV*).
11 Athur Schopenhauer, *The World as Will and Representation*, trans. E. F. J. Payne, 2 vols. (New York: Dover Publication, 1966), 2: 3.
12 Friedrich Nietzsche, "On Truth and Lying in a Non-moral Sense," in *The Birth of Tragedy and Other Writings*, trans. Ronald Speirs (Cambridge: Cambridge University Press, 1999), 141.
13 Heidegger, *Introduction to Metaphysics*, 4–5.
14 Lévi-Strauss, *Tristes Tropiques*, 397.
15 This "secular" symmetry was once articulated by Schopenhauer, but still with the positive twist of the world existing only in man's representation: "The vastness of the world, which previously disturbed our peace of mind, now rests within us; our dependence on it is now annulled by its dependence on us" (Schopenhauer, *The World as Will and Representation*, 1: 205). As we will see, it is possible to reverse this narrative: only after the entire determinacy of the world has proved to be a mere projection of man will he be able to afford to recognize his worldly nothingness.
16 It is also worth noting that a structurally analogous scene is then enacted in the third *Critique* when the subject faces the sublime object.
17 Johann Gottlob Fichte, "Beiträge zur Berichtigung der Urtheile des Publicums über die französische Revolution, 1793," in *Fichtes Werke*, ed. Immanuel Hermann Fichte, vol. 6 (Berlin: de Gruyter, 1971), 117 (hereafter translation mine).
18 Ibid., 127.

19 Ibid., 120.
20 Ibid., 133.
21 As the kind anonymous reviewer pointed out, the argument of this chapter could be strengthened "by showing how metaphors of desert islands function differently in pre-Kantian philosophers." Indeed, it seems that the vast majority of "islands" in the philosophical and pseudo-philosophical literature before Kant play a quite dissimilar, even opposite, role: they represent a perfect setting for the recreation of an ideal political state. Typically, these islands tend to be placed in a warm and mild climate, they are rich in raw materials and natural resources, their cities often exhibit an idealized geometrical architecture, etc. Such is, with some variation, the case with Plato's Atlantis as depicted in *Timaeus* and *Critias*, Thomas Morus' *Utopia*, Campanella's *Civitas Solis*, Francis Bacon's *Nova Atlantis*, Andreae's *Christianopolis*, or the countless utopias of the French late seventeenth and eighteenth centuries, such as Tiphaigne de la Roche's Galligènes, Diderot's *république sauvage* of Tahiti (in *Supplément au voyage de Bougainville*), Denis Veiras' Sevarambia, Fontenelle's Ajao, and many more. These wealthy, fertile, well protected, isolated, fully populated isles are nothing but laboratories for the social utopias of various ideologies and worldviews; far from being nonhuman, they serve as drafting tables for a certain hyper-humanist enactment of society in its purest form: a Calvinist will find there a theocracy and a monarchy, as in the case of Sevarambia, and an atheist a communist democracy of sorts, as in Ajao.

Nevertheless, at some point, these heavens on earth seem to have gone out of fashion; it is perhaps of some interest that Kant himself spoke negatively of the ideal insular cities in a note to *The Contest of Faculties*, mentioning Plato's Atlantis, More's Utopia, Harrington's Oceana, and Allais' (that is, Veiras') Sevarambia (see Immanuel Kant, "The Contest of Faculties," in *Political Writings*, ed. H. S. Reiss [Cambridge: Cambridge University Press, 1991], 188.) Only after Kant, due to both the "logical prohibition" of the absolute Outside and, arguably, the historical circumstance of *terra incognita* disappearing from the maps of the world during the nineteenth century, the fantasy of the island changed its metaphorical value and became a small, barren, desolate, uninhabited, or, at the utmost, scarcely populated land. It would thus appear that the *utopian* island is the supreme pre-Kantian phantom, and the *desert* island the ultimate post-Kantian fantasy.
22 Fichte, "Beiträge zur Berichtigung der Urtheile des Publicums über die französische Revolution, 1793," 116.
23 Ibid., 59.
24 Although, genetically, conscience is more "original" than the practical I.
25 For instance, in *The Vocation of Man*, Fichte calls the voice of conscience "the oracle of the Eternal World" (Johann Gottlob Fichte, *The Vocation of Man*, trans. William Smith [London: John Chapman, 1848], 173).
26 G. W. F. Hegel, "Auszüge aus dem Tagebuch der Reise in die Berner Oberalpen (25. Juli bis August 1796)," in *Werke*, vol. 1: *Frühe Schriften*, ed. Eva Moldenhauer and Karl Markus Michel (Frankfurt am Main: Suhkamp, 1986), 614–15 (hereafter translation mine).
27 Ibid., 618.
28 Karl Marx, "The German Ideology," in *Selected Writings*, ed. David McLellan (Oxford: Oxford University Press, 2000), 191.
29 Friedrich Nietzsche, *Thus Spoke Zarathustra*, trans. Adrian del Caro (Cambridge: Cambridge University Press, 2006), 266.

30 Friedrich Nietzsche, *The Will to Power*, trans. Walter Kaufmann and R. J. Hollingdale (New York: Vintage Books, 1968), 14–15 (§ 15).
31 Our will might be almighty in its projective, perspectival, claim, but it is utterly moot in the face of its existential conditions; the creatural devaluation of man is an obsessive theme in Nietzsche's writings. To quote only two examples: "But how could we reproach or praise the universe! Let us beware of attributing to it heartlessness or unreason or their opposites: it is neither perfect, nor beautiful, nor noble, nor does it want to become any of these things; in no way does it strive to imitate man!" (Friedrich Nietzsche, *The Gay Science*, trans. Josephine Nauckhoff [Cambridge: Cambridge University Press, 2001], 109 [§ 109]). And in his posthumous fragments, Nietzsche calls man "this little eccentric animal species," life on earth "a mere moment, an incident, an exception without consequence," and the Earth itself, "like every star, a hiatus between two nothingnesses" (Friedrich Nietzsche, "Nachgelassene Fragmente," in KSA 13: 16 (25). Translation mine).
32 Nietzsche, *The Will to Power*, 330 (§ 616).
33 Friedrich Nietzsche, "Anti-Christ," in *Anti-Christ, Ecce Homo, Twilight of the Idols, and Other Writings*, trans. Judith Norman (Cambridge: Cambridge University Press, 2006), 49 (§ 15).
34 Nietzsche, *The Will to Power*, 536, (§ 1041).
35 Nietzsche, *Thus Spoke Zarathustra*, 128.
36 Ibid., 66.
37 Ibid., 7.
38 Friedrich Nietzsche, "Dionysos-Dithyramben," in KSA 6: 393–4 (translation mine).
39 Nietzsche, *Thus Spoke Zarathustra*, 64.
40 Ibid., 65.
41 Martin Heidegger, *Sojourns: The Journey to Greece*, trans. John Panteleimon Manoussakis (Albany: SUNY, 2005), 5.
42 Ibid., 9.
43 Ibid., 9–10.
44 Ibid., 30.
45 Ibid., 35.
46 Claude Lévi-Strauss, *The Savage Mind* (London: Weidenfeld and Nicholson, 1966), 172–3.
47 Michel Foucault, *The History of Sexuality*, trans. Robert Hurley (London: Penguin Books, 1990), 93.
48 Jacques Derrida, *Of Grammatology*, trans. Gayatri Chakravorty Spivak (Baltimore, MD: Johns Hopkins University Press, 1976), 158.
49 Roland Barthes, *Mythologies*, trans. Anette Lavers (New York: The Noonday Press, 1970), 107.
50 Lévi-Strauss, *Tristes Tropiques*, 262.
51 Ibid., 398.
52 Barthes, *Mythologies*, 54.
53 Jacques Lacan, *The Seminar, Book II: The Ego in Freud's Theory and in the Technique of Psychoanalysis 1954–1955*, trans. Sylvana Tomaselli (New York, London: W.W. Norton & Company, 1991), 46.
54 Ibid.
55 Ibid.
56 Gilles Deleuze, "Desert Islands," in *Desert Islands and Other Texts 1953–1974*, trans. Michael Taormina (Los Angeles: Semiotext(e), 2004), 9.

57 Ibid.
58 Ibid., 10.
59 Ibid.
60 Ibid., 10–11.
61 Ibid., 13.
62 Ibid., 11.
63 Gilles Deleuze, *The Logic of Sense*, trans. Mark Lester (London: The Athlone Press, 1990), 305.
64 Ibid., 306.
65 Ibid., 311.
66 For the subtitle of the English translation of *Vendredi ou les Limbes du Pacifique* reads *The Other Island*.
67 Deleuze, *The Logic of Sense*, 315–16.
68 In the end the ship that Robinson longed for does arrive, but Friday embarks in his stead and leaves, while Robinson takes into care a young sailor to teach him the technique of staring into the sun. It could well be said that this young man now acts as a representative of the "ideal otherness" of Robinson.
69 It is Charles Taylor's point that the modern, Cartesian mind is already "disengaged" from the given world and governs things "instrumentally." The pre-modern reliance on the world embodying "ontic logos" is lost, and the suturing of ideas to things now requires additional effort: "Knowledge comes not from connecting the mind to the order of things we find but in framing a representation of reality according to the right canons" (Charles Taylor, *Sources of the Self: The Making of the Modern Identity* [Cambridge, MA: Harvard University Press, 1989], 197). Nevertheless, these canons still conform to the strict correspondence between ideas and things, a form that, with Kant, becomes precarious, deferred, and even obsolete.
70 "Sense" being probably the closest concept to "truth" that the Deleuzean truth-scorning attitude can stand up for.
71 Or, in Deleuze's case, where the concept of "subject" is largely obsolete, it is the universe that is only held together by the vitalist energy of perpetual production and creation.
72 René Descartes, "Discourse on Method," in *The Philosophical Writings of Descartes*, trans. John Cottingham, Robert Stoothoff, and Dugald Murdoch, vol. 2 (Cambridge: Cambridge University Press, 1985), 142–3.
73 It seems as if the world was transferred inside man the moment man realized that the world could do well without him. It may be a historical coincidence: hyperbolic theories of the subject appeared when science made man disappear in the farthest corners of the universe. In this light, realism and idealism are no longer in contradiction, but form a subtle equilibrium of man encapsulating the world within the "ideal order," while simultaneously relinquishing his cosmic predestination and rolling toward the indiscernible edge of the "order of reality."
74 After all, the devaluation of man's creatural existence and the strictly correlative "practical" overvaluation of his claim and mission is a typical form of post-Kantian philosophy. Marx, for instance, was a Darwinian, regarding humanity as a historically late and dispensable species. This degradation of man, however, in itself served as a trigger of his projective hubris. The human body may be a bad coincidence, but that does not mean that the world cannot become too small for the efforts of man's labor. In Heidegger, *Dasein* is so superfluous in the world that it is even *thrown* into it. But to this loss of the "organic" place in the cosmos man answers by being the only one capable of bestowing meaning to it.

75 This is ultimately what separates Kant from Hume and announces the dawn of a new era. Hume still at least pretended to set out to catch cause and effect "in the act," so to speak. In Kant, however, the concepts, such as cause and effect, are transcendental "conditions of possibility" precisely because they do not even presume to be "verifiable" in an empiricist way.

76 This fetish of industry and growth also generates a certain inevitable remainder. In the philosophy before Kant, there was nothing "essentially unattainable" about the world; between Descartes and Hume, for instance, the concept of the "thing-in-itself" designated the quality of things that can only be grasped by acts of thought unbound by the senses. In Kant, however, it seems as if the world, confronted with the subject's usurpation, began clinging to this minimal residue of independence and sovereignty. Even if post-Kantian philosophy was quick to dispose of the "thing-in-itself," reality nevertheless put on the mask of some sort of constitutional gap and infinite withdrawal. The "irreducible remainder" either assumed the form of the infinite task of conquering reality, the asymptotic approach to something never fully present, and the mere approximation to the ultimate ground of things, or manifested itself as the torpor of the already accomplished task, the apathy of the world having surrendered its last secret, thus testifying *per negationem* to the innate "unhappiness" of the antirealist stance. It is almost ironic that the eternal receding of reality, or its inversion, the melancholy of the conquered earth, becomes so virulent precisely at the dawn of the antirealist age.

77 One might speculate that if the modern subject was a bit more certain of his place in the world, then the things outside him would get along just fine without his persistent efforts to incorporate them. Instead, he would sooner make the entire world his home than come to terms with his initial homelessness. To put it starkly, the world does not fit into the mind of the subject because he is almighty "by nature," but because he was born a bastard, so he must perpetually swing and splash with his arms so as to hold his head above water.

78 It is this conception of truth as irreducible to reality that we have developed in our *The Untruth of Reality: The Unacknowledged Realism of Modern Philosophy* (Lanham, MD: Lexington Books, 2016).

4

To Make Truth: Ontology, Epistemology, Technology

Maurizio Ferraris

Contrary to what is often argued, new realism is not a return to a pre-Kantian ontology, but proposes an enrichment of the philosophical perspective based on three terms: *ontology*, what there is, which in the case of natural objects is independent of what we know; *epistemology*, what we know, which interferes with what there is only in the case of social objects; and *technology*, what we do—often without concepts, such as when we use tools, speak a language, or perform social acts (promise, pay, confer or receive titles)—which ensures the transition from ontology to epistemology. This chapter will first define these three spheres and then analyze a world in which they interact.

Three theories of truth

At some point in the *Confessions*, Augustine poses an elementary, almost comical question: Why should I confess to God, who knows everything? What is the point of telling one's life to someone who knows more about me than myself? The answer is enlightening: Augustine says he wants to *make truth*, not only in his heart, but also in writing before many witnesses.[1] Does he mean that one makes truth just as one makes post-truth? Of course not: one can hardly pass off fashionable nonsense to an omniscient being. He rather means that truth is not only an inner process, but also a testimony that is made publicly, has a social value, and is, above all, something that entails effort, activity, and technical skill. Let us try to place this position within contemporary philosophy. To this end, I propose three theories of truth: hypotruth, which corresponds to mainstream hermeneutics; hypertruth, which is the mainstream analytic philosophy; and mesotruth, which is the theory I would like to develop in these pages.

Hermeneutic philosophers have developed an epistemic theory of truth that is, in fact, a *hypotruth*, a subordinate truth, as it is disconnected from ontology and rather consists of the conceptual schemes that mediate—and, in fact, constitute—our relationship with the world. In this version, with different degrees of radicality, "true" becomes synonymous with "conforming to a shared belief." Thus, hermeneutic thinkers rightly note that truth does not go by itself, as it requires a context and some actions. However, they go too far when they claim that truth only lies in investigational procedures, and that the idea of a world "out there," independent of our conceptual schemes, is a pre-Kantian naivety. This way, they not only provide a theoretical guarantee for post-truth (which does not know what to do with it), but, above all, they lose the opportunity to give hermeneutics its right dimension, which—as I will argue later on—is technological and not ideological.

Most analytics, instead, develop a very strong notion of truth. I call it *hypertruth*, as it postulates a necessary correlation between ontology and epistemology, in which the proposition "snow is white" is true (epistemology) if and only if snow is white (ontology). This means: if snow is white, then it is true that snow is white, so it would be true that snow is white even if there was not (never was or never will be) any human on the face of the earth. For hypertruthists, if it is true that salt is sodium chloride, then this proposition was true even for an ancient Greek, although he did not have the tools to access this truth. To designate truth as a relationship between the proposition "snow is white" and the fact that snow is white is a thesis that one can hardly disagree with. However, hypertruthists draw the conclusion that this proposition would be true even if there had never been a human being on earth who could formulate it. And that is far from obvious.

This second thesis of hypertruth seems motivated by the concern that one might otherwise fall into hermeneutics and hypotruth. But this is by no means a necessary outcome. For example, Heidegger's thesis that before Newton, the theories of the motions of the planets he enunciated were not true is not relativistic in itself: Newton's laws (epistemology) did not exist, but the reality they referred to (ontology) existed. Newton revealed something that was already there. To say this does not mean—independently of the conclusions drawn by Heidegger—to argue that the motion of the planets was created by Newton, but that the true conception of the planets' motion depends on the apparatus thanks to which Newton could elaborate his laws (in this case, mathematics, unthinkable without paper and pen), applying them to physical reality. In the same way, the true conception of the Medicean Planets depends on the technical device with which Galilei discovered them (in this case, a telescope), and this conception is not so despotic as to turn into planets those which are actually the four main satellites of Jupiter.

That salt is sodium chloride or that dinosaurs existed does not depend in any way on us and our conceptual schemes. However, what depends on us is that we developed chemistry (we did not have to), that we found bones and fossils, and that we proposed classifications and interpretations. Thus, before Newton, there indeed were planets and their interactions, which, of course, were exactly what they were without the intervention of any conceptual scheme. However, to claim, as hypertruthists do, that the laws were true even before they were discovered means either making a meaningless assertion, or—*involuntarily converging with hypotruthists*—making the interactions between planets depend on conceptual schemes.

Against hypotruth and hypertruth I propose what I call *mesotruth*. The point is not so much that mesotruth is halfway between the other two, but rather that it insists on the technical mediation between ontology and epistemology, that is, on the *apparatuses*, *devices*, and *operations* I mentioned earlier. In mesotruth, truth is neither epistemology shaping ontology (as in hypotruth) nor ontology mirroring itself in epistemology (as in hypertruth). Rather, it is a threefold structure, including ontology, epistemology, *and technology*, which is the element—so far widely neglected in philosophy—ensuring the passage from ontology to epistemology and allowing us to *make* truth. For mesotruth, truth is the technological outcome of the relationship between ontology (what there is) and epistemology (what we know).

Let me clarify with a vaguely Peircean example. In a jar, there are twenty-two beans (ontology); I count them (technology); I make the statement: "There are twenty-two beans in this jar" (epistemology). The statement is true. The jar has some weight (ontology); I put it on a scale (technology); I make the statement, "The jar weighs 100 grams" (epistemology). This statement is also true. If I was in the United States, I would say that the jar weighs 3.5 ounces, and it would be equally true, even though 3.5 and 100 are different numbers. Moral of the story: truth is relative to the tools of technical verification, but absolute with respect to the ontological sphere to which it refers and to the epistemological need to which it responds. The terms "relative" and "absolute," in the version I propose, indicate two different forms of the dependence of truth, in relation to technology and ontology, respectively.

In this way, truth depends on propositions, without—for this reason—being relative. There is white snow (or not) regardless of us humans (ontology). There is the phrase "snow is white," which is true (if snow is white), and it depends on the fact that there are beings like us (it is hard to think of the validity of "snow is white" for a bat): this is epistemology, which is not necessarily related to ontology, despite the claims of hypo- and hypertruthists alike. And above all, there are operations that allow us to link ontology and epistemology, which I call "technology." They include observing snow to ascertain whether it is white, the chemical analysis of salt to determine whether it is sodium chloride, finding out that the butler did it, and that the Donation of Constantine is a fake. There are, therefore, two very different spheres and a series of operations that can (though not necessarily will) connect them.

To clarify this theory, I propose a terminological reformation. In the analytic area, it is common to distinguish between truth makers and truth bearers, where the former would be the ontological foundation of a true proposition (snow is white) and the latter would be the epistemological expression of truth (the statement "snow is white"). This distinction, however, rests on the hypertruthist identification between ontology and epistemology. Conversely, in the perspective I propose, there can be reality without truth, but not truth without reality, and truth is something that is made: the set of true propositions that emerge from reality. What do I mean by this? A positive theory of verification. "To verify" comes from the Latin *veritas facere*: to make truth. This has two sides to it: that of invalidation (if snow is not white) and that of convalidation (if the snow is white). In the light of my threefold perspective, I propose a further differentiation: instead of understanding the ontological foundation as a "truth maker," as ontology is what provides the material, I would suggest indicating the ontological layer as a "truth bearer"; the function of "truth maker," instead, for what I have said, goes to technology, which is indeed responsible for making truth; finally, epistemology has the function of "truth teller."

Truth bearers are what (using Peirce in an ontological, not gnoseological, sense) I propose we call "firstness": the first thing that exists and exists independently is ontology, which makes up reality and is composed of individuals. Truth tellers constitute epistemology, what we know, which is always a "secondness" (something that is known, or is believed to be known, *about something* that is there: τι κατὰ τινος), which makes up truth and consists of objects, which are relational concepts that presuppose knowing subjects. Truth tellers are the "thirdness," the technology mediating between ontology and epistemology through interpretations, which serve as diagrams and generate facts. I summarize these terms in the table below and will describe them in greater detail in the following pages.

Truth bearers	*Firstness*	*Ontology*	*Reality*	*Individuals*
Truth tellers	*Secondness*	*Epistemology*	*Truth*	*Objects*
Truth makers	*Thirdness*	*Technology*	*Interpretation*	*Facts*

Truth bearers

Let us start with *firstness*, which, from an ontological point of view, is not the first thing we know (as in Peirce), but is what is there regardless of whether we know it or not. This firstness is not the indeterminate, but the most determinate of things: the individual. From elementary particles to atoms to molecules to organisms, the world is composed of individuals, which are what they are regardless of whatever knowledge one may have of them. Individuals and their interactions constitute ontology, what there is, from which may—much later, or never—emerge epistemology (what we know) and politics (what we do as free or supposedly free agents). Firstness is precisely ontology, whose distinctive characteristic is the alternative between *existence* and *non-existence*. This may seem unimportant, but this alternative is, in fact, the basis of the three fundamental characteristics of what there is: unamendability, interaction, and emergence.

Unamendability defines *negative realism*, which has nothing to do with naive realism, for which perception would grant us truthful access to reality. Perception does not give us infallible access to reality (nor systematically illusory access): it is simply proof of its resistance. With the sole power of thought, I cannot turn a white object into a black object; I must at least take the time to turn off the light. Without this operation, which is an action, not a thought, the white object remains white, which confirms the unamendability of the perceptual with respect to the conceptual, which, in this case, is presented as the unamendability of ontology with respect to epistemology. We know that a stick immersed in water is not really bent, yet we cannot help seeing it bent.

Let us now come to *positive realism*, for which reality is not an indeterminate noumenon, but has positive characteristics. The latter manifest themselves through the fact that beings with different or no perceptual apparatuses, interpretive schemes, and conceptual schemes, can *interact*. For Cartesian negative philosophy (for which the world is cookie dough shaped by the cutters of conceptual schemes), the world has no ontological consistency, and everything is traced back to thought and knowledge, whence the world is reconstructed in epistemology. For positive realism, instead, it is possible to start from ontology to found epistemology. The latter, of course, when it comes to the social world, can and must be constitutive (it is clear that laws are made by people, not atoms), while it cannot be such in the natural world, as posited by negative philosophy from Descartes to postmodernism. For our purposes, this means at least two things. First, that ontology is a solid space that does not need the forms imposed by epistemology. Secondly, that in order to interact and to live in general, there is no need for epistemology or concepts. Concepts serve the extremely rare and specialized function typical of some living beings, which is called "knowledge" (between the sphere of knowledge and that of being there is a disproportion that the constructionists have left unaccounted for: the first is enormously smaller than the second).

Unamendability and interaction are what characterizes the real as something that hurts us, escapes us, or meets us. That is what I call "emergence." Its main characteristics, in the light of negative realism, are *resistance* and *persistence*: unamendability is the reason why individuals do not get out of the way or disappear very easily. Its traits related to positive realism,[2] instead, are variously linked to interaction: the *direction* of a movement, the *fixation* of traces, the *invitation*, the *affordances* coming from the individuals (to use Eco's example: I can use a screwdriver to open a package, but not to drink). Unamendability, interaction, and emergence define the character of reality, which precedes truth. Between the first and the second there is an ontological and logical dependence, as well as a chronological difference: if reality is only potentially relational (if there were humans, then reality would smack them in the face and say "talk about me"), truth is thematically relational (in the perspective that I am defending, there is truth if and only if there are humans capable of making truth). The fact that being is different from, and prior to, knowledge is *a priori* material stronger than any conceptual *a priori*, and is as material and as *a priori* as the axiom for which there is no color without wavelength. If knowledge did not refer to something other than and prior to itself, then the words "subject," "object," "epistemology," "ontology," "knowledge," and "reflection" would not make sense, or rather, they would be inexplicable synonyms.

Given that it is previous to and independent of our knowledge, reality (which we are part of ourselves) is composed of individuals: unities that are what they are independently of other factors (senses, concepts, past experiences). The first characteristic of individuals is that they are *external* to other individuals. By "external" I mean external to epistemology, so that exteriority qualifies as a non-topological but functional independence. We are surrounded by separate existences on which, in large part, we have no influence at all (and that, fortunately, largely have no influence on us). Despite the opinion of Berkeley and his many followers, there is no need to be known or to know in order to exist. These followers include not only hypotruthists but also hypertruthists, since both, although in different directions (the former from left to right, the latter from right to left), postulate an analytic correlation between truth and reality.

Truth tellers

Truth tellers always come second, and their field is therefore secondness. The term *secondness* is to be understood in an ontological and chronological sense (this may not be evident in "snow is white," but it is very clear in "salt is sodium chloride") since, as we have said, knowledge, being the knowledge of something, necessarily comes after the known thing. Knowing that snow is white means having the concepts of "snow" and of "white," and linking them in a judgment, which is true if and only if snow is white. The sphere in which judgments take place is epistemology, which, however, depends not only on ontology but also on technology, which is the way through which epistemology has access to ontology, and which will be discussed later.

If ontology is about presence and absence, epistemology is about *truth*, *falsehood*, and *non-knowledge* (what is neither true nor false). It is neither an inert sphere, which only mirrors what there is, nor an overactive sphere, which fabricates everything there is. Rather, it is the field in which concepts take shape. The concepts of "number" or "disabled" do not exist in nature. They are sedimented and culturally selected: concepts like "calories" and "phlogiston" survive, but as historical and non-physical notions; with time, new concepts are formed. In the case of social objects, concepts have not only a descriptive, but also a performative value, as they highlight ontological layers still unseen: workers will discover that they are the victims of surplus value, people of color will find out they are discriminated against, and the bourgeois gentleman will find that he has spoken in prose all his life. But even in this case, truth refers to an ontological layer that is independent of epistemology, which merely gives it a form. Hypotruthists would object, saying that without epistemology there would be no ontology, as the characteristics of individuals are defined by knowledge and concepts. Which is obviously nonsense. Hypertruthist nonsense is less obvious, arguing that ontology and epistemology come at the same time: if salt is sodium chloride, then it is true that it is sodium chloride even if there are no humans on the face of the earth, or even if the humans that are there (say, Homer) have no knowledge of modern chemistry.

It seems strange that the proposition "salt is sodium chloride" would be true *in* Homer's world, i.e., to be more precise, at Homer's time, so many hypertruthists claim that it was rather true *of* Homer's world, i.e., to be more precise, for us today considering Homer's world. Now, if by "Homer's world" one means the earth, that world is neither Homer's nor ours nor anybody else's, so saying that "salt is sodium chloride" is true of Homer's world is meaningless. If, however, one means Homer's age, saying that the proposition "salt is sodium chloride" is true of Homer's era is false. Being true (today) of the world we know—and which probably has many characteristics in common with the world in which Homer lived, although we cannot be absolutely certain—does not equal being true (consequently) of an epoch in which, among other things, it was not known that salt is sodium chloride.

It also seems strange that a proposition like "salt is sodium chloride" (not to mention "stalking is a crime," "practicing Christians do not eat meat on Friday," "Nelson won the Battle of Trafalgar") can have meaning regardless of language, and therefore of humankind. So, some hypertruthists insist on the non-linguistic but logical nature of propositions. However, I do not think that this changes much, not only because hypertruthists themselves often speak of propositions as linguistic expressions (and one could hardly do otherwise), but especially because logic, like mathematics and language, is a technique whose existence depends on the existence of humans. We will see this shortly in my own theory, which, incidentally, is not very original as it is shared by all non-Platonist philosophers, i.e., most philosophers. Unless one is worryingly anthropocentric, and attributes properties of today's age to very ancient times, the proposition "there were dinosaurs on the earth" only appeared at a certain point in time: before, dinosaurs had still existed, but nobody knew it. And saying that for Homer it was true that salt is sodium chloride is like saying that "dinosaurs exist" (in the present) is true for us.

Finally, coming to the idea, shared by both hypo- and hypertruthists, of a necessary correlation between ontology and epistemology, it is worth observing that this correlation (which is, in fact, simultaneous) would deprive epistemology of its meaning. In fact, virtually all the beliefs held true 10,000 years ago, as far as we know, have now changed, so much so that Ramses II never suspected that he was dying of tuberculosis, although he did indeed die of tuberculosis. This is not only true of scientific knowledge. The whiteness of snow is a perceptive datum that applies to humans but not to bats. The proposition does not express a necessary fact: if there were no humans, snow would have all the properties it has, but the proposition "snow is white" would not be there, and would seem meaningless to anyone disagreeing with the hypetruthist belief that reality and truth are correlated. Even more so if "snow is white" stood for "snow appears to be white to the human perceptual apparatus" or (to complicate things even further) for "snow has the dispositional property of appearing white to the human perceptual apparatus."

As I said, *secondness is an essential characteristic of truth*. Truth comes after reality because it refers to it, differs from it, and depends on it. This is clear from a chronological perspective: from the point of view of truth, reality is not a starting point but a point of arrival, something that only comes later (if all goes well). In this way, truth is not archaeologically founded in reality; *it is teleologically oriented toward it*. Ontological emergence proceeds from the past to the present; the epistemological operation goes from the present to the past. This—anticipating the point I will deal with in the last part of this chapter—is the principle of making truth: finding out how things are, starting from a situation of not knowing. Truth, therefore, does not take place at the same time as reality, but always comes next. In this sense, truth has a teleological dependence on ontology (its purpose is to enunciate the truth about ontology), and a causal dependence on technology (without some form of technology we would have no truth).

If ontology is made up of individuals, epistemology refers to *objects* (*objectum*: a thing placed in front). These may be classic individuals (individuals in the strict sense), as is the case with natural objects, which exist in space and time independently of knowing subjects,[3] and with *social objects*, which exist in space and time, but depend on knowing subjects—in fact, social objects manifest a general dependence on subjects, as they do not depend on a particular subject (10 euros do not cease to be such if I ignore the fact that they are 10 euros). However, objects may also be atypical individuals, as is the case with *ideal objects*, which exist outside time and space, independently of subjects. The fourth (and last) family of epistemological objects is that of *artefacts*, which depend on subjects for their production (like social objects) but continue to exist even in the absence of subjects (like natural objects).

Truth makers

Epistemology concerns what we know, or think we know; it is a form (syntax, judgment, concepts) and has the values of truth and falsehood. Ontology concerns what there is; it is a force (something effective, an agent: resistance, unamendability, etc.) and has the values of existence and nonexistence. *Technology*, finally, concerns what we do, and its values are *success* or *failure* (or, if you prefer Austin's terminology, happiness or unhappiness).[4]

If ontology is firstness and epistemology is secondness (as it always refers to ontology), technology is *thirdness*, indicating the mediation between the former and the latter. There are, of course, reasons to say that technology is secondness and ontology is thirdness, but I prefer the above choice for three reasons. First, it allows me to re-link technology to the tradition of "thirds": the interrelations between reality and concepts, which are so common in the philosophical tradition (in order of appearance: the *chora* in Plato, the scheme in Kant, the dialectic in Hegel, the *différance* in Derrida). Secondly, it is the most interesting thing, so I prefer to keep it last. Finally, there is a third reason that suggests that technology should be allocated to the sphere of thirdness: technology is *becoming*, as it is no longer being (which is or is not) and is not yet knowledge (which is true or false). It is doing: it expresses a competence that can, though not necessarily will, lead to understanding[5] (I only have a very vague idea of the psychophysical mechanisms that are activated by me typing these very words, and if I were a neurophysiologist, I would not type any better).

By "technology" I mean the wide range of actions we perform in a competent way without prior knowledge. These actions are varied, ranging from lighting a fire without any notion of physics to speaking a language without grammatical and syntactical knowledge, to creating works of art without having the ability to figure out why they were made exactly that way. In this sense, technology has a privileged relationship with gestures (though, of course, there can be technologies of thought, such as logic, mnemotechnics, arithmetic).

We act before thinking, and that way, new truths are discovered, while comprehension is necessarily linked to the formulation of analytic reasonings, which belong to the sphere of ascertained knowledge. This action allows for the emergence of truth from reality. This knowledge comes from doing and often surprises us (unlike analytic judgments, which make up knowledge that emerges from further knowledge, and are therefore not surprising). Competence is, in fact, a *praxis* that can result in *poiesis*, a practical attitude that leads to a result: the bee makes honey, the termite builds the termite mound, Michelangelo sculpts Moses, Maradona scores goals. But *poiesis*, the more-or-less ritualized action, may also happen for no reason, as shown by people who knit, scrabble on a piece of paper, or play with their phone. Without hands, and the experience of handling and grasping, thought would not exist; without the competence of manuality, there would be no comprehension.[6] Hands are prehensile, they grasp things (as Hegel knew very well, seeing the noun *Begriff*, "concept," as related to the verb *greifen*, "to grasp"). Hands indicate and, when they indicate without grasping, making gestures, they start the production of symbols.

Speaking a language, lighting a fire, writing a novel, counting, interacting socially: these skills do not rely on conceptual schemes but on *interpretive schemes*, which, in some cases (as in, for example, finding a four-leaf clover in a meadow), mediate between concept (abstract and general) and perception (concrete and individual), but in many others—in fact, in the vast majority of cases—apply to perceptions or operate in the world independently of concepts. This is not surprising: we have a disposition that manifests itself from the most elementary devices and evolves in increasingly complex formations, like a reproductive faculty that transports ontology into epistemology. Conversely, technology is not only related to the remote origins of humankind but also to our highest intellectual achievements: it shows itself in mathematics and logic, in the creation of scientific experiments and artistic works, in the actions and rites that accompany our social lives.

New realist hermeneutics

The interpretive scheme is not a conceptual scheme (whatever this desperately vague expression means), but a practical rule through which we interact with individuals. In most cases, the rules are neither known nor explicit (I walk, play with my cat, apologize), in others the rules are explicit but not "understood." What do I really understand when I count the beans in the jar? I follow a rule ("add one") I learned as a child. At the same time, this operation is an interpretation not in the sense that it defines some conceptual horizon, but because it fulfills the practical function that traditionally belongs to hermeneutics, which, not coincidentally, is defined as *hermeneutikè techne*: the technique of carrying messages, capable of mediating as a link between the ontological layer of being and the epistemological layer of knowledge.

Hermes is the messenger of the gods, and the hermeneut is a mailman, one who performs the task of carrying messages (a hieroglyph, a Hungarian novel, a threatening letter, a love letter), which he almost never understands. And all the meanings of hermeneutics, ancient and modern, are easily attributable to practical operations: expression (the meaning of Aristotle's *hermeneia*) means taking outside, translation means transporting, comprehension means grasping—all manual operations. Even deconstruction, typical of nineteenth- and twentieth-century hermeneutics, has a clear technical connotation. By understanding interpretation as an operation, I refer to two aspects. The first is the practical character of interpretation, namely the fact that it is perfectly possible without understanding—as we have seen, the latter is just one of the traditional functions of hermeneutics. For Plato, poets are messengers of the gods (*hermenes*),[7] and considering his poor opinion of the poets' knowledge, this is not a compliment.

The second, though, is that this operation allows for judgments: that is, technology can turn into epistemology. Consider the case of *a priori* synthetic judgments, which were Kant's ultimate goal. They are indeed operations, as is clear in the arithmetic example made by Kant himself: 7 + 5 = 12, where 12 is synthetic and not analytic because it cannot be obtained from the analysis of 7 and 5, since I can achieve that result even by adding 6 to 6, 8 to 4, etc. Kant was so interested in *a priori* synthetic judgments because, in his conception, they depended on concepts that were independent of experience and therefore certain. Now, we can easily note that informative *a posteriori* synthetic judgments do indeed come from *operations*: we get the number of beans by applying the rule "add one," and many pieces of information (for instance, what time it is or how much we weigh) come from machines, which have no concepts, only mechanisms regulating their functioning.

On the one hand, Kant offers us a hyper-conceptualist view ("intuitions without concepts are blind"), by which even the most distracted of intuitions depends on concepts. And Kant's world is made up of epistemology (conceptual schemes with which we order the world) and ontology (the world that we order, and which we never really know, as it is made of things in itself, which we can only access as phenomena). On the other hand, however, in the chapter on schematism, Kant mentions a third term that lies between concepts and intuitions (that is, between epistemology and ontology): the scheme, defined as a "hidden technique" (*verborgene Kunst*, which usually translates as "hidden art," but of course has the same meaning as "hidden technique"). The scheme performs operations (Kant defines it as a "construction method").

Translating Kant's proposal into my own terms, I suggest we invert the succession epistemology/technology/ontology (with the latter being inaccessible as such) into ontology/technology/epistemology. First there is ontology, with individuals that are not inaccessible as such because they manifest clear characteristics in interaction (among themselves and with us). That is, first there are individuals, e.g., snow, whose properties are independent of me, of you, of my cat, and of whomever: this is the ontology of what, later, we will recognize as natural objects. Then there are interpretive schemes, namely those operations that generate facts and are not free or subjective: I see snow with my visual apparatus and note that it is white (the operational aspect appears more clearly if we think of salt, which I have to taste to realize it is salty, or of beans, which I have to count). Finally, there are judgments, which constitute objects: snow is white; salt is salty (and, much later, salt is sodium chloride); there are 22 beans in this jar. If I said that snow is black, salt is sweet, and there are 21 beans in the jar, this would not be an interpretation but a mistake. What I do when I interpret something—I repeat—is not apply a conceptual scheme to some formless matter ("there are no facts, only interpretations"), but rather note the emergences of ontology (the properties of snow, salt, or the beans in the jar independently of me), through technological procedures (looking, tasting, counting), which may, though not necessarily will, produce epistemological judgments.

In so doing, mesotruth recovers hermeneutics without falling into the correlationism of hypo- or hypertruth. The mistake made by postmodernists was twofold: they treated hermeneutics as epistemology (the entirety of knowledge would be the outcome of interpretation) and as ontology (there are no facts, only interpretations, or, more modestly, every fact can be interpreted). The hyperbolic (and false) statement that "there are no facts, only interpretations" should be replaced with the principle that the existence of interpretations does not exclude the existence of facts, individuals, and objects. As radical and attractive as it may be to think of undoing truth (which has fascinated philosophers and non-philosophers after Nietzsche), making truth seems to be a better idea, even though it is harder. Indeed, the saying "so easy to criticize, so hard to create" also applies to the art of interpretation.

Notes

1. See Augustine, *Confessiones*, X, 1.1.
2. Maurizio Ferraris, *Positive Realism* (London: Zero Books, 2015).
3. Compared to them, epistemology only adds an external property: the fact of being known. In this sense, natural objects are individuals because they are known as existing in space and time independently of subjects.
4. John L. Austin, *How to Do Things with Words* (Cambridge, MA: Harvard University Press, 1962).
5. Daniel C. Dennett, *From Bacteria To Bach and Back: The Evolution of Minds* (Cambridge, MA: Bradford Books/MIT Press, 2017).
6. Colin McGinn, *Prehension* (Cambridge, MA: MIT Press, 2015).
7. See Plato, *Ion*, 534 e.

5

The Real Scandal

Lee Braver

The question of thinkability

First we asked what reality was. What is the nature of all this stuff around us, we wondered, and what is higher than it? What can withstand the ravages of time, rise above the imperfections of matter, to achieve a more real reality, a truer truth? This inquiry into the timeless sustained us for quite some time. But at some point the nature of the question changed. It became more reflexive, turned inwards, turned on itself. The questioning came to question the question itself. Rather than just asking about reality, we started to ask why we asked about the nature of reality. Not just the material stuff around us, but the loftier matters, that which is *meta* the *physis*—the transcendent, the necessary, the *a priori*, God, the soul, everything, 42. We asked whether this inquiry was impossible; we asked whether this inquiry was necessary. Kant, perhaps the originator of this phase of metaphysics, answered yes to both questions, casting metaphysics as a Greek tragedy where we are fated to do that one thing that we must never do. For Heidegger, on the other hand—the other great figure from this period[1]—being does not so much trap us in metaphysics as seduce us into it, lure us with its scintillating charms. Metaphysics then becomes a rather clumsy set of love letters, as Derrida portrays them, sent from brilliant but awkward lovers, rather how Nietzsche depicts philosophers.[2]

And today, what is our question today? Is it just this—this question as to what is our question? That seems so feeble, like a pale shadow of true inquiry cast upon the wall of the history of philosophy. If that were our main preoccupation, would that not be an outrageous waste of our efforts, a squandering of our rich inheritance, something of a scandal?

There have, of course, been many scandals concerning reality and its investigation throughout the centuries. Kant found it scandalous that we still had no proof of an external world, surely the one thing the world should have expected our profession to have supplied them. Heidegger, in response, was scandalized at the notion that such a passé question could still generate a scandal. But they reach back much farther. Plato's metaphysics, the very birth of Western philosophy, arose in response to the twin scandals of the best man of his generation being condemned to death, and of the very existence of death, the degradation of matter, the corrosion of time. How could reality, the self, knowledge, all be here only to disappear? Surely such an outrage cannot be, so there must be a realm where it is not; hence transcendence. Augustine was scandalized that we mortals prefer to shore up these worldly rotting treasures rather than investing in the incorruptible divine. Descartes was shocked at the poor education he had paid so much for and set out to reform the schools by re-forming knowledge itself. Perhaps philosophy begins in scandal rather than in wonder.

And philosophy's response to this shock, whether it be scandal or wonder, has always been to attempt to defuse it. The quintessential philosophical attitude is summed up in Aristotle's analysis of questioning: philosophy begins in wonder but "must end up in the contrary and (according to the proverb) the better state, the one that people achieve by learning."[3] Wonder is useful as an initiating motivation because it starts us investigating, but it's like an itch that needs to be scratched. If reality presents us with a scandal, we must set up a political war room that will come up with a solution that dispels it. Questions are to be answered, puzzles to be solved, confusions resolved. Wonder, perplexity, inquiries—ladders to be climbed and then discarded.

But this modus operandi, no matter how obvious and natural, rests on an assumption—precisely the things we philosophers are trained to root out and question. It assumes that answers are preferable to questions, that the natural life cycle of a question is to seek its *telos* and fulfillment in coming to rest, or even dissolving itself in an answer. This view is not innocent or isolated but finds its place in a larger sense of cosmos, humanity, and their relationship, one that buys into what Leibniz called a pre-established harmony between mind and world, albeit without Leibniz's own Rube Goldbergesque mechanisms for its operation. At bottom, philosophy has generally seen reality as intelligible, as that which is intelligible, which underwrites the project of understanding it. Just think of the way Plato's divided line analogy from the *Republic* correlates degrees of realness with degrees of comprehensibility, or Descartes's determination that the quantifiable aspects of the world—those which can be captured in formulae and the webs of Cartesian grids—are the only ones we can be sure are out there the way we perceive them, or Hegel's neat summation that the real is the rational and the rational is the real. The world is at its most real where our understanding penetrates it most fully, where its ways of being fit our ways of thinking best, such that the two gear into each other seamlessly. We know we have struck the hard rock of reality when we can know it, when it makes sense to us.

Questions naturally lead into answers, then, because the world, in some sense, is made to make sense, is meant to have meaning. Whether that is simply how reality is, or God is communicating with us through the language of existence, or we ourselves have, as enlightened autonomous agents, made the world over in our minds' image—however it is accounted for, we have traditionally called real what confirms our expectations, what responds to our call, what slips tamely into our taxonomies. This underlying epistemo-metaphysical principle is what I call the Parmenedean Thinkability Principle, as Parmenides implanted this concept in philosophy in embryo at conception, an idea that has guided it ever since: that being and thinking are one. That which is is that which is thinkable, and that which is thinkable, is. In one way, it is a tremendously hubristic assumption. Why should we presume world and mind to be compatible? In another, it seems unavoidable. If there isn't at least some compatibility between the two, then all thought is futile, all knowledge illusory. It's just common sense: the world and mind must have sense in common if they are to communicate with each other.

This notion, like so many others, took rather a sharp turn with Kant. For an Enlightenment thinker helping humanity finally reach maturity, simply taking up a world laying there predigested for us maintains us in our tutelage. No, we must light the light of knowledge ourselves; we must *make* sense of the world by making it sensible. We do this by fomenting the Copernican Revolution whereby the comprehensible world is rendered comprehensible by us, and so becomes a correlate of our transcendental faculties. The world becomes part of the subject, or the inextricable context of the subject, or the subject's meaning or posit or reification or constitution or historical situation—various forms, but all concluding that the world is the subject's. It is what gives meaning, and what receives it, both what overhangs and precedes and situates the subject, and what the subject projects and forms and transforms. And thus is born what is sometimes called anti-realism or correlationism.

But let us note that Kant left us another legacy alongside this anti-realist one, or rather underside it. For noumena, the world as we *don't* constitute it, are the other side of phenomena. Noumena are the conceptual shadows of phenomena since Kant believes that we cannot think the latter without the former although, at the same time, phenomena are the shadow cast by noumena when the blinding light of the in-itself hits our transcendental faculties. If we make over the world in order to render it intelligible, then the world as it is in-itself, as it *really* is, is fundamentally unintelligible to us. At its deepest level, where it is most independent of us, where it is most real, this view says, reality makes no sense to us, *can* make no sense to us in principle no matter how much we learn, no matter how far we extend our perception, knowledge, or understanding. Although he does occasionally say that noumena are thinkable, just not knowable—they must obey the laws of logic and be amenable to the concepts of the understanding even though they do not pass through the intuition to actually have concepts applied to them—this seems both unwarranted (how do you know, Kant?) and against the basic thrust of his system, since the only way to secure concepts' necessary, universal status is to place their origin in the mind, not in the world. At one point, Kant says that even if angels were to whisper the true physics of the universe to us, noumenal mechanics if you will, we should ignore it and continue our phenomenal experiments for it could be nothing but gibberish to us.[4] Newton or Einstein would find their minds going blank, or perhaps they would be driven mad like the protagonists in a Lovecraft story when too much of the old gods' ways are revealed to them.

Kant set up an impervious shield against this mad, maddening, literally unnatural reality: our faculties automatically transform all incoming data into a familiar, digestible phenomenal form, thus making sure we can never make contact with anything that breaks the laws of Newton or Euclid, just as Midas can touch nothing but gold. There can be no cognitive indigestion for Kant, no unanswerable questions, for if it is a legitimate question then it must have a real answer, one that is, in principle even if not in practice, available to us. As we saw above, question and answer are suited to each other since mind and phenomenal world are. We can never be truly, deeply, radically surprised, for anything that conflicts with our set ways of thinking and experiencing would either be filtered out or mashed into them. The *a posteriori* truly does follow the *a priori*, inexorably. No one can escape themselves.

But what if we could? What if the old gods could contact us, not for extended conversations, for that would make them contemporary, but what if we could get brief glimpses of a world that lay beyond the furthest reaches of our grasp? What if our experience outran our understanding, our thinking, our reasoning? And what if these experiences, these experiences that transgress our best and possibly inescapable ways of making sense of the world, turned out to be our most valuable? What if they mark our best, most unadulterated contact with reality, even if such contact outrages and scandalizes the mind?

I believe along with the anti-realism that has dominated continental thought since Kant, there has been a counter-strain of a peculiar kind of realism, one which I call transgressive realism. In many ways, this theory inverts Parmenidean realism. Whereas that view tracks reality with intelligibility, as in Plato's divided line, transgressive realism locates the most persuasive encounters with reality in those experiences that are unintelligible, that go against the grain of the mind, the ones that poke through the phenomenal cocoon that Kant's idealism weaves around us. If the real is that which is other to us, that which breaks in on us from outside, then the more other it is, the more outsider, the more it trails transcendence as it crashes into us. That which is beyond us conceptually is that which we could not have created ourselves, and hence cannot be an extension of our selves, thus breaking with all forms of idealism, anti-realism, or correlationism. Breaking with these ideas has taken a number of recent forms.

Transgressive realism

An exorcism is haunting twenty-first-century philosophy—the exorcism of the specter of anti-realism. It seems that a number of thinkers, from a variety of backgrounds, all woke up around the same time (2007) thinking that the last two centuries of anti-realism have been, or at least have become, a dead end. The way forward lay not through some more subtle extension or refinement of anti-realism, the most common strategy for progress over the last two centuries,[5] but rather by some form or other of realism.

My version, transgressive realism, differs from speculative realism, perhaps the most prominent of these recent oppositions to Kant's anti-realist legacy, because I am still talking about experiences. I don't know how to talk about that which we never can and never will come into contact with; it's hard enough philosophizing about the things we can. The noumenal in the sense of that which stays on the dark side of the real, always on the other side of things, fundamentally outside our horizons—horizons of time, of space, of perception—to me, this smacks of that world well lost, the unheard tree falling in the forest, the object that vanishes just before you look at it. Philosophizing about such matters veers between fruitless speculation and the loss of meaning entirely, at least it does when I try to do it. I'm just not sure what or how much it means to talk about entities we can in principle never have any experience of. One of the ways Kant's successors improved upon his noumenal ruminations was to insist that any reality worthy of the name, any reality which we can understand how to apply the term to and understand what it means to do so, must be something we can encounter in some way or other. We are rooted in Heidegger's clearing, confined to talking only about being as we have some experience of it, which I think leaves me still an anti-realist in their eyes.

Meillassoux's anti-correlationist ancestral thinking, on the other hand, uses our capacities to reason, especially scientific and mathematical reasoning, to surpass our horizons of experience.[6] Astrophysics apparently enables us to reach back before all humans existed to the beginnings of the universe, as well as to what will happen after all have been extinguished. Meillassoux argues, among other things, that these modes of thinking are formal and impersonal enough to escape anthropomorphic and anthropocentric limitations. As Galileo had it, math allows us to listen in on the murmurings of the universe in its own language rather than remaining confined within our own, human-all-too-human speech. But how does one know from within these ways of thinking whether they succeed in touching the world as it escapes these ways, since the only way to compare the two is still through these very ways of thinking? As McDowell says, we cannot see our way of seeing and the world seen "sideways-on" to evaluate how we affect what we see; we only see what we see through our own ways of seeing.[7] Thus, it seems to me that Meillassoux's strategy retroactively imposes our concepts onto the universe's past, such that his attempt to escape the bubble of human experience merely extends human conceptuality, making our escape into the great outdoors somewhat less adventuresome than it initially appears.[8]

Unlike speculative and Meillassoux's realisms, the transgressive version sticks to experiences. I am enough of a phenomenologist to want to philosophize only about what I can encounter, although encountering occurs in all kinds of wildly diverse ways. The first philosophical idea that Heidegger ever learned was that being is said, and is, in many ways; this notion guided a considerable portion of his thinking throughout his long career. I'm just not interested in analyzing anything falling entirely outside the cone of potential contact, and I'm not confident that we can. Nor am I interested in the scientific analysis of the long, long ago or ahead, as the scientificity of the analysis renders it conceptually, if not chronologically, contemporaneous. It is our concepts, our modes of temporality, our ways of understanding that roll out these horizons, making them transcendental rather than transcendent.

I am interested in what is intellectually transcendent but phenomenologically immanent, so that we do in fact encounter it but in moments of utter bafflement. These are impossible for Kant's transcendental idealism since for him, the encounter itself renders the phenomena encountered intellectually digestible, but they are the heart and soul of transgressive realism. These are the wild, untamed experiences, the bewildering, captivating and uncapturable, unanticipatible and unforgettable, inexplicable, sometimes headshaking, sometimes life-changing events. These are the times you know you're alive, you know that something has happened. These are the thoughts that can re-form your mind into strange new shapes and reveal heretofore unnoticed dimensions of the world. These are the moments that try humans' minds but, by that very trial, constitute our fullest, least-mediated contact with something other.

The dominant strain of continental philosophy has played out in some variation of an idealist, anti-realist, or correlationist key which, following Kant, rules out such transgressions. If we encounter something, it must be meaningful, these philosophies say, for meaningfulness is the medium, the atmosphere, the gravitational field of experience. Even something surprising or confusing represents merely a temporary hiccup that necessarily can be smoothly assimilated into our ways of understanding reality. Phenomena must be Euclidean and Newtonian, or imbued with some degree of Spirit, or constituted as part of a harmonious and anticipated coalescence of adumbrations, or integrated into a holistic world, or text, or language, or epoch, or something—but however it happens, it must present itself as meaningful if it is to present itself to us at all. These philosophies emphasize holistic contexts which give meaning and are given meaning and in which everything finds its place and thereby has its sense. These senses may change in different contexts or historical periods or strategies or interpretations, yet all there is lives in meaning like fish in water: outside of it, it cannot.

The problem with this view, as a number of recent thinkers have pointed out, is that this makes external reality not very external. It makes the world in some sense an extension of the self, an appendage, a correlate, an effect of our transcendental faculties or will or everyday activities or interpretations, and these constructions can never really get us outside of ourselves. We never touch on something that has nothing of us to it, the transcendent, the fully non-human, what Meillassoux calls "the Great Outdoors," Levinas "infinity," Heidegger "earth." The world narrows to a Potemkin village that we have unconsciously built to fool ourselves, behind which philosophy teaches us to find ourselves. Thus does idealism inflate the self to encompass all; thus does all dwindle down to our small selves. Thus is the astounding, prodigious world, with its shocks and mysteries, its spirits from the vasty deep and strangers from strange lands, its bazaar of the bizarre, its gods and monsters—thus is all this richness reduced to what the mind is prepared to process through its prior forms. What a loss. As Levinas, one of the great transcendental realists, says, "focusing on being, [thought] is outside itself, but remains marvelously within itself, or returns to itself. The exteriority or otherness of the self is recaptured in immanence.... One learns only what one already knows."[9]

But the thing is, we don't actually learn only what we already know, the eternal recurrence of recollection that Plato condemns us to; in fact, that's precisely what we cannot learn, for that's when learning by definition does not happen. We meet ideas and people and places that do not just bring us new facts to toss onto the homogeneous pile of already-gathered knowledge but new *kinds* of facts, genuinely new ideas that, as the phrase has it, expand our horizons, warping and distending the mind's previous structure such that it can never simply reassume its old shape. And why would you ever want to go back, now that you have seen the open sea that Nietzsche speaks of, once you have practiced the gay science, a way of thinking deeply and questioning evilly that is to previous philosophizing as alchemy is to chemistry?[10] Isn't this literal changing of one's mind precisely what we aspire to induce in our Intro students if, perhaps, quixotically? Isn't this the high we scholars have been chasing all of our professional lives, with, as all junkies know, ever-diminishing success? Isn't this why we got in this business in the first place (besides for the money, of course)?

What's so external about external reality?

Now these transgressive experiences are, of course, not proof of the external world, nothing like that. I take it that we no longer are concerned with such matters. To borrow Lyotard's term, we live today in an age of incredulity towards proofs of this kind, greeting an allegedly successful proof of the external world with as much of a raised eyebrow as a skeptical argument. Today, Heidegger's scandal is surely more on target than Kant's.

Rather, it is a matter of where we find external reality most genuinely external, and what we mean by this externality after all, and why we care about it in the first place. Why does it matter, as the old freshman head-scratcher goes, if you're in virtual reality with everything great but fake? What would it matter, as long as the Cubs win the World Series, Donald Trump gets impeached, and peanut butter still tastes good with chocolate? To move Nietzsche's question about truth one sub-discipline over to metaphysics,[11] why should external reality matter to us? And what do we mean when we apply this term, "external," to reality?

It seems to me that it is its externality that makes reality real, vital, and important. It is the fact that it is not us, that it can surprise us, change us, teach us something that we could not find out on our own. The problem with the way all idealisms slide into solipsisms is not that we know them to be false; it is that they would be hellishly dull. Sartre got it exactly wrong: hell is the *absence* of other people, and other things, and otherness in general. That's why solitary confinement is a worse punishment than being locked up with others. The transcendental hamster ball that Kant's idealism locks us into where the basic outline of all discoveries for all time have been sketched out in advance isn't the protection of science, as he thought, but its death by suffocation. For without discovery, without the conquest of the unknown, what is science? The extension of Kuhnian normal science forever would deserve the scorn Hegel pours on the bad infinite. It's the revolutions, the times we radically revise our most basic concepts, that rejuvenate the endeavor. As Heidegger says, anticipating Kuhn by some decades, "[t]he real 'movement' of the sciences takes place when their basic concepts undergo a more or less radical revision which is transparent to itself.... In such immanent crises the very relationship between positively investigative inquiry and those things themselves that are under interrogation comes to a point where it begins to totter."[12] Although here he is describing the positive sciences, what else is *Being and Time*'s destruction of the tradition and proposal of the new ontological categories of readiness-to-hand, presence-at-hand, and existence but an attempt to make philosophy totter and undergo an epochal revolution? What else but the promise of such a shake-up stirred up so much excitement?

Kierkegaard captured this idea in *Philosophical Fragments* where he contrasted two epistemologies: Greek recollection and Christian incarnation. For the former, the teacher can be nothing more than a midwife, essentially gratuitous—simply a useful catalyst for touching off an internal self-discovery. Thus, for recollective epistemology, all inquiry can be summed in the Delphic maxim, "Know thyself." Kierkegaard held that this structure informed most philosophy. Some version of spiritual ascent marches in lockstep with epistemological education: as one ascends from the physical individuals to the Forms, one becomes more soul and less body, and hence more akin to the Forms, and so more attracted to them upon death, thereby increasing the odds of a heavenly afterlife. Or one aspires to the more divine and less sinfully worldly, or more rationally scientific and less superstitiously dependent on society, tradition, the senses, emotions, etc. All of this occurs essentially on one's own, through recalling oneself to one's own inner resources, redirecting one's energies, rewiring the faculties.

In that case, though, why did the living category mistake, the God-man, come to earth and suffer crucifixion? What would be the point of a divine epiphany were this infinite being merely telling us what we already know, what we can find out for ourselves? Kant's morality, for example, ensures universality by placing the source of moral knowledge within rational creatures. This allows us to hold pre-Christian pagans as responsible as those who came afterwards and benefit from his teachings, but then, of course, no external authority, not even God, can teach us anything about morality. We come into this world with its lessons hard-wired into our reason, and Kant argues that if we encounter what we think might be God, we must match this apparent apparition against our pre-existing notions of goodness to see if He measures up to our standards: "Even the Holy One of the Gospel must be compared with our idea of moral perfection before He is recognized as such."[13] Such a transcendent entity could not even teach us anything about religion: "there can be no religion springing from revelation alone."[14] Not just morality, but religion too must be located entirely within the boundaries of mere reason.

Nothing outside of ourselves can tell us anything; as the etymology of "autonomy" tells us, we must give the law to ourselves rather than taking it from anywhere outside. "The whole of human existence is in that case entirely self-enclosed, as a sphere," Kierkegaard writes, "and the ethical is at once the limit and completion. God becomes an invisible, vanishing point, an impotent thought."[15] Then there is only us, only the human, what our reason must tell us, which can in a sense over-rule what God in fact tells us. Kant thinks that Abraham failed his test since he should have told God that because the command to kill Isaac fails the test of the categorical imperative, it is his duty to disobey it.

But the very idea of the incarnation, of the infinite breaking into the immanent, finite horizons of this earth demonstrates the need for something beyond our comprehension, for it would be pointless otherwise. Thus Kierkegaard's life-long fascination with the paradoxical and absurd: this is how the transcendent must strike our reason, else it is not truly transcendent. "The new which he [the apostle] may have to proclaim is the essential paradox. However long a time it may be preached in the world, essentially it remains equally new, equally paradoxical, no immanence can assimilate it."[16] Compare Derrida's analysis: "God doesn't give his reasons.... Otherwise he wouldn't be God, we wouldn't be dealing with the Other as God or with God as *wholly other*. If the other were to share his reasons with us by explaining them to us, if he were to speak to us all the time without any secrets, he wouldn't be the other."[17] As Nietzsche says, the new in morality is, by definition, evil at first, for its novelty means that it must contravene previous standards.[18] Now combine that with Derrida's claim that it is in the history of philosophy, even the nature of the discipline (to use a decidedly un-Derridean phrase) to forever question the nature of philosophy, of what counts as philosophical reasoning.[19] Together, the two points mean that every great philosopher becomes great at least partially by redefining how to philosophize, stretching and remolding the very contours of reason. Transferring Nietzsche's claim about morality, we can say that each new form of rationality necessarily appears irrational at first, for its newness means that it violates what had been taken as self-evident and necessary.

Transgressive philosophers and philosophizing

Transgressive realism neatly inverts traditional takes on philosophical questions, exposing and questioning their deeply held common assumptions, as all good theories do. Starting with Parmenides and Plato, intelligibility has always been a hallmark of realness; transgressive realism finds it in opacity, resistance to understanding, even its violation. Aesthetics had praised harmony and beauty but, finding our inspiration in the sublime—again left to us in an alternate inheritance from Kant—we seek out art that doesn't settle down peacefully, "anxious objects" in critic Harold Rosenberg's term. These are objects that call themselves into question—their status, their meaning, and by doing so, unsettle larger aesthetic ideas—the entire category of art, the notion of meaning itself. They resist attempts to settle "what they mean," all the while still beckoning us to interpret them; indeed, it is this very struggle against meaning something that captivates us and makes us feel sure that they do mean something. Duchamp, Kafka, Beckett, Beckmann—that sort of thing.

In epistemology, as discussed, inexplicable mysteries are preferred over answered questions, puzzles rather than solutions. It is the mystery that keeps the drowsy mind attentive and alert, that keeps the clearing open and bright and prevents forgetfulness of being in Heidegger's thought, for all is question-worthy. In logic, it is the meta-logical question that Heidegger and Derrida took up, the alogical fact that there is logic at all, the lack of a sufficient reason for the principle of sufficient reason, the groundless grounds of all reasoning. This is not a battle cry to abandon reason and embrace ... what? Emotion? Irrationality? Intentional obfuscation? Whatever the misological caricature of continental philosophy of the day has it. Rather, it's to reason about reason, to become aware of it as reasoning, and to express thankfulness for our thinking. Its gratuitousness instills gratitude.

Heidegger often says in his later work that being calls us—being calls on us, calls to us, calls us to our essence, our destiny, our authentic selves if openness to being is later Heidegger's heir to authenticity. But being also prods us, provokes and unsettles us. In *Being and Time*, Dasein seems perpetually unsettled, not-at-home—*unheimlich*. Anxiety reveals that while we always are-in-a-world, we can never be-of-the-world; we can find no home in this world even after we have chosen our place in it for ourselves. Whereas being in the later work comes to comfort, to throw us instead of abandoning us,[20] to possibly overcome "the homelessness of contemporary man"[21] as a temporary, historical phase we can surpass, the early work discourages us from ever feeling settled; our being is essentially unsettled, always already and always forever an issue for us.

Perhaps we can read this early acknowledgment of essentially anxious unsettledness into the later work, so that instead of seeing being as like a benevolent giver (the "like" is important here, lest we fall into onto-theo-logy), we instead view it as an unending provocation. Rather than calling us to rise to our destiny as thinkers, it can serve as an incitement, a spur, a refusal of any destiny as final, settled. The way being is beyond reason (not irrational) is what draws us to reason endlessly about it. That's what the historical epochs amount to, after all—various attempts to conceptualize contemporary revelations of beings, to understand as a response to that which confuses, to draw up and systematize what rises up and presents itself to us.

This is what each epoch does, but just as consciousness on Hegel's highway of despair constantly forgets previous self-assurances that it finally has things aright once and for all, so each epochal understanding claims to surpass its epochal limitation to grasp the underlying structure of all that is and can be. Even if it were to master the beings around it—technologically and intellectually—as well as the epoch's beingness or basic understanding of what it is to be, no epoch can truly settle what being is. This is the "source" or giving of beings in their periodic beingness, and it cannot be captured within the concepts of any given understanding. It is *essentially* mysterious, incomprehensible as the wellspring of all comprehensibility and comprehension. This is one reason why Heidegger treasures thinking of being over understandings of beings or beingness: it will never exhaust its ability to provoke. This is one reason why it is better captured in irresolvable questions than any kind of answer.[22]

Furthermore, the deep historicity of being that suffuses Heidegger's later thought ensures that there can be no final answer. Whatever we come up with will be overturned at the next turning. We don't understand better than previous generations, with the implicit promise of at least asymptotically approaching the one correct understanding; we understand differently, anew, and this is the most correct way to understand it. After all, being is said in many ways, diachronically. This awareness is what breaks the filtering circle of recollection that Kierkegaard warned us against but which *Being and Time*'s pre-ontological understandings seemed to trap us in.

Heidegger's thought didn't so much turn from early to late, as it turned to and into turning itself. "I have left an earlier standpoint, not in order to exchange it for another one, but because even the former standpoint was merely a way-station along a way. The lasting element in thinking is the way."[23] Our being as thinkers is a "counter-resonance of en-ownment ... to become itself: the preserver of the thrown projecting-open";[24] we are those who receive what being gives, becoming ourselves in the receiving and responding because we become the receiving and responding, just as being gives itself in giving the given because it is only the giving. So we, in our being, echo and respond to being. And perhaps the essential point of his later ruminations on being is that it is historical, history itself in one sense. As it continually releases different kinds of beings, we must respond to them with new forms of thinking if we are to continue to dovetail with being like yin and yang to make up the clearing. The one thing we know about being is that there cannot be just one thing to know, one way to know it. Knowledge and understanding must also be said in many ways.

This lack of conclusions can be a boon rather than a burden. Heidegger enigmatically says that "*most thought-provoking in our thought-provoking time is that we are still not thinking.*"[25] Let us recall the inconspicuousness of ready-to-hand equipment from *Being and Time*. It is our familiarity and facility with tools that renders them virtually invisible, withdrawing from our attention as we go about our business. It is only when they break down or behave unexpectedly that our attention gets drawn to them and our world is "lit up ... The world announces itself."[26] In the more existential Division II, this inconspicuousness spreads throughout our selves and our world which supplies the place where and materials with which we make our existence, leading us to sleepwalk through life. Once again, what wakes us up to our ephemeral existence and to the capacity, obligation, and dread of choosing ourselves is a breakdown. Here, anxiety slices the futural pull of our pro-jects so that our world as a whole falls slack, like a circus tent deflating after the center pole has been removed, and we are in a sense ejected from our world, our lives, our selves for a time. When we take these back up after the miasma clears, we do so in changed way. Indeed, in an important sense, we *take* them up for the first time.

Applying this analysis to thinking, we can say that our thinking is thoughtless—automatic, careless—while we encounter the straightforwardly thinkable. As long as our concepts grasp reality and experiences smoothly and unproblematically, they remain inconspicuous; our thinking, thoughts, and the very capacity to think—the clearing—go unnoticed. This happens above all for Heidegger in science since it "always encounters only what *its* kind of representation has admitted beforehand as an object possible for science,"[27] the hermeneutic circle weaponized. Like the Kantian subject, science filters out what does not conform to its conceptual expectations, which is what he means when he says that science does not think—it takes its basic concepts for granted.[28] Heidegger is surely thinking here of what Kuhn calls normal science; he praises the moments of revolutionary upheaval.

On the other hand, where concepts break down, where they run into dead-ends they cannot get through—*Holzwege*, or Derrida's *aporiai*—here the resistance to our Ideas throws off sparks that light them up.

> Where beings are not very familiar to man and are scarcely and only roughly known by science, the openedness of beings as a whole can prevail more essentially than it can where the familiar and well-known has become boundless, and nothing is any longer able to withstand the business of knowing, since technical mastery over things bears itself without limit.[29]

It is where thought fails in understanding beings that it can successfully hint at being. The two calls Heidegger talks about are the call of conscience in *Being and Time* and the call of thinking in the later work. Just as the former breaks in on our ongoing living in the familiar, comforting, reassuring tracks laid down by *das Man*, so the latter breaks through our normal, generally ontic and static ways of thinking. After all, for speaking and thinking about being, "we lack not only most of the words but, above all, the 'grammar.'"[30] Both calls allow the intentional, mindful, actively aware taking up of what had previously been done on autopilot. The difference, as Kierkegaard discussed a century earlier, is that the call of conscience comes from ourselves, reinforcing the hermeneutic circle of pre-understanding, whereas the call to thinking comes from outside and beyond us, calling us forth into the unknown, to think the heretofore unthinkable.

Levinas comes to a similar conclusion but, instead of looking to history for inspiration, he mines ethics. It is the face of the other that provokes us, that even first opens us up to allow encounters with anything, making it the essential experience, what Levinas calls "experience preeminently,"[31] or "the great experience."[32] "The idea of infinity exceeds my powers (not quantitatively, but, we will see later, by calling them into question); it does not come from our *a priori* depths—it is consequently experience par excellence."[33] This is the experience of the personal other and of what is wholly Other. It is this experience of the unexperiencable that defies what Husserl had considered the necessary formal anticipations of all experience. Like Heidegger, Levinas sees reason and knowledge as perhaps the crucial enforcers of homogeneity between thought and being, what he calls the assimilation of the other into the same. "The achievement of knowledge consists of grasping the object. Its strangeness is then conquered. Its newness, the opening up of its otherness, is reduced to the 'same', to what has already been seen, already known."[34] What exceeds and violates our grasp is what can truly be other, so encounters with it can count as touching on something truly outside of ourselves. "The idea of being does not therefore suffice to sustain the claim of realism, if realism is equivalent to affirming an alterity outside the Same. Only the idea of the infinite renders realism possible."[35]

Thus, the success of knowledge means the elimination of the otherness of the object of knowledge. Alternately, like Heidegger's thinking of being, its failure is what could actually put us in touch with that which can never be known. "What was taken as an imperfection of human knowledge measured by a certain ideal of self-evidence and certitude becomes a positive characteristic of the approach of a certain type of reality that would not be what it is if it were revealed in another way."[36]

And why would we think about reality in the first place, why philosophize at all, except in reaction to its perplexing us? We eat because we are drawn to food's enticing us, drink when liquids like Alice's potion call out "Drink me." So too we think because what is other calls us to think it, and this call is one of challenge. Were being to open itself up transparently, with self-evident significance, we would have no cause to think it, just as one need not chew IV liquid nutrition. This is what Hegel mocked as

> a philosophical utopia in which the Absolute itself readies itself for being something true and known, and surrenders itself for total enjoyment to the passivity of a thinking which only needs a mouth agape. Strenuous creative construction, in assertoric and categorical statements, is banished from this utopia. A problematic and hypothetical shaking of the tree of knowledge, which grows in a sandy grounding, brings the fruit of knowledge down, already chewed and self-digested.[37]

In such a pre-understood utopia, there would be no call for wrestling with reality, creating new concepts and thoughts to grasp and settle it.

But our thought, cast out of pellucid perfection into this opaque, perplexing world, suffers a happy fall, forcing us to work to pull down and cut up the fruit of knowledge by the sweat of our brow. This disharmony is what awakens us to our task and to our privilege of being the being who thinks the real. This goes against the perpetually renewed task of philosophy to settle down into an established way of thinking that one has concluded is Truth, but it preserves and responds more faithfully to its original provocation. Perhaps what is scandalous today is how scandal-less thought aspires to be.

Notes

1 See my *A Thing of This World: A History of Continental Anti-realism* (Evanston, IL: Northwestern University Press, 2007).
2 Friedrich Nietzsche, *Beyond Good and Evil: Prelude to a Philosophy of the Future*, trans. Walter Arnold Kaufmann (New York: Vintage Books, 2011), 1–3.
3 Aristotle, *Metaphysics* 983a 18–20. The quotation is from *A New Aristotle Reader*, ed. J. L. Ackrill (Princeton: Princeton University Press, 1987), 259.
4 Immanuel Kant, *Religion within the Limits of Reason Alone*, trans. Theodore M. Greene and Hoyt H. Hudson (New York: Harper & Row, 1960), 101n.
5 See my *A Thing of This World*.
6 Quentin Meillassoux, *After Finitude: An Essay on the Necessity of Contingency*, trans. Ray Brassier (Bloomsbury, 2017).
7 John Henry McDowell, *Mind and World* (Cambridge, MA: Harvard University Press, 2003).
8 For more on this, see my "Before Infinitude: A Levinasian Response to Meillassoux's Speculative Realism," in *Continental Realism and its Discontents*, ed. Marie-Eve Morin (Edinburgh: Edinburgh University Press, 2017).
9 Emmanuel Levinas, *Entre Nous: Thinking-of-the-other*, trans. Michael B. Smith and Barbara Harshav (London and New York: Continuum, 2006), 125.
10 Friedrich Nietzsche, *The Gay Science: With a Prelude in German Rhymes and an Appendix of Songs*, ed. Bernard Williams (Cambridge: Cambridge University Press, 2004), Preface, §300.
11 See Nietzsche, *Beyond Good and Evil*, §1.
12 Martin Heidegger, *Being and Time*, trans. John Macquarrie and Edward Robinson (Oxford: Blackwell, 2013), 29/9 (§3).
13 Immanuel Kant, *Foundations of the Metaphysics of Morals*, trans. Lewis White Beck, 2nd edn (Upper Saddle River, NJ: Library of Liberal Arts, 1995), 24, see also 60.
14 Kant, *Religion within the Limits of Reason Alone*, 157n., see also 82, 143, 175.
15 Søren Kierkegaard, *Fear and Trembling: Dialectical Lyric by Johannes de Silentio*, trans. Alastair Hannay (New York: Penguin Books, 1985), 96.
16 Søren Kierkegaard, *On Authority and Revelation: The Book on Adler, or a Cycle of Ethico-Religious Essays*, trans. Walter Lowrie (New York: Harper & Row, 1966), 107.
17 Jacques Derrida, *The Gift of Death; Literature in Secret*, trans. David Wills, 2nd edn (Chicago and London: University of Chicago Press, 2008), 57.
18 Nietzsche, *The Gay Science*, §4.
19 Jacques Derrida, *Points . . .: Interviews, 1974–1994*, trans. Peggy Kamuf et al. (Stanford: Stanford University Press, 1995), 217, 376, 411. See also Jacques Derrida, *Eyes of the University: Right to Philosophy 2*, trans. Jan Plug et al. (Stanford: Stanford University Press, 2004), 138, 147–8.
20 Martin Heidegger, *Basic Writings: Ten Key Essays, plus the Introduction to Being and Time*, ed. David Farrell Krell, rev. edn (San Francisco: HarperCollins, 1993), 234.
21 Ibid., 241.

22 See my unpublished paper, "Questioning Heidegger: The Question of the Question in Late Heidegger."
23 Martin Heidegger, *On the Way to Language*, trans. Peter D. Hertz (New York: Harper & Row, 1982), 12.
24 Martin Heidegger, *Contributions to Philosophy (From Enowning)*, trans. Parvis Emad and Kenneth Maly (Bloomington and Indianapolis: Indiana University Press, 1999), 169 (§122).
25 Martin Heidegger, *What is Called Thinking?* trans. Fred D. Wieck and J. Glenn Gray (New York: Harper & Row, 1968), 6 (emphasis original).
26 Heidegger, *Being and Time*, 105/75.
27 Martin Heidegger, *Poetry, Language, Thought*, trans. Albert Hofstadter (New York: Harper & Row, 1971), 170.
28 Heidegger, *What is Called Thinking?*, 8.
29 Heidegger, *Basic Writings*, 129.
30 Heidegger, *Being and Time*, 63/39.
31 Emmanuel Levinas, *Totality and Infinity: An Essay on Exteriority*, trans. Alphonso Lingis (Pittsburgh: Duquesne University Press, 1969), 109.
32 Emmanuel Levinas, *Is It Righteous to Be? Interviews with Emmanuel Levinas*, ed. Jill Robbins (Stanford: Stanford University Press, 2001), 234.
33 Levinas, *Totality and Infinity*, 196.
34 Levinas, *Is It Righteous to Be?*, 191.
35 Martin Heidegger, *Basic Writings*, 21.
36 Emmanuel Levinas, *Discovering Existence with Husserl*, trans. Richard A. Cohen and Michael B. Smith (Evanston, IL: Northwestern University Press, 1998), 68.
37 Georg Wilhelm Friedrich Hegel, *The Difference between Fichte's and Schelling's System of Philosophy*, trans. H. S. Harris and Walter Cerf (Albany: SUNY Press, 1977), 185.

6

Realism with a Straight Face: A Response to Leonard Lawlor

Graham Harman

In the closing weeks of 2017, my Argentine friend Laureano Ralón conducted an interview of Leonard Lawlor that I read with great interest.[1] Lawlor is currently Edwin Earle Sparks Professor of Philosophy at Penn State University, and has long been one of the most influential members of his generation in the American continental philosophy establishment. He has distinguished himself as a scholar of established classics in philosophy, but also as someone unusually alert to such relatively recent trends as the philosophies of Jacques Derrida and Gilles Deleuze. In short, he has always been near the cutting edge of wherever American continental philosophy happens to be. For this reason, his views on some of the latest developments in continentally inspired philosophy need to be taken seriously. Nonetheless—as will be seen in what follows—I think he gets these developments largely wrong. I hope that Lawlor will take these pages in the spirit of friendly disagreement in which they are intended, though inevitably there will be some friction when two views of the future of continental philosophy as different as ours confront each other.

We begin with the third-to-last question of the interview, in which Ralón asks Lawlor about "the new realism of the 2000s." More specifically, Ralón wants to know if "Deleuze is more of a realist than, say, Heidegger, Foucault, or Derrida."[2] This seems like a reasonable question, given the broad spectrum of views on this topic: ranging from Manuel DeLanda's provocative claim that Deleuze simply *is a realist* to Ray Brassier's rather vitriolic account of Deleuze as one of the great *anti*-realists of recent philosophy.[3] Rather than answering directly, Lawlor challenges the question itself:

> When I hear the word "realism" today, I'm really not sure what it means.... If realism means that we seek the ontological conditions of consciousness, of the subject, then of course Heidegger is a realist. But if realism means that reality exists in itself, separate from experience, then I think this is a return to the "old metaphysics."... I guess if the debate now is between realism and transcendentalism, then I am a transcendentalist. Simply, I do not see how one can return back beyond Kant's Copernican Revolution. As Kant showed, if there is a reality beyond the forms in which things are given to us, the noumenal, then we can say nothing about it. And to say anything about reality in itself amounts to falling prey to an illusion.[4]

Here we lodge a first point of disagreement with Lawlor. For object-oriented ontology (OOO, pronounced "Triple O") just as for DeLanda himself, realism definitely does not just mean that "we seek the ontological conditions of consciousness, of the subject," which is the deflationary sense of realism that Lawlor offers.[5] Although I do read Heidegger as a realist, this involves a much more stringently classical definition of the term.[6] That definition—also used by DeLanda when he calls Deleuze a realist—happens to be the very one rejected by Lawlor as a form of the "old metaphysics," which he rejects in favor of "transcendentalism." Hence, in the first part of this article, I will defend realism against transcendentalism. But it will be necessary to do a bit more than that: for unlike DeLanda, I regard the notion that "reality exists in itself, separate from experience" to be a necessary condition for realism, but not a sufficient one. The reason for this is that reality exists not just "separate from experience," but separate from *any relation at all*, including the sort that is so ontologically primitive that we might hesitate even to call it experience. Finally, I will challenge Lawlor's rather mainstream assumption that "if there is a reality beyond the forms in which things are given to us, the noumenal, then we can say nothing about it." For there is actually quite a bit that can be said about the noumenal, paradoxical though it may sound.

The second interesting passage from Lawlor's interview, and thus the topic of the second section below, concerns OOO's connection with the philosophy of Quentin Meillassoux. The link is not at all how Lawlor portrays it; nor does he get Meillassoux quite right. I speak of the following passage:

> While I find Meillassoux's *After Finitude* to be an interesting work, the argument he makes for ancestral time is very weak. How could we speak about anything that is prior to givenness, when what we are speaking about must have been given to us somehow? If it was not given somehow, we would know nothing about it. Therefore, it seems to me that Meillassoux and his followers—object-oriented ontologists— are dogmatists. What must be explored first of all, as Husserl showed, are the modes of givenness.[7]

Several problems arise in this passage even before we reach the key point of philosophical interest. First, though I am happy to hear that Lawlor finds Meillassoux's *After Finitude*[8] to be an interesting book, he seems to get the basic argument of that book wrong. Lawlor claims that Meillassoux makes a "very weak" argument for ancestral time, and that the French philosopher thereby mistakenly assumes we can speak about something beyond its givenness. Yet, this is not actually what Meillassoux does. His entire book is based on the assumption that *both* the claim of science to speak of a world independent of givenness *and* the correlationist claim that there is no way to speak of anything prior to givenness are persuasive.[9] He does not simply belittle correlationism at the expense of scientific realism, but employs considerable finesse in trying to find a novel solution that incorporates the insights of both. Though I happen to think his solution fails, it is not the simplistic "naïve realist" solution that Lawlor seems to imagine, but something far more intricate.[10] Furthermore, in no sense are object-oriented ontologists "followers" of Meillassoux, as even a cursory reading of my criticisms of Meillassoux's position would show. And finally, it is hard to see how

Lawlor can call object-oriented philosophers "dogmatists" when the entire OOO position is based on the acceptance and amplification of Kant's notion of the thing-in-itself: the very kryptonite of all dogmatism. In the second section of this article, then, I will show how Lawlor misreads: (a) Meillassoux's approach to realism, (b) Meillassoux's relation to OOO, and (c) OOO's position with respect to dogmatism.

The third and final passage from Lawlor's interview that I wish to consider is the following, which concerns the status of the human being in recent continental philosophy:

> Here too, one more comment: as far as I can tell, the object-oriented ontologists do not really understand what the transcendental is, especially as this idea develops in 20th century phenomenology. The transcendental and even the transcendental subject are not human. The whole 20th century discourse of anti-humanism develops from the recognition that Dasein in *Being and Time* is not human, not human existence or human reality. Fundamental ontology and transcendental phenomenology are not forms of anthropology. While not equating the two, Dasein in Heidegger and transcendental subjectivity in Husserl refer, respectively, to the conditions for human existence and the conditions for human subjectivity— but these two kinds of conditions are not identical with human existence and human subjectivity. If they were, they would engage in the kind of circular reasoning we discussed earlier. Already in transcendental phenomenology, humans are "actants," as I think some of the object-oriented ontologists say, along with objects.[11]

Having already declared himself on the side of transcendental philosophy, Lawlor preemptively critiques OOO for misunderstanding what that position entails. Specifically, Lawlor holds that OOO is wrong to find transcendental philosophy guilty of a human-centered standpoint. He does get one thing right: OOO does, in fact, claim that transcendental philosophy is anthropocentric. Making unexpected use of the terminology of Bruno Latour (who still seems little known among American continental philosophers) Lawlor claims that Heidegger's *Dasein* is already an "actant," thereby implying that OOO is reinventing the wheel when it tries to outflank Heidegger on the side of anti-anthropocentrism.[12] The third section of this chapter, then, will address Lawlor's view that Heidegger is already as "anti-humanist" as one can possibly be.

I Realism and the "old metaphysics"

We have seen that Lawlor expresses some perplexity about the meaning of the word "realism" in its contemporary usage. This is not entirely his fault, since countless attempts have been made in recent years to redefine "realism" in a less robust sense than is usual. In American continental philosophy, we have John D. Caputo making the nearly inedible claim that Jacques Derrida is a realist; the impossibility of this will be seen shortly.[13] I interpret this as resulting from a wish to make Derrida impregnable to the objections frequently thrown his way by philosophical realists of a more standard sort. The important thinker Karen Barad uses the term "agential realism" for her position, even though she explicitly denies that either subject or object can exist independently of one another; her views are basically those of the physicist Niels Bohr, one of her intellectual heroes.[14] This is more of a correlationist or even idealist view than a realist one, to such an extent that "agential idealism" would be a better term for Barad's position than "agential realism." And finally, there is my own favorite living philosopher, Bruno Latour, who uses the opening pages of *Pandora's Hope* to try to remove the term "realism" from the hands of his—admittedly thuggish—opponents in the 1990s "science wars."[15] Yet as someone who has probably spent thousands of hours studying the writings of Latour and conversing with him in person, I can safely declare that Latour has not an ounce of sympathy for anything traditionally called "realism."[16]

Only against the background of these many imprecise uses of "realism" is it possible for Lawlor to say that "if realism means that we seek the ontological conditions of consciousness, of the subject, then of course Heidegger is a realist." For obviously enough, this is not what "realism" means when used by speculative realism and object-oriented ontology, by DeLanda in his realist interpretation of Deleuze and Guattari, or indeed by anyone who would normally be called a realist: Maurizio Ferraris, for example, who for years has been one of the most hardcore realists among continental philosophers.[17] In any case, the sort of realism that interests me is the more traditional sense of the term that Lawlor rules entirely out of play: "But if realism means that reality exists in itself, separate from experience, then I think this is a return to the 'old metaphysics.'" We will consider the theme of the "old metaphysics" shortly. But first, I want to contest briefly Lawlor's suggestion that Heidegger is primarily about "seeking the ontological conditions of consciousness," and that he might count as a realist only in this rather un-realist sense of realism. For the purpose of comparison, let's consider the case of Immanuel Kant. Kant holds, of course, that rational beings have no direct access to the things-in-themselves, and therefore the primary theme of Kantian philosophy does amount to "seeking the ontological conditions of consciousness." But obviously enough, there is nothing about the study of consciousness that could count as "realist" in any normally accepted sense of the term. If we are nevertheless inclined to call Kant a "realist"—as I am so inclined—then this clearly has nothing to do with his pursuit of the transcendental categories of experience, but only with what *escapes* such categories: namely, the infamous *Ding an sich*, or thing-in-itself. Returning from Kant to Heidegger, an analogous point holds true. If we want to consider Heidegger a realist, then this has nothing to do with the transcendental structures of *Dasein* as uncovered in *Being and Time*, but with that which escapes or eludes *Dasein*.[18] The first example of what thus eludes *Dasein* comes in the tool-analysis, where it is not just a question of a practical use of things preceding a direct perceptual or conceptual awareness of them—as too many readings have it—but of the tools themselves being deeper even than our practical use of them. Without such a surplus of being in the tools, they could never possibly break, and breaking is the most illuminating thing that equipment does in *Being and Time*. Beyond this, *Being itself* is always characterized by Heidegger in terms of its withdrawal from any direct presence. In sum, I would argue for reading both Kant and Heidegger as realists: not because they think there is a reality to which we have direct access, but because they are committed to the notion that reality means that which *escapes* any such access. It is a sense of realism directly opposed to that of dogmatic or naïve realism, which takes an interest in the real only insofar as it can be known. On this point, OOO can be likened to the positions of Kant or Heidegger: not insofar as these great thinkers are preoccupied with the structures that make human reality possible, but insofar as they point unmistakably beyond such knowable structures into the darkness of the real.

We turn now, as promised, to the "old metaphysics." Here Lawlor speaks in a somewhat accusing voice with a markedly Derridean accent. Let's recall some key passages from Derrida's *Of Grammatology* to show what he means by the old metaphysics, which—I hold—is not quite the same thing as what Heidegger wants to combat under that name.[19] On one level there is an obvious similarity, as seen from Derrida's Heideggerian-sounding wish to "undermine an ontology which, in its innermost course, has determined the meaning of being as presence."[20] There can be no question that Heidegger is an enemy of the metaphysics of presence, which he treats as the hereditary flaw of Western philosophy since Plato; for Heidegger no less than for Derrida, nothing can ever be made directly present. What can be questioned is whether Heidegger would agree to Derrida's additional embellishments on this theme. For instance:

> Heidegger's insistence on noting that being is produced as history only through the logos, and is nothing outside of it, the difference between being and the entity— all this clearly indicates that fundamentally nothing escapes the movement of the signifier, and that, in the last instance, the difference between signified and signifier is nothing.[21]

This sounds less like Heidegger than like the linguistics of Ferdinand de Saussure, with its famous claim that meaning arises only from relation and differentiation. But the view that Heidegger's Being is nothing apart from its various meanings to *Dasein* is not a plausible reading of Heidegger, for whom Being is always that which withdraws from any attempt to thematize it. Yet Derrida doubles down on this point, insisting that nothing exists at all apart from its relations with anything else: "The so-called 'thing itself' is always already a *representamen* shielded from the simplicity of intuitive evidence. The *representamen* functions only by giving rise to an *interpretant* that itself becomes a sign and so on to infinity."[22] Stated differently: "The thing itself is a collection of things or a chain of differences."[23] We learn further that those who disagree with this premise are guilty of "logocentric repression": an astonishing act of political intimidation aimed by Derrida at realists, who are portrayed as patriarchal oppressors of those liberated ones who celebrate chains of difference and the mirroring of signs unto infinity.[24]

But some of this is beside the point. For whether or not the reader agrees with my brief account of the chief distinction between Heidegger and Derrida, it should be easy enough to see the difference between my own position and Lawlor's. I am in total agreement with Lawlor that the "old metaphysics" ought not to be revived, but we disagree as to what was harmful about that metaphysics. For OOO, the old metaphysics failed through its assumption that the thing itself can somehow be brought to direct presence: an error found not only in pre-Kantian dogmatism, but even in the philosophy of Edmund Husserl, whom I admire at least as much as Lawlor does. From a OOO standpoint, the problem with Husserl's much-maligned "intuition of essences" is not the "essence" part, but the "intuition" part. The essence really is there: not just at the level of the given phenomena—where Husserl acknowledges it—but also in a layer of the cosmos withdrawn from all access, and hence impenetrable to "intuition" or to any other form of relation. But for Derrida, and evidently for Lawlor, the very *existence* of a thing-in-itself outside all relations to human meaning is incoherent. This is not just an anti-presence view, but a bluntly anti-realist one. While it is certainly true that Heidegger emphasizes the permanent co-existence of *Sein* and *Dasein*, it does not follow from this correlation that *Sein* is nothing more than how it appears to *Dasein*, despite Derrida's groundless claim that Being is nothing outside of how it comes to presence in history at various times. To summarize, Lawlor's effort to link philosophical realism with the old metaphysics of presence fails, just as Derrida's own effort in this direction fails. Derrida complains that any identical thing would be "self-present" and would therefore run afoul of the Heideggerian strictures against presence. But this notion of "self-presence" is found nowhere that I can recall in Heidegger and is simply an attempt to impose Derrida's own ultra-relational ontology onto the rather different Heideggerian landscape, where it is not altogether applicable.

We now turn to Lawlor's attempt to deploy Kant against OOO. We recall that his words were as follows: "Simply, I do not see how one can return back beyond Kant's Copernican Revolution. As Kant showed, if there is a reality beyond the forms in which things are given to us, the noumenal, then we can say nothing about it. And to say anything about reality in itself amounts to falling prey to an illusion." While basically correct, Lawlor's gloss of Kant contains an added drop of contraband German idealism. For it is by no means true that Kant holds that "we can say nothing about" the reality beyond the forms. He at least says we can be sure that the in-itself is really there, which is more than most contemporary philosophers are willing to concede. But more importantly, what Kant thinks about the thing-in-itself is not the most important matter here.

First, it is odd to claim that OOO slips back into dogmatism, when it makes perhaps the most ardent defense of the inaccessibility of the thing-in-itself since the days of Kant himself. Dogmatism means the claim to gain direct knowledge of the in-itself, and while this is a perfectly accurate description of what Meillassoux aims to do by mathematical means, OOO is resolute in its defense of Kant on this point: finitude is insurmountable, not something we can pass beyond. Yet there is a second point on which OOO *disagrees* with Kant, though both Lawlor and Meillassoux agree with him. Namely, OOO holds that the thing-in-itself is not just something that haunts human perception and cognition. Instead, the thing-in-itself is the excess or surplus outside of any relation between *any* two terms, including inanimate ones. When fire burns cotton, these entities interact with only a small portion of each other's reality, not with the whole of it; here we can see that finitude is not a uniquely human burden but is the name of the game in any relation whatsoever. Now, Meillassoux dismisses this aspect of OOO for an odd taxonomical reason: he holds that only natural science should be able to tell us how to deal with inanimate beings, and that philosophy should not be imposing what he calls "hyperphysics" onto terrain that is the rightful property of the sciences.[25] But I suspect that Lawlor would offer a different reason for rejecting OOO's treatment of inanimate objects, one that is closer to what would probably be Kant's own. Namely, while we can justifiably speak about human access to the world, since that is the space that each of us always occupies, we cannot have any idea of what the experience of fire or cotton is like, or even if such experience exists at all. Therefore, to make any claim at all about inanimate interactions is to step illegitimately into something beyond our direct access, and thus to commit the crime of dogmatism. But to say this is to conflate two separate issues. For it is one thing to ask whether we can speak of the thing-in-itself directly, and quite another to say whether we can speak about the relation of non-human things to the world that is outside of them. From a OOO standpoint, the answer to the first is no, while the answer to the second is yes. One need not be able to experience the world as a lizard or a stone experiences it in order to deduce that they cannot experience the thing-in-itself: not because they possibly lack experience, but because even sub-experiential relations cannot make any contact with the thing-in-itself. OOO does not claim to be able to step into the shoes of other beings in order to determine whether they can grasp the thing-in-itself. Rather, OOO claims that it is not through experience that I conclude that an in-itself exists beyond that experience. The thing-in-itself is something we *deduce* from the fact that—contra Merleau-Ponty—no number of views of a house suffice to add up to a house.[26] Nor would any number of *causal impacts* with the house add up to a house. On this basis I deduce that I have no access to the thing-in-itself, that my wife has no such access, that Lucy in the primeval Awash Valley did not, and that every animal, bacterium, fire, cotton ball, and asteroid in the history of the cosmos has not had access to the thing-in-itself.

The other problem with Lawlor's views—though it is certainly common enough—can be found in his deceptively logical-sounding assumption that if the thing-in-itself is beyond all direct access, then we cannot say anything about it at all. Note that this all-or-nothing approach to speaking would render *philosophia* as practiced by Socrates impossible, and would even annihilate philosophy altogether. It is true enough that we can never know the thing-in-itself in the manner of confronting it directly and face-to-face; in this sense, there is no wisdom. But there is always *love of wisdom*, and herein lies the entire justification of philosophy. Socrates tells us famously that a god can have knowledge and an animal none at all; though both parts of this claim are more than dubious, we can accept them for the sake of argument. The real import of the claim can be found in its third part: humans can have something without having it. There is no passage in the Platonic dialogues where Socrates successfully defines anything, but this hardly means that Socrates does not succeed in saying anything of value. Only the overemphasis on scientific knowledge since the 1600s has browbeaten us into the assumption that the only options are knowledge on one side and ignorant gesticulation on the other. This crude vision of human cognition has never made any sense in the arts, for instance: for an artwork is a reality autonomous from whatever any human opinion of it may be, and there can be no final adequate critical knowledge of any given artwork.[27] This was Kant's point in the *Critique of Judgment* when he separated art from the realm of concepts and rules.[28] To summarize, the claim that philosophy need not deal with things-in-themselves because there is nothing we can say about them is a false one.

II Meillassoux, OOO, and dogmatism

We now turn to Lawlor's discussion of OOO, its link with Meillassoux, and the relation of both to the metaphysical dogmatism effectively ended by Kant. Let's begin with Meillassoux, whom Lawlor misreads in the same way as virtually all mainstream continental philosophers in the United States (the situation seems somewhat better in Great Britain and Australia): "While I find Meillassoux's *After Finitude* to be an interesting work, the argument he makes for ancestral time is very weak. How could we speak about anything that is prior to givenness, when what we are speaking about must have been given to us somehow? If it was not given somehow, we would know nothing about it." The mistake here results from a misunderstanding of Meillassoux's aim in introducing the concepts of "ancestrality" and the "arche-fossil," which he does in the early pages of *After Finitude*.

Surely the most famous concept in Meillassoux's book is "correlationism." Here is the initial definition of the term, taken from page 5 of the English translation:

> the central notion of modern philosophy since Kant seems to be that of *correlation*. By "correlation" we mean the idea according to which we only ever have access to the correlation between thinking and being, and never to either term considered apart from the other. We will henceforth call *correlationism* any current of thought which maintains the unsurpassable character of the correlation so defined. Consequently, it becomes possible to say that every philosophy which disavows naïve realism has become a variant of correlationism.[29]

There are two points worth noting here. The first is that Lawlor himself, at least in his interview with Ralón, defends what is in effect a correlationist position. In Lawlor's own words: "What must be explored first of all, as Husserl showed, are the modes of givenness." For my own part, I actually see Husserl—great philosopher though he is—as an outright *idealist* rather than just a correlationist. But there is no reason to have that argument with Lawlor in the present article. What is relevant here is that, even by Lawlor's own admission, his position and Husserl's are both *at least* correlationist if not idealist. "What must be explored first of all, as Husserl showed, are the modes of givenness." In other words, Lawlor admits that both he and Husserl adhere to the following principle that Meillassoux ascribes to correlationism:

> Correlationism consists in disqualifying the claim that it is possible to consider the realms of subjectivity and objectivity independently of one another. Not only does it become necessary to insist that we never grasp an object "in itself," in isolation from its relation to the subject, but it also becomes necessary to maintain that we can never grasp a subject that would not always-already be related to an object.[30]

To claim that we can never grasp a subject that would not always-already be related to an object (in Meillassoux's terms), and the reverse, is the same as to say that we must "first of all" explore the way that the object is given to the subject (in Lawlor's terms). In short, Lawlor cannot claim to be exempt from being called a "correlationist," though of course we have no textual evidence that he would wish to exempt himself.

That brings us to the second important point in the initial passage quoted from Meillassoux: "it becomes possible to say that every philosophy which disavows naïve realism has become a variant of correlationism." Lawlor seems to read Meillassoux as a naïve realist rather than a correlationist, and to view this as Meillassoux's cardinal error. But this is not what is going on in *After Finitude*: by no means does Meillassoux aspire to overturn correlationism in the name of what many continental philosophers would call "naïve scientific realism." Instead, Meillassoux is trying to develop the consequences of the paradox that *both* naïve realism and correlationism have an important point to make. His entire philosophical enterprise amounts to a rather complex effort to overcome the limitations of both options, and I happen to think this effort fails.

In one sense, it is true that Meillassoux has tremendous respect for the work of the natural sciences. He finds it utterly implausible that the astronomical statement "the Big Bang occurred 13.5 billion years ago" could be rewritten in terms of "givenness" by saying "the Big Bang occurred 13.5 billion years ago *for us*." The philosophical problem this presents is not merely hypothetical. No less a thinker than Bruno Latour argues that Ramses II could not have died of tuberculosis, as Egyptologists now claim, since, in the time of Ramses, tuberculosis had not yet been discovered. For Latour, the most we can say in this case is that *from our standpoint today*, Ramses II died of tuberculosis.[31] Now, it is true that Meillassoux has no sympathy for correlationist-sounding statements of this sort. As he sees it, the "naïve realist" has a good point, and this is why ancestral statements about arche-fossils—entities that pre-exist the emergence of all consciousness—must be taken seriously in a *literal* sense, rather than correlationized into "arche-fossils for us."

But this is only half of Meillassoux's concern. The other half, usually forgotten, is that he also thinks the correlationist has a point: Meillassoux *is not* a naïve realist. As he puts it in *After Finitude*: "we cannot go back to being dogmatists. On this point we cannot but be heirs of Kantianism."[32] To some extent it is true that *After Finitude* emphasizes the strength of ancestrality and the arche-fossil more than the equal strength of correlationism, perhaps because this book's primary enemy is the rampant correlationism of continental thought. But any doubts about Meillassoux's respect for correlationism quickly evaporate as soon as one reads his remarks from the inaugural 2007 Speculative Realism Workshop at Goldsmiths, University of London. As he puts it there:

> I insist on this point—the exceptional *strength* of this argumentation, apparently and desperately implacable. Correlationism rests on an argument as simple as it is powerful, and which can be formulated in the following way: No X without givenness of X, and no theory about X without a positing of X. If you speak about something, you speak about something that is given to you, and posited by you.[33]

This is not a stray or misfired remark. The whole point of Meillassoux at Goldsmiths was to show that there is no easy way to escape the correlational circle, that it represents the permanent horizon of all serious philosophy. Let's now place two previous citations side by side for purposes of comparison.

> **Lawlor** "How could we speak about anything that is prior to givenness, when what we are speaking about must have been given to us somehow? If it was not given somehow, we would know nothing about it."
>
> **Meillassoux** "No X without givenness of X, and no theory about X without a positing of X. If you speak about something, you speak about something that is given to you, and posited by you."

When it comes to givenness, it should now be obvious that Lawlor and Meillassoux are very much in agreement. The difference is that Meillassoux is still somewhat uncomfortable with the situation. For this reason, he tries to radicalize what he calls "strong correlationism" into a position he calls "speculative materialism." For the speculative materialist, even though we cannot think a thing outside thought without turning it into a thought, something might exist outside thought anyway. Although I have argued in print more than once that this position is impossible,[34] it is important that we not confuse it with naïve scientific realism, as Lawlor seems to do. Meillassoux's speculative materialism is actually in far greater danger of slipping into idealism than into naïve realism.

This brings us to Lawlor's mistaken assessment of the relative allegiances of the speculative realist philosophers. Namely: "it seems to me that Meillassoux and his followers—object-oriented ontologists—are dogmatists." It is hard to know where this came from. Simply put, the object-oriented ontologists *are not* followers of Meillassoux. How could Lawlor have formed such a notion? The most charitable interpretation I can think of is that my own enthusiasm for writing frequently about Meillassoux has been mistaken for a symptom of OOO having actually derived from Meillassoux.[35] While this inference may be understandable, even a quick scan of what I have written on this important French thinker will show severe disagreement with the foundations of his work, which obviously does not preclude admiration and interest.[36] It is also worth mentioning that the term "object-oriented philosophy" (the predecessor of "object-oriented ontology") has been in public use since 1999, some years before I first became aware of Meillassoux's existence in 2006.[37]

But it may be more helpful simply to give a brief list of the major differences between OOO and Meillassoux's speculative materialism. First, whereas Meillassoux thinks that the correlationist argument ("you can't think something outside thought without turning it into a thought") is a formidable one, OOO finds it to be extremely weak. Second, Meillassoux regards mathematics as the exemplary form of cognition, while for OOO aesthetics enjoys that role; a great deal follows from this disagreement. Meillassoux dismisses the principle of sufficient reason, though for OOO it is of crucial importance that it be retained. Third, for Meillassoux, the thing-in-itself is not beyond all thought, but is simply that which can exist before thought rises and after it disappears;

for OOO, more along the lines of Kant, the thing-in-itself exists right now and is beyond all thought. Nonetheless, for Meillassoux—as for Kant—the thing-in-itself is something that exists outside *thought*, while OOO departs from Kant in treating the thing-in-itself as existing outside *any relation at all*, including causal relations between inanimate beings. These are some of the chief differences between speculative materialism and OOO, whose originators were born just over six months apart, and whose dice were already cast years before the two currents of thought came into contact.

III *Dasein*, actants, and humanism

We should conclude by speaking, more briefly, of Lawlor's claim that OOO misunderstands the respective places of *Dasein* and the human being in twentieth-century continental philosophy. Here is one of his shorter remarks on this topic: "Already in transcendental phenomenology, humans are 'actants,' as I think some of the object-oriented ontologists say, along with objects." The term "actant" is borrowed by OOO from Latour, who took it from the semiotics of Algirdas Greimas but pressed it beyond the limits of semiotics; "actor" is one of Latour's synonyms for "actant."[38] The important thing to recognize about the term "actor" is that it is not used by Latour just to say that something acts, but to say that everything is *equally* an actor, and in the same way. In Latour's actor-network theory human beings act, as do giraffes, trains, protons, cartoon characters, square circles, along with "golden Mountains, phlogiston, unicorns, bald kings of France, chimeras, spontaneous generation, black holes, cats on mats, and other black swans and white ravens."[39] In other words, the primary function of the term "actor" or "actant" for Latour is to be *ontologically democratic*, along the lines of what is often called a "flat ontology." Please note that no such thing exists in Heidegger's work, at least not according to Heidegger's interpretation of his own work. Central for Heidegger is the correlation between *Dasein* (human being) and *Sein* (being). Though he occasionally speaks about other types of beings, none of them rise to the level of *Dasein*, to which Heidegger always accords a special status. There can be no question of a flat otology in Heidegger of the sort that we find in Latour, however inconsistently the latter may carry it out at times. For this reason, it is impossible to speak of Heideggerian *Dasein* as an "actant," no matter how many actions one may ascribe to it.

This leaves us with a final, related point by Lawlor. I speak of the following:

> as far as I can tell, the object-oriented ontologists do not really understand what the transcendental is, especially as this idea develops in 20th century phenomenology. The transcendental and even the transcendental subject are not human. The whole 20th century discourse of anti-humanism develops from the recognition that Dasein in *Being and Time* is not human, not human existence or human reality. Fundamental ontology and transcendental phenomenology are not forms of anthropology.

Here, rather than engaging in a genuine philosophical dispute, Lawlor plays the authority card by saying that OOO simply "does not understand" a crucial point, which he goes on merely to assert rather than to argue: the purportedly vast chasm between the transcendental and the human. In response, I should say first that the "20th century discourse of anti-humanism" does not interest OOO very much, since the inauguration of this discourse has done absolutely nothing to move human beings away from the center of philosophy. You can claim all you like that the transcendental is not the human, but until you are also willing to ascribe a "transcendental" structure to an animal, citrus fruit, or stone, then you are still linking the transcendental to just one specific type of entity: the human being. And if you claim that this is inescapable, insofar as we cannot step out of the human categories into the experience of animals, citrus fruits, or stones, since it will always be *we* who think of them, then you have simply repeated Kant's unfortunate ambiguity about dogmatism already discussed in Section I above. What we must overleap is not the pointless low hurdle of "humanism," but the more serious obstacle of the widespread assumption that *givenness to thought* is the starting point for all philosophy.

Notes

1 Laureano Ralón, "Interview with Leonard Lawlor," *Figure/Ground*, December 11, 2017. Available at: http://figureground.org/conversation-leonard-lawlor/.
2 Ibid.
3 Manuel DeLanda, *Intensive Science and Virtual Philosophy* (London: Continuum, 2002); Ray Brassier, *Nihil Unbound: Enlightenment and Extinction* (London: Palgrave, 2007).
4 Ralón, "Interview with Leonard Lawlor."
5 Manuel DeLanda and Graham Harman, *The Rise of Realism* (Cambridge, UK: Polity, 2017).
6 Graham Harman, *Tool-Being: Heidegger and the Metaphysics of Objects* (Chicago: Open Court, 2002).
7 Ralón, "Interview with Leonard Lawlor."
8 Quentin Meillassoux, *After Finitude: Essay on the Necessity of Contingency*, trans. Ray Brassier (London: Continuum, 2008).
9 Meillassoux's underpublicized respect for correlationism was the central theme of his contribution to the April 2007 Speculative Realism Workshop. See Ray Brassier, Iain Hamilton Grant, Graham Harman, and Quentin Meillassoux, "Speculative Realism," *Collapse* III (2007): 306–449, in which Meillassoux's presentation runs on pages 408–49.
10 See Chapter 1 of Graham Harman, *Quentin Meillassoux: Philosophy in the Making*, 2nd edn (Edinburgh: Edinburgh University Press, 2015).
11 Ralón, "Interview with Leonard Lawlor."
12 Bruno Latour, *The Pasteurization of France*, trans. Alan Sheridan and John Law (Cambridge, MA: Harvard University Press, 1988).
13 John D. Caputo, "For Love of the Things Themselves: Derrida's Phenomenology of the Hyper-Real," in *Fenomenologia hoje: significado e linguagem*, ed. Ricardo Timm de Souza and Nythamar Fernandes de Oliveira (Porto Alegre, Brazil: EDIPUCRS, 2002), 37–59.

14 Karen Barad, *Meeting the Universe Halfway: Quantum Physics and the Entanglement of Matter and Meaning* (Durham, NC: Duke University Press, 2007). For a more detailed critique of Barad's position see Graham Harman, "Agential and Speculative Realism: Remarks on Barad's Ontology," *rhizomes* 30 (2016). Available at: www.rhizomes.net/issue30/harman.html.
15 Bruno Latour, *Pandora's Hope: Essays on the Reality of Science Studies* (Cambridge, MA: Harvard University Press, 1999), 1–23.
16 See Graham Harman, *Prince of Networks: Bruno Latour and Metaphysics* (Melbourne: re.press, 2009); Graham Harman, *Bruno Latour: Reassembling the Political* (London: Pluto, 2014).
17 Maurizio Ferraris, *Introduction to New Realism*, trans. Sarah De Sanctis (London: Bloomsbury, 2015).
18 Martin Heidegger, *Being and Time*, trans. John Macquarrie and Edward Robinson (New York: Harper, 2008).
19 Jacques Derrida, *Of Grammatology*, trans. Gayatri Chakravorty Spivak (Baltimore: Johns Hopkins University Press, 1997). For a more detailed critique of these passages from Derrida and others, see Graham Harman, "The Well-Wrought Broken Hammer: Object-Oriented Literary Criticism," *New Literary History* 43, no. 2 (Spring 2012): 183–203.
20 Derrida, *Of Grammatology*, 70.
21 Ibid., 22–3.
22 Ibid., 49.
23 Ibid., 90.
24 Ibid., 51.
25 Quentin Meillassoux, "Iteration, Reiteration, Repetition: A Speculative Analysis of the Meaningless Sign" (a.k.a. "The Berlin Lecture"), (unpublished version, trans. Robin Mackay, 2012), 13–14. Available at: https://cdn.shopify.com/s/files/1/0069/6232/files/Meillassoux_Workshop_Berlin.pdf.
26 Maurice Merleau-Ponty, *Phenomenology of Perception*, trans. Colin Smith (London: Routledge, 2012), 79.
27 See Graham Harman, "The Third Table," in *The Book of Books*, ed. Carolyn Christov-Bakargiev (Ostfildern: Hatje Cantz Verlag, 2012), 540–2.
28 Immanuel Kant, *Critique of Judgment*, trans. Werner Pluhar (Indianapolis: Hackett, 2002).
29 Meillassoux, *After Finitude*, 5.
30 Ibid.
31 See Bruno Latour, "On the Partial Existence of Existence *and* Non-existing Objects," in *Biographies of Scientific Objects*, ed. Lorraine Daston (Chicago: University of Chicago Press, 2000), 247–69.
32 Meillassoux, *After Finitude*, 29.
33 Meillassoux, in Brassier, Grant, Harman, and Meillassoux, "Speculative Realism," 409.
34 Graham Harman, *Speculative Realism: An Introduction* (Cambridge, UK: Polity, 2018), 123–65.
35 Graham Harman, "Quentin Meillassoux: A New French Philosopher," *Philosophy Today* 51, no. 1 (Spring 2007): 104–17; Graham Harman, "Meillassoux's Virtual Future," *Continent* 1, no. 2 (2011): 78–91; Harman, *Quentin Meillassoux: Philosophy in the Making*.

36 See especially Chapter 15 of Graham Harman, *Bells and Whistles: More Speculative Realism* (Winchester, UK: Zero Books, 2013).
37 See Chapter 6 of Graham Harman, *Towards Speculative Realism: Essays and Lectures* (Winchester, UK: Zero Books, 2010).
38 For an interesting account of Latour's relation to semiotics, see Hennig Schmidgen, *Bruno Latour in Pieces: An Intellectual Biography*, trans. Gloria Custance (New York: Fordham University Press, 2014).
39 Latour, *Pandora's Hope*, 161.

7

A Return to the Pre-critical? On Meillassoux's Speculative Realism and a More General Problem[1]

Zdravko Kobe

Throughout the second half of the twentieth century, France continuously took center stage in contemporary philosophy. Existentialism, structuralism, post-structuralism, theoretical psychoanalysis, deconstruction, and so forth—these are only the most celebrated schools of thought setting the tone of theoretical debate all around the world. The conceptual productivity of French theory in that particular period was so massive that Badiou declared it one of the three "moments" in the history of philosophy, along with Greek philosophy from Socrates to Aristotle and Classical German philosophy from Kant to Hegel.[2]

But an event is essentially determined in space and time. As the last philosophical giants little by little disappeared, the heroic era was evidently coming to an end. Not that French theory is done and dusted. However, due to various reasons, and in spite of the multinational academic apparatus built around it, its inheritors have been unable to show the same theoretical incisiveness. Even Badiou, the only one still reputed to be the proper inheritor of the school, increasingly acts only as the appointed manager of the legacy rather than its true theoretical continuer.

In this constellation, the publication of the book *After Finitude* by Quentin Meillassoux in 2006 triggered a sigh of relief. Finally, it seemed, there was again a powerful author who indisputably dared to walk his path alone and pretended to institute his own philosophical project, "speculative realism," which might eventually develop into a complete theoretical platform.

The spatial and temporal vicinity of Meillassoux's work to French theory must not mislead us, however. Both in style and content, Meillassoux is the very opposite of what one would expect under the heading "French theory." While the latter is usually marked by an ornamental train of thought, packed with self-indulgent phrasing and flirtation with poetry, Meillassoux follows a far more traditional ideal of rigorous, almost deductive reasoning. Similarly, if there is anything that French theory constantly derides as an erroneous theoretical stance, it is the pretension to grasp the world as it is in itself. From the Copernican turn onward, the doctrine of naive realism has been considered the foundational assumption to be abandoned if we are to enter into the realm of thought. But if this represents the standard post-Kantian pattern of thought,

Meillassoux turns vehemently against it. His goal is no more and no less than to rehabilitate the absolute into philosophy: to justify our ability to cognize the things as they are in themselves, independently of our cognition, and to reclaim the univocity of language so that no philosophical subtlety could transform it into its alleged true meaning.

The task is enormous and the stakes are high. Meillassoux tries to kill two birds with one stone: post-Kantian philosophy in general and contemporary French thought in particular. In this respect, there can be no common denominator between French theory and his project. And if we were to seek something "French" in his philosophy, we would have to go very far back into the past, up to Descartes —who, in his long winter night that was to become the inauguration scene of modern philosophy, relying only on the power of clear and distinct ideas, tried to achieve completely certain knowledge of things in themselves.

Where does Meillassoux's radicalism come from?

Meillassoux does not hide his conviction that Kant's so-called Copernican turn is misguided. While Copernicus, Darwin, and Freud all gradually deprived man of his privileged status, Kant, on the contrary, placed the thinking subject back into the center around which all objects of possible cognition rotate. This fundamental deviation from the Enlightenment project has inevitably had far-reaching theoretical consequences, providing external motives for Meillassoux's project of speculative realism. By renouncing the absolute, philosophy has given up what has always constituted the goal of all its endeavors, and in this way, it has given up itself. As Meillassoux would put it, a thought is either strong or it is not a thought at all. In addition, the restriction of the domain of certain knowledge has further deepened the split between philosophy and science (and partly between philosophy and common sense) up to the point that nowadays they seem to inhabit two completely separate worlds, with no bridges to connect them. At this point, Meillassoux re-emphasizes that it is only in science that philosophy can find its true ally, which is why it has to retain a positive relation towards it. Even if philosophy does not share the same spontaneous faith in the capacity of science to grasp the world as it is in itself, it should still be able to explain where the relative success of science in handling the world stems from.[3]

Finally, the self-imposed limitation of reason championed by various strains of post-Kantian thought conferred philosophical dignity on conspiracy theories, undermining the very foundations of rational argumentation. If our knowledge is filtered through subjective forms of thought, which have their real foundation in positive elements of the world—for example in the class struggle, in the will to power, in various drives—then the legacy of rational argumentation is bound to be nothing but a pretext for something else. Accordingly, when confronted with rational arguments, we first ask ourselves why someone is asserting what they are asserting, and instead of dealing with the reasoning in their argumentation, our primary philosophical task is to unmask the true forces behind their assertions, the hidden motives of rational discourse in general. Philosophy is thus reduced to detective work.

If, on the other hand, subjective forms of thought remain without any firm justification, as is mostly the case today, the situation is actually much worse: rational discourse becomes but one of the many language games, which, in principle, has no priority over any other language game. The difference between philosophical geniality and rational discourse becomes blurred, and eventually even mystical experience can be recognized as an equally proper means to grasp the truth. Along these lines, inspired speech might even gain the advantage over rational argumentation. For while reason is sometimes bound to acknowledge that the knowledge obtained under its own criteria cannot be completely justified, non-rational knowledge is burdened with no inner deficiency of such kind. Since its criteria of truth are far more modest and much less rigorous, they can also be satisfied far more easily. Thus a paradoxical situation can occur, where non-rational knowledge pretends to be more rational than rational knowledge itself, and where understanding gives legitimacy to every kind of assertion, no matter how eccentric, provided that it does *not* acknowledge the requirements of rationality.

It seems that this sort of self-imposed blockade of rational discourse is one of the main external reasons for Meillassoux's endeavor to give philosophy back its taste for the absolute. In what follows, we are first going to sketch a basic outline of Meillassoux's project as presented in his first book and some of his later writings; then we are going to verify the internal and external coherence of the project as a whole; and finally, we are going to sketch some general implications of its failure for contemporary philosophy.

I

1. As far as we can estimate, three observations lie at the very core of speculative realism. Whilst they do not enter into the construction of the argument proper, they act as external guidance and tacitly establish criteria that have to be met by every system of thought that would be able to come forward as philosophy.

The first observation formulates the fundamental result of the Kantian turn: an object can be grasped only through the subject's thinking, and so it is always already thought from the standpoint of the subject (and not as it is in itself). The thesis, in its straightforwardness, appears to be irrefutable, since the very insistence on the accessibility of the "in-itself" brings about a pragmatic contradiction. As soon as we start thinking the object as something in itself, it is us, the thinking subjects, that think the object, which thereby ceases to be "in itself." Meillassoux calls this the correlationist thesis.

The second observation highlights a banal yet neglected fact, which has, according to Meillassoux, the most far-reaching theoretical implications. The scientific practice and everyday language both strongly suggest that we are nevertheless capable of thinking states which imply a non-existence of the subject and consequently of the correlation as such. To begin with, there are assertions and facts pertaining to a time before the appearance of the human species and the formation of intelligent life on Earth in general. Such statements—for instance, that our planet was formed 4.5 billion years ago—are distinguishable in the respect that in the time they describe, there was no possible subjective standpoint from which they could be formulated. Thus, they imply an a-subjective and absolute world. Structurally equal situations can be adduced both for the present and the future. However, since the distant past has the advantage of being more obvious when compared to the present, we shall follow Meillassoux in calling this thesis the ancestral thesis.

The third and final observation concerns the major rupture in the conception of philosophy brought about by Kant's refutation of the ontological proof. In his critique, Kant demonstrated that it is impossible to infer the existence of a necessary being from concepts alone—but for Meillassoux, he demonstrated much more. According to his reading, Kant's critique of the ontological proof implies that the very concept of a necessary being is indeed impossible. There can be no thing that exists necessarily. But as according to Meillassoux, metaphysics is characterized precisely by postulating a being that is, as *causa sui*, absolutely necessary, the above claim is tantamount to the impossibility of metaphysics. This does not mean that there is no longer any room for necessity in philosophy; it does mean, however, that this necessity must not imply *some thing* that would be necessary. Since Meillassoux considers this type of philosophy as speculative philosophy, we can call the thesis on the impossibility of something existing by necessity the speculative thesis.

The three theses—the correlationist, the ancestral, and the speculative thesis—raise a peculiar problem, however. They are not compatible. The first two, in particular, are in obvious contradiction. Whereas the first one asserts the essential subjective mediateness of every (known) object, the second one implies the (known) object's independence of any kind of subject. And since the two theses logically exclude each other, yet at the same time seem to be equally well justified, we are, in a sense, faced with a typical Kantian antinomy, the antinomy of ancestrality.

Of course, Meillassoux knows very well that many correlationist systems, from transcendental idealism to phenomenology, denied the soundness of this antinomy. Consequently, they developed more or less sophisticated strategies to allow for the inclusion of ancestral statements into our always already subjective world. It is possible to claim, for instance, that the true subject of our statements does not refer to us, finite rational beings, but to some supra-individual subject—call it god, or the absolute spirit—who exists eternally and is immediately present to each and every event. And since we ultimately belong to him, this world proves to be ours nonetheless! Similarly, it is possible to introduce various discursive finesses and uncover the deeper meanings underneath the literal meanings of statements, which can be brought to the surface precisely by the efforts of philosophy. This would imply that, strictly speaking, there were no ancestral events after all, at least not in the literal, naive meaning of the word. In this sense, we could speak about them only from our current (essentially subjective) standpoint and to the extent to which it is possible for us to re-construct the relevant past by moving backwards.

But if the first defense strategy proves to be unfeasible since it is manifestly metaphysical (contrary to the third thesis, it introduces the existence of a necessary being), Meillassoux points out that the second strategy, too, has devastating consequences: it threatens the complete collapse of the world of sense and meaning. For the ancestral assertions, taken literally, do not refer to some distant past, they refer to the past that is supposed to have existed before our time in its entirety. Having that in mind, we can easily see how the alleged philosophical explanation, far from deepening the literal meanings of those assertions, rather turns them upside down. If we accept this kind of retrojection, we have to infer the peculiar idea that, in the past, time lapsed in two directions simultaneously—from the past to the present, and vice versa. Furthermore, we have to allow for the idea of a specific category of the past, a past that, contrary to the familiar past that once used to be present, has never been present, an eternal past, as it were, without being able to explain when and how (in which direction) the transition between the two temporalities took place.

The proposed solution thus turns out to be even worse than the problem itself. Far from saving the phenomena, the introduction of the two levels of meaning produces a pile of nonsense and in the end literally "goes mad."[4] Consequently, if the world of meaning is to be preserved, we should take the ancestral assertions seriously and accept the obvious—that their literal meanings are their true meanings after all.

It is worth considering this idea a little closer. Meillassoux is well aware that philosophical systems cannot be refuted by appealing to empirical facts. He does not build his argument on the fact that our planet came about 4.5 billion years ago; what he relies on in his inference is rather the mere possibility that this fact could be true. The question he asks is: How are ancestral assertions possible? What are the conditions under which they can possibly make sense? Like Kant in the case of *a priori* synthetic judgments, Meillassoux indicates philosophy would have resolved its questions much earlier had it noticed the existence of this special class of ancestral propositions.

After these preliminary remarks, we are now in a position to give a more detailed formulation of the task that Meillassoux is up against. What he wants is simply to propose a philosophical system that could incorporate all three theses. Since in the antinomy of ancestrality he gives a clear preference to the intelligibility of the absolute in itself, his task is, more precisely, to develop such a version of theoretical access to a-subjective objectivity that would not simply dismiss the correlationist thesis—after all, it is assumed to be justified but would, on the contrary, appear as a positive consequence of its very acceptance. Such a system would earn the name of speculative realism, standing for the intelligibility of the absolute in itself without having to allow for the existence of a necessary being of any kind.[5]

2. Meillassoux's argument for breaking through the correlationist circle can be summarized in four steps. Interestingly, the four steps in a sense recapitulate the development of contemporary philosophy in the sequence of Kant, Hegel, Heidegger, and Meillassoux.

In the first step, we simply accept the validity of the correlationist thesis: the object is an essentially subjectively conditioned object, it is always already thought by a subject, and due to pragmatic contradiction, it is impossible even to think that something a-subjective is possible. What is not thinkable is not possible either.

By accepting the correlationist thesis, we seem to have successfully excluded the possibility that the absolute could be grasped by thought. Yet this is not entirely true. Within the correlationist closure, the absolute is out of reach solely on condition that it is conceived as something that is essentially *uncontaminated* by any subjectivity and is consequently *in itself* exactly to the extent to which it is *not for us*. It is only the outside absolute that is thus excluded. If, therefore, in the second step, we assume that the relation between the absolute and ourselves is one of mutual inclusion, then we should no longer need to seek the absolute in the beyond, for the absolute is now the correlation as such. We will, of course, continue to speak about the absolute from a subjective point of view; but since the absolute is now supposed to include a subjective dimension, thinking it subjectively will turn out to be the only possible way of grasping it adequately. In a similar vein, we will continue to use the expression "in itself" to refer to the ultimate reality; however, since the "in-itself" is now for the subject, it will cease to be understood in opposition to subjective mediation.

Meillassoux calls this philosophical standpoint subjectivist metaphysics: metaphysics in so far as the correlation assumes the usual features of a necessary being, and subjectivist, one could imagine, because from that standpoint the in-itself is not independent of the subject.[6] Here, Meillassoux obviously aims at Hegel. It is important to note, however, that under the same heading of subjectivist metaphysics he can include many other philosophical systems as well—from vitalism to Marxism. For that purpose, the absolute spirit simply needs to be replaced by some other absolute subject. It also needs to be emphasized that the standpoint of subjectivist metaphysics insists on the intelligibility of the absolute even after the original correlationist turn. So if we understand correlationism as an endeavor to relativize thought by setting an unsurpassable barrier between the absolute and ourselves, then with subjectivist metaphysics this attempt has been successfully neutralized.

In the third step, there appears a new correlationist attack, this time trying to de-absolutize thought by using the principle of factuality. When we speak about correlation, we have to carefully distinguish between two different aspects of it: correlation as the mere fact that an object is always thought by a subject, i.e., from a subject position, and correlation as the notion that the subject's thinking is bound to include certain forms of thought which partly condition and determine his relation to the object. It is these forms that subjectivist metaphysics tried to absolutize, ground in some real feature of the world, and thereby demonstrate their necessity. This procedure is bound to fail, the correlationist now adds, since these forms can only be described as facts. In order to establish their real necessity, we would have to step out of them—and that is impossible. What is more, adds Meillassoux as he continues his advances, even if we assume that it is not possible to provide a positive demonstration of the impossibility to prove the necessity of our forms of thought, there still remains the fact that due to our finitude, due to the irreducible facticity of our forms of thought, we can always imagine that those forms of thought could be different than they actually are. Even if we cannot think differently than we actually do, we can still acknowledge the possibility that under different circumstances it would, in principle, be *possible* for us to think differently. We therefore admit that what is "unthinkable for us" is not "impossible in itself," that something can occur which we cannot think of.

In the correlationist attack, this thesis is not put forward as positive knowledge. We cannot really wrench ourselves from our circle as we cannot think the forms in which, and only in which, it is possible for us to think at all, and if we talk about their facticity, it is their inner facticity we are discussing. We cannot know what lies beyond them, and in the end we cannot really know if there is anything beyond them at all. What we know for certain, however, is that we are finite, limited beings, and from that point we can justifiably infer that these limitations could be different than they are. Although we cannot explain how it could happen, we also know that, in the end, we cannot know that it could not ever happen. This is roughly how the present state in philosophy could be described: in our postmodern era there is virtually no philosophical school that would dare grant absolute validity to rational thought, calling instead for a humble reservation in thinking which often comes with obscurantism at its back.

It is at the fourth step that Meillassoux finally intervenes in the argument in person. His wager is that subjectivist metaphysics is not the only way to break the correlationist closure. Or, more precisely, that the breaking of the closure, if it was possible once, should be possible at least once more. The first break was achieved by a gesture of absolutization directed at the very point that used to constitute the strength of correlationism—the correlation itself. Meillassoux suggests that a similar gesture should now be undertaken once more, with regard to what correlationism relied on to refute the first absolutization—we should now absolutize facticity itself.

By claiming that the forms of thought could be different than they are, correlationism did two things. First, it asserted a notion which, in its pretension, went quite beyond the correlationist circle—it pretended to speak about the absolute. Second, correlationism allowed for this possibility without being able to provide a positive reason for it, which means that it had no reason. In short, it stated something allegedly absolute without a reason. Meillassoux now asks himself: What if, as a matter of fact, this *is* an adequate description of the absolute in-itself? What if the world is in itself such that everything happens absolutely contingently, without a reason? In this case, the correlationist's previous assertion would not be an expression of our inevitable ignorance regarding the in-itself; on the contrary, it would help us express fundamental knowledge about the world as it is in itself.

This is exactly what Meillassoux affirms! For him, the absolute is facticity. The truth of objects in themselves lies ultimately in the fact that when they are, they are without a reason, and when they start or cease to be, this too happens in an absolutely contingent way and without any reason (or cause, for that matter). The absolute truth of the world is that it is absolute chaos, a chaos so chaotic that it is able to present itself as a completely lawful world, since its only necessity lies in the fact that everything is merely factual. Meillassoux calls this principle the principle of factuality.

At this point, a common objection is bound to arise. Even if things in themselves are ultimately without reason, correlationists may insist, even if they are subjected to a contingency so absolute that anything can indeed happen at any moment, we still cannot *know* this. Since the reasonless picture of the world was not deduced by us, but simply proposed, our assertion can, at best, correspond to the absolute by mere accident. Besides, we can never assert anything positive about things in themselves. However, as Meillassoux points out, it is precisely the correlationist who cannot formulate such an objection (and he seems to be the only one who would want to do it), at least to the extent that he conceives his position to be *not* a matter of mere opinion but the *positive* result of rational derivation. In order to see why a correlationist is not allowed to use the above argument, we have to remind ourselves that, in his view, he has refuted subjectivist metaphysics by applying the principle of factuality, which claims something with absolute pretension. If this were not so, as a philosopher, he would have remained at the standpoint of subjectivist metaphysics. Conversely, if this is a valid argument for him, if he really considers it possible that the forms of thought could be different than they are, then he is equally obliged to recognize the validity of the next step, forcing him to acknowledge the principle of factuality. The correlationist cannot claim something that is inscribed in the order of the in-itself, even if he does it *per negationem* or under the guise of ignorance, and then again insist on the absolute inaccessibility of the in-itself. He cannot, without any reason, allow some possibility with regard to the absolute, and then again state that it is absolutely inadmissible to claim anything pertaining to the absolute. In any case, he cannot affirm the validity of the refutation of subjectivist metaphysics without at the same time being obligated to make one step further towards the standpoint of speculative realism.

Thus, after the two correlationist attempts at de-absolutization, access to the absolute has been regained. The picture of the absolute has been altered in the process, however. The absolute thus gained is not the one that was conceived by subjectivist metaphysicians such as Hegel, for instance, which was always already permeated by thought and always already included the subjective standpoint: now, it is a materialistic absolute that exists in itself outside any kind of subject. In that respect, the absolute of speculative realism is surprisingly similar to the usual absolute of naive realism, which can be found in everyday consciousness. In another respect, however, it is the very opposite of it. Instead of the world being subjected to the principle of causality, where any event has a sufficient reason why it is so and not otherwise, we now have a world where there is no reason, a world "governed" by the principle of unreason. It is interesting to note that Meillassoux has undergone a similar experience as Hegel before him. If traditional metaphysics was based on two principles, the principle of contradiction and the principle of sufficient reason, it seems that there is a price to be paid for the absolute after its demise. In exchange for the absolute, we are now forced to give up either one or the other. Hegel gave up the principle of contradiction. Meillassoux has given up the principle of reason.

3. Until the project is carried out to its completion, it is impossible to say if the price is perhaps not too high. Meillassoux knows very well that by breaking the correlationist closure, we have come to a point where it seems that all hope inevitably fails in the face of the abyss of reasonless chaos. However, he is strongly convinced that this little piece of the absolute that has been gained will, after the initial phase of destruction, prove sufficient to produce a reconstruction of the fundamental elements constituting the accustomed picture of the world. To conclude the outline of Meillassoux's framework, let us briefly look at the idea behind his reconstructive derivation, which is supposed to follow the first, destructive, phase.

In this respect, we must first address the reservation regarding the very idea of derivation after the collapse of the traditional framework of rationality. As its name implies, the distinctive feature of rational argumentation is giving reasons. But once an occurrence does not and cannot have any reason, it seems that rational argumentation is out for the count. To counter this kind of hesitation, Meillassoux stresses convincingly that *irraison* is not synonymous with *déraison*. If accepting the principle of unreason definitely involves some changes in the prevailing conception of rationality, it by no means implies complete abandonment of rationality. In order to see this, we should remind ourselves that the principle of factuality was not introduced arbitrarily, but rather imposed itself as a *consequence* of a positive argument. It was brought about by the binding force of thought, as an expression of its strength, not its weakness; that is why we can further rely on the same power of thought in order to give a more detailed account of the unreasonable world.[7]

For although the principle of factuality seems to be infinitely scant in its content, it nonetheless contains some conditions which are not trivial at all. And because the principle has presumably been established already, we can start from the basic fact of its truth, and from there on derive all the propositions that constitute the necessary conditions of its possibility. Absolutely true will therefore be everything we have to necessarily assume as true in order to assert the validity of the principle of factuality in its full account—that is to say, that everything in every moment can cease or commence without any reason. Meillassoux calls these conditions of the principle of factuality figures or forms. For now, only two of them have been given an explicit derivation: first, that the principle of contradiction applies to the thing in itself; and second, that in every moment of time there necessarily is, or exists, at least one thing (which, of course, is not a necessary thing itself).

How much of a world can be constructed with such figures is still open. Some assertions made by Meillassoux on various occasions indicate that he wanted to reaffirm Locke's distinction between primary and secondary qualities, and to give a new foundation to Descartes's claim regarding the absolute truth of everything mathematically thinkable. His reliance on Locke also suggested that he might introduce an analogous distinction between the "in-itself" and "appearance." And since, under the name of the two figures of factuality, he substantiated the absolute validity of the principle of contradiction and the existence of things in themselves—precisely those two propositions that Kant, having limited cognition of the realm of appearances, nonetheless affirmed as true in regards to the very things in themselves—we can assume that Meillassoux intended to develop a dual picture of the world, structurally similar to what we know from Kant's transcendental idealism. However, since Meillassoux no longer seems to be interested in the project, this is nothing but speculation.

II

Proceeding to an immanent examination of speculative realism, let us begin by pointing to a rather peculiar ambiguity. To name his antagonist, Meillassoux coined the word correlationism. Since he uses it repeatedly and without special warning in various key moments of his argumentation ("correlationist circle," "correlationist offensive," etc.), this may give rise to an impression that correlationism refers to a unique and coherent philosophical position. Yet, on a closer look, it soon becomes apparent that this common designation brings together rather diverse elements. Meillassoux, for instance, almost in the guise of definition, writes: "[B]y this neologism, in the first approximation, every position is understood as affirming that it does not make any sense to access a thing independent of thought, on the ground that we cannot extract ourselves from the essential correlation of thought and being that we are always already in."⁸ Further on he adds that "we call, more precisely, 'correlationism' every endeavor of the de-absolutization of thought."⁹ The problem is, of course, that the alleged more precise description is not simply a closer specification of the initial approximation, it rather introduces a new feature, which does not have much in common with the original one. As a consequence, it may well happen that a philosophical system which takes the correlationist circle very seriously and even emphasizes its inescapability—up to the point of declaring the very idea of an independent outside thing meaningless and impossible—ends up being described as having exited the correlationist closure. As a symptom of this classification, subjective metaphysics and Hegel, who, "in the first approximation," represent a paradigmatic correlationist position, then, "more precisely," show to be its opposite, both fall out. Such weird paradoxes indicate that under the common denominator of correlationism, Meillassoux is, in fact, fighting against two enemies at once—against the standpoint affirming that the absolute is in itself and inaccessible, and against the standpoint claiming that the absolute is not in itself (in the sense of being uncontaminated by us), yet it is accessible. We will return to this point.¹⁰

In the execution of the project there are some difficulties worth mentioning, for instance regarding the correct interpretation of Kant,¹¹ or the unclarity concerning the exact derivation of positive conditions of the principle of factuality.¹² But since they do not affect the conclusiveness of the general argument, they may be left aside. There are three technical problems which do, however, call for a closer examination. The first refers to the validity and effective range of the ancestral example; the second to the consistency of the argument designed by Meillassoux with the intention to break the correlationist closure; and the third, finally, to the conditions of the validity of his argumentative strategy in general.

1. Ancestral events—and "arche-fossils" as their present traces—are not used by Meillassoux as empirical facts. He cites them to testify that there is a certain level of meaning that is effectively and rather regularly attained by common sense and science alike, whereas it remains necessarily inaccessible to philosophy, that is, as long as it continues to persist within the correlationist circle.

Common sense is a dangerous ally, however. Philosophy has always been the one to question precisely what appears to be the most obvious and natural to common sense. In this regard, philosophy is always at least a bit "insane." The admonition that the entire world of meaning would collapse should philosophy fail to accept the authority of common sense may to that extent even prove to be correct, yet it is of no consequence taken in itself. Rather, this is the normal condition for philosophy, which constantly (and one is tempted to say constitutively) walks on the edge of nonsense and sophistry.¹³

Moreover, it seems that little was actually gained for Meillassoux by transposing the argumentation from the level of possible facts to the level of meaning. Nowadays, common sense and science do not enjoy the privilege sometimes accorded to children—namely, that in their naivety they speak nothing but the truth. Confronted with a certain proposition, philosophy is therefore not obliged to take it in the sense attributed to it by the author; on the contrary, its first task should consist in examining under what conditions such an affirmation could possibly be true, and, consequently, whether it can be taken seriously in its literal meaning at all. The criteria for that may, of course, vary across different systems. It is important to note, however, that such criteria have to be met if we are to take a proposition seriously; and it is pertinent to remind ourselves that, among philosophers, one of the most prominent criteria was furnished by Kant with his contention that it is only through relation to possible experience that our concepts acquire sense and meaning.[14] Yet if this is the case, then the transposition from the level of possible facts to the level of meaning brings no advantage by itself, since in order to justify the very meaningfulness of ancestral propositions, we have to first show that they do indeed refer to a possible experience. It turns out that this is precisely what we cannot do.

An ancestral proposition is supposed to refer to an event that took place *before* the very appearance of subjective temporality, thus before the existence of correlation as such. Confronted with the task of explaining this event, the correlationist will indeed find himself in deep waters. No matter how far into the past he is prepared to retreat from his present position, he will, by his very moving back, do nothing but extend his present, that is, phenomenal, subjective temporality; nowhere will he possibly come across anything belonging to the realm of the ancestral in-itself. The same holds true in the opposite direction: if he were to start from the ancestral event and proceed towards the future, at no point would he reach the moment where another, subjective, time could start, so that up to the present moment he would remain trapped within the same temporality as it is in itself. To this extent, the ancestral event is contradictory indeed, as it both denies and affirms the existence of correlation.

But if this is so, we have to ask ourselves: How do we know that the ancestral event *in this sense* is not merely an empty word?[15] More precisely, how can we show to the correlationist that events of this kind are really possible, that they could actually have taken place? Once again, the problem stems from the fact that we can do it solely by integrating these events into the temporality that we are currently in; but by doing so, we prove to the correlationist that the event in question is, in fact, located within the phenomenal temporality—and, therefore, that the ancestral event is not ancestral after all. The result is that the reasons which make the correlationist unable to think the possibility of the ancestral event are also the reasons which make the realist unable to prove the reality of this possibility.

The problem of Meillassoux's argument is that the ancestral notion involves a transition from one temporality into the other, from the external in-itself into the phenomenal internality. The realist and the correlationist both agree that this kind of transition is impossible: there is but *one time*. Proceeding from this common ground, however, they reach opposite conclusions. The realist will claim that the correlationist is wrong in attributing a phenomenal character to the present; the correlationist will, in turn, insist that it is the realist who is wrong in assuming the existence of ancestral events or of temporality in itself. Both will reproach each other that the other's view is wrong because it implies a transition into the other temporality. But instead of refuting each other mutually, what manifests is that their argument is circular, presenting their presuppositions in the form of the conclusion.[16] In the end, we are thus forced to admit that the ancestral event is unable to provide a concrete illustration of the inconsistency of correlationism.

While in this respect the ancestral example proves to be unsuccessful, it can give us some valuable insight into the realist's implicit conception of correlationism. There are many clues to suggest that "Meillassoux's correlationist" remains devoted to the myth of presence, and that, at least implicitly, he still relates the authentic being to some *Urszene* of pure givenness in the form of a direct face-to-face between the subject and the object. It is only within such a framework that cognition can be considered certain on the mere basis of the subject's direct testimony, while in every other case it has to be additionally justified, usually by being related to some possible or actual immediate experience. Such a theory has many inherent problems. From the standpoint of actual presence, there is in principle no difference between remoteness in space and remoteness in time, since both are something not present here and now; from that standpoint, there is no real difference between the ancestral event, the remote past, and the moment just passed either, since they are all equally gone in the present moment.[17] For this reason, in addition to the primacy of the present, Meillassoux's correlationist has to advocate a version of absolute time containing all real temporal moments and constituting, as the ultimate criterion of authenticity, the stock of possible truth. Only such a criterion would enable him to treat the not-present past differently from the not-present future and to introduce the duality required for the validity of the ancestral example within the not-present past. In short, it is only on the basis of such absolute temporality—with rather realist traits—that Meillassoux can talk of a certain "past that existed as a temporal succession in correlation to the transcendental subject even before we happen to descent back to it" and some other "past that was never present."

We cannot examine here to what extent a correlationism of this kind is still consistent. Suffice it to say that the idea of retrojection endangers the existence of meaning only for the philosophical systems falling under the description given above. And if the latter may, perhaps, apply to some varieties of phenomenology (which appear to be Meillassoux's target here), we find it profoundly alien to Kant. For with Kant, nothing in experience is immediate, everything is brought about by a presupposed act of constitution. The original scene of the pure givenness of appearances is in Kantian theory nothing but a retroactive reconstruction, as a list of necessary conditions that must have been met in order for experience to be materially possible. Moreover, this manifold cannot genuinely be called appearance, as it becomes one only by its subsumption under categories. Since the transition from the presumed point of pure givenness to phenomenal objectivity has always already taken place, it is equally not possible to speak of the transcendental subject in the sense of a being facing an object and guaranteeing its objectivity by its immediate testimony.

True, the very use of the term "appearance" implies that we have to accept the idea of a subject to whom the world appears. Yet this relation does not need to be a forcible one-to-one relation of the object-type entities. According to Berkley's *esse est percipi*, for instance, a thing would indeed cease to exist unless constantly supported by an actual presence of the perceiving subject. For Kant, however, the role of the subject is far less Stakhanovite: its intervention is in principle limited to the introductory gesture, which opens the very realm of appearing. But once a fragment of the phenomenal world has thus been established, no matter how small—and as already mentioned, it is established by the given manifold being subjected to lawful relations—with Kant, the entire phenomenal world emancipates itself and starts to live its own life, in complete independence of any subject (this is precisely what "objective" means). The transcendental subject can now self-confidently take its leave, without having to worry that the things might fall into the abyss of nothingness: for it knows that the things are hereafter kept together by the universal laws of nature.

The fact that the existence of appearance is not grounded in the subject's immediate and actual presence enables Kant to attenuate the ontological difference between the past and the present, between space and time, and even to abandon the notion of closeness altogether. If no experience is immediately given, then the transcendental subject is equidistant from every phenomenon integrated in the world. Kant has no problem whatsoever with speaking about the past that existed well before the emergence of the human species, since, due to the laws governing the phenomenal world, the past is equally close to him as the present.[18] Moreover, by following the same pattern, Kant can provide a successful explanation for the present that is too distant in space to become the object of immediate observation (the case of "inhabitants of the moon").[19] This also applies to what is intimately close, but is for some reason or other not directly observable (the problem of the ultimate constitutive parts of composed substances on the one hand,[20] and the question of magnetic matter on the other).[21] Using the same argument, we could easily add many other manifest features of what exists in the present, and even more so, what will exist in the future. To make these kinds of projections, one simply has to take into account the general Kantian constraint that the subject is essentially finite and therefore unable to cognize any single phenomenon in its complete determination.[22]

Surprisingly enough, the structure of Meillassoux's argument suggests that, in his argumentation, he himself is covertly prone to naive realism since he gives a pronounced privilege to the present.[23] But in the end, the decisive conclusion is, in general, that the ancestral example is by itself unable to make the inconsistency of correlationism evident, and, in particular, that it is of no avail against transcendental idealism.

2. While the ancestral example doubtlessly plays a role in Meillassoux's project, it is by no means decisive. The key step in breaking the correlationist closure is performed independently of it and does not mention it at all.

The entire argument has, as already indicated, the structure of two correlationist offensives aimed at the de-absolutization of thought, followed by two attempts at its absolutization, the first being undertaken by so-called subjectivist metaphysics and the second by speculative realism itself. Every subsequent step is, as is appropriate for a historical perspective, justified in the Hegelian manner of "determinate negation"; that is, not simply by demonstrating the nullity of its immediate predecessor but by trying to establish its own position precisely on the assumption of the correctness of its predecessor. The next step in the argument accepts the soundness of what, in principle, constitutes the strength of the previous standpoint, adding, however, a small yet decisive comment: when the argument is fully developed, its consequences prove to be exactly the opposite of what was first claimed. This is particularly true of the speculative realist who wants to break the correlationist closure by turning the second correlationist attack against itself. Because the correlationist evidently accepts the validity of the inference used to refute subjectivist metaphysics, so the argument goes, he also has to admit that he is actually able to think the in-itself—namely, as the absence of any reason. If, for that reason, he is justified in taking a step away from subjectivist metaphysics, then he is, for the very same reason, obliged to take one step further.

As in every argument of this type, the fundamental problem lies in the fact that its validity depends on the strength of the opponent. Paradoxically, and somehow schizophrenically, Meillassoux first has to argue that correlationism is right on the grounds presented in his reconstruction to be able to demonstrate its ultimate invalidity on that very basis further on. He has to affirm that subjectivist metaphysics can refute the original correlationism and that correlationism can refute subjectivist metaphysics; further, he has to claim that these refutations can be carried out in the way and on the grounds presented in his reconstruction; and, finally, he has to assert that these grounds are actually valid, not only for the correlationist but by themselves, without qualification. If but one step in the above chain of reasoning turns out to be defective, Meillassoux's entire argument breaks down.

Unfortunately, this is not the place to examine the entire sequence.[24] We will pay closer attention only to the crucial third step, since that is the point at which a correlationist is supposed to touch the absolute and by that, unknowingly and unwittingly, break the correlationist closure. In this regard, our claim is the very opposite of Meillassoux's. If we suppose that from the third step indeed follows the fourth, as argued by Meillassoux, then the assumed validity of the fourth step retroactively invalidates the third step, used by correlationism to refute subjectivist metaphysics. Or, alternatively, if Meillassoux indeed reads the correlationist's argument correctly, then this argument can have no validity for the correlationist. Therefore, instead of justifying the standpoint of speculative materialism, it in fact, unknowingly and unwittingly, finally succeeds in defending subjectivist metaphysics. Let us explain.

The paradigmatic correlationist statement asserts that what is unthinkable for us is not impossible in itself. Because we know we are finite, we cannot allow ourselves to limit things in themselves by our forms, and so we cannot exclude the possibility that something may happen, even if it is utterly impossible for us to conceive. As already noted, the correlationist does not pretend that this statement refers to something in itself. In his modesty, he insists he is speaking merely about his awareness of his limits, which is positive, but he does not dare to conclude that there actually is anything beyond these limits, let alone the in-itself.[25] The correlationist's modesty is misplaced, however, argues Meillassoux. By recognizing his limitedness, he actually manages to open a realm beyond our forms of thought, the realm of the in-itself; and although the correlationist has indeed no reason whatsoever to think of anything in it in a positive way, he thereby, as a matter of fact, does think something in it in a positive way—that is, insofar as the in-itself is indeed without any reason: "For even if I cannot think the unthinkable, I can think the possibility of the unthinkable by dint of the unreason of the real."[26]

Both moments of the above breakthrough can be shown to be invalid. If we take the correlationist stance seriously, as Meillassoux insists we should, then we know in advance that we cannot know anything about the a-subjective in-itself—with one exception, namely, *that* we cannot know anything about it. For us, it is an empty and contradictory concept. Even when we think of something beyond the realm of our cognition, we still think it through our forms of thought, and if we decide to name this the "in-itself," this is still the in-itself for us. At this point, the reminder of our finitude may lead us to think that the forms of our thought could be different from what they in fact are. Exactly how far their possible or thinkable changeability extends is hard to determine in advance; we can assume that throughout every change a certain core has to remain unchanged, so that it is finally still possible to speak of a gradual series of transformations, establishing a kind of continuity between the initial and the finale state. But in any case, we do know that this possible continuity has a *bottom limit*: since we constitutively think in subject form and from a certain subjective standpoint, finite forms of thought cannot be such to imply the non-existence of every subjective standpoint (and correlation along with it). This remains an unsurpassable obstacle, which no consequent correlationist will be prepared to overstep, no matter how eager he is to refute subjectivist metaphysics.

Meillassoux would perhaps even agree with the above assessment. For him, the correlationist closure is indeed impossible to penetrate in a direct attack. It is for that reason that he sets out to break it indirectly by thinking "the possibility of the unthinkable by dint of the unreason of the real."²⁷ Yet, here, such meandering is to no avail. For if such a stratagem may well permit one to achieve a revolution within an already existing space, it can never open a space that did not exist before. We are thus bound to admit that this introduction of the principle of unreason is still thought in our forms of thought, designating only the unreason for us, not unreason in itself.

But as already noted, this is exactly what, according to Meillassoux, a correlationist cannot allow himself to say if he wants to successfully refute subjectivist metaphysics. He has to assume that he actually and effectively thought the absolute in itself, "since were this not the case, it would never had occurred to you not to be a subjective (or speculative) idealist."²⁸ More precisely:

> Let me make myself clear, for this is the crux of the matter. So long as you maintain that your scepticism towards all knowledge of the absolute is based upon an argument, rather than upon mere belief or opinion, then you have to grant that the core of any such argument must be *thinkable*. But the core of your argument is that we *can* access everything's capacity-not-to-be, or capacity-to-be-other; our own as well as the world's.²⁹

Let us then try to understand and, for the sake of the argument, let us suppose that the interpretation of the third step given above is correct. For if Meillassoux is really right in this respect, then we are simply forced to find out that, for the correlationist, the third step cannot be conclusive. The mere fact that the correlationist *erroneously accepts* this argument cannot provide a sufficient ground for Meillassoux's triumph. It would be truly remarkable indeed if access to the absolute as it is in itself were ultimately conditioned by someone's factual mistake.

In justifying true cognition, it does not suffice to have reasons; one has to have the right reasons. Descartes, too, started with reasons in favor of his affirmation that everything can be doubted. But as he later touched upon those completely evident truths, which we are not even able to think about without inadvertently producing an unshakable certainty about their truth, he was forced to recognize that there indeed are things that are impossible to doubt. Descartes was consistent enough to acknowledge that his initial claim was—despite all the reasons—wrong. Meillassoux does not do this. His standpoint cannot pass for knowledge, even if *per impossibilem* we suppose it to be correct, since he is unable to show that he has the right reasons. We can see this if we now *per impossibilem* suppose that the world in itself, unknown to us, in fact obeys the most classical, pre-determined necessity: this fact would at no point disturb the speculative realist's argumentation.

In the end, the shortcomings of Meillassoux's argument could be aptly illustrated by using Kant's distinction between the logical and the real possibility. The standard requirement for the possibility of thought is the absence of contradiction—but for Kant, as we know, this is by far not enough for the possibility of a thing corresponding to that thought. In order to establish the real possibility, something more is needed: it is necessary to exhibit positive conditions for the possibility of the existence of the thing, ultimately, to show that the thing in question is possible in its complete determination.[30] Until this additional requirement is met, it can always turn out that our thought is possible simply because it is empty and has no sense and meaning (empty thoughts lack contradiction by virtue of their very emptiness). With regard to our case, we would have to show in a positive way not only how the thought of the reasonless in-itself is free of contradiction, but also how it is possible at all. Meillassoux does not provide anything of the sort. On the contrary, at the critical points where our ignorance is supposed to transform into an insight into the inner structure of things in themselves, and where one would expect the speculative realist to display the greatest possible certainty, Meillassoux often employs discursive attenuators ("on se demande si") and incentive calls ("il nous faut comprendre," "nous devons saisir"). Long gone are the times "when the empty possibility to represent something in a different way was sufficient to refute a view."[31]

3. Meillassoux presents his argument as a succession of two parallel gestures of the absolutization of thought, following two equally parallel attempts of its relativization. This parallel duality is of crucial importance for his discursive strategy. Only thus can he claim that for a successful correlationist de-absolutization it does not suffice to insist on one but two characteristics of correlation; only thus can he provide a structural analogy between the first, provisional, and the second, final, break of the correlationist closure; and only thus can he show how something that is impossible when attempted directly can nonetheless be done by using a deviation. Throughout the entire argumentation, he relies on the following parallelism: Just as subjectivist metaphysics absolutized the very correlation that was initially used by correlationism to limit our access to the absolute, so speculative realism absolutizes that very facticity that was used by correlationism to relativize the first absolutization. This second absolutization, argues Meillassoux, is at the same time the final one. For, in the correlationist circle, there are no more than two constitutive elements: the fact of its existence and the determinacy of its forms. And besides, any further attempt at de-absolutization would

have to make affirmative use of the principle of unreason and would therefore only absolutize what it has set to de-absolutize.

The discursive structure of double duality is distinguished by its aesthetic elegance, a quality characteristic of all great conceptual achievements. Moreover, it has the advantage of allowing for further applications. One can legitimately ask, for instance, what the results would be if the argument were carried out in reverse, starting with the absolutization of facticity and following with the absolutization of the correlation. Be that as it may, we have to take into account that the use of the same argument on two different occasions requires that the conditions of its validity as well as the circumstances of its application remain, at least as regards their essentials, the same. With Meillassoux, this is hard to affirm.

The first gesture of absolutization of the correlation is in principle acceptable simply because we stay within the correlation throughout. The basic environment remains unaltered; the change affects only the implicit conception of the absolute, which turns from something essentially a-subjective into an absolute that already includes the subjective dimension. This is why, in this case, it is acceptable to use dialectic argumentation: here, our relation to the absolute is something that directly and trivially affects the absolute itself, and when our stance towards it changes, this is bound to make an impact on the absolute. In the second case, however, the previous conditions no longer apply. If we suppose that the correlationist closure indeed gets demolished, this produces a substantial transformation of the entire environment, which invalidates the analogy and prohibits further use of the previous argument—at least until it is substantially adapted. In the second attempt at absolutization, it is equally not possible to use a Hegelian type of argumentation, which consists in unveiling all the consequences of an affirmation. Since the absolute is now perceived as an a-subjective entity, quietly lying in its self-sufficiency at the end of the road, the absolute is completely indifferent to what a certain subject might think of it. To such an absolute, all the subtleties of dialectics are of no avail.[32]

Drawing on remarks concerning the implicit conception of the absolute, we are now in a position to give a more accurate description of the structural crack in the argument presented above. We have already noted that Meillassoux is fighting two opponents at once: the correlationist affirming that we are always already contained within the subjective circle, and the relativist affirming that the absolute is out of our reach. It is often the case that both of these propositions happen to be advocated by the same philosophers. Yet we have to notice that they are, in principle, independent of one another. Someone who insists that we always already think from our subjective position cannot solely on this ground jump to the conclusion that, therefore, the absolute is unthinkable for us. In fact, this is a new presupposition, concerning the nature of the absolute. Such a presupposition can be made from different perspectives. If we suppose that the absolute is a kind of thing in itself located beyond our thought, what we get is "relativist correlationism"; but if we, on the contrary, assume that the thing in itself in the usual sense is an empty concept (since we ourselves are already within the absolute), then what emerges could be called "absolutist correlationism."

Both alternatives are originally on equal footing. Meillassoux, however, arranges them into an ordered succession, and this makes his presentation biased from the very beginning. He is later bound to struggle as he searches for an adequate definition of correlationism, since, as a consequence of his strategy, there is no proper place to be found for Hegel. And if Meillassoux's correlationist is immediately deprived of the absolute, then, as we have learned from Hegel, it is his conception of the absolute to blame, not the correlationist circle.[33]

Meillassoux's project could be understood as an attempt to draw an inference from thought to being even after the demise of metaphysics. As an ontological argument for the new era, this argument is designed to justify not a necessary being, but rather the necessity of being without anything being necessary. But in order to make such an inference possible at all, it is necessary to presuppose a basic identity, a fundamental continuity holding the two orders together. As Schelling wrote: "The first presupposition of all knowing is that that which knows and that which is known is one and the same."[34] Meillassoux seems unwilling to accept this.

III

As speculative realism seems to remain an unfinished project that has been abandoned by its author way before its completion, it is bold to give a general assessment of it. Every attempt to that effect is bound to make inevitably premature assumptions, subjecting itself to reproaches about, for instance, simply missing the target.[35] This is a risk we will readily assume.

1. If we start by comparing the declared goals of speculative realism with what it did manage to achieve, we can note a series of inner incongruities or pragmatic contradictions.

The project was designed to defend common sense (and science) from philosophical subtleties that tend to turn the literal meaning upside down. But if we now look at what can be said about the world as it is conceived by speculative realism, we get a rather strange picture: in front of us is a world where punctual entities emerge and disappear without any order of their own; a world where in any moment and for no reason anything can happen; a world where, unless it contradicts the principle of mathematics, everything is possible, including the possibility that the natural laws may in the very next moment alter and that, for example, the sun will not rise in the morning. In short, we are confronted with a world (a "hyper-chaos") that could not be more alien to common sense (and science), but that is, for that matter, perfectly familiar to the most traditional of metaphysics, together with all its picturesque eccentricities. Where being naive in philosophy leads to!

In a similar vein, Meillassoux rejects the idea of retrojection on the ground that it would imply the existence of a past that was never present, destroying the very possibility of meaning. To object to retrojection is strange, however. In fact, a very similar procedure is used by science itself, such as in determining the age of organic matter based on the half-life of a carbon isotope, or in calculating the exact date of a solar eclipse that happened in the past. In the latter case, the eventual availability of written documents is certainly exciting, yet it does not significantly affect the results obtained by simply rolling back the present state of the solar system in accordance with the laws of nature. What is more, if we now accept the results of Meillassoux's speculative realism, we are obliged to allow for the real possibility that common sense and science alike speak of a past that never existed. All the statements made by science about the past (or the future) are valid solely under the condition of *ceteris paribus*, that is, that the system of natural laws retains at least its basic stability. In speculative realism, however, this very presupposition is no longer certain. If the laws may indeed change, in any given moment and for no reason, then it is absolutely possible that they actually changed in the past. It is therefore perfectly possible that the entirety of science describes an imaginary past. And, to that extent, it is also possible that the configuration of the world as we know it today was in fact established around 6,000 years ago, exactly as insisted by those "picturesque believers" derided by Meillassoux.

The presented paradoxes suggest that, at a certain point, speculative materialism would be forced to reintroduce the common distinction between the in-itself and appearance. As we have seen, this distinction is possibly going to be built along the lines of either Locke's or Kant's model. Hyper-chaos would in this case refer primarily to the world of the in-itself, while the phenomenal world would display far more familiar traits and would fall under stable laws. But in this case, Meillassoux would have found himself in another pragmatic paradox. The project of speculative realism was originally introduced in the name of common sense and in support of the affirmation that science describes the world as it is in itself. Now, however, it would have turned out that, on the contrary, it speaks primarily of the world of appearance.

Another paradox relates to the fact that speculative materialism developed its project in order to curb the light-mindedness of contemporary philosophy, which, at least in part, bears responsibility for the perverse situation in which any fideistic claim can appear to be more rational than the requirements of rational explanation. In this sense, Meillassoux's goal is definitely to fight for the cause of reason. But if he finds himself defending the principle of unreason within this process, the cure may just be worse than the disease. What is left of the idea of rational explanation if we accept that there is no reason for why things are the way they are? If indeed everything is possible, any proposition regarding the future is *a priori* on equal footing, which widely opens the door to every kind of *Schwärmerei* and empty fiction.[36]

At this point, Meillassoux protests that *irraison* is not *déraison*. To abandon the principle of reason does not imply giving up rationality as such; for him, it rather stands for the call to develop a different kind of rationality. But the problem is that this "logique de l'irraison" is far from being developed, and for now, there is no guarantee that it is even possible to develop it. In this respect, the use of mathematics is more an attempt to shift the problem to a subcontractor, a great expert in his field, rather than a promising strategy.[37] And here we are tempted to ask, together with Lessing, whether it is really wise to throw the baby out with the bathwater.

2. Another group of questions concerning the project as a whole pertains to its implicit ontology. The field of the undefined here is even larger than usual, and the risk of false assumptions even greater. Nevertheless, we believe that Harman was basically right in referring to speculative realism as hyper-occasionalism.[38]

The term occasionalism is used to designate a particular system which explains how the extended and the thinking substance can affect one another without having common attributes. However, this kind of interaction is but a special case of the more general question of how a substance can produce a change in the state of another substance at all if the substance is something that essentially exists independently. Universalized occasionalism is consequently a system in which substances are completely isolated from one another, having no real interaction. If correspondence does occur, it is typically produced by the intervention of a benevolent God, who, at the occasion of change in one substance, spontaneously produces a corresponding change in some other substance. As a result, an outward impression that one substance is the cause of the effect in the other is created.[39]

In a sense, Meillassoux proposes a radicalized version of such a system. If in general occasionalism God is constantly kept busy by ordering appearances along the principle of reason, in Meillassoux, he can now take his leave. For, a change in the state of one substance is no reason why any change should be produced in some other substance—there is no relation among them now, be it real or ideal. But what is even more important, in Meillassoux, the substance has lost every relation *to itself* as well. A change in its state is henceforth not a reason for why anything else should happen within it: the substance's state in one moment in no way affects its state in the following moment. In this way, however, the substance eventually loses what used to constitute its very virtue—the capacity to preserve its identity. It turns into an essentially momentous, punctual entity, which is what it is, comes to be when it does, and is while it is, without any reason. Such hyper-occasionalism might suitably be described as Hume inverted, where the role of ideas has been filled by "things" themselves.[40]

It goes without saying that such ontology has an extremely heavy argumentative burden to sustain. If, in the final analysis, the absolute consists of entities which originally exist for a moment only, without constitutive duration, and which by themselves do not entertain any relations to other entities of the same order or to themselves in the next moment, then it indeed becomes difficult to show not only how a phenomenal world featuring familiar traits can arise out of this, but also how the predicate of being could be attributed to something like this at all. Is this still something rather than nothing? How can it acquire any positive qualities? What might be its conditions of identity? Can it be said to have any identity at all? In spite of Meillassoux's repeated insistence on how in any moment anything can change into something else, it could well be that he is actually not able to think the concept of change or alteration at all, since alteration presupposes the identity of what is being altered.[41] For that reason, the above conception of being cannot represent an original state.[42] If the world indeed consisted of such relationless entities, its objects would be left devoid of qualities. In order to achieve minimal consistency, they would have to be additionally furnished with some kind of eternal essences and supported by some higher being. Hyper-occasionalist ontology would thus turn out to be profoundly metaphysical in the most traditional sense.

We claimed that in a hyper-occasionalist world God becomes idle, not that he simply disappears. Due to the punctual nature of basic entities, Meillassoux is bound to face difficulties when it comes to providing a proper foundation for space,[43] and particularly for time. He seems to be obligated to assume the existence of some absolute time that is independent of anything in it on the one hand, while it provides the ultimate verification of any present actuality on the other. Only such divine time can enable Meillassoux to draw a demarcation line between the past that was once present and the one that never existed as the present. It goes without saying that such a conception of time has serious metaphysical consequences as well.

3. The examinations conducted so far suggest that Meillassoux endorses basic presuppositions of pre-critical ontology, where the absolute is still conceived according to the model of a thing and truth is defined as an external correspondence between the atom of thought and the atom of the object. In short, it seems that Meillassoux still relies on the regime of rationality that Hegel called *Vorstellung*. It is in reference to this conception that Lessing once commented that, for it, truth is like a coin to be taken ready-made out of the pocket.

Meillassoux is well aware that such a monetary conception of thinking and being is obliged to accept various assumptions that have nowadays lost their former self-evidence. Indeed, this is why he wants to develop a different, speculative philosophy, which, for instance, forsakes the principle of reason. He is equally familiar with the propositions that were developed as possible alternatives to representational thought by authors such as Kant, Fichte, Schelling, and Hegel. Therefore, if he does not accept them, this is simply because he finds them inconclusive. This is particularly the case with Hegel. Meillassoux seems unwilling to forgive that in his attempt to reach the absolute, Hegel has renounced the principle of contradiction. But if it is possible not to agree with the proposed solutions, it is impossible to ignore that the problems they respond to—problems, paradigmatically exposed by the so-called Spinozism controversy, ranging from the proper conception of subjectivity to the status of reason and truth—are real. The failure to show an adequate understanding of these problems is in our view one of the main reasons for the ultimate failure of Meillassoux's project.

This nearly "voluntary," self-imposed sightlessness is well discernible in the strategy developed by Meillassoux to refute one of the "parades" made from the standpoint of transcendental idealism. In an addition written specially for the English edition of *After Finitude*, Meillassoux flawlessly recapitulates the objection according to which "a transcendental condition is not an object."[44] He then begins his counter-argument by introducing what appears to be, again, a very correct distinction between the subjective and the objective mode of being. However, in developing his argument further, he simply seems to forget this crucial distinction. What are, he asks, "the conditions under which there is a transcendental subject"?[45] And in spite of knowing only too well that the transcendental subject is in its very concept the unconditioned, he still treats its being as conditioned in the most outward manner possible. Making the transcendental subject dependent on the pre-existing conditions of its "incarnation," he concludes by explicitly reducing it to something that exists in the manner of things (that is, "takes place" at a determinate point in space and time), thereby simply evading the fundamental question of the subject's mode of existence.[46]

A similar sightlessness, in the sense of a specific configuration of the visible and the invisible, can be observed in relation to the question of the necessity of the correlation.

Meillassoux begins by highlighting the position of subjectivist metaphysics according to which the correlation is necessary in the sense that we cannot think but within it. This conceptual necessity, which is unconditional in exactly the same sense as the subject, is then interpreted by Meillassoux in the sense of the necessity of a thing; and since there is no external condition that could possibly determine it, he comes to the conclusion that the existence of the correlation is not necessary. As if the inner necessity could be thought from the standpoint of its outer conditions! As if the subject of thought could have accompanied the transition that made it into a subject! As if Fichte's I were something else beyond its self-positing! At this point, it becomes manifest that Meillassoux is not prepared to accept any other necessity than the necessity of the substantial type, understood as a relation between two objects, and that he is therefore unable to see how Hegel, for instance, tries to develop a different kind of necessity, one that would arise out of facticity as a sort of accidental absolute lacking any outer ground, but not being any less absolute because of it. In this respect, Meillassoux's fight against correlationism actually bears a striking resemblance to the struggle of the Enlightenment against superstition as portrayed by Hegel.

As we have seen, in a decisive moment and against his implicit assumptions, Meillassoux in fact argues in a Hegelian manner—to that extent, he is half-Hegelian. Perhaps he would have become completely Hegelian had he realized that Hegel was trying to develop a new mode of conceptuality and that, for this very reason, his system was called speculative idealism, not subjectivist metaphysics. If this were the case, he would have probably also noticed that when confronted with Jacobi's anti-philosophical objections on the one side and romantic endeavors to bypass them on the other, Hegel had a similar goal as himself in his struggle against what is the *Schwärmerei* of our times.

IV

In a rather short period of time since the publication of his book, Meillassoux managed to attract enormous theoretical interest. By virtue of his inventiveness, his courage of thought, his search for clarity, and finally the greatest possible goals he has set for himself, there is no doubt that the attention was warranted. However, the gaps in his project, and some of them are rather serious, suggest that the admired response cannot be solely due to the inner strength of his argument. To conclude, let us therefore take a brief look at what the events surrounding the publication of the book could tell us about the state of contemporary philosophy, French philosophy in particular.

The reasons for the popularity of a certain philosophical program are, even within philosophical circles, often related to factors external to philosophy proper. A discipline called "the political economy of theoretical production" would probably lead to the conclusion that the public success of certain philosophemes depends on a vast array of factors, ranging from institutional infrastructure to market demands, which may eventually affect the very content of philosophical thinking. It could also be established that the chances of success significantly increase when the thought has strong connections to some social group or when it occupies a place that is, as it is said, waiting for it in the spirit of the times. This is nothing new. Even in Fichte's case his vertiginous ascension to prominence was, probably more than for philosophical reasons, related to the political revolution in France and the early fermentation of Romanticism in Germany.

In the case of Meillassoux, his extraordinarily positive reception undoubtedly resonates with a certain discontent, with feelings of weariness and fatigue, which have obviously spread within contemporary philosophy. The call for the absolute, which, as a matter of fact, exploits the means of old metaphysics and in many aspects acts in direct opposition to dominant philosophical views, would not be heard, at least not to such an extent, had the idol not already been close to falling. In this sense, the general enthusiasm triggered by Meillassoux indeed had a prognostic power.

Another important circumstance of the public response to Meillassoux refers, in our view, to the fact that he explicitly stood up for naivety in philosophy. This is probably the reason why he was given such a warm reception precisely in those philosophical circles that used to be renowned for their subtle games of incessant cross-referring. Had he come out within the analytical theory of meaning or reference, for instance, he would have easily been dismissed with a simple wave of the hand as yet another one of those common sense metaphysicians, who, like Putnam,[47] still bother to prove that the world exists. But because Meillassoux is one of us, and because we are oh-so-subtle, his naivety can be (another turn of the screw) understood as the ultimate level of subtlety. We may not agree completely with the author, yet his argument is without a doubt refreshing and worthy of the closest reading, and besides, we can now associate with common sense while, if we want to, at the same time flirting with metaphysics.

This, however, is precisely the kind of reception that would not have been possible had Meillassoux really been taken seriously. We must therefore stress that naivety has two dimensions. It can present itself in the form of the favorable acceptance of the views of common sense, so that the first task of philosophy becomes to give them proper justification in their literal meaning. The other, and rather different, use of naivety in philosophy requires, on the contrary, that we are able to treat every single thought as a bastard, that we are prepared to start anywhere and without presuppositions, relying on nothing but the strength and necessity of thought. To be naive in philosophy in this sense means that no question seems too banal not to be worth tarrying with and no answer so evident that it cannot be questioned. To be naive means simply to refrain from logical geniality and to acknowledge nothing but the binding force of understanding as the right path to the science of thinking, which is equally available for all. Finally, to be naive in philosophy means having the courage to take up thought. This courage was demonstrated by Meillassoux—and in this we support his naivety.

One final remark. Meillassoux's project, as we have seen, grew out of dissatisfaction with the postmodernist strain of thought that lost all connection to both common sense and science while making it impossible to conceive any viable emancipatory program. As it was Kant who was designated the ultimate culprit for the deplorable state philosophy is presently in, it comes as no surprise that Meillassoux, as it were, performed a pre-critical turn. This is not to say that in the process of justification of his speculative realism he did not deploy, very skillfully, some decisive arguments that clearly come from the post-Kantian tradition. Our point is rather that his argumentation, the very form of the concepts he uses, pertain to a pre-critical conceptual regime that Hegel once called *Vorstellung*. Indeed, not only are thoughts treated as if they were mental atoms, the very picture of the world produced in the end bears an unmistakable resemblance to seventeenth- and eighteenth-century philosophical systems—together with all their eccentricities of, for instance, worlds disappearing behind our backs, objects just popping up, etc.

But as we have equally seen, everything suggests that Meillassoux's project of speculative realism is going to remain unfinished. In this conjunction, the realist banner has been taken up by authors such as Graham Harman, Markus Gabriel, Maurizio Ferraris, and others, each defending their own variety of this new realism. However, while these authors largely share the basic anti-postmodern thrust—both theoretically, as regards the need to reconnect to the sciences, and politically, as a request to formulate a feasible emancipatory strategy[48]—we must not overlook that there is a profound difference separating them from Meillassoux. For if Meillassoux defends the most rigorous form of argumentation, taking its criteria from mathematics, the new realists tend to satisfy themselves with what is more or less convincing, natural, witty, or well-formulated. In one of his latest books, Maurizio Ferraris, for example, proposes a version of naturalistic epistemology, suggesting that it makes no sense to engage in a hair-splitting inquiry on how it is possible for us to know things when it is obvious that, as time goes by, more or less everything happens to occur and more or less everything happens to be known. "Sooner or later, the truth comes out," as indeed the proverb says. In this sense, observes Ferraris, "perfect epistemology is therefore history," adding that, "if awarded with an eternal life," one would be in a position to "realize historic knowledge as absolute knowing regarding the past."[49] This is undoubtedly nicely put. However, although this kind of argument may be perfectly useful for everyday life, and even successful in movies such as *Groundhog Day*,[50] in the field of philosophy, it brings us no closer to answering the question of how we can know anything at all. From this perspective, new realism constitutes yet another return to the pre-critical, this time to the so-called *Popularphilosophie*, which flourished in Germany in the second half of the eighteenth century. Again, this is not an argument against popular philosophy as such, then or now, for it definitely has its merits. It is only that, insofar as it takes the place of philosophy, it gives up what constitutes its proper task.

Interestingly enough, in order to exit the postmodern entrapment, both Meillassoux and the new realists in a sense returned to the pre-critical. But given that the situation in question is very much like the early Romanticist one, with its exaltation of feeling or art against the limitations of rational knowledge, it seems at hand that instead of returning to the pre-critical, one should rather repeat Hegel's gesture. This is especially so since what can be seen as the main premises of Meillassoux's project—the correlationist, the ancestral, and the speculative thesis—can all be shown to be defective: the first arbitrarily assumes that thought and the absolute are external to each other (Hegel); the second fails to allow for the distinction between logical and real possibility (Kant); the third disregards the capacity of subjective concepts to think a non-metaphysical necessity (Fichte, Hegel). Consequently, it might be more realistic, and more promising, to propose a speculative version of absolute idealism instead.

Notes

1. The research included in this chapter was funded by the Slovenian Research Agency (ARRS) under the research project "Language and Science: the Possibility of Realism in Modern Philosophy" (J6-7364).
2. I would like to thank Žana Stefanović for the incitement and valuable suggestions. In addition, I would like to thank Bojana Jovićević, Sabina Žakelj, and Tanja Dominko for the English.
3. Here, one can finally find a kind of continuity between Meillassoux's project and some aspects of French theory. Structuralism, too, explicitly relied on the most recent insights of linguistics. On this basis, it even set out to develop a general theory of knowledge that would include both the science of nature and the science of man (see Jean-Claude Milner, *Le périple structural: figures et paradigme* [Paris: Seuil, 2002]). In spite of all the divergences that profoundly separate Meillassoux from the main figures of French Thought, in this regard he does retain a clear proximity to Lacan and Badiou, who equally, although each in his own way, mathematized ontology. It may be noted that Meillassoux's implicit understanding of science appears to be rather narrow, shaped after the ideal of physics, and is as such likely to exclude the science of man and large portions of the science of nature.
4. Cf. Quentin Meillassoux, "Métaphyisique, speculation, correlation," in *Ce peu d'espace autour: six essais sur la métaphysique et ses limites*, ed. Bernard Mabille (Chatou: La Transparence, 2010), 83.
5. Later on, Meillassoux increasingly used the name of speculative materialism, intended to convey that the absolute is independent of thought. We will use both expressions interchangeably.
6. This reading is assumed throughout the entire chapter. It is certainly possible that Meillassoux understood the absolutization of the correlation in such a manner that the subject of correlation was itself an absolute being that, as such, was somehow capable of grasping the things in themselves. That would justify the conclusion that the impossibility of the ontological proof makes it unattainable to ground the necessity of such a subject. This interpretation will, however, not be taken into account, since it is not worth a closer examination.
7. In this respect, Meillassoux's philosophical procedure is comparable to Descartes's treatise on the creation of eternal truths; there is a structural similarity between Descartes's argumentation and Meillassoux's breaking of the correlationist closure that one can hardly call a coincidence.
8. Meillassoux, "Métaphyisique, speculation, correlation," 75–6.
9. Ibid., 76. Meillassoux makes further comments that consequential correlationist philosophy would be the one to not only declare that we cannot say anything, by means of concept alone, but also refuse every absolutization *of the correlation itself*.
10. The question of nomenclature is a rather delicate one for Meillassoux. Since, in his argumentation, he relies heavily on typified philosophical positions, he is, on the one hand, compelled to use rather rough categories, which are necessarily insensitive to the finer details. It seems, for instance, that he uses thinking and cognition (or, the in-itself and the absolute) synonymously, to denote something like "successful access to ...,"

although, in a way, Kant built his entire philosophical system precisely on this differentiation. On the other hand, the characterization of these philosophical positions has to be very concise in order to include all the relevant positions that actually appeared in the history of post-Kantian philosophy. The fact that he uses his categories both as descriptive and normative at the same time does not contribute to the conclusiveness of his argument.

11 Let us mention but two major issues. Meillassoux assumes that, with Kant, the ontological proof was rejected on the grounds that being was not a predicate. According to our view, on the contrary, for Kant, the ultimate reason for its failure lies in the fact that no conceptual connection can be established between the necessary being and the most perfect being, leaving the concept of necessary being empty. Meillassoux further claims that in Transcendental Deduction, Kant based his argument on the apparent stability of natural laws: were appearance not subject to necessary laws, the world would have often changed its course, and since this is obviously not the case, appearance is indeed subjected to the categories and their lawfulness. Although this argument proves to be invalid, Meillassoux actually stands in defense of Kant, adding that he did not have the necessary conceptual tools at his disposal—at the time, Cantor had not yet discovered the transfinite calculus—and was therefore unable to see the shortcomings of his proof. In this decisive point, our disagreement with Meillassoux is triple. In our view, the Transcendental Deduction, far from pretending to justify the apparent stability of the world, wants rather to provide a rational foundation for the very possibility that there can be any kind of immanent relation between phenomenal objects, ultimately for the very possibility of the existence of something similar to a phenomenal object; in this sense, the fact of the existence of a unified representation of an object is by itself sufficient proof of the application of the categories. Similarly, we do not believe that Kant would have had to wait for Cantor in order to understand the inconclusiveness of Meillassoux's reading of his argument: all that was needed was already at his disposal in his conception of "infinite judgments." And contrary to Meillassoux, we hold that Kant's argument in the Transcendental Deduction is perfectly valid.

12 It is obvious, as Meillassoux seems to acknowledge himself in his later presentations, that his original derivation of the principle of contradiction cannot justify the impossibility of a contradictory being but only the impossibility of a *universally* contradictory being, as *ens sibi contradictissimum*. Only for a being that includes the predicate itself as well as its opposite for *all* the predicates is there no otherness to change into. It is a long way to go from here to the exclusion of every partial contradiction.

13 Meillassoux admits something similar. Cf. Quentin Meillassoux, *After Finitude: An Essay on the Necessity of Contingency*, trans. Ray Brassier (London: Bloomsbury, 2008), 76: "Philosophy is invention of strange forms of argumentation, necessarily bordering on sophistry, which remains its dark structural double." Concerning the sense and meaning attributed by everyday consciousness and science to each other, Hegel makes a similar comment—cf. Georg Wilhelm Friedrich Hegel, *Phenomenology of Spirit*, trans. Terry Pinkard (Cambridge: Cambridge University Press, 2018), 17: "For the natural consciousness to entrust itself immediately to science would be to make an attempt, induced by it knows not what, to walk upside down all of a sudden."

14 Cf. Immanuel Kant, *Critique of Pure Reason*, trans. Paul Guyer and Allen W. Wood (Cambridge: Cambridge University Press, 1998), hereinafter cited as *KrV* according to the pagination of original German editions. *KrV*, B148–9: "But this further extension

of concepts beyond *our* sensible intuition does not get us anywhere. For they are then merely empty concepts of objects, through which we cannot even judge whether the latter are possible or not—mere forms of thought without objective reality—since we have available no intuition to which the synthetic unity of apperception, which they alone contain, could be applied, and that could thus determine an object. *Our* sensible and empirical intuition alone can provide them with sense and significance."

15 If ancestral propositions are understood solely as judgments referring to the time before the emergence of intelligent life, their meaningfulness and truth are undisputed. However, this is not what Meillassoux is after. These propositions acquire their intended ancestral dimension only when combined with the additional affirmation that the correlationist cannot speak of the existence of the objective world without the *simultaneous* existence of intelligent life.

16 In this respect, there is an evident analogy to the famous Leibniz–Clarke dispute and to Kant's presentation of antinomy. The difference being that our "antinomy" undermines the soundness of the ancestral example.

17 Let us put a naive question. Suppose it turned out that there is no substantial difference between travelling through space and travelling through time. It is irrelevant whether such a journey is actually viable or not, since, similarly to Meillassoux, we are tackling the realm of possible sense, and we by no means want to limit science in advance. The question for Meillassoux is: If, and under what conditions, would the ancestral example still function?

18 Cf. Kant, *KrV*, B523/A495: "Thus one can say: The real things of past time are given in the transcendental object of experience, but for me they are objects and real in past time only insofar as I represent to myself that, in accordance with empirical laws, or in other words, the course of the world, a regressive series of possible perceptions (whether under the guidance of history or in the footsteps of causes and effects) leads to a time-series that has elapsed as the condition of the present time, which is then represented as real only in connection with a possible experience and not in itself; so that all those events which have elapsed from an inconceivable past time prior to my own existence signify nothing but the possibility of prolonging the chain of experience, starting with the present perception, upward to the conditions that determine it in time." Interestingly enough, Meillassoux often quotes this very reference.

19 Cf. ibid., B521/A492–3: "That there could be inhabitants of the moon, even though no human being has ever perceived them, must of course be admitted; but this means only that in the possible progress of experience we could encounter them; for everything is actual that stands in one context with a perception in accordance with the laws of the empirical progression."

20 Cf. ibid., B553/A505: "Hence I will have to say: the multiplicity of parts in a given appearance is in itself neither finite nor infinite, because appearance is nothing existing in itself, and the parts are given for the very first time through the regress of the decomposing synthesis, and in this regress, which is never given absolutely wholly either as finite nor as infinite."

21 Cf. ibid., B273/A226: "However, one can also cognize the existence of the thing prior to the perception of it, and therefore cognize it comparatively a priori, if only it is connected with some perceptions in accordance with the principles of their empirical connection (the analogies). For in that case the existence of the thing is still connected with our perceptions in a possible experience, and with the guidance of the analogies we can get from our actual perceptions to the thing in the series of possible

perceptions. Thus we cognize the existence of a magnetic matter penetrating all bodies from the perception of attracted iron filings, although an immediate perception of this matter is impossible for us given the constitution of our organs."

22 Kant's conception of the subjectivity of cognition is characterized by this conjunction of a *self-supporting world*, where the function of authentication is taken over by objective laws, and the *subject's finitude*, which makes complete cognition impossible and the notion of closeness inapplicable. In this way, Kant is able to affirm that the subject *is finite* without having to occupy *a determined point* of space and time. A similar point was recently made by Sebastian Rödl in his study on Kant's theoretical philosophy; see, for instance, *Categories of the Temporal*, trans. Sibylle Salewski (Cambridge and London: Harvard University Press, 2012), 73–4: "I have to able to think the same thought at a different time. And this I can do if I can think it *by means of this other time*. There is necessarily a time at which I think it, but no time at which I necessarily think it. The thoughts expressed with situational sentences break free from the given time."

23 Similar observations were made by some commentators close to Meillassoux as well; cf. Ray Brassier, *Nihil Unbound: Enlightenment and Extinction* (Hampshire and New York: Palgrave, 2007), 59.

24 It is not clear, for instance, how exactly Meillassoux understands the *necessity* of correlation, which is supposed to characterize the standpoint of subjectivist metaphysics. Does it refer to the impossibility of its inexistence or to the impossibility of its being different? Further, it is not clear how exactly we are supposed to understand the grounds of this necessity, that is, what are the requirements for their validity.

25 In this respect, Meillassoux relies on Kant's use of the concept of noumenon in the negative sense, as a boundary concept; cf. Kant, *KrV*, B310–11/A256: "The concept of a noumenon is therefore merely a *boundary concept*, in order to limit the pretension of sensibility, and therefore only of negative use." In Kant, of course, this implies that it is forbidden to use the concept of noumenon in a positive sense, as a concept of an existing thing, and, in general, that for us no proposition referring to things in themselves can ever attain the distinctive status of cognition. However, the real question is what status to ascribe to statements such as the following (ibid., Bxxvi–xxvii): "Yet the reservation must also be well noted, that even if we cannot *cognize* these same objects as things in themselves, we at least must be able to *think* them as things in themselves. For otherwise there would follow the absurd proposition that there is an appearance without anything that appears." Meillassoux basically wants to justify this proposition.

26 Meillassoux, *After Finitude*, 56.

27 Ibid.

28 Ibid., 59.

29 Ibid., 58.

30 Cf. Kant, *KrV*, Bxxvi, n.

31 Hegel, *Phenomenology*, 11.

32 For a convincing demonstration showing that Meillassoux's mode of argumentation effectively (and inadmissibly) bears all the hallmarks of the dialectical method, see Aljoša Kravanja, "Po končnosti in dialektika," *Problemi* 48, no. 4/5 (2010): 139–60.

33 How access to knowledge can be spoiled by the apparent thoroughness itself, is well described by Hegel; see Hegel, *Phenomenology*, 50: "In fact, this [apparent thoroughness masking itself as] fear presupposes something, and in fact presupposes

a great deal, as the truth, and it bases its scruples and its conclusions on what itself ought to be tested in advance as to whether or not it is the truth. This fear presupposes *representations* of cognizing as an *instrument* and as a *medium*, and it also presupposes a *difference between our own selves and this cognition*; but above all it presupposes that the absolute stands *on one side* and that *cognition stands on the other* for itself, and separated from the absolute, thought cognition is nevertheless something real; that is, it presupposes that cognition, which, by being outside of the absolute, is indeed also outside of the truth, is nevertheless truthful; an assumption through which that which calls itself the fear of error gives itself away to be known rather as the fear of the truth."

34 F. W. J. Schelling, *System der gesammten Philosophie*, in *Sämtliche Werke* (Stuttgart: Cotta 1856–61), I/6, 137.

35 In his book review, Peter Hallward commented that "Meillassoux's acausal ontology, in other words, includes no account of an actual process of transformation or development.... His insistence that anything might happen can only amount to an insistence on the bare possibility of radical change" (Peter Hallward, "Anything is possible," *Radical Philosophy*, no. 152 [2008]: 51–7). After making this statement, Hallward was harshly criticized for trying "to extend the book's arguments beyond the proper domain of their application and then to hold Meillassoux accountable for the resulting difficulties of the argument" (Nathan Brown, "The Speculative and the Specific: On Hallward and Meillassoux," in Bryant et al., *The Speculative Turn* [Melbourne: re.press, 2011], 146.) This may well be a correct observation. But it is equally true that Meillassoux's project must have certain consequences, and if he has not managed to make them explicit, this is still a sign of weakness, not strength.

36 To illustrate the problem, we can refer to Meillassoux's comment (see Meillassoux, *After Finitude*, 33) that such a refusal of the real necessity furnishes the minimal condition of every critique of ideology, insofar as it always strives to show how the present state of affairs is not necessary. We would affirm the very opposite. The first step in every possible critique of ideology should consist in the attempt to relate the dominant ideology back to the structural constraints of the existing social order, and in this sense, precisely, to demonstrate its necessity. Only once this preliminary step has been made, can the other one follow, consisting in the attempt to change the very conditions that produced the state in question and its concomitant ideology. This is what makes all the difference between scientific and utopian socialism!

37 Meillassoux puts high hopes in mathematics. This is curious enough: from an advocate of the absolute in itself it is unlikely to expect that he would derive knowledge of the world from a science *a priori*. Moreover, mathematics seems to have an additional discursive function in Meillassoux, the function of the "de-subjectivization of sense" and the "de-pathetization of philosophy," as analyzed in Badiou by Simoniti; see Jure Simoniti, "Matematizacija biti in patos dogodka," *Filozofski vestnik* 31, no. 3 (2010): 31–44.

38 See Graham Harman, "Quentin Meillassoux: A New French Philosopher," *Philosophy Today*, 51, no. 1 (2007): 115.

39 For a detailed examination of the problem of causality in German philosophy of the eighteenth century, see Eric Watkins, *Kant and the Metaphysics of Causality* (Cambridge: Cambridge University Press, 2005).

40 Cf. David Hume, *A Treatise of Human Nature*, ed. Peter H. Nidditch (Oxford: Clarendon Press, 1992), 253: "The mind is a kind of theatre, where several perceptions successively make their appearance; pass, repass, glide away, and mingle in an infinite variety of postures and situations."

41 This was justly emphasized by Kant; see *KrV*, B230/A187: "Now on this persistence there is also grounded a correction of the concept of *alteration*. Arising and perishing are not *alterations* of that which arises or perishes. *Alteration* is a way of existing that succeeds another way of existing of the very same object. Hence everything that is altered is lasting, and only its *state switches*."

42 Meillassoux's conception of being comes rather close to the view of Roquentin, the leading character in Jean-Paul Sartre's *Nausea*, for whom objects slip out of their natural web of relations, revealing themselves in their bare being. There is an important difference between the two, however. Whereas in Sartre the de-connection of objects evidently takes place as a retreat from the objective world, as already constituted, in Meillassoux it is supposed to describe the original state of the world. In this respect, oddly enough, Sartre's Roquentin seems more convincing than Meillassoux Quentin.

43 To extend the analogy with Hume, the problem with the space of hyper-chaotic objects seems to be similar to the question formulated by Hume in relation to the nature of mind; see Hume, *A Treatise*, 253.

44 Meillassoux, *After Finitude*, 24.

45 Ibid.

46 For a similar point, see, again, Rödl, *The Categories of the Temporal*, 74–5. Both the concept of the subject in general and the transcendental subject in particular are notoriously ridden with paradoxes, grounded in the subject's self-relating structure and non-fixed mode of being. Indeed, from the standpoint of traditional metaphysics, the conception of the subject is utterly unacceptable since it infringes on its most fundamental postulates of rationality. Nevertheless, we are obliged to accept it due to the necessity of traditional conceptuality itself, since it is only by accepting it that we can solve the contradictions that are both unavoidable und unsolvable within its premises. Meillassoux's reluctance to accept the concept of the subject might be inspired, at least partially, by his apprehension that the concept of the subject would undermine the certainty of scientific propositions. However, this kind of fear is redundant. It is our good fortune that Hegel already introduced the distinction between *Wahrheit* and *Richtigkeit*, providing a sufficiently safe zone for science in its difference to philosophy, thus suggesting a possible solution to the problem Meillassoux raised through the notion of the ancestral. For a succinct presentation of the argument, see Jure Simoniti, *The Untruth of Reality: The Unacknowledged Realism of Modern Philosophy* (Lanham, MD: Lexington Books, 2016), 38–43.

47 Putnam designed an argument in favor of access to the in-itself that, in spite of its eccentricity—we are supposed to imagine that we are not humans made of flesh and bones, living in the middle of the world as we know it, but effectively brains in a vat that have the same sensory input as real humans and that therefore wrongly think they are real humans living in the real world—is in fact similar to Meillassoux's. Cf. Hilary Putnam, *Reason, Truth and History* (Cambridge: Cambridge University Press, 1981), 15.

48 See, for instance, Ferraris's acerbic remarks on the alleged political radicalism of postmodern thinkers: "Given that to really be Marxist involves too many renouncements on the personal and practical level . . ., the intellectuals decided to be Nietzscheans or Heideggerians, claiming that in theses figures of thought, which are perfectly compatible with a bourgeois form of life, a way of revolution transpires which is much more profound and radical than that of Marx." (Maurizio Ferraris, *Emergenza* [Torino: Einaudi, 2016], 82.)

49 Ferraris, *Emergenza*, XIII.
50 *Groundhog Day* (1993), [Film] Dir. Harold Ramis, USA: Columbia Pictures. The movie is about Phil (Bill Murray), who, for some reason, is trapped in time, living through the same day over and over again (keeping track of his previous episodes). At a certain point, he tells his colleague Rita (Andie MacDowell) about it, who, of course, always lives this day for the first time and finds the story crazy. He tries to convince her by showing her that he knows everything about every person present in the bar. Rita first accuses him of playing God, and then, bewildered, asks: "This is some kind of a trick?" To this, Phil replies: "Maybe the real God uses tricks. Maybe he's not omniscient. Maybe he's just been around for so long he knows everything."

8

Meta-transcendentalism and Error-First Ontology: The Cases of Gilbert Simondon and Catherine Malabou

Adrian Johnston

I The anatomy of the spiritual subject is the key to the anatomy of natural substance: transcendental materialism as critical-dialectical naturalism

For a number of years now, I have developed and defended a materialist theory of subjectivity under the heading of "transcendental materialism." The present piece gets underway in its first section here with me explaining why I have come to consider the descriptive label "critical-dialectical naturalism" synonymous with, if not preferable to, this heading. Recasting transcendental materialism as (also) critical-dialectical naturalism signals several things. Starting with the term "critical," I embrace an idealist method (although not an idealist ontology) by beginning with spontaneous subjectivity. I do so with an eye to the sorts of epistemological requirements imposed by Kantian critique on any future metaphysics. Then, the term "dialectical" designates a procedure of moving beyond subjectivity taken as a starting point through delineating and mobilizing intra-subjective antagonisms, conflicts, and the like (i.e., dialectical dimensions of subjects identified by German idealism and psychoanalysis especially). In short, I dialectically reverse-engineer an ontology of pre/non-subjective nature out of a theory of more-than-natural subjectivity—this being the crux of critical-dialectical naturalism.

This chapter is a sequel to, and builds upon, another piece by me entitled "Whither the Transcendental?: Hegel, Analytic Philosophy, and the Prospects of a Realist Transcendentalism Today."[1] This prior piece intervenes in long-running debates, ones arising already between Immanuel Kant and his contemporaries in the late-eighteenth century, about transcendentalism. Therein, I put into conversation three orientations deeply invested in controversies about the transcendental: German idealism and its critics (especially F. H. Jacobi, G. E. Schulze, J. G. Fichte, F. W. J. Schelling, and G. W. F. Hegel); Analytic epistemology, philosophy of science, and Kant scholarship from the mid-twentieth century through today (particularly P. F. Strawson, Barry Stroud, Quassim

Cassam, and Christopher Peacocke); and recent Continental metaphysics (as varyingly represented by, for instance, Gilles Deleuze, Alain Badiou, Slavoj Žižek, and the so-called "speculative realists").

At this peculiar three-way intersection involving permutations of, to paraphrase Sigmund Freud, transcendentalism and its discontents, I plead for the feasibility and value of decoupling the transcendental from Kantian subjectivist transcendental idealism. Against contemporary European calls to abandon transcendentalism altogether, I forge an alliance between the superficially strange bedfellows of, on the one hand, Hegel as constructing a de-idealized, anti-subjectivist transcendental and, on the other hand, Strawson and his ilk as arguing for a promising, workable marriage between transcendentalism and realism. In the process, I address the forms of skepticism both Hegel and Strawson et al. are confronted with in their efforts to save the transcendental from transcendental idealism.

Most importantly for the present chapter, "Whither the Transcendental?" puts forward a necessary supplement to the philosophical sub-discipline of epistemology. To be more precise, I advance a meta-transcendental, genetic-diachronic "error-first ontology" (EFO) as a precursor of and condition for any transcendental, static-synchronic epistemology preoccupied with knowing truly. Before the issue of the thinking of minded subjects achieving knowledge of the being of worldly objects, there is the matter of how subjects susceptible to the false, the illusory, and the like come into existence in the first place. Put differently, the very fact that there is epistemology, that knowledge itself is a problem, presupposes something in need of positing, namely, an ontology containing within itself an account of what makes possible the problem of knowing as a problem to be overcome. Humans must first ontologically become alienated or detached from the pre/non-human Real in order to be faced with the epistemological challenge of, as subjects, bridging the chasm between themselves and objects.[2] The second section of this intervention situates EFO with respect to the critical-dialectical naturalism described in the first section here.

Yet, to clarify something not (or at least not sufficiently) clarified by me in "Whither the Transcendental?" there is a sense in which I remain faithful to a certain aspect of the spirit of Kantian transcendental idealism. Specifically, this would be what arguably amounts to this idealism's proposal of epistemology as first philosophy. On the one hand, I obviously do not accept epistemology as first philosophy insofar as, in a Hegelian fashion, I place ontology/metaphysics prior to and beneath it as more foundational. But, on the other hand, the larger philosophical framework within which I operate—a transcendental materialism I have taken to equating with a critical-dialectical naturalism[3]—accepts at the procedural level the critical-epistemological imperative of Kantian idealism on beginning philosophical inquiries with and from the theoretical and practical spontaneity of *Cogito*-like transcendental subjectivity.

Karl Marx, in his mature critique of political economy, insists upon combining an idealist methodology (i.e., a Hegelian-style logical assembling process moving, within the ideal order of thinking, from abstract categories to ever-more concrete instances) with a materialist edifice (i.e., historical materialism's insistence on the priority, within the real order of being, of concrete instances over abstract categories).[4] For this Marx, a procedural/methodological idealism at the level of epistemology is anything but incompatible with a materialist metaphysics at the level of ontology—so long as one remains careful to distinguish between the orders of ideal thinking and real being. As the first of the eleven 1845 "Theses on Feuerbach" already urges,[5] a viable materialism (as historical and/or dialectical) is obligated to assimilate into itself core aspects of idealist theories of subjectivities.[6]

Following in Marx's footsteps, transcendental materialism as critical-dialectical naturalism likewise sublates (as *aufhebt*) idealism (transcendental idealism in particular) within materialism. I can render this appreciable through unpacking the label "critical-dialectical naturalism." The term "critical" signifies a couple of key dimensions of this position. First and quite obviously, it refers to Kantian critique. The critical side of Kant's transcendental idealism epitomizes a modern epistemological demand, originating with René Descartes (although differently and to a lesser degree also with Francis Bacon), for grounding knowledge-claims on foundations resistant to various forms of skepticism (with Kant approving of Bacon's methodology and its accompanying epistemology[7]). In the varying guises of Descartes's *Cogito, ergo sum*, Kant's "transcendental unity of apperception," Fichte's "self-positing I," and Hegel's logical "thinking about thinking," the spirit of epistemological modernity is paradigmatically represented by critique in the form of a methodological necessity of embarking on philosophical inquiries beginning with and from inquiring subjectivity itself. A dictum along the lines of "no matter where you start, there you are" arguably holds even for the most radical of skeptics who might want, despite the performative contradiction involved, to deny even this.

Accordingly, transcendental materialism as critical-dialectical naturalism, in line with the modern epistemological spirit of critique, proceeds in its order of thinking from subject to substance (as Hegel would put it). Starting with the *Es gibt* or *Il y a* of subjectivity, I ask: Given this "there is," how must pre/non-subjective being be such as to permit and make possible this subjective procedural starting point? Asked differently, what sort of ontology of nature does the positing of subjectivity presuppose? I raise these queries in tandem with three interlinked lines of argumentation (laid out by me on numerous other occasions): One, subjects, at the levels of natural history, phylogeny, and ontogeny, emerge out of pre/non-subjective being(s); Two, this pre/non-subjective ontological dimension should be identified as "nature"; And, three, emergent subjective dimensions are non-epiphenomenal, causally efficacious realities unto themselves not to be reduced to or eliminated in favor of a-subjective nature alone.

The second significance of the adjective "critical" for my stance is its association with Kant's ban on any and every recourse to the suspect epistemological power of intellectual intuition. Amongst the "big four" of German idealism, this prohibition pits Kant and Hegel on one side against Fichte and Schelling on the other side. The latter two indeed help themselves, in the teeth of Kant's critical prohibition, to versions of a purported direct and immediate insight into the Absolute itself. By contrast, Hegel's philosophical maturation during his Jena period, culminating with the 1807 *Phenomenology of Spirit*, involves in no small part his abandonment of intellectual intuition and replacement of it with dialectics as first systematically deployed in the *Phenomenology*. These Hegelian moves are inspired specifically by Kant's "Transcendental Dialectic" in the *Critique of Pure Reason*.

Earlier during Hegel's stay in Jena, in 1802, he writes that, "we need a roundabout way [*eines Umwegs*] to sneak the Absolute in [*um es einzuschwärzen*]"[8] (although this line occurs in a text written in collaboration with Schelling, Hegel almost certainly is responsible for it). Of course, this "roundabout way" turns out to be, just a few years later, the historically and textually drawn-out "way of despair" (*der Weg des Verzweiflung*),[9] the long and painful dialectical detour (*Umweg*), of the entirety of the *Phenomenology* itself. That said, the just-quoted line from Hegel's introduction to the *Kritisches Journal der Philosophie* he co-edits with Schelling can be interpreted as, among other things, Hegel "sneaking in" (*einzuschwärzen*) a criticism of Schelling's epistemology (or lack thereof) within the pages of their collaborative project. Only subsequently, in wounded reaction to the lines of the *Phenomenology*'s preface about the "night in which all cows are black"[10] and supposedly knowing the Absolute "like a shot from a pistol,"[11] does Schelling come to register the conflict between his and Hegel's *modi operandi*.

Yet, the 1802 statement above conveys Hegel's straddling of the epistemological divide between, on the one hand, Kantian critique and, on the other hand, Fichtean and Schellingian intellectual intuition. Like Fichte and Schelling, Hegel refuses to confine speculation within Kant's critical "limits of possible experience," to de-absolutize and deflate philosophy thusly. But, like Kant, Hegel repudiates as epistemologically dubitable any and every pretense to be able to instantaneously leap at will into the Absolute as an abruptly accessible starting point for speculative investigations.

Hence, as the *Phenomenology* first exhibits in excruciating detail, "absolute knowing" (*das absolute Wissen*) is arrived at solely in and through the protracted and arduous process of the philosopher "tarrying with the negative."[12] Specifically, this is the negativity of all not-yet-absolute figures/shapes of consciousness immanently critiquing themselves and thereby forming the "pathway of *doubt*" (*der Weg des Zweifels*)[13] eventually leading to the beginning of dialectical-speculative Science *als Wissenschaft* ("To help bring philosophy closer to the form of Science [*Wissenschaft*], to the goal where it can lay aside the title '*love* of knowing' [*der* Liebe *zum Wissen*] and be *actual* knowing [*wirkliches Wissen*]—that is what I have set myself to do"[14]). Hegelian dialectics is a means of conforming to the epistemological strictures of Kantian critique (in particular, its problematizations of and prohibitions on intellectual intuition) while rebelling against Kantian transcendental idealism's anti-realist, subjectivist barring of access to the absoluteness of *das Reale an sich*.

For me, following in Hegel's footsteps, post-critical philosophy likewise involves eschewing appeals to anything along the lines of intellectual intuition. Examples of what is being repudiated here would include: before Kant, the unmediated, instantaneous insights into the substantial-in-itself claimed by the rationalist metaphysicians of the European continent; and, after Kant, the epistemologically insouciant assertions about the a-subjective Real put forward by such current orientations as "new materialism" and speculative realism. These insights and assertions, in their differences with each other (for instance, those between Baruch Spinoza and G. W. Leibniz in the seventeenth century or between, for instance, Deleuzians, neo-Schellingians, speculative materialists, and/or object-oriented ontologists nowadays), are readily vulnerable to being played off against one another and thereby cast into serious doubt. Such maneuvers of playing-off indeed are carried out by ancient equipollence skepticism, Humean modern empiricist skepticism, and both Kantian and Hegelian dialectics alike.

Moreover, inevitable and crucial questions can and should be raised about, first, from where the knowledge-claims of intellectual intuition are made as well as, second and relatedly, what ontologically/metaphysically makes possible the very locus of these same knowledge-claims. Failing to ask and answer the second line of questioning in particular more often than not results in lapsing into what Marx, again in the first of his "Theses on Feuerbach," criticizes as purely "contemplative" stances. These are rendered incomplete by their inability to account for themselves, for how they have been arrived at within and out of the very reality they purport to describe.

Despite the preceding, the rationalist substance metaphysicians, Hegel, the new materialists, the speculative realists, and I nonetheless share in common certain antisubjectivist ontological ambitions. So, what is the epistemologically conscientious, critique-meeting alternative to the "abracadabra!" magic and mystery of intellectually intuitive communing with the *an sich*? As I already underscored, Hegel replaces intellectual intuition with dialectics as the motor driving philosophical speculation. He all too frequently is wrongly accused of being the epitome of the arrogant, know-it-all philosopher legislating in an *a priori* manner over everything under the sun from the complacent comfort of his armchair. But, against this falsifying caricature, Hegel's sprawling System shows his speculative dialectics to be bound up with, fed by and dependent upon, non-philosophical forms of knowledge, experience, and consciousness (as well as other philosophies). By sharp contrast with the cheap and easy instant gratifications of an intellectual intuition bypassing all things *a posteriori*, dialectical processes laboriously work in and through the more-than-philosophical materials also dealt with by the full range of human disciplines.

In this Hegelian spirit, the epistemology and methodology of critical-dialectical naturalism *qua* critical similarly places the philosophical, including itself, in a position of being parasitic upon (Badiou would say "conditioned by") the extra-philosophical— albeit without simply collapsing the distinction between the philosophical and the extra-philosophical. The dialectical mill needs grist in order to produce anything. For me, this grist is provided by the empirical and/or experimental findings of bodies of knowledge ranging from the natural sciences through history, economics, and psychoanalysis, among other fields. Unlike intellectual intuition, these various bodies of knowledge implicitly and/or explicitly hold themselves accountable to defensible epistemological criteria. As critical, critical-dialectical naturalism prefers to pass through these disciplines, rather than sit back and indulge in undisciplined speculation. In so doing, its speculations are tempered by the frictions generated via its contacts with the evidence and facts divulged by its interdisciplinary partners.

Insofar as Kantian critique and Hegelian dialectics are closely related for Hegel himself, I already have provided some indications of the significance of the adjective "dialectical" in the label "critical-dialectical naturalism." However, a few further clarifications are warranted at this juncture. To begin with, the dialectics deployed by my position are immanent-critical interpretations of the just-mentioned extra-philosophical disciplines.

Arguably, even the most empirical of extra-philosophical disciplines cannot avoid resting upon a set of presupposed or posited metaphysical commitments. Such commitments open these disciplines to philosophical interventions. As exemplified by the narrated recollections of the various *Gestalten* by Hegel in the 1807 *Phenomenology*, the dialectical philosopher can and does put to work the spontaneous philosophies of more-than-philosophical fields, theories, and practices.

The Hegelian philosopher makes explicit the implicit contradictions, inconsistencies, and the like both: one, between the categories and concepts of the spontaneous metaphysics necessarily accompanying each and every given non-philosophical body of knowledge; as well as, two, between the non-empirical (i.e., metaphysical) and empirical dimensions of these same bodies of knowledge. In so doing, the dialectical philosopher puts each extra-philosophical discipline in its appropriate place as contributing towards, but not monopolizing on its own, the building of a larger overarching metaphysical framework. This framework thereby arises from, while nonetheless remaining irreducible to, its ensemble of more *a posteriori* sources providing both epistemological legitimacy and inspiration for well-grounded (rather than capriciously arbitrary) speculation.

An additional aspect of the dialectics of critical-dialectical naturalism, one bound up with my above-mentioned idealist procedure of starting with/from subjectivity, is its role in reverse-engineering, within the order of ideal thinking (as distinct from that of real being), substance out of subject (with the order of real being exhibiting the opposite movement from substance to subject). Already in the mid-1790s, the trio of young friends Friedrich Hölderlin, Schelling, and Hegel raise fundamental questions and objections regarding the subjectivist transcendental idealisms of Kant and Fichte. In such texts as "On Judgment and Being" (Hölderlin) from 1795 and "The Earliest System-Program of German Idealism" (Hegel, Schelling, …?) from 1796, an anti-subjectivist thesis, one putting ontology back before epistemology as first philosophy, crystallizes as a point of consensus for this trio: Even if one begins with subjectivity for compelling epistemological reasons, one cannot forever stay within subjectivity for ultimately unavoidable ontological reasons.

Of course, the fateful choices of names for and further determinations of whatever lies beneath and beyond the subject of Kant's and Fichte's transcendental idealisms (Being, Identity, Indifference, Nature, Spirit, Substance, etc.) mark significant intellectual differences between Hölderlin, Schelling, and Hegel. In the cases of the latter two, their post-1790s intellectual itineraries exhibit each of them undergoing changes of mind about the names and determinations of this Beneath/Beyond of subjectivity. That said, Hölderlin, Schelling, and Hegel concur, despite their differences, that the issue of real genesis is a major problem for the sort of static subjectivism championed by Kant and Fichte.

From the early 1800s onward, Hegel in particular elaborates and hones a post-Kantian dialectical reverse-engineering of the substantial out of the subjective in ways informing my critical-dialectical naturalism. Two features of Hegel's corpus exemplify this. First, the evolution of his mature thinking runs from the *Phenomenology of Spirit* through the *Science of Logic* and on into the *Encyclopedia of the Philosophical Sciences*. Setting aside scholarly exegetical debates about whether or how the *Phenomenology* remains crucial to the mature Hegel after 1807, Hegel's philosophical trajectory, as a matter of history-of-philosophy fact, moves from the subjects of pre/non-philosophical figures/shapes of consciousness (*Phänomenologie*) to the trans-subjective dimensions of absolute idealism and the foundations of its *Realphilosophie* (*Logik* and *Naturphilosophie*) and back to the *Gestalten* of spiritual mindedness and like-mindedness (*Geistesphilosophie*).

What does the architectonic sequence of the Hegelian System indicate in relation to my endeavors? Answering this requires a bit of explanation. To begin with, both Phenomenology and Logic, as Hegel conceives these philosophical sub-disciplines, are designed to meet the epistemological demands of Kantian critique. Phenomenology clears the way for Logic (with the latter as the start of Hegel's System proper) by traversing the immanent (self-)critiques of all other perspectives that actually do or potentially could compete with the presuppositionless position from which Logic's pure "thinking about thinking" initiates itself.

This thus-initiated Logic then proceeds to unfurl a web of fundamental categories that themselves eventually prove to form not only epistemological conditions of possibility for thinking and knowing, but also ontological conditions of possibility for being and existing. The latter conditions get actualized only in and through the natural and spiritual Reals of the Philosophy of the Real, Reals in relation to which the logical categories are always-already immanent and inseparable (with Hegel strongly preferring Aristotle to Plato and correspondingly rejecting anything along the lines of classical metaphysical realism). At the Logic's end *qua* a closing of a circle returning to its opening, the category of Being at the opening of the Logic reveals itself to be, in truth and hindsight, something more than (just) thinking, namely, the being of pre/non-subjective Nature (first in the guise of the objectively real, rather than merely subjectively ideal as per Kant, categories of space and time).

The immediately preceding leads into the second feature of Hegel's corpus informing the dialectical aspects of critical-dialectical naturalism. At various points in the *Phenomenology*, *Science of Logic*, and *Encyclopedia*, Hegel deploys multifaceted (immanent) criticisms of Kant's theoretical and practical philosophies, including the anti-realist subjectivism of Kantian (as well as Fichtean) transcendental idealism. As regards Kant's and Fichte's subjective idealisms, Hegel, to cut a long story short, reveals their anti-realisms to be untenable by their own lights, to rely upon images and notions undoing or nullifying themselves by virtue of their inner inconsistencies and inadequacies.

But, in good post-critical fashion, Hegel introduces his robustly realist Philosophy of the Real only after both, within Phenomenology, eliminating all alternative presuppositions and posits as well as, within Logic, initially setting out to deduce non-dogmatically all categories with a transcendental status relative to thinking. However, in the logical process of thinking reflecting upon the categorial conditions for its own possibility, thinking discovers that it cannot reduce or confine everything to or within itself alone. Hegel's anti-subjectivism is the outcome of subjectivism's self-critique. Hence, his realism is post-, rather than pre-, critical.

The immanent criticisms of Kantian- and Fichtean-style subjective idealism in the Logic trigger a peeling apart of transcendentalism from such idealism. Through this separation, a transcendental dimension (represented by Logic) compatible with a realism (represented by the Philosophy of the Real) comes into view. Additionally, the earliest and most basic levels of the Real are natural as per Philosophy of Nature.

Before finally explaining the particular naturalism of critical-dialectical naturalism, I should point out that the architectonic trajectory of Hegel's System, as I have just glossed it, involves not only the movement from subject to substance, but also the complementary reverse. More precisely, after passing through the "substances" formed by the logical and natural categories (as more-than-subjective and pre/non-subjective respectively), the third and final part of the *Encyclopedia*, the Philosophy of Spirit, returns to subjectivity, including circumnavigating to certain *Gestalten* from the *Phenomenology*.

In moving from subject to substance and back again, Hegel, on the one hand, rises to the modern epistemological requirements epitomized by Kantian critique (in moving from phenomenological subjects to the "substances" of logical and natural categories) while simultaneously, on the other hand, putting idealist epistemology in its circumscribed place by situating it within a wider set of de-idealized natural and cultural ontological conditions (in going back again to spiritual subjectivities both individual and collective, both mentally internal and extra-mentally external). Hegel thereby respects what critique commands within the ideal order of thinking while at the same time indicating, against the subjectivist transcendental idealism associated with critique, that the ideal order of thinking inverts the real order of being. This Hegelian lesson is taken to heart by critical-dialectical naturalism.

I at last come to the noun "naturalism" as modified by the hyphenated adjective "critical-dialectical." As I noted at the outset here, the label "critical-dialectical naturalism" is intended by me as a further clarification of what I have in mind with the phrase "transcendental materialism." And, as I have insisted on multiple occasions, any *bona fide* materialism also necessarily involves naturalism. In other words, an anti-naturalist materialism is a contradiction-in-terms.[15]

This insistence that materialism cannot be without some naturalism, combined with what I have spelled out above in connection with the adjectives "critical" and "dialectical," commits me to grounding a materialist theory of *Cogito*-like transcendental subjectivity in an ontology of nature. In this ontological sense, nature would be the name for being as both prior and irreducible to any and all subjects. It is the a-subjective Real out of which subjects happen to arise. However, as per the hybrid critical-dialectical sensibilities of my qualified naturalism, this ontology of nature must be, at the epistemological level, reverse-engineered out of (the theory of) subjectivity.

Furthermore, I deliberately retain the modern associations of the word "nature" with the natural sciences. This nature of modernity is the region, the set of domains, of the Real falling within the explanatory jurisdictions of such *a posteriori* disciplines as physics, chemistry, and biology. My gesture of tying fundamental ontology to such ontic disciplines not only deliberately defies anything in the vein of an insufficiently dialectical Heideggerian conception of ontological difference—it also dovetails, as does Hegelian dialectics, with Kantian critique's barring of intellectual intuitions of any sort whatsoever.

The natural sciences, specifically as empirical and/or experimental, place sobering checks on (without for all that stifling) philosophical speculation, up to and including fundamental ontology. By tethering the ontological to the natural, with the latter as it reveals itself via *a posteriori* knowledge-practices capable of providing intersubjectively recognizable reasons for their claims, no *a priori* flights of intuitive fancy are allowed. The epistemological weight of such interdisciplinary anchoring prevents drifting off into dark mists imagined to cloak ineffable Being or beings.

By way of summary, the label "critical-dialectical naturalism" reflects, condensed into a single phrase, transcendental materialism's combination of an idealist epistemological method/procedure (to which is tied an idealism-inspired conception of subjectivity) with a realist and materialist ontology of nature. Especially in the context of contemporary Continental metaphysics and political theory, the naturalistic dimension of transcendental materialism sets it apart from most of what presently passes itself off as materialist. What is more, the phrase "critical-dialectical naturalism" captures much of what I am after: a materialism, informed by the natural sciences, of an auto-denaturalizing (i.e., self-dialecticizing) nature dramatically transforming itself in and through its more-than-natural human offspring—a materialism whose objective ontology of pre- and non-subjective nature is arrived at through a reverse-engineering process beginning with(in) this nature's immanently-generated denaturalized subjects (hence the adjective "critical").

At this juncture, it would be appropriate to ask: How is transcendental materialism as critical-dialectical naturalism related to error-first ontology? In the next section of this intervention, I will address precisely this query.

II Being human is erring: better an ontology of stupidity than a stupid epistemology

In the fourth and final section of "Whither the Transcendental?" I delineate the core features of error-first ontology.[16] The fundamental mystery, especially for a materialist or naturalist, is not how (if at all) human thinkers come to have true knowledge of things-in-themselves. Instead, if sentient and sapient subjectivity is immanent (even if also irreducible) to the a-subjective Real, then the genuine enigma is how subjects arise and persist in detaching themselves from their pre/non-subjective ontological grounds. From this perspective, the human capacity for falsity and ignorance unmoored from objectivities is at least as important to explain as the capacity for truth and knowledge somehow or other moored to them (this counter-emphasis runs as much against the industry of Analytic epistemology after Edmund Gettier as it does speculative realism). I even would go so far as to claim that it is more important to explain, since, arguably, without such loss, detachment, and the like, i.e., the fall into errancy, there simply is no subject to (re)connect with being(s) *an sich*.

In "Whither the Transcendental?" I focus on Analytic epistemology as the main foil for EFO. Here, apropos speculative realism, I can take Quentin Meillassoux's approach as a foil. For Meillassoux, the top philosophical priority after the "Kantian catastrophe"[17] is to figure out how to get from the idealist/anti-realist subjective *Innenwelt* back to the realist/materialist objective *Umwelt*. Meillassouxian speculation is obsessed with rejoining what he baptizes "the *great outdoors*."[18]

Without diving into the details of Meillassoux's philosophy—I have done so at length on previous occasions[19]—suffice it for my present purposes to note that EFO involves an inversion of the Meillassouxian problematic, an inversion asserted as prior to (and even making possible) this problematic. That is to say, before asking how one moves from inside to outside, one must first ask, at least if one shares some of Meillassoux's own materialist commitments, how the outside produces out of itself this very inside in the first place. On one occasion, Meillassoux expresses astonishment at the possibility that the objective *an sich* might really resemble the subjective *für sich*— "We cannot go outside our skin to know what is out there. Maybe the irony would be that this world is in itself exactly as it is for us—wow!"[20] If this is the wonder in which Meillassoux's speculative philosophy begins, it is the exact opposite of what induces question-provoking wonderment for a genuinely materialist immanentism. The latter must inquire instead: How does pre-subjective material being come to erect within itself the prison of (transcendental) subjectivity from which someone like Meillassoux wishes to escape? In a way, figuring out how to reconstruct this prison in theory is already to escape it.

This sort of questioning lies at the heart of transcendental materialism as critical-dialectical naturalism with its error-first ontology. Likewise, certain of Jacques Lacan's turns to topology, in which the pure externality of a lone surface generates interior spaces through movements of folding, can be interpreted as addressing this topic. As will be seen in the third section below, Gilbert Simondon's philosophy of individuation has recourse to things topological for exactly these reasons.

As I argue in "Whither the Transcendental?" any non-idealistic, anti-subjectivist immanentist/monist philosophical project presupposing a subjectivity distinct from, and in need of a bridge to, objectivity must be led in the consequent end to posit the real genesis of this very subjectivity and, along with it, the gap between it and objectivity. Certain things must already have transpired at the level of being in order for knowing to be a problem for thinking. This can be connected to a thesis according to which it is impossible to have an epistemology entirely without a corresponding ontology.

More precisely, a static-synchronic epistemology of transcendental subjectivity must be embedded within a grounding genetic-diachronic ontology of meta-transcendental objectivity. In the case of critical-dialectical naturalism, this objectivity would be pre/non-subjective nature—specifically, a contingently self-denaturalizing nature just so happening to have eventuated in sentient and sapient human beings. For transcendental materialism as critical-dialectical naturalism, if the thinking subject is transcendental in the sense of instantiating conditions of possibility for knowing, then pre/non-thinking material nature is meta-transcendental in the sense of constituting in turn the conditions of possibility for the very existence of such a transcendental subject as emergent (and not, as per subjective idealisms, always-already given). One might characterize this as a meta-transcendentalism of anthropogenesis, of the becoming-transcendental-subject of the human animal (an account even Kant himself felt compelled to flirt with in his *Anthropology from a Pragmatic Point of View*[21]).

In the final stretch of "Whither the Transcendental?" I invoke both Martin Heidegger and Deleuze. In particular, I make Heidegger's "ontological errancy" and Deleuze's "transcendental stupidity" cross-resonate with each other as recent historical precursors of EFO. I will return to Deleuze as part of my treatment of Simondon in the next section. For now, I ought to underscore an important difference between EFO's and Heidegger's conceptions of what the latter calls "errancy" (*die Irre*). This difference has everything to do with my reliance upon psychoanalysis and corresponding rejection of core features of phenomenology. In addition, there is my above-mentioned Hegelian aversion to sharp distinctions between the ontological and the ontic. Heideggerian ontological difference seems to depend upon something akin to intellectual intuition (such as the supposed romantic genius of "poetic thinking") *vis-à-vis* Being apart from beings.

Heidegger's phenomenological ontology associates the fundamental being of humans with a "clearing" or "opening" for Being itself as ontological rather than merely ontic. *Dasein* is the site for the manifestation of Being, for the latter's self-disclosure. Of a piece with this, the discussion of errancy in "On the Essence of Truth" proposes that erring is essential to being human insofar as *Dasein* has an inherent, irresistible tendency to veer towards and fixate upon ontic beings. The non-empirical "error" here would be *Dasein*'s mistake of repeatedly turning away from ontological Being as it reveals itself in and through the light of its being-there. In its fallen, everyday inauthenticity, *Dasein* allows the ontic to obscure the ontological, beings to eclipse Being. It thereby drifts into existing in untruth, wandering away from Being's truth as its unconcealedness.[22]

Although Heidegger elevates errancy into an intrinsic attribute of *Dasein*, he nonetheless holds onto a very traditional image of human thinking as, at its most essential core, openness to the world. For him, mindedness is, at root, receptivity to the truth of Being as *aletheia* (and only secondarily a deviant sealing off of this porosity and shutting down of this responsiveness). The phenomenological field of lived experience is expressive of this presumed underlying stance of embracing the outside, the ontological "great outdoors," with arms and eyes wide open. With reference to the cliché "to err is human," first there is the human, i.e., *Dasein* as ontological clearing, and then there is the erring, i.e., *das Man* as ontic closure.

In this respect, as in many others, Freud differs from someone like Heidegger and offers a strikingly non-traditional picture of the cognitive, affective, and motivational fundaments of human subjectivity. At its ontogenetic, zero-level base, the psyche of Freudian metapsychology (as Freud's avowed alternative to metaphysics[23]) is the exact opposite of a receptive openness to external realities. The psychical apparatus of analysis exhibits, at its genetic and structural basis, a recoiling from and being closed to any and every extra-psychical Real. Humans are born fighting against being. To combine words from Jean-Paul Sartre and Lacan, humanity is a passion for ignorance. If there really is also a love of wisdom, it must struggle mightily and ceaselessly against a countervailing and perhaps more primordial inclination. This might help explain epistemology as the problem(s) of knowledge, the problematic nature of knowing, being a central concern of *philia sophia* from Plato onwards.

By Freud's lights, human beings are thrown into the world wildly hallucinating at it, entangled in spectral cobwebs of fantasies and dreams (a thesis much recent neuroscientific research appears to corroborate). Only gradually and secondarily, after repeated slaps to the face by natural and social externalities, does the fiction-loving psyche partially and grudgingly make concessions to what contradicts its impulses and illusions. Even in the wake of these half-hearted concessions, a lifelong tendency to erect barriers, dams, filters, screens, shields, and the like persists. On the analytic image of psychical life, first there is the erring, and then there is the human—namely, the humanization *qua* taming and domesticating subjection of this initial *Ur*-errancy.

Lacan's confrontations with Heidegger's depiction of truth as *aletheia* hint at some of what I am asserting. In his third seminar on the topic of the psychoses (1955–6), Lacan already discretely signals his divergence from the Heidegger who equates the essence of human beings (as *Dasein*) with openness.[24] Later, in *Seminar XIII* on *The Object of Psychoanalysis* (1965–6), Lacan maintains that analysts have more to say about *aletheia* than Heidegger himself.[25] He proceeds to specify that Freudian primal repression (*Urverdrängung*) is the "basis" (*le fond*) of *aletheia* (a claim also to be found in the *écrit* "Response to Jean Hyppolite's Commentary on Freud's 'Verneinung'"[26]). In other words, an originary closure (i.e., *Urverdrängung*), as the passionate ignorance of wanting not to know from the very beginning, precedes and enables (i.e., grounds *comme fond*) a secondary opening or clearing (i.e., Being's self-disclosure as the unconcealedness of *aletheia* within the ecstatic horizon of being-there).

Even later, in the twenty-second seminar (*R.S.I.* [1974–5]), Lacan begins another discussion of Heidegger by expressing a certain fondness for the German thinker based on their personal acquaintance. He then offers qualified praise for Heidegger, saying that, "[t]here is something in him like a presentiment" of psychoanalysis, "[b]ut, it is only a presentiment, because Freud does not interest him"[27] (a lack of interest painfully evident from Heidegger's *Zollikon Seminars*, the lone occasion when he reluctantly and uncharitably attempts to engage with a few snippets of Freud's thought). In this April 8, 1975 session of *Seminar XXII*, speaking (i.e., linguistic mediation) is said to be the errancy (*erre*) essential to the human animal as a speaking being (*parlêtre*) adrift along chains of signifiers.[28]

Still in the same session of the twenty-second seminar, Lacan, describing Heidegger's ways of speaking to him in their private conversations, insinuates that Heidegger insists excessively (along the lines of "methinks thou doth protest too much") on the worldliness, the *In-der-Welt-sein*, of a being-there involving both *Umwelt* and *Innenwelt*.[29] Lacan's contemporaneous appearance on French state television, with its explicit reference to Jakob von Uexküll (to whom Heidegger turns in his pivotal text *The Fundamental Concepts of Metaphysics* of 1929–30[30]), warns that the worldly "reality" (*réalité*) constituted by von Uexküll's *Innenwelt-Umwelt* couple is a phantasmatic, fictionalizing distortion, namely, "a grimace of the real" (*grimace du réel*).[31] This very well might be a subtle swipe at Heidegger. The likelihood of this is quite high given that the Lacan of this period pointedly derides philosophical efforts, Heidegger's included, to formulate fundamental ontologies.[32] Indeed, in . . . *ou pire* (*Seminar XIX* [1971–2]), Lacan flirts with describing ontology as "the grimace of the One" (*le grimace de l'Un*),[33] a phrase with which his 1973 "grimace of the real" clearly resonates.

Similar critical glosses on von Uexküll (and, by implication, on Heidegger too) to the one occurring in *Television* crop up in other portions of the Lacanian corpus. Following Lacan's indications, it could be claimed, against Heidegger (but with Hegel and Freud), that the human animal is, in specific ways, even poorer in world than nonhuman animals. As François Balmès, someone deeply invested in the stakes of Lacan's rapport with Heidegger, phrases things, "psychoanalysis leads" Freud "to forbid himself from admitting a spontaneous affinity of the human mind with the truth."[34] Balmès portrays this dimension of Freud's discovery as of even greater importance to Lacan.[35]

Panning back to a broader perspective, for a quasi-naturalist materialism taking on board Freud's psychoanalytic insights into an ontogenetically primary passion for stupidity—I will address Deleuzian *bêtise* in the subsequent section on Simondon—if the mind is a mirror of the world, it is, more precisely, a funhouse mirror (or a darkened glass). Sentient and sapient humanity not only is nature reflecting upon itself—it is (also) nature's inability to reflect on itself accurately, faithfully, etc. Human beings are nature's auto-distorting self-reflections, its failure to be either, at one extreme, wholly non-reflective or, at the opposite extreme, fully transparent to itself.

Such a quasi-naturalism, with its EFO, perhaps could be called a materialism of stupidity. But, it definitely is not a stupid materialism, i.e., a mechanical, reductive, and/ or eliminative one of the sort by comparison with which even V. I. Lenin prefers (intelligent) idealism.[36] What is more, in a suitably Hegelian-style convergence of opposites that Hegel himself subtly suggests in several manners, human *Ur*-errancy is a stupidity that nonetheless makes possible peculiarly human intelligence.

In Hegel's work, this shows up in such varied guises as the withdrawn "night of the world," the chaotic capriciousness of the human imagination, the sinking down to the automatic mechanics of habit, the dialectical *faux pas* of mistakes absolutely necessary for arriving at truth, and the essential roles violently inaccurate abstractions play in facilitating concepts' precise grips on thereby-known objectivities. Similarly, one might hypothesize that humans' sensory-perceptual capacities as blunted and diminished relative to many other sentient animals (i.e., the dumbness of human sentience) helps to permit the rise of more detached categorial and conceptual abstractions (i.e., the smartness of human sapience). To supplement a Hegel-inspired Kojèvian one-liner beloved by the Lacan of the 1950s, the word is able to murder the thing only because the latter already is fatally weakened, vulnerable, and oblivious.

In "Whither the Transcendental?" I promised to engage specifically with Simondon and Catherine Malabou along the lines of critical-dialectical naturalism with its EFO. Both figures, not unrelated to each other (thanks to Deleuze as an intermediary), recast transcendentalism in relation to processes of genesis: Simondon through his accounts of individuation and Malabou via her naturalization of the transcendental. The next two sections deal with Simondon's and Malabou's contributions respectively in these veins. Then, the fifth and final section asks and answers questions regarding what, if anything, remains of the more traditional conception of the transcendental in the aftermath of my and certain others' revisions of it.

III The idiocy of individuation: Simondon and the becoming-subject of substance

Deleuze himself, during his discussion of transcendental stupidity in *Difference and Repetition*, invokes the notion of individuation. Although Simondon is not mentioned explicitly as part of this invocation, his name subsequently surfaces in Deleuze's 1968 book (a book for which Lacan, as is well known, had the highest regard[37]). This later direct reference highlights Simondon's theory of individuation,[38] thus indicating that Deleuze already has him in mind while reflecting on the link between individuation and *bêtise*. Additionally, two years prior to the publication of *Difference and Repetition*, Deleuze publishes a review of Simondon's *L'individu et sa genèse physico-biologique* in the journal *Revue philosophique de la France et de l'étranger*.[39] In 1969's *Logic of Sense*, Simondon's account of individuation is mobilized again by Deleuze.[40]

What, in Deleuze's mind, is the relationship between stupidity and (Simondonian) individuation? Perhaps his clearest explanation states:

> Stupidity is neither the ground [*le fond*] nor the individual, but rather this relation in which individuation brings the ground to the surface without being able to give it form (this ground rises by means of the I, penetrating deeply into the possibility of thought and constituting the unrecognised [*le non-reconnu*] in every recognition).[41]

As Deleuze is acutely aware, the three interlinked terms "ground," "individuation," and "individual" have very precise technical senses in Simondon's framework. A full appreciation of their significances, and, hence, of Deleuze's just-quoted statement, demands a reconstruction of the Simondonian theory of individuation. I will engage in such a reconstruction momentarily.

For the time being, suffice it to say a few preliminary things in order provisionally to illuminate Deleuze's association of stupidity in his sense with Simondon's theoretical apparatus. For Simondon, all individuals (i.e., individuated beings) are secondary products arising within and out of a pre-individual ground (i.e., non-, or not-yet-, individuated being). Furthermore, Simondon asserts that no processes of individuation and no thereby-produced individuals ever exhaustively appropriate, assimilate, digest, incorporate, master, sublate, etc. their anonymous, un-individuated background conditions for surfacing into existence. Therefore, internal to each and every individual, as a sort of "extimate" ineliminable remainder, there are to be found persisting residues of pre-individual bases. The un-individuated ground permanently accompanies the individual and its ongoing dynamics of individuation as a virtual dimension of non/not-yet-realized potentialities.[42] For the sub-set of individuals qualifying as subjects, this means that, as Simondon puts it, "the subject is individual and other than individual; it is incompatible with itself."[43]

As just seen, Deleuze associates his *bêtise* with the kinetics of individuation as mediating between pre-individuated being (i.e., ground) and individuated beings (i.e., individuals). More precisely, the Simondonian individual is (transcendentally) "stupid" insofar as, on the basis of the ongoing acts and movements of its individuation by which it comes to be and continues to exist as the individual that it is, it cannot "recognize" all of its pre-individual grounds and accompanying virtual potentialities. Individuation unavoidably brings about blind spots rendering portions of the pre-individual opaque to the thus-individuated individual. Deleuze appears to tie transcendental stupidity to such blindness and opacity.

But, what about Simondon himself? What is it that interests me in his corpus from the angles of EFO and my related reconsiderations of the transcendental? In the remainder of this section, I will set about answering this line of questioning. In light of my specific perspective and agenda in the present context, my engagement with Simondon will be highly selective. In particular, I will focus on what arguably is Simondon's *magnum opus*, namely, his massive 1958 dissertation *L'individuation à la lumière des notions de forme et d'information* (originally published as two separate books: *L'individu et sa génèse physico-biologique* from 1964, reviewed by Deleuze in 1966, and, quite belatedly, *L'individuation psychique et collective* from 1989). My rapprochement between the EFO of transcendental materialism as critical-dialectical naturalism and the Simondonian account of individuation will be anchored in targeted interpretations of certain relevant moments within *L'individuation*.

To be yet more precise, my reading of Simondon is driven by a perhaps somewhat contentious underlying thesis: Despite Simondon's wariness of Hegel (so typical of post-war French thinkers), his theory of individuation can be construed as unwittingly very Hegelian. Less controversially, I also will bring out the psychoanalytic debts of the Simondonian model of individuation. Hegel's motif of the becoming-subject of substance and this motif's incarnations, in the Philosophy of the Real, at the levels of both Nature and Spirit delineate in advance much of what is to be found in modified terminological guise in *L'individuation*. Similarly, both Freud and Lacan anticipate quite a bit of what Simondon's labors advance.

Curiously, Simondon *circa* 1958 recognizes Fichte and, especially, Schelling as historical forerunners of his own philosophy.[44] But, failing to register the affinities between Schelling and Hegel in terms of joint foreshadowings of individuation—these affinities continue to reverberate between Schelling's and Hegel's intellectual itineraries even after they part ways following the publication of the latter's *Phenomenology of Spirit*—Simondon is unwilling and/or unable to acknowledge the Hegelian precedents for his position. Indeed, as will be seen below, he even takes occasional swipes at what he (mis)understands Hegel's positions to be.

Given the preoccupations of transcendental materialism (as critical-dialectical naturalism) with animal-organic and human-subjective structures and dynamics, these same layers of Simondon's multi-layered delineation of various processes of individuation will be my main concerns throughout much of the rest of this section. But, before turning to the Simondonian examinations of the biological (as in *L'individu et sa génèse physico-biologique*) and the psychical (as in *L'individuation psychique et collective*), I will preface my treatment of these topics with a brief overview of some of the conceptual and argumentative fundaments of Simondon's general systematic edifice. Doing so will go a long way towards substantiating my (partial) Hegelianization of Simondon (a Hegelianization with interesting consequences for a Deleuze who, as a vehement anti-Hegelian, relies upon the very same Simondon of interest to me here). Then, at the end of my treatment of Simondon in this section, I will highlight Simondon's recasting of the transcendental and its relevance for anyone (including me) devoted to retaining a transcendentalism free of subjectivist transcendental idealism.

Early on in *L'individuation*, Simondon links any and every instance of individuation to tensions within non/not-yet-individuated being.[45] The latter is depicted as shot through with asymmetries, disequilibriums, imbalances, and so on. Hence, the Simondonian pre-individuated ground is both an internally fractured and conflicted foundation as well as always-already perturbed from within by various sorts of negativity.[46] Correlatively, in the absence of such pre-individual instabilities and tensions, there would be no individuation. As Simondon expresses it at one point, symmetry would equal lifelessness[47] (a profoundly Schellingian and Hegelian observation). Therefore, his theory of individuation entails, at its foundation, an ontological commitment to a monism of out-of-synch multiplicities.[48]

However, in what I cannot help but interpret as a case of classical Freudian *Verneinung*, Simondon insists that the immanent ontological agitation underlying and catalyzing individuations is different from and prior to dialectical negativity (as per Hegelian dialectics).[49] The contrasts Simondon likely has in mind between himself and Hegel can be best introduced by me first noting several additional general theoretical commitments of Simondon. These other commitments reveal significant differences between Simondonian metaphysics and what Simondon seems to take Hegelian "idealism" to be about.

Four cardinal features of Simondon's position imply oppositions on his part to Hegel as (mis)represented in post-war French philosophy. I already mention the first feature immediately above: the embrace of a monism of multiplicities. Simondon probably views Hegel as a totalizing thinker of the All, One, or Whole dissolving all individuals into the unity of the Absolute, Idea, World Spirit, or the like. Hence, *L'individuation* strongly hints at a clash between Hegel's monism of unity and Simondon's monism of multiplicities.

Second, Simondon is adamant about the realism (*qua* anti-subjective-idealism) of his account of various possible and actual processes of individuation.[50] As a realist, Simondon rejects epiphenomenalisms that would reduce individuations and individuals to any pre-, non-, or trans-individual "x."[51] A key ingredient of Simondon's anti-epiphenomenalism is endorsement of what more recent Analytic metaphysics and philosophy of mind refers to as "downward causation." For this Simondon, emergent individuations and individuals can and do react back upon the pre-individual being(s) from which they emerged.[52] As I noted in the prior paragraph, Simondon seems to suspect Hegel of being a monist of unity. As such, Hegel would be seen to collapse all individuals without exception into the One-All of the Absolute. Given this, Simondon may (mis)construe his anti-epiphenomenalism of downward causation as also anti-Hegelian.

Third, *L'individuation* emphasizes the key role of "accidental encounters" as crucial mediators of dynamics of individuation.[53] Of course, for many philosophers and theorists of the past two centuries through today, including the majority of denizens of French intellectual milieus of the past half-century or so, Hegel all too often is viewed as the metaphysician of teleological necessity *par excellence*, a sort of post-Kantian Leibniz with his own theodicy of a God-like *Weltgeist*. Along with certain others, I reject this picture of Hegel as a one-hundred-eighty-degree inversion of the truth, arguing instead that contingency, and not necessity, is the *Ur*-category in Hegel's doctrine of the modalities (along with me underscoring Hegel's often unappreciated rejections of Leibnizianism). Nonetheless, Simondon, with his concept of "the accidental encounter, totally fortuitous,"⁵⁴ tacitly pits himself against, among other things, the image of Hegel-the-necessitarian.

Fourth, Simondon's critical remarks apropos the philosophical concept-term "substance" subtly entail divergence away from what Simondon understands a philosopher like Hegel to mean when employing this term. For Simondon, the substantial would be homogeneous, self-identical/consistent, and internally undifferentiated. Therefore, his pre/non-individuated being or ground, as already fragmented into multiplicities and traversed by negativities, would not be a substance comprehended in this sense. Likewise, Simondon's rejections of pre- and non-dialectical versions of materialism partially overlap with his criticisms of more traditional substance metaphysics.⁵⁵ However, as I indicated a short while ago, Schelling, in some of his incarnations, and Hegel, consistently throughout his career, both posit substance(s) as pervaded by (self-)disruptive antagonisms, conflicts, tensions, etc.

Ironically, these four apparently anti-Hegelian aspects of the Simondonian philosophy of individuation actually help identify the real Hegel as perhaps Simondon's closest philosophical ancestor. Indeed, Hegel's absolute idealism (as opposing itself to the subjective idealisms of, for instance, Kant and Fichte) is itself a robust realism. Moreover, Hegel advances an anti-epiphenomenal, neither-reductive-nor-eliminative vision of substance-also-as-subject. This vision is made possible by a desubstantializing reconception of substance, namely, a dialectical depriving that subtracts from substance its substantiality *qua* cohesiveness, harmony, solidity, and the like (e.g., as in the "weakness of nature" [*die Ohnmacht der Natur*] of Hegel's Philosophy of Nature with its *Naturdialektik*, not to mention various other logical and spiritual forms of dialectical negativity in the Hegelian System). As now can be registered, some of Simondon's core tenets inadvertently testify to his unwitting Hegelianism.

This perhaps unconscious Hegelianism is further on display at the levels of Simondon's inquiries into biological and psychical individuations. Starting at the level of the individuals of inorganic physics, but also encompassing individuals as animal organisms, Simondon offers a "chrono-topological" delineation of the very formation of individuals.⁵⁶ That is to say, both physical and biological individuals are produced through the flat immanence of the surface of pre-individuated being folding and twisting itself (hence topology) in movements that, as movements, necessarily unfurl over time (hence chronology). Apropos this self-contorting immanence, being itself is, for Simondon, the ultimate author of acts of individuation.⁵⁷ Along these lines, he asserts, "*the individual is self-constitution of a topology of being which resolves an anterior incompatibility by the appearance of a new systematic*"⁵⁸ (an assertion embellished upon subsequently in *L'individuation*⁵⁹). Simondon's theory of individuation combines, on the one hand, a dimension of the static, synchronic, and structural and, on the other hand, a dimension of the kinetic, diachronic, and genetic. What is more, and again like Hegel, Simondon, with his chrono-topology, outlines a dynamic in which resolutions of old negativities generate new negativities in processes forming open-ended trajectories.

Interestingly in relation to Simondonian chrono-topology, Lacan's twenty-sixth and final seminar of 1978–9 is entitled *Topology and Time*. Similarly, Žižek, in the content of staging an encounter between Hegel and Deleuze, offers an implicitly chrono-topological delineation of the emergence of individuated organisms through the self-organizing (i.e., autopoietic) kinetics of cell formation.[60] Žižekian autopoiesis is quite compatible with Simondonian individuation.

At one point in *L'individuation*, Simondon maintains that individuation (specifically, the emergence of organic from inorganic individuals) comes before adaptation.[61] As regards, for instance, (post-)Darwinian evolutionary biology, this explanatory discourse presupposes and applies itself to already-constituted biological individuals. In order for there to be the problems of organisms having to adapt to environmental challenges and pressures, such individuals already have to have arisen. Therefore, individuations going from the inorganic to the organic would be ontological conditions of possibility for the very real struggles to survive of biological individuals. Likewise, a Simondonian delineation of these same individuations would be an epistemological condition of possibility for evolutionary theory as a body of knowledge.

But, what about the crucial transition from animal organism to human subject? How, according to Simondon, do psychical individuations arise out of biological individuals? *L'individuation* has a great deal to say about processes of individuation running from soma to psyche. Moreover, Simondon draws extensively from psychoanalysis in particular for his renditions of psychical life.

Elsewhere, and starting from indications surfacing in Hegel's philosophy of nature and philosophical anthropology, I forge a distinction between the organic and the "anorganic."[62] The latter is not equivalent to the inorganic *qua* pre- and non-organic. Rather, anorganicity is a lack of inner consistency and harmony, an immanent (self-)negation, inherent to the (human) organism (with the etymology of the word "organism" linking it to order, organization, etc.). While the inorganic gives rise to the organic, the organic in turn gives rise to the anorganic.

Something similar to my (Hegelian-Lacanian) anorganicity is to be found in Simondon's psychoanalysis-informed ontogenetic narratives about the emergence of the subjective from the biological. For Simondon, ontogeny itself is driven by negativities.[63] Implicitly in line with Freud and Lacan, *L'individuation* emphasizes the biological fact of distinctively human prolonged prematurational *Hilflosigkeit* as pivotal here.

Much like with the *corps morcelé* of Lacan's mirror stage, the Simondonian infant, as an individuation-in-process between the somatic and the psychical, is both anatomically and physiologically helpless (uncoordinated and unable to fend for itself) as well as affectively troubled by this initial condition into which he/she is thrown by birth. The negativity of the young human organism's lack of self-sufficiency is registered by corresponding negative affects.[64] Indeed, Simondon immediately proceeds to claim that the psyche itself is born out of the dissatisfaction so powerfully felt by the flailing, immature creature.[65] Lacan likely would not agree that the psychical as a whole comes together in this way; his theory of the mirror stage accounts for the genesis of the ego specifically, not the individuation of the entire psyche or subject generally. Nevertheless, the Lacanian and Simondonian reflections on the ontogenetic significance of *Hilflosigkeit* partially but powerfully resonate with each other.

Simondon goes on to posit that organic dysfunctions (in my parlance, anorganic structures and dynamics) catalyze but do not determine the psyche.[66] This echoes, however intentionally or not, Schelling's and Hegel's deployments of the notion of illness, namely, their shared theme of the human being as a sick animal, as the by-product of problems generated within organic nature (with Lacan, among others, picking up on this German idealist theme⁶⁷). What is more, Simondon, as just seen, is careful to stipulate that biological dysfunctionality prompts the emergence of a psychical reality that itself, despite arising thusly, thereafter does not deterministically reduce back down to its organic base. Such a stipulation is an important feature of transcendental materialism too.

Once psyche has thereby sprung out of soma, the tail starts to wag the dog, so to speak. That is to say, the *zoē* of animal vitality becomes the exception under the rule of the *bios* of psychical individuality.⁶⁸ In line with Simondon's overarching theory of individuation, he maintains that the psychical individual preserves within itself unsublated remainders of the pre-individual grounds of its individuation, including the biological being(s) out of which it surfaces. Although mind comes to dominate the body (partly) generating it, the latter occasionally is able to reverse this relationship, at least temporarily.

Simondon speaks of a predisposition (but definitely not a fate or destiny) of being itself towards opening out onto socio-cultural mediations.⁶⁹ This is most readily appreciable in connection with *Hilflosigkeit*. Indeed, *L'individuation* pinpoints ontogenetically primary prolonged prematurational helplessness as making the newborn human animal vulnerable and receptive *vis-à-vis* external, more-than-biological mediators.⁷⁰ Freud's 1895 *Project for a Scientific Psychology* already says as much.

Hilflosigkeit leads Simondon, following Freud, to stress the centrality of intersubjective and trans-subjective influences in the ontogenetic taking-shape (i.e., chrono-topological individuation) of the individual psychical subject. Yet, *L'individuation* contains a distinction enabling its author to avoid concluding that the individual psyche is exhaustively determined by and heteronomous with respect to social mediators. Simondon differentiates between, on the one hand, "autonomy" as the internal self-relating of an individual and, on the other hand, "independence" as non-relatedness to other individuals.⁷¹ For him, individuals can be, and usually are, (partially) autonomous but not (fully) independent. One finds the same distinction in different terminological garb in Hegelian Logic too. Apropos the relations between the psychical and the social in Simondon's philosophy, this distinction entails that inter/trans-subjective mediations do not thoroughly override the intrasubjective self-relating of the individual psyche *qua* locus of autonomous subjectivity.

Simondon sees his account of individuation as critically supplementing psychoanalysis. In particular, he adds to the individuated unconscious of analysis the pre-individual one of his philosophy.⁷² Analytic theory and practice arguably presuppose as already established a singular psyche within which discrete representations (i.e., Freud's signifier-like representations, *Vorstellungen*) are submitted to various operations, including the repressions constituting that psyche's unconscious. But, the pre-individuated being out of which the individuated psyche itself congeals would be, according to Simondon's model, an even more radically occluded and opaque (i.e., "repressed" in a looser, broader sense) dimension for this same psyche. Of course,

Deleuze, along with Félix Guattari, readily can be understood as further developing the suggestions of *L'individuation* along these lines, namely, theorizing a "productive," "molecular" unconscious of virtual potentialities prior to, for instance, the "produced" individual actors of the Oedipal family drama or the well-defined "molar" agencies of a psychical topography.

By mentioning Deleuze, I bring things back to the start of this section on Simondon. Having opened this section with reference to Deleuze's concept of transcendental stupidity, a concept he associates with Simondonian individuation, I will close it by examining what *L'individuation* has to contribute to a reconsideration of transcendentalism. Simondon's dissertation puts forward several propositions in this vein worth underscoring for my purposes.

With psychical ontogeny as the process generative of minded subjectivity, this structured dynamic of individuation is a precondition for knowledge.[73] In other words, the knowing subject of an epistemology is made possible by the genetically emergent psyche of an ontology (here, Simondon's ontology of individuation). Ontological ontogeny comes before and makes possible epistemological subjectivity; without the former, the latter would not exist in the first place. In the case of a transcendental epistemology, such an ontology would therefore be meta-transcendental.

In this vein, Simondon advances a thesis with respect to transcendentalism resonating with my efforts both in "Whither the Transcendental?" and here. He claims that, "the *conditions of possibility* of knowledge are in fact the *causes of existence* of the individuated being."[74] On the heels of this claim, Simondon aligns the distinction between transcendental and empirical subjects with that between the individuated (*l'être individué*) and the individualized (*l'être individualisé*) respectively.[75]

Simondon's just-quoted thesis is especially important to appreciate in the present context. Simondon is once again surprisingly proximate to Hegel. Specifically, his reflections related to transcendentalism are strikingly close to Hegel's decoupling of the transcendental from transcendental idealism in particular and, relatedly, his anti-subjectivist absolute idealism in general. Both Hegel and Simondon are realists. As such, they consider really true knowledge, in order for the very phrase "true knowledge" to mean anything, as having to do with mind-independent entities and events in themselves. Some of Hegel's criticisms of Kant have as an upshot that Kant's subjectivist idealism is fundamentally incompatible with any theory of knowledge whatsoever (including the epistemology Kant intends to establish) insofar as Kantian anti-realism, with its unknowable things-in-themselves, deprives the word "knowledge" of any coherent meaning.[76]

Hegel's and Simondon's alternative is to argue that what ultimately makes possible thinking-as-knowing on the side of ideal subjectivity is being-as-knowable on the side of real objectivity. Put differently, Hegel, with his substance-also-as-subject, and Simondon, with his theory of individuation, are both monists for whom the transcendental subjectivity of epistemology immanently emerges out of the meta-transcendental grounds of ontology. Thanks to this, the categorial and conceptual structures of mind are akin to the pre/extra-mental structures of an already-structured-in-itself world (with Hegel fiercely attacking Kant's subjectivist notion of the formlessness of the *an sich*[77]). The isomorphisms between subjective and objective forms make knowledge possible by enabling cross-resonances back-and-forth between thinking and being. Mind can know world because the former is of this same world.

Yet, at the same time, the contractions and separations that individuate transcendental subjectivity within meta-transcendental objectivity introduce differences between these levels of thinking and being. After passing through the idiocy of individuation, the estrangements and withdrawals from pre-individuality constitutive of individuality, the epistemological challenge for individuated mind is to regain the trans-individual world partly, but never completely, lost. As Hegel would put it, the regained ontological identity (as per his absolute idealism as full knowledge of the logical forms cutting across the subject-object divide and realized in both natural and spiritual incarnations) between the thinking of subjects and the being of objects is an identity of identity and difference (with, for me, EFO doing justice to the "difference" side of this equation).

As will be seen in the next section, Malabou's recent work on the topic of the transcendental can be situated in the same lineage to which the Simondon just examined belongs too. This is not coincidental, since Malabou could be said to be indirectly influenced by Simondon due to Deleuze's direct influence on her philosophy. However, what she adds to this discussion, additions especially close to and valuable for my own transcendental materialist endeavors, is a careful reassessment of the possible relations between transcendentalism and naturalism.

IV Against preformationism: Malabou's genesis and structure of the transcendental

Malabou's two most recent books, *Avant demain: Épigenèse et rationalité* from 2014 and *Métamorphoses de l'intelligence: Que faire de leur cerveau bleu?* from 2017, are centrally concerned with radically transforming, while not jettisoning altogether, the Kantian transcendental. In *Avant demain*, she contends that, "*it is with Kant, and not against him, that it is necessary to negotiate his abandonment.*"[78] What is more, for her, this passing through, rather than bypassing, of Kant's critical philosophy must mobilize tensions internal to the Kantian apparatus itself—"there is in Kant himself, within critique, the organizing of an encounter between the transcendental and that which resists it."[79]

Malabou offers a similar set of observations in a 2017 interview. Speaking of her current efforts to reinvent transcendentalism, she therein remarks:

> I was so interested in exploring whether the transcendental could be transformed. I don't think we can keep it as it is, but I also don't think we can do without it, so the challenge was to see if Kant himself offered the necessary resources to transform it.... Meillassoux thinks that Kant cannot explain the genesis of the a priori categories. There can be no transcendental deduction of the transcendental. But this is not true: in the deduction of the categories Kant is explicit that there *cannot* be a genetic account of the a priori categories as a genesis is always empirical, and transcendental conditions are independent of all experience. But at the same

time he has to prove that our categories are not *innate* or given by God, so he has to open a very subtle space between innateness and empiricism. And this is where the idea of epigenesis comes in—the categories are not given ready-made but have in themselves the principle of their own development, and this is what he calls the epigenesis of pure reason in paragraph 27 of *The Critique of Pure Reason*.[80]

In good Hegelian fashion, Malabou is proposing an immanent-critical (self-)reworking of Kantian transcendentalism. She finds within the first *Critique* an internal tension "between innateness and empiricism." Malabou's core thesis here is that, within this "very subtle space" of in-betweenness, Kant outlines a notion of "epigenesis" as the non-empirical genesis, amenable to a peculiar (meta-)transcendental deduction, of transcendental subjectivity itself. I would add that, as I mention in the second section above, the problem of the non-empirical genesis of the transcendental subject is to be found in Kant's *Anthropology* as well as *Critique of Pure Reason*.

Consistent with the arc of Malabou's pre-2014 intellectual itinerary, *Avant demain* and *Métamorphoses de l'intelligence* both associate Kant's epigenesis with the recent life-scientific field of epigenetics. Malabou avowedly engages in a project of "biologizing the transcendental."[81] As she admits, this is tantamount, in relation to some of Kant's categories, to positing the *a posteriori* emergence of the *a priori*.[82] In other words, Malabou's concern is with the problem of the ontogenetic ascension to logic and logical subjectivity, namely, the emergence of the transcendental dimension itself.[83] As the end of the preceding section shows, this already is a concern of Simondon too, among others.

As Malabou herself is painfully aware, proposing any sort of rapprochement between transcendentalism and biology faces stiff resistance from various Kantian and post-Kantian strains within the Continental European philosophical tradition. She pleads for this tradition to set aside its anti-naturalist, science-phobic biases and reengage with the natural sciences.[84] Correlatively, Malabou pushes back against Heideggerian-style dismissals of epigenetics and neurobiology as merely "ontic" disciplines well below the dignity of philosophy and/as fundamental ontology.[85] One could say that, for her, interfacing the transcendental and the biological does not lower the former but, instead, elevates the latter. Expressed in Hegelian fashion, Malabou seeks to raise her life-scientific sources to the dignity of their philosophical Notions.[86]

At a general level, Malabou characterizes the problematic of the transcendental as the question of the coming-to-be of the self-relating subject.[87] I see this as meta-transcendental rather than transcendental. Why? Assuming that the self-relating subject at issue here overlaps or is coextensive with Kantian-style transcendental subjectivity, its non-empirical "epigenesis" would be meta-transcendental *qua* the conditions of possibility for this subject (which itself in turn comes to function as a set of distinct possibility conditions for other things). Simondon likewise would distinguish between the productive becoming of individuation (as meta-transcendental) and the produced being of the individuated (as transcendental).

That said, Malabou's approach to transcendentalism assumes its separability from transcendental idealism and outlines its compatibility with naturalism (as itself inseparable from a realist materialism). Of course, I explicitly argue for these points both here and in "Whither the Transcendental?" I will return to them in the fifth and final section of the present intervention. At this juncture, I need to lay out in greater detail the biology to which Malabou has recourse in connection with the transcendental.

In Malabou's 2014 and 2017 books presently under consideration, the term "epigenesis" serves as the *point de capiton* stitching together, on the one side, Kant's non-empirical taking-form of transcendental subjectivity and, on the other side, the life-scientific sub-field of epigenetics. As is now common knowledge, the latter deals with the biological mechanisms through which milieus outside the organism influence the translations of genotypes into phenotypes. In the case of human organisms, these milieus are not just natural environments but, more importantly, social, cultural, linguistic, historical, political, etc. surroundings. Hence, epigenetics could be interpreted as illustrating particular instances of the entangling of nature and nurture, of the more-than-natural mediation inherent to the natural itself. With respect to Kant's subject, this would be to suggest that its forms, categories, concepts, and the like take shape at the active intersection between the genetic and the extra-genetic, between first and second natures. Indeed, for Malabou, thinking belongs to a peculiar creature that is simultaneously a transcendental subject and a living being (with the latter as, in her view, more than a merely empirical status).[88]

Malabou situates epigenetics in relation to the notion of "plasticity" guiding her endeavors from her doctoral thesis on Hegel onwards. Epigenetics thus would be a species of specifically biological plasticity, along with the neuroplasticity dear to Malabou too. In this vein, she remarks, "Biological plasticity is, if one wants, programmed in order not to be programmed."[89] In light of this remark, epigenetics would amount to genetic preprogramming for extra-genetic reprogramming, namely, a natural determination not to be (entirely) naturally determined. Or, to risk an oversimplification, one could describe this as a natural inclination towards the dominance of nurture over nature. Such a depiction of epigenetics is of a piece with Malabou's earlier treatments of plasticity generally and neuroplasticity especially.

On this basis, Malabou employs epigenetics (as she does neuroplasticity) so as to undermine the tendency to associate naturalism with determinism. Just as neuroplasticity dissolves the cerebral determinism of a preprogrammed neural machine, so too does epigenetics blow holes in the genetic determinism of an innately coded DNA destiny. On Malabou's assessment, both of these biological phenomena involve natural science pointing to an underdetermination or indeterminism within nature itself (at least in the case of *homo sapiens*).[90]

Although indetermination is not full-fledged self-determination—disrupting determinism is not tantamount to demonstrating freedom—it is a necessary, albeit not sufficient, condition for autonomy. And, of course, transcendental analyses are concerned with necessary conditions of possibility. Thus, Malabou's Kant-related philosophical appropriation of biological epigenetics has implications for another portion of the *Critique of Pure Reason*: the famous third of Kant's "Antinomies of Pure Reason."

As is well known, this Kant accepts a Newtonian vision of nature, with its efficient-causal determinism *à la* Laplace's demon. Therefore, in order to leave room for a free *qua* autonomous, self-determining subject, Kant feels compelled to reinforce a strict dualism between natural objectivity and anti-natural subjectivity. Natural objectivity is dealt with by the empirical, experimental sciences epitomized by mechanical physics. By contrast, anti-natural subjectivity is dealt with by transcendental philosophy both theoretical and practical.

Biological plasticity as per Malabou strongly implies a reconfiguring of the terms of Kant's third antinomy through liquidating the Newtonian image of nature. This image already is in jeopardy for the Kant of the *Critique of the Power of Judgment*, saved only by the later Kant's quarantining of biological final causes within the confines of the deontologized limbo of the regulative "as if" (*als ob*).[91] Of course, Malabou's thinking is profoundly colored by Hegelian speculative dialectics. Hence, it would seem fair to discern in the background of her philosophical reassessments of the life sciences Hegel's (and Schelling's) playing off of Kant's third against his first *Critique*. Specifically, this would be the Hegelian (and Schellingian) gesture of combatting the Newtonian metaphysics of nature by ontologizing the third *Critique*'s presentation of biological teleology, by transforming the 1790 Kant's final causes from regulative into constitutive ideas. Hegel, Schelling, and Malabou share in common an approach to the third antinomy of the first *Critique* in which its antinomic character is taken to arise from a mistaken picture of nature.

Despite Malabou's anti-Newtonian solidarity with late-eighteenth- and early-nineteenth-century German idealism and Romanticism, she definitely is not opposed to biology utilizing the languages of mathematics in describing its objects of investigation. As she is well aware, the various sub-fields of the life sciences upon which she draws employ mathematical and formal delineations of the entities and dynamics falling within their explanatory jurisdictions. However, just because Galilean-style mathematized modern physics has tended to be paired with a determinism of mechanical efficient causality does not entail that the application of mathematics to biology automatically brings about the confinement of life within the iron chains of deterministic mechanisms. For Malabou, one does not have to choose between a mathematical determinism and an anti-mathematical indeterminism. This would be a false dilemma. Life can be modeled mathematically without, for all that, being turned into a preprogrammed clockwork automaton.[92] At the same time, Malabou is sensitive to the risks of encouraging either physicalist or metaphysical-realist reducing-away of living beings and events via the mathematization of biology.[93]

Returning to Malabou's weaving together of Kantian epigenesis and biological epigenetics, she contends that the latter enables liberating the transcendental from the lingering traces of the early modern rationalist doctrine of innate ideas coloring Kant's transcendental idealism. In relation to the recent biology Malabou relies upon, she proposes that, "The epigenetic is ... the origin born of the absence of origin."[94] Assuming the justifiability of linking contemporary life-scientific epigenetics back with the epigenesis of the first *Critique*, this suggests that at least some of the possibility conditions for the emergence of the Kantian subject would be the inbuilt blanks, the determined indeterminacies, of a plastic nature. These clearings, as innate absences (rather than innately present ideas) *qua* encodings for re-codings, are structural spaces making possible the (epi)genetic processes that might happen to arise out of them. Therefore, Malabou posits that a synthesis of transcendentalism's epigenesis with naturalism's epigenetics opens out onto the theoretical option of a transcendental *sans* the preformationism of Kant's rationalist hangover.⁹⁵

In connection with the issue of preformationism, Malabou distinguishes between two versions of the transcendental: a hyper- and a hypo-normative transcendentalism. The more rationalist Kant, inclined towards an innateness that itself enforces an absolutely strict separation of the *a priori* transcendental from the *a posteriori* empirical, would be hyper-normative. As seen, this hyper-normativity makes it difficult for Kant to do justice to his own notion of epigenesis as non-empirical yet non-innate too. If the transcendental is *a priori* innate and the empirical is *a posteriori* acquired, then it indeed seems impermissible to try to conceive of a transcendental genesis, an *a priori* acquisition, without preformations.⁹⁶

So, Malabou herself clearly cannot endorse a hyper-normative transcendentalism. Instead, she opts for the other variety, namely, the hypo-normative one. The biological plasticity she deploys in her biologization of the transcendental indeed involves constraining, configuring forms and structures. Neither rewirable neurons and synapses nor extra-genetically modulated genes are formless, unstructured beings imposing no shape upon that to which they give rise. There indeed is a minimal "normativity" to these biological conditions of possibility for the more-than-biological subject of transcendentalism. However, not only are the built-in openings to external mediators represented by neuroplasticity and epigenetics different from the hyper-normativity of anything along the lines of innate ideas in the classical sense—these biologically plastic forms, in their plasticity, are the very forms in and through which transformations are allowed to transpire. They are preformations permitting reformations. As Malabou puts it regarding these hypo-normative biological transcendentals, "the transcendental certainly is a constraint—of form and of structure—but, paradoxically, this is synonymous with freedom."⁹⁷

To be more precise, such hypo-normative biological transcendentals are, for Malabou, necessary preconditions for the possibility of the emergence of an autonomous subjectivity defying all determinisms and reductivisms.⁹⁸ Although she turns away from the rigid hyper-normativity accompanying orthodox Kantian transcendentalism, her heterodox reworking of Kant in an immanent-critical fashion enables her to hold onto the transcendental after decoupling it from transcendental idealist preformationism. Instead of opposing a straightforward, garden-variety empiricist naturalism to traditional transcendentalism, Malabou opts for dividing the transcendental from within so as to play off one form of it (i.e., the hypo-normative) against the other (i.e., the hyper-normative). In so doing, she conveys that there is something of enduring merit to the term "transcendental." For her (and for me too, as will be seen in the fifth section to follow), one of the virtues of this term is its designation of implacable resistance to anything and everything deterministic or reductive.⁹⁹

I wish to touch upon a final set of points contained specifically in *Avant demain* before concluding my consideration of Malabou's recent labors in relation to the topic of the transcendental. In the context of criticizing Meillassoux's attempted problematizations of Kant's theoretical philosophy, Malabou insists that Kant himself affirms the ultimately factical status of the transcendental itself.¹⁰⁰ She suggests that

Kantian critique accepts the necessity of contingency, namely, the hybrid modality Meillassoux tries to turn against Kant and his legacy.[101]

This move of Malabou's goes against not only Meillassouxian speculative materialism, but also the three major post-Kantian German idealists, namely, Fichte, Schelling, and Hegel. In the wake of some of Jacobi's and Schulze's challenges to Kant, these three, despite their many differences, all strive in their own manners to eliminate the factical, contingent qualities of Kant's transcendentalism through more systematic deductions of such things as the categories of cognition and the faculties of human mindedness. Malabou, in her countering of Meillassoux, transforms what the post-Kantians see as a vice into a virtue. For her, Kant's failure/refusal to provide systematic deductions all the way down, his leaving of core features of the subject as un-grounded givens, is an essential acknowledging and indication of the irreducible contingency/facticity of the very existence of transcendental subjectivity.

Additionally, Malabou extends the contingency/facticity of the transcendental subject to the biological being (i.e., the human organism) she posits as the natural condition of possibility for this subject. Life itself is both ontologically contingent, as evolutionary theory from Charles Darwin onward shows, as well as a real-material transcendental (or, as I would say, meta-transcendental) *vis-à-vis* transcendental subjectivity. This is what Malabou intends when she identifies life as a "contingent transcendental."[102]

Taking a step further back to an even more sweeping perspective, Malabou gestures at a general ontology involving a combination of facticity, contingency, necessity, and irreducibility. Specifically, she sketches a picture of real being in which there exists a factically given plurality of different levels of existences (such as the physical, chemical, and biological strata of nature). These levels are irreducible in relation to each other. Moreover, necessities are internal to particular levels (for instance, intra-physical, intra-chemical, and intra-biological "laws"). Necessities do not emanate from a foundational level in relation to which other levels are secondary, reducible determinations (such as a standard physicalist reductivism in which everything boils down to the physics of the smallest constituents of material nature). There is an *Ur*-contingency to the givenness of this dispersed multitude of ontological regions. Likewise, the domain of thinking covered by transcendental philosophy would itself be an irreducible and factically given level with respect to physical, chemical, and biological domains.[103]

From the start, Malabou has situated her work in the lineage of dialectical materialism. Her just-summarized vision of a stratified ontology of irreducible layers indeed is in line with aspects of a tradition including Friedrich Engels, the later Nikolai Bukharin, and the mature Georg Lukács (not to mention the non-Marxists Émile Boutroux and Nicolai Hartmann). I deal with Engels *et al.* along these lines elsewhere.[104]

Here, I want to conclude my discussion of Malabou with a line of questioning leading straight into the subsequent fifth section of my intervention. These queries are directed at a feature of Malabou's thinking setting it apart from what often is associated with dialectical materialism. Due to this orientation's debts to Marx's historical materialism, with its profound historicist sensibilities, both Kant and his transcendental usually appear anathema to most Marxists, including most self-avowed dialectical materialists (such as Engels, Lenin, etc.). Yet, as seen, Malabou passes through via immanent critique, rather than bypasses via external critique, Kantian transcendentalism.

So, a more conventional dialectical materialist might ask of Malabou: Why continue speaking of the transcendental after its naturalization? Especially in light of Malabou's reliance on the empirical, experimental sciences of nature, why not replace transcendentalism wholesale with an empiricist naturalism, perhaps supplemented by a variant of historical materialism aiming to encompass the distinguishing peculiarities of human histories both phylogenetic and ontogenetic? What, if anything, is left of the transcendental after the revisions and alterations to which Malabou submits it?

The following final section of my intervention attempts to answer precisely these questions. It is intended as a friendly supplement to Malabou's efforts apropos transcendentalism, ones for which I have deep sympathy. My replies to the preceding queries also will serve to encapsulate the key philosophical upshots of both "Whither the Transcendental?" and this present sequel piece.

V Between history and eternity: what is left of transcendentalism today?

From Kant himself, with his subjectivist idealism, onwards, transcendentalism often has been bound up with philosophically and/or politically problematic larger theoretical projects. It has been made to aid and abet a range of dubious enterprises: artificially and conservatively limiting the scopes of legitimate human inquiry; protectively rationalizing and perpetuating religious dogmas and superstitions; sometimes hastily eternalizing and essentializing what arguably are transient historical phenomena; at other times trying to rule out claims to any sort of theoretical or practical knowledge not always-already qualified as contextualized *qua* socially, culturally, historically, linguistically, etc. conditioned and localized ... I pose the questions with which I end the preceding section as much to myself as to Malabou. Moreover, another, similar question should be raised at this moment: Burdened with all its accumulated baggage, is it even worth the trouble to attempt salvaging something from transcendentalism?

Addressing these concerns, as I am about to do, will allow me to enumerate the results of "Whither the Transcendental?" and the present sequel piece. Taken together, these two texts of mine are meant to justify retaining the term "transcendental" as signifying a set of points of enduring validity and contemporary importance. These points would be in danger of being conceded or abandoned if transcendentalism in its entirety were to be rejected.

I will begin through a *via negativa*, stipulating three things that the transcendental is not, despite commonly being associated with them. First, transcendentalism is not synonymous with or equivalent to subjectivist transcendental idealism. To be transcendental is to be a necessary condition of possibility for subjectivity. Therefore, the transcendental is not, by definition, inherent to already-constituted ideality *qua* subjective mind as separate from reality *qua* objective world. Consequently, there is nothing oxymoronic about pairing transcendentalism with realism, materialism, naturalism, or the like. A phrase such as "transcendental materialism" is not a contradiction-in-terms; it would be so only for those who falsely conflate the transcendental with transcendental idealism. Neither Kant's opposition to realism, etc. nor certain of his descendants' aversions to such stances are dictated by the very idea of transcendentalism. On the contrary—the transcendental can and should be divorced from all subjective idealisms.

Second, the transcendental need not be treated as timeless. As seen, even Kant himself (partially) concedes that the subject of his critical philosophy is emergent, that there is a process of genesis through which a passage occurs from pre-subjectivity to subjectivity proper (for instance, a transition from a nature devoid of subject to a nature containing a more-than-natural subject). In short, there are comings-to-be of transcendental subjects. Therefore, since the bearers and instantiations of the dimension of the transcendental are not eternally existent, this dimension itself arguably is not eternal either.

Third, and closely linked to the second point, transcendentals do not have to be (and ought not to be) taken as absolute necessities. More precisely, the ideal-epistemological transcendentals of subjectivity, although necessary for the subject and its thinking, are not themselves absolutely necessary at the level of the real-ontological meta-transcendentals of substantiality. That is to say, transcendentals can be relative necessities, with their relative necessity itself being contingent (as per the Hegelian thematic of the contingency of necessity). Nevertheless, despite the contingency of even transcendental necessity, such necessity, although historically emergent (whether from natural history, phylogeny, or ontogeny), is still really necessary relative to certain other things. As Hegel convincingly demonstrates, necessity is not inherently eternal and not categorically opposed to contingency.

With these three negative stipulations put forward, I turn now to specifying the positive features of the modified transcendentalism I consider worthy of defense in the present and preservation in the future. I will spell out these features in eight points. To begin with, and as the first negative point above indicates, transcendentals, as nothing more and nothing less than (relatively) necessary conditions of possibility, can be real-ontological as well as ideal-epistemological. By definition and in principle, nothing rules out pursuing a theoretical identification of pre- and non-subjective possibility conditions for (transcendental) subjectivity itself. Of course, transcendental materialism, with its critical-dialectical naturalism, pursues an account of precisely such conditions.

Second, any static ideal-epistemological transcendentalism of transcendental subjectivity (such as the standard image of Kant's critical philosophy as transcendental idealism) cannot remain within its own confines, whether it wants to or not. At the most fundamental of levels, there can be no epistemology without ontology. In other words, even if a philosophical endeavor strives to be purely epistemological and thus to avoid any and all ontological posits, it still cannot help but fall back on ontological presuppositions (as both John Locke and Kant each reveal to varying degrees despite themselves). In line with core aspects of Hegel's multifaceted critique of Kant, a static epistemological transcendentalism of an ideal subject must be led by immanent (self-)critique to a genetic ontological meta-transcendentalism of a real substance (or substances) prior to and independent of this subject.

Third, the status of being transcendental or meta-transcendental is, at least sometimes, retroactive. As the third negative point above specifies, the necessity of any condition of possibility is relative rather than absolute. Hence, being (meta-)transcendental depends upon being related to something else as condition to conditioned. And, what holds for Hegel's speculative dialectics of causality holds here too. For Hegel, there is a retroaction of effect on cause; the effect causes its cause to be a cause in the first place.[105] Likewise with condition and conditioned: The conditioned conditions its condition to be a condition. Therefore, a necessary condition of possibility will have been such (in the mode of the future anterior) only if and when what it conditions happens to arise and exist. The condition and its necessity come to be after-the-fact of the conditioned and its contingency.

Fourth, situated within an ontological meta-transcendentalism, the genetically emergent transcendental subject is, however long it endures, ultimately transient. Hence, transcendentals, as carried and realized by subjects who arise and pass away, neither always have been nor always will be. However, they remain necessities for so long as there are subjects as such.

Fifth, the transition from meta-transcendental substance to transcendental subject involves "error" as per EFO. Both here and in "Whither the Transcendental?" I already have delineated features of EFO by tying it to sources of inspiration to be found in the works of such thinkers as Hegel, Freud, Heidegger, Lacan, Deleuze, and Simondon. Similarly, Hegel and Schelling alike, through their overlapping manners of comparing evil to illness as both involving a part withdrawing from and rebelling against its encompassing whole, could be said to gesture at an evil-first ethics (EFE) that would be to practical philosophy what error-first ontology (EFO) is to theoretical philosophy. The fall into a subjectivity practically (as evil) as well as theoretically (as erring) alienated from substantiality precedes and makes possible the redemptions of both the Good of ethics and the True of epistemology. In Schelling's and Hegel's footsteps, one could say that humans are exceptionally sick (as per EFE) as well as exceptionally stupid (as per EFO) animals.

Sixth, although the terms "transcendental" and "transcendent" are far from equivalent, playing with their false synonymy enables emphasizing something else of value in transcendentalism. As Malabou observes (as seen in the preceding section), transcendentals are worth retaining for their resistances to all reductivisms and determinisms. Transcendental subjectivity is at least transcendent in the sense of being neither reducible to nor, after its emergence, thoroughly determined by its meta-transcendental, pre-subjective grounds. The main caveat to be attached here is that, for any monistic materialism or naturalism, this transcendence would have to be a strange transcendence-in-immanence, namely, a more-than-material or denaturalized dimension nonetheless internal to matter or nature.

Seventh, the word "transcendental" is a fitting name for something in history more than history itself, to paraphrase Lacan. An example of one version of this is Marx's conception of the nature-initiated and mutually modifying subject-object dynamic of social laboring. For Marx, so long as there is human history, a constant possibility condition for this history's continued unfolding is labor as *praxis* broadly speaking. Hence, labor, according to Marx's historical materialism, is a transhistorical condition of possibility for history itself. Although thoroughly immanent to history, it is not merely one historical detail among others, but that which continually propels the movement of history along. Additionally, on my reading of the relationship between Logic and the Philosophy of the Real in Hegel's mature, encyclopedic System, with Hegel as neither a metaphysical realist of the logical nor a nominalist of the real, the categories of Logic play similar roles as transhistorical possibility conditions for the movements of historical Reals.

An example of another version of "in history more than history itself," one inspired by Badiou, would be truth-events such as mathematical discoveries. On the one hand, these discoveries, like everything else in human history, occur in specific historical contexts, arising within determinate times and places. On the other hand, after they happen in their given socio-historical locales, these truth-events achieve a sort of transcendence *vis-à-vis* their particular sites of origin. Although surfacing within history, these advents thereafter detach from their birthplaces and become transhistorical, cutting across an indefinite number of subsequent times and places.

Therefore, "in history more than history itself" can designate either the history-immanent motor of history itself (for example, labor *à la* Marx) or the historical generation of the thereafter transhistorical (for example, truth-events *à la* Badiou). Such instances occupy a peculiar liminal position in-between the temporal and the eternal (as does Kantian epigenesis on Malabou's reading of the first *Critique*, as I explained in the prior section). A transcendentalism recast along the lines I have been urging is meant to be able to do justice to this neither historical nor timeless region.

Eighth and finally—this is closely tied to the preceding seventh point—any vulgar, reductive pan-historicism, including bastardized versions of Marxian historical materialism, is self-refuting. If unreserved historicizers refuse to recognize any sort of transcendental dimension with the contours of what I already have traced, then their cry of "Everything is historical!" runs up against the same type of paralyzing paradox as radical empiricism and logical positivism. Put in the form of a question, is the claim "Everything is historical" itself historical? If so, then not everything is historical, since this claim's universality is denied in the claim itself being historicized. If not, then at least one thing, the claim itself, is not historical, thus contradicting the very content of the same claim. Either way, the claim itself turns out to be false.

A genuine historical materialist with a proper appreciation of Marx's theory avoids the self-refuting paradox of crude, unqualified historicism by granting that, once again to have recourse to Lacanian locution, not all is historical. This *pas tout* includes cases of transcendences-in-immanence relative to natural and social histories, the transhistorically necessary conditions for historical sequences to unfold as they do. I would go so far as to say that a true historical materialist must also embrace an appropriately qualified transcendentalism.

In addition to the philosophical reasons for revising and retaining the category of the transcendental I have provided, there is the never-more-timely political need for a vigorous defense of precisely the sort of universalism inseparable from Kant's transcendentalism—a universalism Marx inherits from the great German idealists. The transcendental can and should be fashioned into a weapon with which to arm authentic Marxist materialism in its struggles against the ongoing proliferation of identitarianisms and relativisms. A materialism that leaves itself without such a weapon is in danger of finding itself unable to win the fights it continues to face against its many foes.

Notes

1 Adrian Johnston, "Whither the Transcendental?: Hegel, Analytic Philosophy, and the Prospects of a Realist Transcendentalism Today," *Crisis and Critique* 5, no. 1 (March 2018): 162–208. Available at: http://crisiscritique.org/2018h/aj.pdf.
2 See Adrian Johnston, "On Transcendental Materialism: An Interview with Adrian Johnston," *Ex Nihilo*, 2018 (forthcoming).
3 Ibid. See also my *Prolegomena to Any Future Materialism, Volume Two: A Weak Nature Alone* (Evanston: Northwestern University Press, forthcoming).
4 See Karl Marx, *Grundrisse: Foundations of the Critique of Political Economy (Rough Draft)*, trans. Martin Nicolaus (New York: Penguin, 1973), 88, 100–2, 104–6.
5 See Karl Marx, "Theses on Feuerbach," trans. S. Ryazanskaya, in *Selected Writings*, ed. David McLellan (Oxford: Oxford University Press, 1977), 156.
6 See Adrian Johnston, "Transcendental Materialism: A Conversation with Adrian Johnston," in *The Kantian Catastrophe? Conversations on Finitude and the Limits of Philosophy*, ed. Anthony Morgan (Newcastle-upon-Tyne: Bigg Books, 2017), 191, 202–4.
7 See Immanuel Kant, *Critique of Pure Reason*, trans. Paul Guyer and Allen Wood (Cambridge: Cambridge University Press, 1998), 108–9 (Bxii–xiv). See also Adrian Johnston, *A New German Idealism: Hegel, Žižek, and Dialectical Materialism* (New York: Columbia University Press, 2018).
8 G. W. F. Hegel and F. W. J. Schelling, "The Critical Journal of Philosophy, Introduction: On The Essence of Philosophical Criticism Generally, and its Relationship to the Present State of Philosophy in Particular," trans. H. S. Harris, in *Between Kant and Hegel: Texts in the Development of Post-Kantian Idealism*, ed. and trans. George Di Giovanni and H. S. Harris (Indianapolis: Hackett, 2000), 281.
9 G. W. F. Hegel, *Phenomenology of Spirit*, trans. A. V. Miller (Oxford: Oxford University Press, 1977), 49.
10 Ibid., 9.
11 Ibid., 16.
12 Ibid., 19.
13 Ibid., 49.
14 Ibid., 3.
15 See Adrian Johnston, "Preface: From Nonfeeling to Misfeeling—Affects Between Trauma and the Unconscious," in Adrian Johnston and Catherine Malabou, *Self and Emotional Life: Philosophy, Psychoanalysis, and Neuroscience* (New York: Columbia University Press, 2013), xi. See also Adrian Johnston, "Confession of a Weak Reductionist: Responses to Some Recent Criticisms of My Materialism," in *Neuroscience and Critique: Exploring the Limits of the Neurological Turn*, ed. Jan De Vos and Ed Pluth (New York: Routledge, 2015), 166.
16 Johnston, "Whither the Transcendental?," 162–208.
17 Quentin Meillassoux, *After Finitude: An Essay on the Necessity of Contingency*, trans. Ray Brassier (London: Continuum, 2008), 124.

18 Ibid., 7.
19 See Adrian Johnston, *Prolegomena to Any Future Materialism, Volume One: The Outcome of Contemporary French Philosophy* (Evanston: Northwestern University Press, 2013), 129–209. See also Adrian Johnston, *Adventures in Transcendental Materialism: Dialogues with Contemporary Thinkers* (Edinburgh: Edinburgh University Press, 2014), 14–16.
20 Quentin Meillassoux's presentation in Ray Brassier, Iain Hamilton Grant, Graham Harman, and Quentin Meillassoux, "Speculative Realism," *Collapse* III (2007): 449.
21 See Immanuel Kant, *Anthropology from a Pragmatic Point of View*, trans. Victor Lyle Dowdell (Carbondale and Edwardsville: Southern Illinois University Press, 1978), 9–10, 85, 176; Michel Foucault, *Introduction to Kant's Anthropology*, trans. Robert Nigro and Kate Briggs (Los Angeles: Semiotext(e), 2008). 22–3, 67; Adrian Johnston, *Time Driven: Metapsychology and the Splitting of the Drive* (Evanston, IL; Northwestern University Press, 2005), 79–93.
22 See Martin Heidegger, "On the Essence of Truth," in *Basic Writings: Ten Key Essays, plus the Introduction to Being and Time*, ed. David Farrell Krell, rev. edn (San Francisco: HarperCollins, 1993) 132–5.
23 See Sigmund Freud, "The Psychopathology of Everyday Life," in *The Standard Edition of the Complete Psychological Works of Sigmund Freud*, ed. and trans. James Strachey et al., 24 vols. (London: Hogarth Press and the Institute of Psycho-Analysis, 1953–1974), 6: 259.
24 See Jacques Lacan, *The Seminar of Jacques Lacan, Book III: The Psychoses, 1955–1956*, ed. Jacques-Alain Miller, trans. Russell Grigg (New York: W. W. Norton and Company, 1993), 295–6.
25 See Jacques Lacan, *Le Séminaire de Jacques Lacan, Livre XIII: L'objet de la psychanalyse, 1965–1966* (unpublished typescript), session of January 12, 1966.
26 See Jacques Lacan, "Response to Jean Hyppolite's Commentary on Freud's 'Verneinung,'" in *Écrits: The First Complete Edition in English*, trans. Bruce Fink (New York: W. W. Norton and Company, 2006), 323–4.
27 Lacan, *Le Séminaire de Jacques Lacan, Livre XXII: R.S.I., 1974–1975* (unpublished typescript), session of April 8, 1975 (translation mine).
28 See ibid. See also François Balmès, *Le nom, la loi, la voix* (Ramonville Saint-Agne: Érès, 1997), 53.
29 See Lacan, *Le Séminaire de Jacques Lacan, Livre XXII*, session of April 8, 1975.
30 See Martin Heidegger, *The Fundamental Concepts of Metaphysics: World, Finitude, Solitude*, trans. William McNeill and Nicholas Walker (Bloomington: Indiana University Press, 1995), 192–3, 263–4.
31 Jacques Lacan, "Television," trans. Denis Hollier et al., in *Television/A Challenge to the Psychoanalytic Establishment*, ed. Joan Copjec (New York: W. W. Norton and Company, 1990), 6.
32 See Jacques Lacan, *The Seminar of Jacques Lacan, Book XI: The Four Fundamental Concepts of Psychoanalysis, 1964*, ed. Jacques-Alain Miller, trans. Alan Sheridan (New York: W. W. Norton and Company, 1977), 29; Jacques Lacan, *Le Séminaire de Jacques Lacan, Livre XIX: . . . ou pire, 1971-1972*, ed. Jacques-Alain Miller (Paris: Éditions du Seuil, 2011), 222–3; Jacques Lacan, *The Seminar of Jacques Lacan, Book XX: Encore, 1972–1973*, ed. Jacques-Alain Miller, trans. Bruce Fink (New York: W. W. Norton and Company, 1998), 30–1. See also Johnston, *Adventures in Transcendental Materialism*, 209.
33 Lacan, *Le Séminaire de Jacques Lacan, Livre XIX: . . . ou pire*, 223.

34 Balmès, *Le nom, la loi, la voix*, 48.
35 See ibid., 54.
36 See V. I. Lenin, "Conspectus of Hegel's Book *Lectures on the History of Philosophy*," in *Collected Works,* vol. 38: *Philosophical Notebooks*, ed. Stewart Smith; trans. Clemence Dutt (Moscow: Progress Publishers, 1976), 274.
37 See Jacques Lacan, *Le Séminaire de Jacques Lacan, Livre XVI: D'un Autre à l'autre, 1968-1969*, ed. Jacques-Alain Miller (Paris: Éditions du Seuil, 2006), 218-19.
38 See Gilles Deleuze, *Difference and Repetition*, trans. Paul Patton (New York: Columbia University Press, 1994), 246-7.
39 See Gilles Deleuze, "On Gilbert Simondon," in *Desert Islands and Other Texts: 1953-1974*, trans. Michael Taormina (New York: Semiotext(e), 2004), 86-9.
40 See Gilles Deleuze, *The Logic of Sense*, trans. Mark Lester with Charles Stivale (New York: Columbia University Press, 1990), 103-5.
41 Deleuze, *Difference and Repetition*,152.
42 See Gilbert Simondon, *L'individuation à la lumière des notions de forme et d'information* (Grenoble: Éditions Jérôme Millon, 2005), 166, 197, 248, 316.
43 Ibid., 248. All translations from Simondon's *L'individuation* are mine.
44 See ibid., 513-19.
45 See ibid., 25, 307.
46 See ibid., 32, 95.
47 See ibid., 90.
48 See ibid., 266.
49 See ibid., 34, 308.
50 See ibid., 60, 128.
51 See ibid., 68.
52 See ibid., 82.
53 See ibid., 127.
54 See ibid.
55 See ibid., 158-60.
56 See ibid., 149-151, 163-4, 224-7.
57 See ibid., 190.
58 Ibid., 256-7.
59 See ibid., 316-17.
60 See Slavoj Žižek, *Organs without Bodies: On Deleuze and Consequences* (New York: Routledge, 2004), 111-18.
61 Simondon, *L'individuation*, 208.
62 Johnston, *Prolegomena to Any Future Materialism, Volume Two*.
63 See Simondon, *L'individuation*, 206-7, 316-7.
64 See ibid., 163.
65 See ibid., 165, 276.
66 See ibid., 166.
67 See Adrian Johnston, "Humanity, That Sickness: Louis Althusser and the Helplessness of Psychoanalysis," *Crisis and Critique* 2, no. 2 (2015): 217-61.
68 See Simondon, *L'individuation*, 165.
69 See ibid., 288, 290.
70 See ibid., 173, 197, 204-6, 302.
71 See ibid.,194.
72 See ibid., 242-3.
73 See ibid., 278.

74 See ibid., 257.
75 See ibid., 257–8.
76 See G. W. F. Hegel, *Science of Logic*, trans. A. V. Miller (London: George Allen & Unwin, 1969), 45–7.
77 See G. W. F. Hegel, *Faith and Knowledge*, trans. Walter Cerf and H. S. Harris (Albany: SUNY Press, 1977), 76–7.
78 Catherine Malabou, *Avant demain: Épigenèse et rationalité* (Paris: Presses universitaires de France, 2014), 25. All translations from Malabou's *Avant demain* are mine.
79 Ibid.
80 Catherine Malabou, "Transcendental Epigenesis: A Conversation with Catherine Malabou," in *The Kantian Catastrophe?*, 241–2.
81 Catherine Malabou, *Métamorphoses de l'intelligence: Que faire de leur cerveau bleu?* (Paris: Presses universitaires de France, 2017), 163. All translations are mine.
82 See ibid., 165.
83 See ibid., 96, 98.
84 See Malabou, *Avant demain*, 319–20.
85 See ibid., 261, 303–4.
86 See ibid., 264.
87 See ibid., 158.
88 See ibid., 300.
89 Malabou, *Métamorphoses de l'intelligence*, 118.
90 See Malabou, *Avant demain*, 153, 157, 170.
91 See Immanuel Kant, *Critique of the Power of Judgment*, trans. Paul Guyer and Eric Matthews (Cambridge: Cambridge University Press, 2000), §61 (234), §67 (250-1), §76 (273-4), §78 (280).
92 See Malabou, *Métamorphoses de l'intelligence*, 90.
93 See Malabou, *Avant demain*, 25, 261.
94 Ibid. 170.
95 See ibid.
96 See ibid., 223.
97 Ibid.
98 See ibid.
99 See ibid., 223–5.
100 See ibid., 294.
101 See ibid., 297.
102 Ibid. 296.
103 See ibid., 298.
104 See Johnston, *Prolegomena to Any Future Materialism, Volume Two*.
105 See Hegel, *Science of Logic*, 559, 562–3; G. W. F. Hegel, *The Encyclopedia Logic: Part I of the Encyclopedia of the Philosophical Sciences with the Zusätze*, trans. T. F. Geraets, W. A. Suchting, and H. S. Harris (Indianapolis: Hackett, 1991), 227-30 (§153–4); G. W. F. Hegel, *Lectures on Logic: Berlin, 1831*, trans. Clark Butler (Bloomington: Indiana University Press, 2008), 167–9.

9

On the Essence and Existence of So-called "Fictional Objects"[1]

Markus Gabriel

Jed Martin is a fictional character, a *dramatis persona*. He is the protagonist of Michel Houellebecq's *The Map and the Territory*.[2] In *The Map and the Territory* he is an artist who becomes famous for turning Michelin maps into artworks. Yet, by the same token, Damien Hirst and Jeff Koons are also fictional characters. They too are *dramatis personae* in Houellebecq's *The Map and the Territory*. This raises the question how we can avoid drawing the conclusion that Damien Hirst and Jeff Koons after all do not exist because they are fictional characters. If we assume without further ado that non-existence is a hallmark of fictional objects, we could destroy reality by writing novels about it.

Evidently, we, modern philosophers, should begin by drawing an important distinction here. There are different ways of giving voice to the relevant distinction, but (almost) all parties agree that there has to be one way or another of putting the distinction center stage. If there is not, the theorist's mental economy is threatened with incoherence at best and madness at worst. It seems like there simply has to be an *ontological* distinction between Jed Martin, who is merely a fictional character, and Damien Hirst, who is a living artist present in flesh and blood. Jed Martin and Damien Hirst, according to this thought, cannot and must not exist on the same plane.

The most classical attempt to make sense of the relevant distinction is the founding gesture of Western philosophy in Eleatic times. According to this founding gesture, Jed Martin does not exist whereas Damien Hirst does exist. The relevant distinction would then be a distinction between something non-existent (Jed Martin) on the one hand and something existent (Damien Hirst) on the other hand. For various linguistic and historical reasons, this distinction in Ancient Greek philosophy and beyond was mapped onto a reality/appearance-distinction. One could then say that Jed Martin does not *really* exist (that he is only an appearance), whereas Damien Hirst does *really* exist. Back in the days of archaic Greek poetry, Hesiod already charged Homer with making things up that were not real—a thought radicalized in Plato's critique of art as a source of illusions.[3] In this vein, one could argue then that Jed Martin is somehow essentially a fictional object, whereas Damien Hirst merely happens to be entangled in Houellebecq's web of lies.

In what follows, I will challenge this inherited wisdom on various fronts. In Part I of my chapter I will sketch a central part of the landscape occupied by the most prominent members of the family of views concerning fictional objects. I will conclude that the category "fictional objects" is ill-formed. On closer inspection, the mainstream debate about fictional, non-existent objects is almost completely devoid of ontological content. In Part II, I will rehearse my reasons for believing that Jed Martin exists. He is no less real than Damien Hirst. In Part III, I will present a brand of fictional realism according to which in our field of sense Jed Martin is essentially fictional in that he can only exist in our field of sense to the extent to which we complete his character in exercises of imagination. In this context, I will briefly sketch the outlines of my view that some significant ontological parts of Emmanuel Macron resemble *Le Bureau des légendes* (a famous contemporary French TV series dealing with the French secret service) more closely than one would expect. However, this does not mean that politics should be understood as an extension of aesthetics.

I There are no fictional objects

Ever since the Presocratics and their game-changing echo in book X of Plato's *Republic*, the majority of philosophers have agreed that fictional objects are a subset of non-existent objects. Of course, one might wonder whether all non-existent objects are fictional. But let us assume for the sake of the argument that there is a point in calling some of the allegedly non-existent objects "fictional."

Let an "object" be anything we can think about or mention in the context of truth-apt belief formation. Let us call this the "formal theory of objects." It is often ascribed to Meinong, clearly held by Carnap in *The Logical Structure of the World* and fully articulated in Graham Priest's Neo-Meinongianism.[4] I have many problems with this notion of a formal object, but let us put these aside for the time being. Today, I am more interested in the other half of the spurious concept of a fictional object, namely the "fictional."[5]

In a recent collection of essays on the topic of fictional objects, Stuart Brock and Anthony Everett claim about Jed Martin, Emma Bovary, Gretchen, and their ilk that these kinds of things are typically called "fictional," where this means that they "are individuals first introduced in a work of fiction."[6]

This formulation raises many problems. One general problem is: What is it for an individual to be introduced? A more specific problem concerns the question: What is it to be first introduced? Let us address the specific problem. If the thought behind the expression that some individuals are first introduced within a work of fiction is that an individual is introduced by being referred to or mentioned for the first time in human linguistic history, then far too many objects would have to count as fictional and, therefore, non-existent. Imagine that astronomers from now on formulated their theories in the form of novels, such that every astronomic object discovered from now on accordingly is first introduced in a novel. Or think of the actual fact that a lot of clearly existing objects (including natural kinds such as water or celestial bodies) were first introduced in fictions (mythologies and so forth). If "fictional" is tied to "fiction" in the sense of a genre of writing, it is hard to see why exactly anything which is first introduced in a work of fiction would have to count as non-existent at all, unless one smuggles in the assumption that works of fiction as such only introduce non-existent objects. But this would mean that the only philosophical maneuver performed by our formulation is simply to *call* all objects that are first introduced in a work of fiction non-existent.

But now we are owed an answer to the question why something that is first introduced in a work of fiction automatically counts as non-existent. What exactly is it about works of fiction that accounts for their alleged association with non-existence? Of course, Hesiod, Parmenides, Solon, and Plato's Socrates gave answers to that. But these are not the ones we find anywhere in the recent philosophical debate. So, what is the trouble with fiction then?

One answer to our question is nicely summed up and accepted by Jody Azzouni in his *Talking About Nothing: Numbers, Hallucinations and Fictions*. Here is what Azzouni says:

> I claim that we (collectively) subscribe to a particular criterion for what exists. This is that anything exists if and only if it's mind- and language-independent. Dream figures, fictional characters that authors have made up, and hallucinated objects are all, in the sense meant, mind- and language-dependent. Dinosaurs, protons, microbes, other people, chairs, buildings, stars, and so on are (purported) examples of mind- and language-independent objects. . . . In my sense of "mind-independent" and "language-independent," no one can dictate such an object into existence by (merely) thinking it or symbolizing it as so.[7]

In the quoted passage, Azzouni deploys a standard conception of ontological realism, i.e., realism about "existence" according to which the term "existence" picks out a property that objects have in a mind- and language-independent way. Let us call this *naïve ontological realism*. It is naïve in that it seems to make sense due to certain entrenched ways of thinking but breaks down as soon as we take a closer look at its theoretical commitments.

The first big problem of naïve ontological realism is that it leaves out too many objects that evidently exist and should be counted as existing by any contribution to ontological debate. For instance, the thought expressed by this sentence as well as this sentence exist. But I seem to dictate them into existence by (merely) thinking them or symbolizing them as existing. And what about mind and language themselves? What would it even mean to say that *they* are mind- and language-independent in Azzouni's special sense of the term?

Azzouni could reply by specifying his ontological realism criterion along the following lines: merely thinking something as being a certain way means to undermine the distinction between something being true and something being taken to be true, between *Wahrheit* and *Fürwahrhalten*, to use the German terms here. I call this distinction "the realist contrast of objectivity."[8] Accordingly, one counts as a realist about some domain of objects D if what is true of the objects in D potentially differs from what someone takes to be true of them. To exist would then mean to be such that one can potentially be wrong about an object in question.

Yet such a criterion, to which I myself subscribe *mutatis mutandis*, does not help Azzouni's case. Because now "dream figures, fictional characters that authors have made up, and hallucinated objects" satisfy the existence criterion. I can be wrong about what you dream about. I can be wrong about fictional characters made up by an author. It is not hard to mistake a marginal fictional character in a classical Russian novel for another one given the usual complexity of their names, which often makes it hard to follow a plot if one is not generally acquainted with Russian names.

Hallucinated objects clearly seem to exist, as is shown by the fact that a psychiatrist might ask a person who hallucinates certain shapes, whether they are more like triangles or more like circles. Maybe there is a sense in which the subject of a hallucination is not fallible with respect to hallucinated objects (if there is such a thing!). But there is a sense in which the psychiatrist is in a fallible position. Let us call this overall realism criterion "objectivity of stance." If objectivity of stance were sufficient for ontological realism in general as well as for ontological realism about a particular domain of objects, Azzouni's naïve ontological realism would evaporate.

A second set of problems pertains to social objects such as institutions or artifacts like chairs. Is the fact that Macron is the president of France mind-dependent? And what does that mean? And what about his office? Are the chairs and tables in Macron's office mind-dependent? Famously, John Searle and, in a more extreme manner, Maurizio Ferraris believe that the French Republic is mind-dependent.[9] Arguably, this makes it hard for them to make sense of the fact that artifacts can only exist in social contexts of cooperation, as they would then be in danger of having to accept the claim that chairs and tables are mind-dependent too.

This raises the twofold question: what exactly is "mind-dependence" supposed to be and why is it related to non-existence at all?

In this context, it may be tempting to draw a distinction between *weak mind-dependence* and *strong mind-dependence*. Something is weakly mind-dependent if it would not exist, had no one ever thought of it. Trivially, one has to make a plan to produce a chair. The chair would not exist *en chair et en os* if no minded animals had ever existed who decided to produce chairs. Chairs are artifacts and not aggregates of matter that spontaneously emerge in the universe. Chairs do not grow on trees. But that should not really be a philosophical point. It should be a boring matter of fact that some things are produced by animals in light of some intention or other, whereas some other things are not thus produced.

Unfortunately, Nietzsche in his worst moments, some mad postmodern sociologists, and some neuroscientists have challenged the assumption that there are objects that are not artifacts of human intentions, but I take that to be not worthy of refutation. Weak mind-dependence and weak mind-independence are, therefore, basically a theoretical free lunch.

But what about *strong mind-dependence*? Might there not be another sense of "mind-dependence" which Azzouni and other participants in the mainstream debate about fictional objects are after? At this stage, I want to point out that I have serious doubts about the coherence of any proposal concerning strong mind-dependence.

Let me just mention some of my worries concerning the coherence of a model for mind-dependence proposed by Searle and adopted by Ferraris. According to this model, some object O is strongly mind-dependent if it is socially constructed.

According to them, if something is strongly mind-dependent, it satisfies the following two conditions:

1. To be such that someone declares something to be so and thereby makes it so (*the production condition*).
2. To be such as to remain in existence only as long as there are relevant social/mental traces of it (*the maintenance condition*).

Strongly mind-dependent social facts come into existence in a specific way, and they remain in existence in a specific way. I believe both conditions are problematic. The production condition assumes that there is a special class of propositions that match reality by bringing it about. If the priest utters the words: "I hereby baptize you John," John is therefore called John. If the right person (the authority) says that John is called John, he thereby makes it the case that John is called John.

However, what the authority achieves is not the miraculous feat that a proposition makes itself true by being uttered. For, the act of uttering is not identical to the fact that John is called John as a consequence of a certain action which might or might not include the act of uttering words. If the priest *writes* it down that John is called John, or if there were a community which does not use words at all in the contexts of baptism, it could still be the case that John is called John because someone (a representative of an institution) did something. The act of uttering the words "I hereby baptize you John" is neither a proposition nor an assertion that makes itself true. It would be a confusion to believe that the act of uttering words in this case is almost like the assertion of a proposition, except for the fact that the act of uttering and the being true of the proposition in this case coincide.

Notice in this connection that a fact is something that is true. It is true that John is called John. Yet, that it is true that John is called John is not a logical consequence of the further fact that someone uttered the words: "I hereby baptize you John." Frege in his 1897 *Logic* famously said: "Whether it is true that Julius Caesar was assassinated by Brutus cannot depend on the nature of Professor Mommsen's brain."[10] My argument against the production condition is similar. Whether John is called John cannot depend on the act of uttering the words "I hereby baptize you John." The fact that John is called John might very well be explained with reference to the fact that someone at some point uttered certain words. However, this does not contribute anything to an enhanced understanding of the obscure notion that there is strong mind-dependence after all. Clearly the fact that John is now called John (however that came about) is not strongly mind-dependent on this construal and it is, thus, far from clear what, if anything, the claim that there are declarative speech acts could contribute to an understanding of mind-dependence.[11]

The maintenance condition is in worse explanatory shape. Ferraris believes that we can destroy past social facts by eradicating any physical trace of them in the present. If everybody forgot the ancient Greeks after we destroyed all present evidence of their past existence, then, according to Ferraris, they did not even exist in the past. Therefore, he models his social ontology on an anti-realism similar to Dummett's anti-realism about the past.[12] For Searle it is the case that we can immediately destroy the Federal

Republic of Germany if we all stop believing that it exists. If we all do not recognize its existence, it therefore does not exist. To be sure, this does not mean that we destroy Germany's past existence.

However, this raises the question how could anyone in the future rediscover a social fact from the past? Imagine again that everyone forgets (and, hence, stops believing in) the ancient Greeks. Now, a future archeologist finds some non-linguistic traces of an ancient Greek social fact, such as a column of a temple. According to the anti-realist maintenance condition, the archeologist would not be in any position to recognize the same entity as the Greeks, for he could not get himself into the frame of mind of its maintenance, as there is no fact in mind-independent reality which his thought could latch onto, only a set of past beliefs to which the archeologist has no access. And this would not merely be an epistemological problem like the one we face with non-linguistic documents, such as cave paintings from the deep past of humanity. It would be *metaphysically* impossible to figure out what cave paintings mean if Searle and Ferraris were right. For they would not mean anything according to Searle, and they will not even have meant anything according to Ferraris if we destroy all traces of their meaning.

I conclude that it does not help the case of identifying fictional objects with a subset of the non-existent on the basis of the claim that real existence is related to mind-independence. Mind-independence is simply a red herring in the context of the question of ontological realism. This comes out if we look at the spurious notion of strong mind-independence. It also does not help the case of the mainstream denial of the existence of fictional objects to think of them as first introduced in a fiction, as this concept is ill-framed as well and in need of ontological support.

The philosophical category of fictional objects is devoid of content specific enough to serve as the basis of an account of their non-existence or existence. In my view, the positions on the spectrum from fictional realism (à la van Inwagen, Amie Thomasson, etc.) at the one end, via make-believe and pretense accounts (à la Kendall Walton), to straight fictional irrealism (à la Anthony Everett, Jody Azzouni, etc.) at the other end are prey to the traps of a pseudo-concept.[13]

Arguably, they operate within the parameters of unexamined assumptions about the ontological status of fictions which are a consequence of prior decisions concerning large-scale metaphysical categories such as "mind," "reality," and "existence." They seriously downplay the ontological commitments of academic literary criticism and straightforward aesthetic experience. Watching a movie or reading a novel commits the interpreter to there being certain objects and facts to which she is responsive in the specific way of an aesthetic experience. The disciplines which study the material conditions for aesthetic experience (film studies, literary criticism, theatre studies, musicology, art history, etc.) in turn have ontological commitments that we should not ignore on account of pre-theoretical assumptions concerning what ought and what ought not to count as "real" and "mind-independent." Given that the debates concerning fictional objects assume the truth of some kind of ontological realism, one would expect an argument from the reasons to adopt a relevant form of ontological realism to there being or not being fictional objects. And yet, these thorny ontological issues are largely avoided in the philosophical literature on fictional objects, because the community has agreed to treat fictional objects (or a subset of objects dealt with in the mode of fiction) as a subset of the non-existent. This agreement is not fully earned by explicit ontological theorizing. Actually, it stands on shaky ground as long as the concept of existence that drives the different accounts is not put center stage so that we can begin to evaluate the different proposals against the background of their actual ontology.

A major problem of the recent philosophical literature on (the metaphysics of) fictional objects is that its manifold metaphysical and semantic assumptions about fiction do not result from engaging with actual literary studies. The literature on fictionality is largely ignored, as if we could settle the ontological score of literary criticism without bothering to look at its own articulation of its ontological commitments. This is not an innocent mistake but one that parallels the case of armchair metaphysics deriving claims about the structure of the physical universe without engaging with actual cosmology or advanced theoretical physics. Given that there are actual disciplines studying fictional objects, philosophers should not ignore what they have to say about the fiction/reality-distinction simply because many philosophers like to believe that "medium-sized dry goods" clearly exist whereas Harry Potter clearly does not.

II Jed Martin, Macron and his bureau exist

Famously, there is another way of approaching the topic of the non-existent that does not rely on the bogus notion that any fictional object as such is mind-dependent and, thus, non-existent. It consists in generating the following *Eleatic riddle*. Here is a slightly inflated paradox, as I state some presuppositions in the form of further premises just to be clear about what is going on.

(I) An object, o, is whatever can be thought about in a truth-apt manner.
(II) Paradigmatically, if I think about an object in a truth-apt manner, I ascribe a property to it, such as Π. I think: oΠ.
(III) I can think oΠ iff I can also think ¬oΠ.
(IV) Let E be the property of existence. If I can think: oE, I can think: ¬oE.
(V) "o" in ¬oE refers to o.
(VI) If a term "t" refers to t, there is something, namely t, to which it refers.
(VII) Whenever I truly think of any object o that it does not exist, there is something, namely o, which does not exist.
∴ There are (infinitely) many objects which do not exist.

At first glance, someone confronted with the paradox could attempt to shrug her shoulders by resorting to the scholarly remark that, for true ancient Greek Eleatics, this only seemed to be tantamount to a full-blown paradox because they had a hard time distinguishing between being and existence due to the polysemy of the words ὄν, εἶναι, etc.[14] The paradox would be a linguistic artifact of Ancient Greek to be explained away by distinguishing between being and existence.

This linguistic diagnosis does not cut any ontological ice. The real problem is that the paradox overpopulates *being* in the sense of the overall domain of reference. That both objects that exist and objects that do not exist are part of being, becomes clear when we state that there are objects which exist and objects which do not exist. The domain of reference is, thus, contradictory, because it is now both true that there is no current King of France and that there is a King of France. Hence, there is an unavoidable paradox in the domain of being regardless of the success of any attempt to keep the non-existent beings out of the domain of existence.

To say that fictional objects are non-existent is to say that some objects that are mentioned or characterized in contexts that count as fictional narratives (including movies, works of plastic art, paintings, operas, etc.) are to be counted within the category of ontological troublemakers. On this score, there is nothing ontologically special about them over and above the fact that they are unwelcome intruders in the object domain of our otherwise well-behaved logical systems.

The ontology of fields of sense (FOS) offers a technical solution to the Eleatic riddle based on my personal charity towards all beings. Hence, I am generous enough to accept the obvious: Jed Martin exists. He is an object. What is more, he is an artist, he was born to parents, etc.

This is not paradoxical. In this context, FOS has the formal property of being an ontological relativism. *Ontological relativism* is the view that there is no metaphysically privileged domain of objects such that on the basis of that domain we can count all objects not belonging to it as non-existent. Rather, what rightly counts as existing in one field need not count as existing in another and vice versa. Jed Martin exists in the FOS of *The Map and the Territory*, but he does not exist here in my room. He could not even come here if he had, say, a time machine. It is impossible for him to leave his FOS and to come to this event to prove his existence. He cannot even show up in Paris in order to meet Houellebecq.

However, this obviously raises the following problem. If Jed Martin exists in *The Map and the Territory*, but does not exist in Paris, how about France? France apparently exists in *The Map and the Territory* and it has the property of having Jed Martin as a citizen. France also exists here in the European Union without counting Jed Martin among its citizens. Hence, one cannot say that the same France exists in two fields of sense in order to draw a neat distinction between those fictional objects that exist *only* in the novel and those that *also* exist in our FOS. This makes it hard to see how the same fictional text could deal with Jed Martin and France at the same time.

To put it in familiar philosophical jargon: is there a counterpart theory for fields of sense ontology, and if so, how does it work? Is there a counterpart of France in *The Map and the Territory*? If there is no counterpart of France in *The Map and the Territory* identical to or strongly resembling France as we know it, we cannot easily think the thought:

(T) Some objects in *The Map and the Territory* (say, France) exist, whereas some other objects in *The Map and the Territory* (say, Jed Martin) do not exist.[15]

The good news is that we cannot and need not think (T). In *The Map and the Territory* the term "France" cannot refer to France but at best to something that is strikingly similar to France in some interpretations of the novel. Fictions deal with something that *seems to* resemble our reality. What the novel calls "France" is something that might be similar to France on an interpretation, but that is another matter. A (rough) way of putting the idea might be this: *a* can be said to resemble *b* given specifiable similarities and differences. So, we might have a set of all true statements about France and a set of all true statements about France in the novel. Some will match, others won't. But this is to think that novels are descriptions of modal variations on our reality, whereas in fact they are ontologically speaking concerned only with themselves. Hence, we cannot properly speak of resemblance here, maximal or minimal. This is what it means for fictional objects to be ontologically isolated from us. Novels are no variation on our world at all, they are not possible worlds—but they are not impossible worlds either.[16] Rather, novels and other artworks are fields of sense which exist in other fields of sense. Yet, given their isolation from the fields of sense within which both the artworks and we exist, the objects of fiction penetrate our reality only in the form of an overlap and vice versa. The specific overlap in the case of fiction has the following form: we do not intentionally relate to Paris when interpreting a novel in which the term "Paris" is used in order to invoke a certain aesthetic experience putting us in touch with an object resembling Paris. We, therefore, relate to something existing in our field of sense as isolated from it in the sense that has parts that do not appear in our field of sense but only in a field of sense appearing in our field of sense.

The power (and, thus, danger) of the kind of fiction produced by Houellebecq in works such as *The Possibility of an Island* or *Submission* lies precisely in the fact that they deal with something that seems to resemble our reality, but departs from it in such a way that it suggests a possibility for us.[17] But the point about fiction, including science-fiction, is not to teach us something about our reality, about a pending possibility, but only to talk about itself. Novels are not statements concerning what could happen in reality but did not or does not happen. They are not modal experiments. Novels are not factual descriptions of possible worlds.

Fictional objects are ontologically isolated from us. We can exercise our imagination by working out the details of works of art, how the objects hang together, etc., by connecting the dots and by adding information to what is explicitly given to us by the score of a work of art in the context of interpretation. We learn something about our reality in aesthetic experience because aesthetic experience is part of our reality.

Ontologically speaking, fiction is maximally separated from reality. There are no fictional counterparts to real objects. Here, a "real object" is meant to be an object that is part of our field of sense, such as Portugal. I do not wish to imply that there is a big metaphysical thing called reality that settles what is real and what is not. Jed Martin and Paris are equally real, but they are real in their respective fields of sense which do not ontologically overlap.

This is what we mean when we say that Jed Martin does not exist. We must, however, not forget that he does exist despite the fact that he does not. This is neither a contradiction nor some other kind of paradox or joke. It is merely a simple consequence of ontological relativism. The utterance "Jed Martin does and does not exist" expresses the non-contradictory proposition:

(JM) Jed Martin exists in *The Map and the Territory* and does not exist in France.

At most, he exists in France in *The Map and the Territory*, which is not tantamount to saying that he exists in France, because France is not identical to France in *The Map and the Territory*.

III Jed Martin, Macron and the imagination

At this point, I would like to sketch my answer to the question why so many believe that fictional objects do not exist. I claim that the background motivation of much of contemporary theorizing about the non-existent is the following: some objects depend for their existence on specific exercises of the imagination. Our best way of learning about Jed Martin is by reading Houellebecq's novel.

In 1978 the distinguished literary theorist and professor of English and American literature Herbert Grabes published an influential paper on our topic which, as far as I can tell, is completely ignored in the philosophical debate. The paper bears the title "How Sentences Turn into Persons ... On the Study of Literary Characters" (*Wie aus Sätzen Personen werden... Über die Erforschung literarischer Figuren*).[18] Grabes reminds us that novels contain sentences which are turned into characters by an interpretation, by a reading of them. Without an interpretation, a novel does not contain anything that has the form of a description.

In order to know anything about Jed Martin, we have to read about him. The novel provides us with different sources of information: the narrator tells us something about Jed, other characters meet him, there is a context in which actions and properties of Jed make sense, and so forth. On the basis of these data, we are entitled to imagine Jed Martin. To imagine Jed Martin need not mean to have a clear mental image of him, as if in a vivid dream. The imagery that pops up as we imagine Jed Martin can have all sorts of psychological effects on the reader. Nevertheless, it plays a role in our understanding of Jed Martin, as it gives us reasons to believe that he is a certain way.

Now my imaginary representation and your imaginary representation of Jed Martin will differ. Yet, I am certain that you and I believe that Jed Martin is a person, that he has two legs, that he knows that Paris has a subway system, that he has heard of the French Revolution, Picasso, the moon, and earthquakes. Nonetheless, the novel nowhere explicitly mentions any of this. If we stick to the explicit information that is provided by the novel, Jed Martin might as well be a giant with superpowers or an alien intruder who pretends to be human. As a matter of fact, it is not even clear to what extent we would be justified in thinking of him as human at all. How do you know that he is not a robot or a hologram from the future send to the past by some wicked Artificial Intelligence System? Maybe *The Possibility of an Island* and *The Map and the Territory* describe the same state of affairs such that the plot narrated in *The Map and the Territory* is a kind of computer simulation that is run as a software on the artificial bodies of the neo-humans in *The Possibility of an Island*.

The point of this train of thought is simply this: Jed Martin essentially exists in our imagination in such a way that we make up answers to many questions that are neither asked nor answered by the novel itself. Without this activity, there would indeed be no such person as Jed Martin in a field of sense appearing in our field of sense. The only way for Jed to make an appearance in our field of sense is via our imagination. Currently, you and I are imagining him to be a certain way. You and I will imagine different details. I imagine him to look quite like Houellebecq, you might imagine him to look like Pierre Lamallatie, or like the actor who played Jed Martin in the play produced on the basis of the novel at the Deutsches Schauspielhaus Hamburg. Everyone is free to imagine him in a variety of ways. The novel itself at most defines a common denominator, a Jed-Martin-Type. This type only has token-instantiation in the form of an exercise of imagination.

Jed Martin is essentially an imaginary object. Had no one ever imagined him, he would not have made an appearance in any field of sense in which *we* exist. Yet, this does not mean that he is mind-dependent in any heavy-weight sense that goes beyond the obvious fact that no one in our field could ever know anything about him, had it not been in virtue of an exercise of imagination. We do not maintain him in existence due to some psychological effort of maintaining his image in front of the eye of our mind or any such thing.

In particular, Jed Martin's imaginary existence does not undermine realism about him. Jed Martin is real. From our point of view, his reality resides is the fact that he exists in manifold ways in different exercises of imagination. We can have true and false beliefs about him. And this is sufficient for realism in the sense of a "neutral realism."[19] Thought about Jed Martin is objective. It satisfies the "contrast of objectivity,"[20] as I call it. The contrast of objectivity holds in a region of thought if there is a semantic gap between holding something to be true and it being true. I can hold something which is false as true of Jed Martin and hold something which is true of Jed Martin as false. Many people have no beliefs at all about Jed Martin. Still, he exists. Jed Martin does not undermine the distinction between believing and being the case. This is why we ought to be realists about him and his ontological family, that is to say, about literary characters that play a role in realistic narratives.

The very reason why we ought to be realists about Jed Martin entails that he is a human being. This is why I disagree with most forms of fictional realism in contemporary analytic aesthetics and metaphysics. Peter van Inwagen, for instance, believes that someone like Jed Martin has the same ontology as the title of the novel in which he makes an appearance. Jed Martin is basically not different from ink on a piece of paper. Clearly, it makes sense to establish a link between various occurrences of the same name, "Jed Martin," within the novel. Yet, according to Peter van Inwagen, this does not entail that Jed Martin is a human being. Similar things have to be said vis-à-vis Amie Thomasson's abstract-object approach. She treats fictional objects as abstract objects. However, no human person is an abstract object. Therefore, either Jed Martin is not a fictional object in Thomasson's sense or is no fictional object after all.

None of this is to deny that Jed Martin is a somewhat strange object if we measure his objectivity by the norm of everyday thought about mesoscopic objects. There are different identity criteria for Jed Martin and for Emmanuel Macron on that front. For instance, I am entitled to imagine Jed Martin to look like Houellebecq and Houellebecq is entitled to imagine him to look like Pierre Lamallatie. There is no fact of the matter beyond the one we can grasp by studying and reading the novel that decides between the two exercises of imagination. However, if I imagine Macron to look like Christian Lindner and Wolfgang Schäuble imagines him to look like Yanis Varoufakis, both I and Wolfang Schäuble would make a mistake if we could not recognize Macron when we meet him. To be sure, I can imagine Macron to look like all sorts of things—in my dreams, in comic strips, in novels, in my everyday fantasy life, etc. However, there are facts of the matter as to how Macron looks. Macron maximally resembles himself and much less resembles, say, Mother Theresa. He resembles Christian Linder more than Wolfgang Schäuble. None of this applies to Jed Martin, the fictional character.

Here we need to pause a minute, because my account is not as simple as I just made it look! Notice that I draw a distinction between Jed Martin, the fictional character, and Jed Martin, the artist. The difference corresponds to the level of *metafictional analysis* on the one hand and the level of what I call an *interpretation* on the other hand. By a "metafictional analysis" I understand a literary study of the text of the novel in which Jed Martin plays the role of a protagonist. To claim that he is a protagonist is a claim that makes sense in the context of a literary study of the novel. Many other things can be said about the fictional character. We can look at the language used to characterize Jed Martin and compare it to the language used to describe his artworks. We can count the sentences about Jed Martin ascribed to the narrator as opposed to the sentences about him ascribed to some fictional character or other (including self-descriptions of Jed Martin by himself). A metafictional analysis relies on conceptual tools developed in different academic branches that deal with literary characters.

There would be no point to metafictional analysis if there were no aesthetic experience of reading a novel, attending an opera, listening to a symphony, enjoying the beauty of the Madonna painted by Raphael or what have you. Aesthetic experience is not some kind of blind rapture. Otherwise, it would not matter which object triggered it. There would be no aesthetic difference between $Madonna_1$ (the pop queen) and $Madonna_2$ (the character as painted by Raphael). The hermeneutic tradition rightly insisted on the objectivity of aesthetic experience against the subjectivist strand in Kant's theory of aesthetic judgment: beauty cannot be identical to subjective titillation; it is not in the eye of the beholder.

In order to circumvent the subjectivism implicit in the notion of aesthetic experience, I prefer to speak of interpretation. I use the term "interpretation" in the sense of performance. A symphony has to be performed in order for it to be part of an aesthetic experience, a novel has to be read, a film has to be watched, etc. In all these cases, the work of art (the score) is realized in the medium of imagination. The medium of imagination gives the work its unity.

A work of art is in need of unity. Without interpretation, Jed Martin would have an open essence. From the standpoint of metafictional analysis, Jed Martin is indeed many objects. The object you imagine being Jed Martin and the one I imagine are simply not the same object. What makes it the case that they seem to be the same object is the existence of Jed Martin, the metafictional object. The metafictional object left by itself is precisely open to interpretation. However, on any acceptable interpretation, Jed Martin has an essence. Thus, there are as many Jed Martins as there are acceptable interpretations despite the fact that there is just one fictional character denoted by the term "Jed Martin" in a metafictional analysis.

Jed Martin splits into many related objects.

On the one hand, *qua* object of aesthetic experience (reading the novel and imaging its events, etc.), we can call him a *hermeneutical object*. Hermeneutical objects essentially are objects of interpretation, where this means that the interpreter (the subject engaged in aesthetic experience) makes sense of what is given to her by the score of the artwork in terms of performance. A performance can have many layers: we can perform the score of a symphony by having an orchestra play it, which does not yet add up to an aesthetic experience if no one makes sense of that performance in the context of an activity of listening to the symphony and of judging it to be a certain way on the basis of past aesthetic experience with similar performances.

On the other hand, the metafictional analysis of the relationship between the score, a performance, and a range of permissible interpretations (responsive aesthetic experience) tells us something about Jed Martin *qua meta-hermeneutical object*. So-called "fictional objects" exist both within the scope of aesthetic experience and as meta-hermeneutical commitments. Metafictional analysis studies the range of acceptable interpretations by teaching us something about the material conditions of a score in its relation to possible performances. There are non-negotiable facts about the scores of artworks that need to be respected by any performance and interpretation that can still count as "faithful" or "responsive" to its objects. In aesthetics it is not true that anything goes. Interpretation is simply not arbitrary. We might believe that it is, as long as we take it for granted that fictional objects do not exist anyway, so that the realist contrast of objectivity potentially separating what is true from what we take to be true cannot apply to them. But that is false given that we can make mistakes both about hermeneutical and meta-hermeneutical objects.

Jed Martin is not an incomplete object. He is only incomplete as long as we do not interpret him. But this is no paradox. For "Jed Martin" refers to, on the one hand, a fictional character studied by literary criticism, and on the other hand, to a person imagined to be a certain way by different readers and relative to divergent readings.

To use Jocelyn Benoist's vocabulary in this context: "Jed Martin," the fictional character, is a norm.[21] This norm leaves many things open. The domain opened up by the norm can be filled by specific interpretations of the norm. Once an actual interpretation is in place, it changes the norm by adding further conceptual elements to it. As soon as we agree that it makes sense to interpret Jed Martin in terms of salient properties of Michel Houellebecq (his mouth, hair, or whatever), some further things will make sense. If we read the novel in a different way, other things will make sense. The novel sets the frame for different interpretations without choosing between any of them. We are free to interpret the novel in many ways. However, the score of the work of art at the same time rules out many interpretations.

We can now introduce a third term of art in order to designate the space between Jed Martin, the fictional character, and Jed Martin, the artist who has certain properties in a given interpretation. I want to call it the SPIELRAUM. The German word "Spielraum" corresponds to the idea of a "room for maneuver." "Spielraum" is hermeneutic wiggle room.[22]

The practice of fiction is grounded in the fact that there is some SPIELRAUM. There is room between the norms set by the work of art itself and the norms defined by a specific performance. The room is not infinite, though. If we stretch our interpretations too much, they will not count as interpretations of a work of art anymore, but maybe as a new work of art or no work of art at all.

IV Concluding thoughts about Macron

I would like to conclude my reflections by coming back to Macron. Macron is the *président de la République*. As such, he resembles a fictional character in the following sense. The rule books of the French constitution, the legal system, the party system, etc., make up a norm we call "président de la République." This norm is interpreted by Macron and by the voters in different ways. Therefore, there is a case of SPIELRAUM separating the legal system from what actually takes place in Macron's and our imaginations. The ontology of social objects such as *le président de la République* involves the ontology of imagination. There is no politics without imagination.

However—and this is crucial!—politics is not a work of art. Macron is not only a fictional character. To put it differently, Macron is not essentially or constitutively a fictional character. On the contrary, Macron, the human being, is responsible for certain actions, looks a certain way, and so forth, in such a way that there is absolutely no room for interpretation on this level.

One of the many problems in our time and age is that too many confuse politics and aesthetics. To be sure, there is an overlap of these fields of sense, but there is absolutely no identity here. Gadamer's student Rüdiger Bubner used to speak of the "aesthetization of the life world" (*Ästhetisierung der Lebenswelt*).[23] This modern process consists in the fact that the actual border separating the fictional from the social becomes more and more invisible to a large group of people. But this does not mean that there is no such border or that the border is evaporating. On the contrary! The fact that there is an ontological border between the imaginary and the social is precisely part of the explanation of the crises of representation we witness today in Western politics. Social facts are produced by actions. These actions are political insofar as they are based on the distribution of economic resources including services, jobs, conditions of productions such as factory machines, banks, tanks, etc. The distribution of economic resources and the negotiations accompanying and justifying it are not fictional at all. However, it could not be justified in the public sphere to the people without an ingredient of fiction. Ideology is thus a necessary byproduct of large-scale social systems that produce economic resources and distribute them in light of a rulebook that cannot be transparent to everyone for whom this distribution has economic consequences. This is why there is such a rich and deluded fantasy life in a globalized economy which, by its very nature, is more opaque than any other economic system humanity has ever witnessed.

The socio-economic realm overlaps with the legal system. The legal system defines norms, which characterize actions and consequences (property law and so on). These norms are then typically interpreted by judges and other sub-systems of nation-states.

There is friction at the intersections of the fields of sense that come to overlap in actual politics. This friction appears in the public sphere as fiction. The news media, for instance, fictionalize the distribution of resources and turn it into narratives. In these narratives, Macron appears as a fictional character which can be studied by our practices of metafictional analysis. However, this does not transform politics or Macron into fictional characters in the sense of Jed Martin. Macron shares many of the same fields of sense with us, such as Paris, France, or Europe. Whereas Jed Martin is only there (in *The Map and the Territory*), Macron is also here (in Paris).

Notes

1 This chapter draws on a research project on the ontology of fictional objects supported by the Lynen Fellowship of the Alexander von Humboldt Foundation and the CNRS (LIA CRNR – UMR 8103). I would like to thank these institutions for their generous support.
2 Michel Houellebecq, *The Map and the Territory*, trans. Gavin Bowd (New York: Vintage International, 2011).
3 On the historical background of the fiction/reality distinction see Hans-Robert Jauss, "Zur historischen Genese der Scheidung von Fiktion und Realität," in *Funktionen des Fiktiven*, eds. Wolfgang Iser and Dieter Henrich (München: Wilhelm Fink, 1983), 423–31; and Martin Hose, "Fiktionalität und Lüge: Über einen Unterschied zwischen römischer und griechischer Terminologie," *Poetica* 28 (1996): 257–74.
4 See, paradigmatically, Rudolf Carnap, *The Logical Structure of the World and Pseudoproblems in Philosophy*, trans. Rolf A. George (Peru, IL: Carus, 2003) and Graham Priest, *Towards Non-being: The Logic and Metaphysics of Intentionality* (Oxford: Oxford University Press, 2005).
5 For details see Markus Gabriel, *Fields of Sense: A New Realist Ontology* (Edinburgh: Edinburgh University Press, 2015).
6 Stuart Brock and Anthony Everett, *Fictional Objects* (Oxford: Oxford University Press, 2015), 3.
7 Jody Azzouni, *Talking About Nothing: Numbers, Hallucinations and Fictions* (Oxford: Oxford University Press, 2010), 14.
8 For more on this see Markus Gabriel, "Neutral Realism," in *The Monist* 98, no. 2 (April 2015): 181–96 and *At the Boundaries of Epistemology: Finitude, Objective Knowledge and the Lessons of Scepticism* (Cambridge: Polity, forthcoming).
9 John R. Searle, *The Construction of Social Reality* (New York: The Free Press, 1995); *Making the Social World* (Oxford: Oxford University Press, 2010); Maurizio Ferraris, *Documentality: Why It Is Necessary to Leave Traces*, trans. Richard Davies (New York: Fordham University Press, 2013).
10 My translation of "Ob es wahr ist, daß Julius Caesar von Brutus ermordet wurde, kann nicht von der Beschaffenheit des Gehirns von Professor Mommsen abhängen." Cf. Gottlob Frege, "Logic," in *Gottlob Frege: Posthumous Writings*, eds. Hans Hermes, Friedrich Kambartel, and Friedrich Kaulbach (Oxford: Blackwell, 1979), 126–52, 148.
11 Of course, Searle does not use his model of social construction in an account of the ontology of fictional objects. Rather, he is one of the most prominent defenders of a pretense-theory, according to which fictional discourse neither contains assertions nor

genuine declarations. For his account of fictional discourse see John R. Searle, "The Logical Status of Fictional Discourse," in *New Literary History* 6, no. 2 (1975): 319–32.
12 See Michael Dummett, "The Reality of the Past," in *Truth and Other Enigmas* (Cambridge, MA: Harvard University Press, 1978), 358–74.
13 Cf. Peter van Inwagen, "Creatures of Fiction," *American Philosophical Quarterly* 14, no. 4 (1977): 299–308; Peter van Inwagen, "Fiction and Metaphysics," *Philosophy and Literature* 7, no. 1 (1983): 67–77; Amie L. Thomasson, *Fiction and Metaphysics* (Cambridge: Cambridge University Press, 1999); Amie L. Thomasson, *Ontology Made Easy* (Oxford: Oxford University Press, 2015); Kendall L. Walton, *Mimesis as Make-Believe: On the Foundations of Representational Arts* (Cambridge, MA, and London: Harvard University Press, 1990); Anthony Everett, *The Nonexistent* (Oxford: Oxford University Press, 2013); Jody Azzouni, *Talking about Nothing: Numbers, Hallucinations and Fictions* (Oxford: Oxford University Press, 2010).
14 See Charles Kahn, *Essays on Being* (Oxford: Oxford University Press, 2009); Graham Priest, "*Sein* Language," *The Monist* 97, no. 4 (October 2014): 430–42.
15 For an analysis of this thought and an associated account of non-committal thought about non-existent objects, see Tim Crane, *The Objects of Thought* (Oxford: Oxford University Press, 2013).
16 I owe most of this paragraph to Alexander Englander, who suggested these formulations as his interpretation of what I was saying in an earlier draft.
17 See Michel Houellebecq, *The Possibility of an Island*, trans. Gavin Bowd (New York: Vintage, 2007), and *Submission*, trans. Lorin Stein (New York: Picador, 2015).
18 See Herbert Grabes, "Wie aus Sätzen Personen werden ... Über die Erforschung literarischer Figuren," *Poetica* 10 (1978): 405–28.
19 See Gabriel, "Neutral Realism" and *Fields of Sense*.
20 See Gabriel, *At the Boundaries of Epistemology*.
21 On the idea of an object as norm, see most recently Jocelyn Benoist, *L'addresse du réel* (Paris: Vrin, 2017), chapters 4 and 5.
22 On this see Hans-Georg Gadamer, *The Relevance of the Beautiful and Other Essays*, trans. Nicholas Walker (Cambridge: Cambridge University Press, 1987).
23 Rüdiger Bubner, "Ästhetisierung der Lebenswelt," in *Ästhetische Erfahrung* (Frankfurt am Main: Suhrkamp, 1989), 143–56.

10

Klein Bottle: *Le tube de caption*, or, the Subject's Snout[1]

Slavoj Žižek

I A Snout in Plato's cave

In October 2017, the media reported that archaeologists had discovered a thirty-meter-long tunnel hidden within the limestone and granite walls of the Great Pyramid of Giza. Since its function was not clear, they simply—and quite adequately—referred to it as "the Void."[2] The pyramid was thus confirmed to be a gigantic *Ding* in the Heideggerian sense, a massive form enveloping a void, which is its true "object." Where does this strange need to redouble the void, to isolate some space in the infinite void of our universe and, in the midst of this enclave, reproduce another void come from? To grasp this, we have to change our most basic view of reality.

The predominant philosophical view today is that of the openness towards the world: we are not separated from external reality through the wall or screen of our mental representations, we are always-already in the world, thrown into it and engaged in it, so (as the early Heidegger put it) the question "How can we reach beyond our representations into reality itself?" is a wrong one, it presupposes a gap (between our representations of things and things themselves) it tries to overcome … This predominant view is right in the sense that the whole image of our Self "inside" and the external reality "outside," with the concomitant problem of how can I step outside my mind and reach external reality the way it is in itself, should be discarded; however, it should not be discarded in this predominant way of asserting our "being-in-the-world" (we are always-already thrown in the world). Following the model of the convoluted space, we should rather explore how, if we go deep "inside" our Self, behind the phenomenal self-experience of our thought, we can again find ourselves in the (immanent) outside of neuronal processes—our singular Self dissolves in a pandemonium of processes whose status is less and less "psychic" in the usual sense of the term. The paradox is thus that I only "am" a Self at a distance not only from outside reality, but also from my innermost inside: my inside remains inside only insofar as I do not get too close to it. We should thus propose another model to replace the couple of my mental life "inside" and the reality "outside": that of the Self as a fragile screen, a thin surface separating the two outsides, that of the external reality and that of the Real.

Against the predominant view, one should therefore shamelessly assert the idea that we live in a closed universe, like prisoners in Plato's cave. We could thus re-tell the story of Plato's cave. In a general approach, we should read Plato's parable as a myth in the Lévi-Straussian sense, so that one has to look for bits of meaning not through its direct interpretation, but rather by way of locating it in a series of variations, i.e., by way of comparing it with other variations of the same story. The elementary frame of the so-called "postmodernism" can effectively be conceived as a network of three modes of inversion of Plato's allegory. First, there is the inversion of the meaning of the central source of light (sun): what if this center is a kind of Black Sun, a terrifying monstrous Evil Thing, and for *this* reason impossible to sustain? Second, what if (along the lines of Peter Sloterdijk's *Spheres*) we invert the meaning of the cave: what if it is cold and windy out in the open, on the earth's surface, too dangerous to survive there, so people themselves decided to dig out the cave to find a shelter/home/sphere? In this way, the cave appears as the first model of building a home, a safe isolated place of dwelling—building one's cave is what distinguishes us from beasts, it is the first act of civilization. Finally, there is the standard postmodern variation: the true myth is precisely the notion that, outside the theatre of shadows, there is some "true reality" or a central Sun—all there is are different theatres of shadows and their endless interplay. The properly Lacanian twist to the story would be that for us, within the cave, the Real outside the cave can only appear as a *shadow of a shadow*, as a gap between different modes or domains of shadows. It is thus not simply that substantial reality disappears in the interplay of appearances; what rather happens in this shift is that the very irreducibility of the appearance to its substantial support, its "autonomy" with regard to it, engenders a Thing of its own, the true "real Thing." Furthermore, there is an aspect of Plato's story of the cave that touches upon the innermost tension of the process of emancipation, bringing out yet another version of the Moebius strip reversal, this time between freedom and servitude:

> The exit from the cave begins when one of the prisoners is not only freed from his chains (as Heidegger shows this is not at all enough to liberate him from the libidinal attachment to the shadows), but when he is forced out. This clearly must be the place for the (libidinal, but also epistemological, political, and ontological) function of the master. This can only be the master who neither tells me what precisely to do nor represents the one whose instrument I could become; instead, he is the one who just "gives me back to myself." And in a sense, one might say this could be connected to Plato's anamnesis theory (remembering what one never knew, as it were) and implies that the proper master just affirms or makes it possible for me to affirm that "I can do this," without telling me what this is, that is, without telling me (too much of) who I am.[3]

The point Ruda makes here is a subtle one: it's not only that if I am left to myself in the cave, even if without chains, I prefer to stay there, so that a master has to force me out—I have to volunteer to be forced out, similarly to the way in which, when a subject enters psychoanalysis, he volunteers to do it, i.e., he voluntarily accepts the psychoanalyst as his master (albeit in a very specific way):

Precisely at this point, the reference to the master in psychoanalytic terms provokes the question: does this mean that those who need a master are—always already—in the position of the analysand? If—politically—one needs such a master in order to become who one is, to use Nietzsche's formula (and this can be structurally linked to liberating the prisoner from the cave, i.e., forcing him out after the chains have been taken off and he still does not want to leave), the question arises how to link this with the idea that the analysand must constitutively be a *volunteer* (and not simply a slave or a bondsman). So, in short, there must be a dialectics of master and volunteer(s): a dialectics because the master to some extent constitutes the volunteers as volunteers (liberates them from a previously seemingly unquestionable position), so that they then become voluntary followers of the master's injunction, whereby the master ultimately becomes superfluous. Of course, the master becomes obsolete only for a certain period of time, for afterwards one has to repeat this very process. One never leaves the cave entirely, so to speak, one constantly has to re-encounter the master, and the anxiety linked to it, such that there must always be a re-punctuation if things get stuck, or mortifyingly habitualized, again.[4]

What further complicates the picture is that

> capitalism relies massively on unpaid and thereby structurally "voluntary" labour. There are, to put it with Lenin, volunteers and "volunteers," so, maybe, one has to not only distinguish between different types of master-figures, but also link them (if the link to psychoanalysis is pertinent in this way) to different understandings of the volunteer (i.e., the analyzand). Even the analyzand as a volunteer must be somehow forced into analysis. This might seem to bring classical readings of the master-slave dialectics back onto the stage, but I think one should bear in mind that as soon as the slave identifies himself as a slave, he is no longer a slave, whereas the voluntary worker in capitalism can identify himself as what he is and this changes nothing (capitalism interpellates people as "nothings," volunteers, etc.).[5]

These two levels of volunteering (which are simultaneously two levels of *servitude volontaire*) are different not only with regard to the content of servitude (to market mechanisms, to an emancipatory cause), but their very form is different. In capitalist servitude, we simply feel free, while in authentic liberation, we accept voluntary servitude as serving a Cause and not just ourselves. In today's cynical functioning of capitalism, I can know very well what I am doing and continue to do it, but the liberating aspect of my knowledge is nevertheless suspended, while in the authentic dialectics of liberation, the awareness of my situation is already the first step of liberation. In capitalism, I am enslaved precisely when I "feel free." This feeling is the very form of my servitude. In an emancipatory process, on the other hand, I am free when I "feel like a slave," i.e., the very feeling of being enslaved already bears witness to the fact that, in the core of my subjectivity, I am free. In other words, only when my position of enunciation is that of a free subject, can I experience my servitude as an abomination. Here, we are thus faced with two versions of the Moebius strip reversal:

if we follow capitalist freedom to the end, the I turns into the very form of servitude, and if we want to break out of the capitalist *servitude volontaire*, our assertion of freedom again has to assume the form of its opposite, of voluntarily serving a Cause.

So, let's add yet another version of Plato's cave, that of the inside of the Klein bottle. A traveler/subject walks on the rounded surface of proto-reality and falls into the abyss (like an atom falling in Ancient Greek atomism); instead of just disappearing into the abyss, the traveler/subject makes a "clinamenesque" turn, redirects the tube into which he is falling aside, then makes a U-turn, and ends up looking up at the rounded space of the cave (which is the same surface upon which he was walking at the beginning, but this time seen from the inside). What a spectator sees inside the bottle is like the monolith depicted in Arnold Böcklin's "Isle of the Dead" (among many other references, it was used by Patrice Chéreau as the model for Brünhilde's rock in his famous 1976 staging of Wagner's *Ring*)—an enclosed space evoking a scene-setting. This closed circular space is of course sustained by a complex stage machinery—but our awareness of it paradoxically does not ruin its magic effect. More threatening than the awareness of this machinery is the protuberance (tube) that functions as a blind spot in the image, the point where we, the spectators, are inscribed into it. If an idiot comes along and wants to erase this protuberance, the result would not be a perfect image but the dissolution of the knot which held it together, and thereby a complete disintegration of (its) reality. "I was the world in which I walked, . . ."[6]—the task is to read these lines in a totally non-solipsist way: it is not that I am the sole source of my reality so that it only exists in my mind, but that me and my reality form a (truncated) whole, which disintegrates if I am cut out of it, and what the Klein bottle model enables us to do is to deploy the process through which this closed whole emerges.

One should note here that this view is confirmed by today's cognitive sciences—Thomas Metzinger proposes a rereading/radicalization of the three standard metaphors of the human mind: Plato's cave, the representationalist metaphor, and the metaphor of a total flight-simulator. As to Plato's cave, Metzinger endorses its basic premise: we misperceive a phenomenal "theatre of shadows" (our immediate experience of reality) for reality, we are constrained by this illusion in a necessary "automatic" way, and we should struggle to achieve true self-knowledge. Where he differs is with regard to a very precise point: there is no self who is tied down in the middle of the cave and can then leave the cave in search of the true light of the sun:

> There are low-dimensional phenomenal shadows of external perceptual objects dancing on the neural user surface of the caveman's brain. So much is true. There certainly is a phenomenal *self*-shadow as well. But what is this shadow the low-dimensional projection *of*? . . . [I]t is a shadow not of a captive person, but of the cave as a whole. . . . There is no true subject and no homunculus in the cave that could confuse itself with anything. It is the cave as a whole, which episodically, during phases of waking and dreaming, projects a shadow of itself onto one of its many internal walls. The cave shadow is there. The cave is empty.[7]

This brings us to the second—representationalist—metaphor: our phenomenal experience is a dynamic multidimensional map of the world—but with a twist: "like only very few of the *external* maps used by human beings, it also has a little red arrow.... [T]he phenomenal self *is* the little red arrow in your conscious map of reality."⁸ Metzinger refers to city, airport or shopping mall maps in which a little red arrow stands for the observer's location within the mapped space ("You are here!"):

> Mental self-models are the little red arrows that help a phenomenal geographer to navigate her own complex mental map of reality.... The most important difference between the little red arrow on the subway map and the little red arrow in our neurophenomenological troglodyte's brain is that the external arrow is *opaque*. It is always clear that it is only a representation—a placeholder for something else.... The conscious self-model in the caveman's brain itself, however, is in large portions transparent: ... it is a phenomenal self characterized not only by full-blown prereflexive embodiment but by the comprehensive, all-encompassing subjective experience of *being situated*.⁹

This "red arrow," of course, is what Lacan called the signifier, which represents the subject for other signifiers; and our total immersion into the map brings us to the third metaphor, that of a *total flight simulator*:

> The brain differs from the flight simulator in not being used by a student pilot, who episodically 'enters' it.... A total flight simulator is a self-modeling airplane that has always flown without a pilot and has generated a complex internal image of itself within its *own* internal flight simulator. The image is transparent. The information that it is an internally generated image is not yet available to the system as a whole.... Like the neurophenomenological caveman, "the pilot" is born into a virtual reality right from the beginning—without a chance to ever discover this fact.¹⁰

There is, however, a vicious circle in this version of the cave argument (a cave projects itself onto the cave-wall, and *it generates/simulates the observer itself*): while the cave can simulate the substantial identity/content of the observer, it cannot simulate the FUNCTION of the observer, since, in this case, we would have a fiction observing itself, like Escher's hand drawing a hand that, in turn, draws the first hand. In other words, while what the observer immediately identifies with the experience of self-awareness is a fiction, something with no positive ontological status, *his very activity of observing is a positive ontological fact*. And it is at this point that we should return to the model of the Klein bottle: what Metzinger ignores is the additional convolution, the "snout," which gives birth to the very observer. Or, to put it in a somewhat simplified way: Metzinger's limit is that his model implies a simple clear-cut distinction between reality (of the neuronal mechanism) and fiction (of the autonomous self as a free agent); while this model explains how fiction is generated by objective neuronal processes, it ignores how these objective neuronal processes have to rely on an efficient fiction, i.e., how they can only function if, in the guise of the "snout" that is the subject, fiction intervenes into reality.

In the second staircase murder (of Detective Arbogast) from Hitchcock's *Psycho* (1960), we first get the Hitchcockian God's-point-of-view, shot from above of the entire scene taking place on the first floor corridor and stairs; when the shrieking creature enters the frame and starts stabbing Arbogast, we pass to the creature's subjective point-of-view, a close-up of Arbogast's face falling down the stairs and being sliced up—as if, in this twist from an objective to a subjective shot, God himself had lost his neutrality and "fallen into" the world, brutally intervening in it, delivering justice. Another exemplary case of such impossible subjectivity is the famous God's-view-shot of the burning Bodega Bay in Hitchcock's *The Birds* (1963), which is then, when the birds enter into the frame (as if from behind the viewer's back), re-signified, subjectivized, transformed from the objective view-from-nowhere of the entire town into the point-of-view of the evil aggressors themselves. A similar reversal should be accomplished in order to effectively break out of Plato's cave: the point is not to penetrate "true" external reality beyond the curved wall, but to take into account how our "objective" view of reality is already subjectivized, how it functions as the view from the standpoint of the impossible/monstrous Thing—the task is not to erase my subjective point-of-view, but to relocate it into the Thing itself, or, as medieval Christian mystics would have put it, the task is not to erase my subjectivity and immerse myself directly into the divine substance, but to become aware of how my view of God is simultaneously the view of God himself upon himself. Again, therein resides the lesson of the Klein bottle: insofar as my view of the curved wall inside the bottle originates in the twisted snout, it is the Real itself which observes itself on the wall of Plato's cave. In a homologous way, Bohr rejected the reproach that his interpretation of quantum physics involves subjectivism since it denies objective reality, making the collapse of the wave function dependent on measurement: he insisted on the objectivity of measurement (independency of the scientist's subjectivity), defining this objectivity as the fact that the measurement, no matter how often repeated at different times and places, always gives the same result. Is this not close to Lacan's early definition of the Real as that which always returns to its same place? Objectivity (of our knowledge), the fact that we are not caught in our subjective representations, is thus not to be looked for in the domain of "objective reality" independent of our activity, but in the whole situation into which we are included.

The feature which is irrepresentable in the Klein bottle (irrepresentable in our three-dimensional space) is the snout-like break through the outer skin, and this snout is the subject. When this snout turns back into the main body, we find ourselves inside, in a cave-like round space, whose openness is disturbed by the same snout seen from the inside and connecting the rounded top with the background circular wall—this inner circular space, like the inside of Plato's cave, is our reality, and looking at this wall of reality, the subject sees it as a complete image, i.e., it doesn't see the snout protruding out of it because the snout is the blind spot of the image, the subject's own inscription in the image.[11] From the inside, this snout is an empty tube, a subject ($), and from the outside (looked upon as it appears in the cave), it is an object, *objet a*, the subject's stand-in. The rounded enclosed surface that is our reality seems the very opposite of the modern scientific notion of an open "cold" universe: it brings back to mind the medieval drawings of the universe as a gigantic finite cupola on which stars are painted, and from where we can break through and see the chaotic infinite outside. Brought to the extreme, this vision gives us the impression of the so-called Concave Earth theory, popular in the obscurantist early twentieth-century pseudo-science, with many advocates among the Nazis. According to this theory, the Earth is on the inner instead of the outer side of a sphere, a hole in the vast eternal ice, and the Sun is in the middle of this hollow. (In Nazi Germany, they actually used mirrors and telescopes to try to look "across" the inside of the Earth and spot British ships in the North Sea.) One should notice that the proponents of this theory saw it as the Aryan answer to the Jewish-scientific vision of an infinite universe. So how can this closed universe generate the illusion of openness? Recall the ridiculously ingenious Christian reply to the Darwinist challenge. One of Darwin's contemporaries proposed a ridiculously perspicuous reconciliation between the Bible and evolutionary theory: the Bible is literally true, the world was created approximately 4,000 years BCE—so how can we explain the fossils? The solution is that they were directly created by God as fossils to give humanity a false sense of opening, of living in an older universe. In short, when God created the universe, he created traces of its imagined past. Post-Kantian transcendentalism answers the challenge of objective science in a similar way: if, for the theological literalists, God directly created fossils in order to expose men to the temptation of denying the divine creation, i.e., to test their faith, the post-Kantian transcendentalists conceive the spontaneous everyday "naïve" notion of objective reality existing independently of us as a similar trap, exposing humans to the test, challenging them to see through this "evidence" and grasp how reality is constituted by the transcendental subject. We should nonetheless insist that the Christian solution—meaningless as a scientific theory, of course—does contain a grain of truth: it provides an implicit adequate theory of ideology. Does every ideology not also directly create fossils, i.e., does it not create an imagined past which fits the present? This is why true historicity is opposed to evolutionist historicism, or, this is why, paradoxically, true historicity always asserts what French structuralism formulated as the "primacy of synchrony over diachrony." Usually, this primacy was taken to mean the ultimate denial of historicity in structuralism: a historical development can be reduced to the (imperfect) temporal deployment of a pre-existing atemporal matrix of all possible variations/combinations. This simplistic notion of the "primacy of synchrony over diachrony" overlooks the (properly dialectical) point, made long ago by (among others) T. S. Eliot, on how each truly new artistic phenomenon not only designates a break from the entire past, but retroactively changes this past itself. At every historical conjuncture, the present is not only the present, it also encompasses a perspective on the past immanent to it—after the disintegration of the Soviet Union in 1991, for example, the October Revolution is no longer the same historical event, i.e., it is (for the triumphant liberal-capitalist view) no longer the beginning of a new progressive epoch in the history of humanity, but the beginning of a catastrophic misdirection of history, which reached its end in 1991.

Thus, our universe of ideological meaning IS closed, its openness is illusory, the result of the invisibility of its limitation. Furthermore, it is not only that we do not perceive the limitation of our ideological universe of meaning; what we also don't perceive is the "snout," the blind spot of this universe. The exclusion of this object-snout is constitutive of the appearance of reality: since reality (not the Real) is correlative to the subject, it can only constitute itself through withdrawing from the object which "is" the subject, i.e., through withdrawing the subject's objectal correlate.

Here, we can see clearly the difference between the Moebius strip and the Klein bottle: in the Moebius strip, we pass from one side of the strip to the other, or from one term to its opposite, while in the Klein bottle, we pass from the hole in the midst of a circular body to the substance of this body itself, i.e., the void returns as the very body that envelops it. Only in this way do we arrive at subjectivity—why? The subject IS pure difference, and it emerges as such when this difference is no longer reduced to a difference between parts of some substantial content.

II The stupid God of quantum ontology

It is crucial to draw the ontological consequences of this metaphor of the Klein bottle, consequences which can be clearly deployed with reference to quantum physics. Let us take as our starting point Carlo Rovelli's advocacy of quantum gravity.[12] Rovelli tries to bring together the theory of relativity and quantum mechanics by positing the quantum nature of space and time: they are not a continuum that can be divided *ad infinitum*, there is a minimal unit of space-time which cannot be further divided. (Incidentally, this makes it easy to solve Zeno's paradox of Achilles being unable to catch up a turtle—Achilles cannot do it only if we presume the infinite divisibility of time and space.) The consequences of this premise are radical. First, they undermine the hypothesis of the Big Bang, the infinitely condensed point of matter, which then exploded and gave birth to our universe. If time and space are quantum entities, they cannot be infinitely condensed. There is a limit of their density defined by the minimal quanta of space and time (they cannot get smaller than their quanta), which means that a different cosmological model imposes itself, that of the "aeons" of the universe and of the Big Bounce: a universe is collapsing into a black hole, but this contraction can never reach its zero-point since its quantum poses a limit, so after a certain point it has to "bounce back" and explode. The ultimate implication of quantum gravity is that space and time are not the basic constituents of reality: if space-time is composed of quantum waves (whose convolutions give birth to gravity, so we get the unity of quantum mechanics and relativity), then the last duality between space-time and the particles or waves which fluctuate IN space-time has to be abandoned. This is how Rovelli answers the big question "What is the world made of?":

> [T]he particles are quanta of quantum fields; light is formed by quanta of a field; space is nothing more than a field, which is also made of quanta; and time emerges from the processes of this same field. In other words, the world is made entirely from quantum fields.
>
> These fields do not live *in* spacetime; they live, so to speak, one on top of the other: fields on fields. The space and time that we perceive in large scale are our blurred and approximate images of one of these quantum fields: the gravitational field.
>
> Fields that live on themselves, without the need of a spacetime to serve as a substratum, as a support, and which are capable by themselves of generating spacetime, are called "covariant quantum fields."[13]

Even the most elementary duality between space-time and the particles (or fields made of waves) which move and vibrate IN space-time thus falls away in this "basic grammar of the world"[14]—at this level, one has to relinquish "the idea of space, and of time, as general structures within which to frame the world."[15] Quantum fields do not vibrate IN space-time, they are themselves segments of space-time—what we encounter here is yet another version of the reversal that characterizes the Moebius strip: if we begin with our common reality, where things and processes take place IN space and time, and then progress in our scientific analysis to the very basic constituents of reality, we encounter in the domain of waves (what we experience in our ordinary reality as) their temporal/spatial form as another element of content, as another quantum wave function. Space-time is (in our reality) the form/container of material processes and (at the most basic level) these processes themselves at their most fundamental—again, form is inscribed into its content as one of its moments. The big question here is, of course, how do time and space—in the usual sense, as the formal containers IN which material processes take place—emerge out of this basic reality of quantum fields? Rovelli's answer:

> What does "the passage of time" mean, if time plays no part in the fundamental description of the world? The answer is simple. The origin of time may be similar to that of heat: it comes from averages of many microscopic variables.[16]

The underlying idea is that "it is always heat and only heat that distinguishes the past from the future."[17] When a process is fully reversible (like moving up and down, etc.), there is no temporality proper in it; the future and the past coincide since we can change the direction of time and the process remains the same. Only when a process is irreversible—say, when we burn a piece of paper to ashes and then cannot change the ashes back into paper—do we get time, i.e., a temporal movement that proceeds univocally from the past to the future. Such temporal processes only take place at the macroscopic level, in our ordinary reality, since at the microscopic level of the "basic texture" of reality (quantum waves), loops are always closed, and processes are reversible. Irreversible processes always and by definition involve heat—when an object burns, we cannot travel back and reconstitute it; when an object loses heat (cools), it cannot be heated again without external intervention; etc. Heat arises when subatomic particles closely mingle and bump into one another, and such processes take place only above the basic texture of the universe, at a macroscopic level where we are not dealing with single particles but with averages of millions of single occurrences:

> As long as we have a *complete* description of a system, all of the variables of the system are on the same footing; none of them acts as a time variable. That is to say: none is correlated to irreversible phenomena. But as soon as we describe the system by means of averages of many variables, we have a preferred variable that functions like common time. A time along which heat is dissipated. The time of our everyday experience.
>
> Hence time is not a fundamental constituent of the world, but it appears because the world is immense, and we are small systems within the world,

interacting only with macroscopic variables that average among innumerable small, microscopic variables. We, in our everyday lives, never see a single elementary particle, or a single quantum of space. We see stones, mountains, the faces of our friends—and each of these things we see is formed by myriads of elementary components. We are always correlated with averages: they disperse heat and, intrinsically, generate time...

Time is an effect of our overlooking of the physical microstates of things. Time is information we don't have.

Time is our ignorance.[18]

In order to account for the passage from quantum reality to ordinary reality, Rovelli thus relies on the notion of statistical average, which is obviously not adequate: when we perceive an object as a chair or a table, or already a letter as a letter, we perceive an idealized form, which persists as the same and is in its identity more than an average. Macroscopic "illusions" based on our ignorance have a status and an efficiency of their own. The key question is therefore: why does a "complete description" not include high-level orders? Rovelli seems to imply that "completeness" covers just the basic texture of quantum reality, without any higher-level phenomena (such as organic life or the universe of signification) since they take place in temporal reality and are thus based on ignoring the physical microstates of things. Just think about language alone: in order to get the meaning of spoken words, we have to ignore their microscopic reality (of sound vibrations, etc.). Or, at a more elementary level, think about desert sand moved by strong wind: it seems to our view that the same form is slowly moving across the desert, although a more "complete" description would have to cover myriads of grains of sand moving and rubbing each other. From the Hegelian standpoint, ignoring the more basic level is a positive condition of perceiving the higher unity, so a truly "complete description" would have to incorporate this ignorance—there is no "synthesis" between the basic quantum wave level and, say, our speech that produces meaning. To get one, we have to ignore the other. This brings us to Hegel's notion of totality, which also includes levels grounded on ignoring parts of reality. Rovelli writes that

> we must not confuse what we know about a system with the absolute state of the same system. What we know is something concerning the relation between the system and ourselves.[19]

But is in this sense the "absolute state" of a system not constrained to the interaction among its basic constituents, without regard to the higher-level orders that arise out of it? So does the "absolute state" not leave out of consideration many "higher" levels? How can we consider a description of language activity that leaves out of consideration the effect of meaning "complete"? To avoid these problems, Rovelli brings in the orderly arrangements of elementary particles:

> As Democritus said, it is not just a question of these atoms but also of the *order* in which they are arranged. Atoms are like the letters in an alphabet: an extraordinary

alphabet, so rich as to be able to read, reflect and even think about itself. We are not atoms, we are *orders* in which atoms are arranged, capable of mirroring other atoms and mirroring ourselves.[20]

Arrangements, of course, begin at the basic quantum level, but—from our standpoint, at least—crucial arrangements take place at higher macroscopic levels, precisely like the letters of an alphabet—so how come that (following Democritus) Rovelli uses the metaphor of the alphabet to describe the arrangements of the very basic quantum level of reality? Let's return to his claim that "we must not confuse what we know about a system with the absolute state of the same system. What we know is something concerning the relation between the system and ourselves." What Rovelli calls the "absolute state" is obviously the "basic grammar of the world" made of quantum waves, in contrast to our knowledge, which is limited to the relations of a given system, to its interactions with its surroundings; however, with regard to man, he simultaneously posits that the nature of man

> is not his internal structure but the network of personal, familial and social interactions within which he exists. It is these which "make" us, these which guard us. As humans, we are that which others know of us, that which we know of ourselves, and that which others know about our knowledge. We are complex nodes in a rich web of reciprocal information.[21]

It is not only that these interactions occur at the higher macroscopic level; one should also add that when Rovelli talks about all the permutations of knowledge (what others know of us, what we know of ourselves, what others know about our knowledge ...), which means all the permutations of the symbolic "registration" of the states of things, he forgets to add the crucial level, that of the "objectivized" knowledge, knowledge embodied in the virtual entity which Lacan calls the big Other. When I talk about other people's opinions, it is never only a matter of what I, you, or other individuals think, but also a matter of what the impersonal "one" thinks. When I violate a certain rule of decency, I never simply do something that the majority of others do not do—I do what "one" doesn't do. Recall sounds like "Oops!," which we feel obliged to utter when we stumble or do something stupid—the mystery here is that it is also possible for another person, one who merely witnesses our blunder, to say "Oops!" *for us*, and it works. The function of the "Oops!" is to enact the symbolic registration of the stupid stumbling: the virtual big Other has to be informed about it. Recall also the typical tricky situation in which all the people in a closed group know some dirty detail (and they also know that all the others know it), but when one of them inadvertently blurts out this detail, they nonetheless all feel embarrassed—why? If no one learned anything new, why do all feel embarrassed? Because they can no longer *pretend* that (or act as if) they do not know it—in other words, because now *the big Other knows it*. Therein resides the lesson of Hans Christian Andersen's "Emperor's New Clothes": one should never underestimate the power of appearances. Sometimes, when we inadvertently disturb the appearances, the thing itself behind them also falls apart. The big Other is fragile, insubstantial, properly *virtual* in the sense that its status is that of a subjective presupposition. It exists only insofar as subjects *act as if it exists*. Its status is similar to that of an ideological cause, such as Communism or the Nation: it is the substance of the individuals who recognize themselves in it, the ground of their entire existence, the point of reference which provides the ultimate horizon of meaning to their lives, something for which these individuals are ready to give their lives, yet the only thing that really exists are these individuals and their activity, so this substance is actual only insofar as individuals believe in it and act accordingly.

So, what does this knowledge of the big Other have to do with quantum physics? Everything, since it directly concerns the so-called collapse of the wave function (which, as Rovelli is right to point out, involves a massive reduction of information): when quantum physicists try to explain the collapse of the wave function, they resort time and again to the metaphor of language—this collapse occurs when a quantum event "leaves a trace" in the observation apparatus, when it is "registered" in some way. We obtain here a relationship of externality; an event becomes fully itself, it realizes itself, only when its external surroundings "take note" of it; and this echoes the process of symbolic realization, in which an event fully actualizes itself only through its symbolic registration, its inscription into a symbolic network, which is external to it. There are large debates about the exact moment of the collapse of the wave function; the three main replies perfectly fit the Lacanian triad of the Real/Symbolic/Imaginary: the Real of measurement (when the result is registered in the measuring machine, establishing the contact between the quantum micro-reality and the ordinary macro-reality), the Imaginary of perception (when this result is perceived by a consciousness), the Symbolic of inscription (when the result is inscribed into the language shared by the community of researchers). Does this debate not signal a kind of ontological inconsistency in quantum physics? Quantum physics accounts for the collapse of the wave function (and thus for the emergence of "ordinary" reality) in the terms of the act of perception/registration (a single reality emerges through the act of measurement), but it then explains (or rather describes) this measurement in the terms of the ordinary reality, which only emerges through it (the measuring machine is hit by electrons, etc.), and this obviously involves a *circulus vitiosus*.

What this means is that the big problem is not how we can pass from the classic universe to the universe of quantum waves, but exactly the opposite—why and how the quantum universe itself immanently requires the collapse of the wave function, its "decoherence" into the classic universe, i.e., why and how the collapse is inherent to the quantum universe. Instead of just standing in awe in front of the wonder of the quantum universe, we should turn our perspective around and perceive as the true wonder the rise of our "ordinary" spatiotemporal reality. It is not only that there is no classic reality which is not sustained by blurred quantum fluctuations; one should add that there is no quantum universe which is not always-already hooked onto a piece of classic reality. The problem of the collapse of the wave function through the act of measurement is that it has to be formulated in classic, not quantum, terms—this is why

> the collapse of the wave function occupies an anomalous position within quantum mechanics. It is *required* by the fact that observations occur, but it is not predicted by quantum theory. It is *an additional postulate, which must be made in order that quantum mechanics be consistent*.[22]

One should note this precise formulation: a measurement formulated in the terms of classic reality is necessary for quantum mechanics itself to be consistent, it is the addition of classic reality which "sutures" the quantum field. Which, then, is the status of "quantum reality," i.e., of the so-called wave function Ψ, which renders the panoply of superimposed states?

> Are we to regard Ψ as actually representing physical reality? Or is it to be viewed as being merely a calculational tool for working out probabilities of the results of experiments that *might* be performed, the results of these being "real," but not the wave function itself?
> ... [I]t was part of the Copenhagen interpretation of quantum mechanics to take this latter viewpoint, and, according to various other schools of thought also, Ψ is to be regarded as a calculational convenience with no ontological status other than to be part of the state of mind of the experimenter or theoretician.[23]

This reticence to concede any ontological status to Ψ "stems from the abhorrence felt by so many physicists that the state of the actual world could suddenly 'jump' from time to time in the seemingly random way that is characteristic of the rules of quantum measurement"[24]: in the act of measurement, the wave function "collapses," it is reduced to just one reality, so how can such an act affect objective reality, erasing the multiplicity of superimposed states? ("In quantum mechanics when we interact with a system, we don't only learn something, we also 'cancel' a part of the relevant information about the system"[25]—this reduction is unthinkable in our standard reality.) The most radical opposite version is that of the MWI (many-worlds interpretation), which admits no such reduction: ALL possibilities contained in a wave function are actualized. However, as we have already seen, the true opposite of the Copenhagen orthodoxy is not MWI, but the interpretation which, on the contrary, reads the wave function (the quantum space-time) as the ultimate reality, and conceives our spatiotemporal reality as a kind of ontological illusion, as a product of our ignorance and cognitive limitation. So which version is the right one, or at least the better one? To paraphrase Stalin, they are both worse, their very alternative is wrong—one should insist on the ultimate undecidability of this choice, none of the two levels should be elevated into the true reality.

This undecidability does not imply a symmetry of the two levels. As materialists, we should posit that there is nothing but quantum waves that forms the "basic grammar" of reality, there is no other reality, but this nothing is in itself a positive fact, which means that there must be some kind of a gap/cut in this "basic grammar," a gap/cut which opens up the space for the collapse of the wave function. This brings us back to the model of the Klein bottle: insofar as its rounded surface stands for the Real, i.e., the "mollusk" of the basic texture of quantum waves, and insofar as this texture is pre-ontological, a "less than nothing," the hole in its midst indicates that something, a kind of abyssal attractor, drags down the field, pushing "less than nothing" to Nothing, to the Void against the background of which something (our reality) may emerge. So we don't just have the duality of "infrastructural" quantum waves and a "superstructural" macroscopic reality: there is a third level, the abyssal Void, through which the pre-ontological Real is transubstantiated into macroscopic reality; through this transubstantiation, all the higher-level entities emerge, including the agents of observation/measurement of quantum waves, but also what we experience as the empty (spatial and temporal) form of macroscopic reality. Kant was right here—time and space are forms, not just the statistic average of space-time oscillations, and the enigma here is: how does this form detach itself from content and impose itself on all content as form? The answer is that the abyssal Void provides the distance from which form can appear as the external container of its content. At the most abstract level, the snout-like twist of the Klein bottle (rendered possible by the abyssal Void, which renders the "mollusk" of quantum waves unstable, incomplete) accounts for the rise of "objective" spatiotemporal reality out of this "mollusk." It is thus not that the "mollusk," the texture of quantum waves, happily vibrates and is just here and there accidentally punctured by an abyssal cut, which gives birth to a snout: in the unoriented closed circularity of the Klein bottle, the snout itself retroactively gives birth to the mollusk of the Real.

Notes

1 The research included in this chapter was funded by the Slovenian Research Agency (ARRS) under the research project "Language and Science: The Possibility of Realism in Modern Philosophy" (J6-7364).
2 See Cassandra Santiago and Sarah El Sirgany, "Scientists discover mysterious 'void' in Great Pyramid of Giza," CNN, updated November 3, 2017. Available at: http://edition.cnn.com/2017/11/02/world/new-void-in-pyramid-of-giza-trnd/index.html.
3 Frank Ruda, email to author, February 19, 2018.
4 Ibid.
5 Ibid.
6 Wallace Stevens, "Tea at the Palaz of Hoon," in *The Collected Poems* (New York: Alfred A. Knopf, 1971), 65.
7 Thomas Metzinger, *Being No One: The Self-Model Theory of Subjectivity* (Cambridge: MIT Press, 2004), 550.
8 Ibid., 551.
9 Ibid., 552.
10 Ibid., 557.
11 When, in a public talk, I have recently projected on the screen a short video clip displaying the gradual emergence of a Klein bottle out of a simple strip, the public reacted with embarrassed laughter—and they were right since the movement of tube-like forms penetrating themselves in a U-turn cannot but generate the impression that "something dirty is taking place, although we don't know precisely what"? (After the presentation, one member of the public approached me and told me that it looked to him as if the scene portrayed a man with a penis long enough for him to be able to twist it and penetrate himself anally...)
12 I must emphasize here two things. Rovelli himself points out that the theory of quantum gravity is one of the theories in competition with others (string theory, for example), and, as such, in no way universally accepted. (One should nonetheless take note that the 2017 Nobel Prize for physics was awarded to Rainer Weiss, Barry Barish and Kip Thorne for their discovery of gravitational waves: the so-called Lido

experiment they conducted detected ripples in the fabric of space-time.) Furthermore, I am, of course, not able to follow the mathematical details of this theory—I merely rely on its general description.
13 Carlo Rovelli, *Reality Is Not What It Seems* (London: Penguin Books, 2016), 167.
14 Ibid., 219.
15 Ibid., 169.
16 Ibid., 220–1.
17 Ibid., 221.
18 Ibid., 222–3.
19 Ibid., 223.
20 Ibid., 226.
21 Ibid., 227.
22 George Greenstein and Arthur G. Zajonc, *The Quantum Challenge: Modern Research on the Foundations of Quantum Mechanics* (Sudbury, MA: Jones and Bartlett, 1997), 187 (italics mine).
23 Roger Penrose, *Fashion, Faith, and Fantasy in the New Physics of the Universe* (Princeton: Princeton University Press, 2017), 198.
24 Ibid.
25 Ibid., 217.

Notes on Contributors

Miran Božovič is Professor of Philosophy at the University of Ljubljana. He has written numerous articles on the early modern philosophy. He is the editor of *Jeremy Bentham: The Panopticon Writings* (1995) and author of *The Utterly Dark Spot: Gaze and Body in Early Modern Philosophy* (2000).

Lee Braver is Professor of Philosophy at the University of South Florida. He is the author of *Groundless Grounds: A Study of Wittgenstein and Heidegger* (2012) and *A Thing of This World: A History of Continental Anti-realism* (2007), among other things.

Maurizio Ferraris teaches philosophy at the University of Turin, where he is President of the LabOnt (Laboratory of Ontology), founded in 1999 in order to revive philosophical realism. He coined the term "new realism" in 2011 and has written hundreds of articles and over fifty books, some of which have appeared in English, such as *Manifesto of New Realism* (2014) and *Positive Realism* (2015).

Markus Gabriel is Chair in Epistemology, Modern and Contemporary Philosophy at Bonn University. His publications in English include *Transcendental Ontology: Essays on German Idealism* (2011), *Fields of Sense: A New Realist Ontology* (2015), and *Why the World Does not Exist* (2015). With Slavoj Žižek, he is a co author of *Mythology, Madness and Laughter: Subjectivity in German Idealism* (2009).

Graham Harman is Distinguished Professor of Philosophy at the Southern California Institute of Architecture. His recent books are *Immaterialism: Objects and Social Theory* (2016), *Dante's Broken Hammer: The Ethics, Aesthetics, and Metaphysics of Love* (2016), and *The Rise of Realism*, co-authored with Manuel DeLanda (2017).

Adrian Johnston is Chair of and Professor in the Department of Philosophy at the University of New Mexico at Albuquerque and a faculty member at the Emory Psychoanalytic Institute in Atlanta. He is the author of *Adventures in Transcendental Materialism: Dialogues with Contemporary Thinkers* (2014). He is the co-author, with Catherine Malabou, of *Self and Emotional Life: Philosophy, Psychoanalysis, and Neuroscience* (2013). His recent books include *Irrepressible Truth: On Lacan's "The Freudian Thing"* (2017) and *A New German Idealism: Hegel, Žižek, and Dialectical Materialism* (2018).

Zdravko Kobe teaches German classical philosophy at the University of Ljubljana. He has published extensively on German classical philosophy, especially on Kant and Hegel. His latest book is *Automaton transcendentale III: Kant's Theory of Subject* (in Slovene, 2014).

Gregor Kroupa is a researcher at the Department of Philosophy, University of Ljubljana, Slovenia. His research focuses on the history of ideas and philosophy of language. He is the editor of the Slovenian translations of the works by Descartes, Bentham, d'Holbach, Condorcet, and Adam Smith. He has published several articles on early modern philosophy and is the author of *The Similar in the Dissimilar: On Metaphor in Early Modern Philosophy* (in Slovene, 2011).

Jure Simoniti is a researcher at the Department of Philosophy, University of Ljubljana, Slovenia. His main research topics are German idealism, philosophy of language, philosophy of science, realism, and theory of truth-values. His latest publications include *Die Philosophie der kleinsten Prätentiösität* (2014) and *The Untruth of Reality: The Unacknowledged Realism of Modern Philosophy* (2016).

Slavoj Žižek is a Senior Researcher at the University of Ljubljana, International Director of the Birkbeck Institute for the Humanities, and Professor of Philosophy and Psychoanalysis at the European Graduate School. His latest publications include *Less Than Nothing: Hegel and the Shadow of Dialectical Materialism* (2012), *Absolute Recoil* (2014), and *Disparities* (2016).

Index

a priori synthetic judgments 81–2, 117
a-subjective Real 148
Aarsleff, Hans 21
absolute
   absolute idealism of Hegel 161
   absolute knowing 148
   absolute otherness 46, 62
   absolute Outside 56–7, 60, 68n.21, 117–18
   absolute state of a system 205
   correlationism and the 122, 128–30
   myth of absolute interiority/exteriority 42
   of speculative realism 120
abyssal Void 207, 208
accidental encounters, key role of 160–1
actants, human beings as 109
actor-network theory 109
aesthetics 93, 108, 187, 190–1, 192
After Finitude 17n.17, 100, 106, 107, 113, 133
agential realism 102
aletheia 53, 54, 60, 155, 156
alteration 142n.41
analytic epistemology, error-first ontology and 153
analytic theory and practice 163
anamnesis theory 196
ancestral time 106
ancestrality 89, 106, 107, 116–17, 122–5
anorganicity 162
anti-humanism 101
anti-idealism 64
anti-natural subjectivity, natural objectivity and 168
anti-realism 42–3, 63–5, 87, 183–4
anti-verism 65
Antinomies of Pure Reason 167
anxious objects 93
appearances, power of 205
arbitrariness thesis 32

arche-fossils 1, 106, 107, 122
argumentation 136
Aristotle 4–11, 16n.4, 17n.16, 86
De arte combinatoria 27, 29, 31
artefacts 79–80
astrophysics 89
Augustine 73, 86
autopoiesis, Žižekian 162
Avant demain: Épigenèse et rationalité 165, 166, 169
Azzouni, Jody 181, 182

Badiou, Alain 113, 174
Balmès, François 157
Barad, Karen 102
Barthes, Roland 55, 56
The Battle of the Books 17n.17
Bayle, Pierre 6
being
   being-in-the-world 195
   existence and 185
   philosophies of 35–6, 93
   thought and 96
   time and 93–4
Being and Time 53, 94, 95, 101, 102, 109
beliefs, false 50
Benoist, Jocelyn 191
Berkeley, George 11–13, 22, 33, 77, 124
Bible 201
Big Bang hypothesis 202
big Other 205–6
biological plasticity 168, 169
biological transcendentals, hyponormative 169
biology 166, 168
The Birds 200
blind thought 28–9
bodies 6
Bohr, Niels 102, 200
Bonnet, Charles 12–13
Božovič, Miran 211 (*see also* chapter 1)

Brassier, Ray 1, 99
Braver, Lee 211 (*see also* chapter 5)
Brock, Stuart 180
Bubner, Rüdiger 192
Le Bureau des légendes 180

capitalism 197–8
Caputo, John D. 101
Carnap, Rudolf 180
Cartesian philosophy 2, 3, 4–5, 8–9, 76–7
categorical imperatives 92
Causes et raisons des îles désertes 57
Chanut, Pierre 2
characteristica universalis (CU) 23, 27, 28, 29–31, 32, 34
characters 28, 30
Christian incarnation, Greek recollection and 91–2
Christianity, the Darwinist challenge and 201
civil contract, domain of 45
classic realism 25
Cogito, ergo sum 147
cognition
    cognitive correlation 22
    cognitive sciences 198
    language and 32
    the subjectivity of 140n.22
Collins, Anthony 12
combinatorial logic 29
common sense 122, 131
communication, perils of 20
competence, as a praxis 80
complete concepts 25
comprehension 80
Concave Earth theory 200–1
concepts
    intuitions and 82
    Kant and 63
    knowledge and 77
    ontology and 78
    primative 29, 30
    pseudo-concepts 184
    reality and 27, 80
    spontaneity and 63, 64
Condillac, Étienne Bonnot de 21, 22, 23
Confessions 73
conscience, domain of 45–6
consciousness

correlationism and 19
    language and 22
    philosophies of 35–6
    realism and 102
Considérations sur les corps organisés 12
continental philosophy 99, 101
contracts in general, domain of 45
contradiction, principle of 120
A Contribution to the Rectification of the Public's Judgment of the French Revolution 44
convalidation 75
Copernican Revolution 87
correlationism
    the absolute and 119, 121–2
    anti-realism and 63–4
    consciousness and 19
    correlationist thesis 115, 116, 117–20
    defined 106
    Kant and 19, 124–5
    language and 19
    Meillassoux and 19, 35–6, 106
    realism and 124
    the subject and 87
    subjectivist metaphysics and 126, 134
    subjectivity and objectivity and 106–8, 118
    the thinking subject and 19
critical-dialectical naturalism 145–53, 153–7, 172
Critique of Judgment 105
The Critique of Pure Reason 21, 147, 166, 167
Critique of the Power of Judgment 168

daimons 7
Daniel, Gabriel 5–6, 13
Darwin, Charles 201
Dasein 101, 102, 103, 104, 109, 155
death
    the minds separation from the body at 13 (*see also* souls)
    Socrates's faking of 7–8
DeLanda, Manuel 99
Deleuze, Gilles 55–9, 60, 66, 99, 154–5, 157–8, 164
Delos, Heidegger's island of 53–5
déraison, irraison and 120, 131
derivation, reconstructive 120–1

Derrida, Jacques 55, 92–3, 99, 101–2, 103–4
Descartes, René
  among the Lapp shamans 2–5
  Aristotle as the reader of 5–11
  epistemology and 35
  ideas and 16n.4, 33
  knowledge and 86
  nature and 61
  quantifiable aspects of the world and 86
  transcendental idealism and 147
  truth and 127–8
  vortex theory 17n.16
desert islands
  as the absolute Outside of human jurisdiction 42
  Deleuze's oceanic islands 55–9
  of Fichte 44–7, 60
  happy isles of Nietzsche 47–53, 60, 66
  Heidegger's island of Delos 53–5
  of Marx 60
  pre-Kantian 68n.21
  as a reality without ideality 65–6
  subjectivity in excess and 60
  as a symptom of the already conquered and occupied world 60
determinism
  linguistic realism and 20–3, 29, 31–2, 38n.20, 38n.21
  naturalism and 167
detranscendentalization of reason 22–3
dialectical materialism 170–1
Dialogus 27
Dictionnaire historique et critique 6
Diderot, Denis 5
Difference and Repetition 157–8
Dionysos-Dithyrambs 52
A Discourse of Free-Thinking 12
Discourse on Method 8
The Diversity of Human Language-Structure and its Influence on the Mental Development of Mankind 21
divine intelligence 33
divine, Leibniz and the 32–4
dogmatism 104, 105, 108–9
domain of civil contract 45
domain of conscience 45–6
domain of contracts in general 45

domain of natural law 45
double expression 29
downward causation 160
Duns Scotus 10

"The Earliest System-Program of German Idealism" 150
Eleatic riddle 185, 186
Éléments de physiologie 5
Eliot, T.S. 201
embodied/disembodied minds 5–6
emergence 77
Encyclopedia of the Philosophical Sciences 150, 151, 152
epigenetics 166, 167, 168–9
epistemology
  Descartes and 35
  as first philosophy 146
  mysteries and 93
  ontology and 74–5, 77, 78, 79–80, 82
  term 73
errancy
  error-first ontology and 155
  ontological of Heidegger 154–5
  Ur-errancy 156, 157
  erring, human beings and 156
error-first ontology (EFO) 146, 153–7, 173
Essay concerning Human Understanding 2, 20, 23, 37n.6
Everett, Anthony 180
evil-first ethics (EFE) 173
evil, illness and 173
existence
  being and 185
  reality as 34
existential realism 42
experiences, transgressive realism and 89
expression, theory of 27
exteriority 77
external maps 199
external reality 90, 91–3, 195

factuality, principle of 118, 119–20, 121
Ferraris, Maurizio 102, 136, 182–4, 211
  (*see also* chapter 4)
Fichte, Johann Gottlob
  ascension to prominence of 135
  desert island of 44–7, 60
  Fichtean I 46, 61, 62, 64, 134

Kant, Hegel and 147, 148, 150, 151–2
Simondon and 159
subject and object and 41
fiction
novels 187, 188
reality and 187, 199
fictional characters 179, 180, 182
fictional, concept of 180–2
fictional objects 179–93
the imagination and 188–92
the philosophical category of 184
as a subset of nonexistent objects 180–5, 186
fictional realism 184
fields of sense (FOS) 186
firstness 76
Forster, Michael 21
Foucault, Michel 55
France
contemporary philosophy and 113
the French Republic as mind-dependent 182
structuralism 55, 137n.3, 201
freedom 43, 44
Frege, Gottlob 183
Freud, Sigmund 155–6, 157, 163
Friday, or, The Other Island 58–9
The Fundamental Concepts of Metaphysics 156
funerals, witnessing one's own 4, 5

Gabriel, Markus 211 (*see also* chapter 9)
Galileo Galilei 74, 89
Gassendi, Pierre 3, 17n.16
Ge-Stell 54, 60
General Science 34
The German Ideology 48
Germany
German hermeneutic philosophy 21, 22
German idealism 104
Popularphilosophie 136
givenness 100, 106, 107, 108, 110, 124
glorified body, philosophy of the 14–15
God
creating the universe 201
in a hyper-occasionalist world 132
ideas and 33
the Other and 92

Grabes, Herbert 188
great outdoors, ontological 153, 155
Greek Eleatics 185
Greek recollection, Christian incarnation and 91–2
Guardian 11
Guattari, Félix 164
Gulliver's Travels 17n.16

hallucinated objects 182
Hamann, Johann Georg 21
Harman, Graham 35–6, 211 (*see also* chapter 6)
Hegel, Georg Wilhelm Friedrich
absolute idealism of 161
critical-dialectical naturalism and 152
as a dialectical philosopher 150
human beings and 157
idealism of 161
Jena period 147–8
Kant, Fichte and 147, 148, 150, 151–2
knowledge and 96
Malabou and 168
nature and 47–8
necessity and 134
philosophical speculation and 149
philosophical trajectory of 150–1
principle of contradiction and 120
the real and 86
reason and 41
Simondon and 159, 160–1, 164
speculative dialectics of causality 173
substance and 161
totality and 204
transcendentalism and 146
Vorstellung 133, 136
Heidegger, Martin
being and 93–4
Dasein and 101, 109
desert island of 53–5, 60
Lacan and 156
later work of 93–4
metaphysics and 85
ontological errancy of 154–5
realism and 100, 102–3
reality and 89
the sciences and 91, 95
second thesis of hypertruth and 74

truth as *aletheia* 156
the world and 41
Herder, Johann Gottfried von 21
Hermann, Brigitte 5
hermeneutic philosophy, German 21, 22
hermeneutical objects 191
hermeneutics, new realist 81–3
Hermes 81
hidden technique 82
Hilflosigkeit 162, 163
Hirst, Damien 179, 180
Histoire de mon esprit ou le roman de la vie de René Descartes 5
historical materialism, of Marx 170, 173–4
historicity 201
Hitchcock, Alfred 199–200
Hobbes, Thomas 27, 32
Hölderlin, Friedrich 150
Homer 78, 179
Houellebecq, Michel 179, 187, 188, 191
"How Sentences Turn into Persons . . . On the Study of Literary Characters" 188
Huet, Pierre-Daniel 2, 4, 5
human beings (*see also* man)
 as actants 109
 continental philosophy and 101
 erring and 156
 human subjectivity 101, 155–6, 157
 intelligence of 157
 the transcendental and 110
Humboldt, Wilhelm von 20, 21, 22, 38n.20
Husserl, Edmund 19, 96, 101, 104, 106
hyper-chaos 130, 131
hypertruth 74, 75, 78–9, 82
hypotruth 73–4, 79, 82

ideal, and the real 16n.4
ideal objects 79
idealism
 anti-idealism 64
 German 104
 of Hegel 161
 of Kant 91
 Lawlor, Husserl and 106
 Leibniz and 34
 re-realization of the ideal 64
 realism and 32–5, 70n.73
 speculative 134

transcendental materialism as critical-dialectical naturalism and 147
ideas
 Descartes and 16n.4, 33
 God and 33
 things and 60
ideology, theory of 201
illness 163, 173
Imaginary of perception 206
imagination 188–92
in-betweenness 166
in-itself 119, 120, 121, 126–7, 131, 148
inanimate interactions 104–5
indetermination 167
L'individu et sa genèse physico-biologique 158, 159
L'individuation à la lumière des notions de forme et d'information 159
L'individuation psychique et collective 159–60, 162, 163, 164
individuation, Simondon and 157–65
infants, Simondonian 162
Innenwelt-Umwelt couple 156
inner voice 46
intelligence 33, 157
intelligibility, realness and 93
interaction 77
interpretation 81, 82, 190, 191
intersubjectivity 58
Introduction to Kant's Anthropology (Introduction à l'Anthropologie) 166
intuition of essences 104
intuitions, concepts and 82
invalidation 75
Inwagen, Peter van 189
irraison, déraison and 120, 131

Johnston, Adrian 211 (*see also* chapter 8)
Jonas, Hans 16n.4
judgments,
 a priori synthetic 81–2, 117
 constituting objects 82

Kant, Immanuel
 anti-realism and 43, 64, 87
 Antinomies of Pure Reason 167
 concepts and 63
 Copernican turn of 114

correlationism and 19, 124–5
critical philosophy of 165–6
Critique of Pure Reason 21, 147, 166, 167
epigenesis and 169
epistemological power of intellectual intuition and 147
Hegel, Fichte and 147, 148, 150, 151–2
the ideal and the real and 16n.4
idealism of 91
knowledge and 87
the logical and the real possibility 128
Malabou and 169–70
Meillassoux and 138n.11
metaphysics and 85
morality and 43–4, 92
noumenon and 87, 140n.25
a priori synthetic judgments and 81–2
realism and 102–3, 104
refutation of the ontological proof 116
spontaneity and 61–2
subject and object and 41
the subjectivity of cognition and 140n.22
transcendental idealism and 89, 146, 147, 174
transcendentalism of 174
Kierkegaard, Søren 91, 92, 95
Klein bottle model 198, 199, 200, 202, 207
knowledge
  absolute knowing 148
  coming after the known thing 78
  concepts and 77
  Descartes and 86
  the elimination of the otherness of the object of 96
  individuation and 164
  Kant and 87
  new 31
  objectivized 205
  scientific 105
  thinking-as-knowing 164
Kobe, Zdravko 211 (*see also* chapter 7)
Kritisches Journal der Philosophie 148
Kroupa, Gregor 212 (*see also* chapter 2; preface)
Kuhn, Thomas Samuel 91, 95

labor
  historical materialism and 173–4
  voluntary 197
Lacan, Jacques 56, 154, 155, 156, 161, 199, 200
Lafont, Christina 21
language(s)
  arbitrariness of 27
  as calculus 27–31
  cognition and 32
  conceptual character of 31–2
  consciousness and 22
  correlationism and 19
  the mind and 22
  natural 28, 29
  philosophy of 19, 20, 36
  symbols of a 27
  things and 27
  thought and 21, 22
  truth and 27–8, 31, 34
  universal 30
Lapland, Lapp shamans 2–5
Latour, Bruno 101, 102, 107, 109
Lawlor, Leonard 99–110
legal legitimacy 45
Leibniz, Gottfried Wilhelm von 27–34, 86
Lessing, Gotthold Ephraim 131, 133
Lévi-Strauss, Claude 41, 55–6
Levinas, Emmanuel 90, 96
life, as a contingent transcendental 170
linguistic correlation 22
linguistic determinism
  language, consciousness and 22, 23
  linguistic realism and 20–3, 29, 31–2, 38n.20, 38n.21
linguistic idealism 21
linguistic ontology, of Leibniz 23–7
linguistic philosophy, new 21
linguistic realism 20–3, 29, 31–2, 38n.20, 38n.21
linguistic relativity, principle of 20
linguistic turn 19, 21, 37n.6
lived experience 155
Locke, John 2, 16n.4, 20, 22, 23–4, 25, 36
logic
  combinatorial 29
  divine intellect and 33
  Phenomenology and 151
  Philosophy of the Real and 174

The Logic of Sense 57, 158
The Logical Structure of the World 180
Logics 183
Lunar philosophy 10

Maat, Jaap 26
Macron, Emmanuel 180, 182, 189–90, 192–3
maintenance condition, anti-realism 183–4
Malabou, Catherine 165–71
Malebranche, Nicolas 8–9, 60, 61
man (*see also* human beings)
    without body 1–2
    the world and 41–2, 56
The Map and the Territory 179, 186, 188
Martin, Jed 179, 180, 186, 187–92, 193
Marx, Karl
    desert island of 60
    historical materialism of 170, 173–4
    idealist methodology of 146–7
    nature and 48
    reason and 41
    social labouring and 173–4
    "Theses on Feuerbach" 147, 149
master-figures 197
materialism, dialectical 170–1
mathematics 28, 108, 168
McDowell, John Henry 89
meaning, not determining reference 26–7
meaningfulness, of encounters 90
Meditations on First Philosophy 2, 8
Meillassoux, Quentin
    anti-correlationist ancestral thinking 89
    correlationism and 19, 35–6, 106
    the great outdoors and 34
    inanimate objects and 104–5
    Kant and 138n.11
    Malabou and 170
    naïve realism and 107, 125, 135
    object-oriented ontology (OOO), dogmatism and 106–9
    realism and 100–1
    speculative realism and 1, 136, 153
    (*see also* chapter 7)
Meinong, Alexius 180
Mersenne, Father 3, 7
mesotruth 74–5, 82

meta-hermeneutical objects 191
meta-transcendentalism 173
metafictional analysis 190, 191
Metakritik 21
Métamorphoses de l'intelligence: Que faire de leur cerveau bleu? 165, 166
metaphysics
    Heidegger and 85
    impossibility of 116
    metaphysical theory 2
    old: realism and 101–6
    in philosophy 85–6
    subjectivist metaphysics 118, 119, 126, 134
Metzinger, Thomas 198–9
"Michel Tournier and the World without Others" 57, 58
Milner, Jean-Claude 55
minds
    autonomy from language 20
    and bodies 6
    embodied/disembodied 5–6
    language and 22
    mind-dependence 182–3
    separation from the body at death 13
    as a thinking thing 6
modernity 60, 63, 147, 152
Moebius strip 196, 197–8, 202, 203
moral law 43–4, 46
morality, Kant and 43, 44, 92
MWI (many-worlds interpretation) 207
myth 196
Mythologies 56

naïve realism 19, 103, 107, 113, 120, 125, 135, 181, 182
natural languages 28, 29
natural laws 45, 130, 131
natural objectivity, anti-natural subjectivity and 168
natural objects 79, 80, 82
natural sciences 152–3, 167
natural substances, spiritual subjects and 145–53
naturalism 136, 145–53, 153–7, 167, 169, 172
nature
    Descartes and 61
    Hegel and 47–8

Marx and 48
non-existence of 56
nurture and 167
philosophy of 152
negative realism 76, 77
Neo-Meinongianism 180
neuroplasticity 167
neutral realism 189
New Essays on Human Understanding 24, 27, 31
Newton, Isaac 74
Newtonian cosmology 17n.16
Nietzsche, Friedrich 41, 47–53, 60, 66, 92–3, 182
nihilism 49–50
nominal definition, of a thing 26
non-existence
    Eleatic riddle and 185, 186
    fictional objects and 179
nonhuman objects 44
noumenon 87, 140n.25
Nouveaux mémoires pour servir à l'histoire du cartésianisme 2, 5
novels 187, 188
nurture, nature and 167

The Object of Psychoanalysis 156
object-oriented ontology (OOO) 100, 101, 103–4, 106–9
object-oriented philosophy 108
objective reality 200
objectivity 181, 182, 189
objectivity, correlationism and 106–8, 118
object(s)
    anxious objects 93
    artefacts 79–80
    formal theory of 180
    hallucinated 182
    hermeneutical 191
    ideal objects 79
    inanimate objects 104–5
    judgments constituting 82
    meta-hermeneutical objects 191
    natural objects 79, 80, 82
    nonhuman objects 44
    object relations 42
    social objects 78, 79–80, 182
    subjects and 41, 49, 51–2, 53–5, 118
    that exist and do not exist 186

occasionalism 132
Of Grammatology 103
"On Judgment and Being" 150
"On the Essence of Truth" 155
ontology
    epistemology and 74–5, 77, 78, 79–80, 82
    error-first ontology (EFO) 146, 153–7, 173
    firstness as 76
    object-oriented ontologists 101
    ontological ontogeny 164
    ontological proof 116, 138n.11
    ontological realism 181, 182
    ontological relativism 186
    ontology-first approach to philosophy 36
    term 73
    truth and 79
organic, and the anorganic 162
organic dysfunctions 162–3
Others/otherness
    absolute 46, 62
    assimilation of into the same 96
    big Other 205–6
    God and 92
    of the world 44
Outside, absolute 56–7, 60, 68n.21, 117–18

Pandora's Hope 102
paradise 14–15
Parmenedean Thinkability Principle 86
Parmenidean realism 88
Parmenides 86
perceptions 76, 81
Peripateticism 3, 4–5
persistence 77
phenomena 87, 90
phenomenal self 199
phenomenology 21, 151
Phenomenology of Spirit 147, 148, 150–1, 159
The Phenomenon of Life: Toward a Philosophical Biology 16n.4
Philaletes 24
Philosophical Fragments 91
Philosophical Snuff 6, 7, 11–12
Philosophical Souls 11
philosophical speculation 116, 149, 153–4

Index

philosophy of life 16n.4
Philosophy of Nature 152
Philosophy of the Real 151–2, 159, 174
philosophy(ies)
    Cartesian philosophy 2, 3, 4–5, 8–9, 76–7
    of consciousness and being 35–6, 93
    continental philosophy 99, 101
    German hermeneutic 21, 22
    of language 19, 20, 36
    ontology-first approach to 36
    post-critical 148
    post-Kantian 49
    science and 114
pineal gland 12, 13
plasticity
    biological 168, 169
    epigenetics and 167
Plato 7–8, 16n.4, 31, 85–6, 105, 179, 180, 196
Plato's cave 196, 198, 200
poiesis 80–1
politics, imagination and 192
Popularphilosophie 136
positive realism 76–7
The Possibility of an Island 187, 188
postmodernism 196
power 55
praxis, competence as a 80
preformationism 169
pretense-theory 193n.11
Priest, Graham 180
primitive concepts 29, 30
principle of contradiction 120
principle of factuality 118, 119–20, 121
principle of linguistic relativity 20
Principles of Philosophy, Part One 8
Project for a Scientific Psychology 163
property rights 45
propositions 78
pseudo-concepts 184
psyche 163
Psycho 199–200
psychoanalysis, individuation and 163
public sphere, as fiction 193

quantum gravity 202
quantum mechanics 207
quantum physics 200, 202–8

quantum waves 206, 208
questioning 86
Quid sit idea 24

Ralón, Laureano 99–110
rational argumentation 120
rational discourse 115
rationalism, early modern 19
real, and the ideal 16n.4
real definition, of a thing 26
realism (*see also* anti-realism)
    agential 102
    classic 25
    consciousness and 102
    correlationism and 124
    dogmatic or naïve 103
    existential 42
    fictional realism 184
    Heidegger and 100, 102–3
    idealism and 32–5, 70n.73
    the infinite and 96
    linguistic realism 20–3, 29, 31–2, 38n.20, 38n.21
    meaning of 99–100, 101
    Meillassoux and 100–1
    naïve realism 19, 103, 107, 113, 120, 125, 181, 182
    negative realism 76, 77
    neutral realism 189
    new realism 73
    and the old metaphysics 101–6
    ontological realism 181, 182
    Parmenidean realism 88
    positive realism 76–7
    pre-critical naïve 19
    Simondon and 160
    speculative realism 1, 107–8, 153 (*see also* chapter 7)
    subjectivization of 200
    transcendentalism and 100
    transgressive realism 88–90, 93
reality
    concepts and 27, 80
    as existence 34
    external 90, 91–3, 195
    fiction and 187, 199
    Heidegger and 89
    objective reality 200
    the subject and 201

totalization of 66
truth and 64, 65, 66, 77, 79, 80
reality-appearance-distinction 179
Reals 148, 151–2, 159, 174, 206, 207
reason, detranscendentalization of 22–3
reason, Hegel/Marx and 41
reasoning 27, 29
relativism, ontological 186
reminiscence 31
Republic 7, 86, 180
resistance 77
retrojection 130
Revue philosophique de la France et de l'étranger 158
Rorty, Richard 19
Rosenberg, Harold 93
Rosicrucians, Brotherhood of the 3, 4
Rovelli, Carlo 202, 204–5, 206

Sartre, Jean-Paul 155
Saussure, Ferdinand de 103
scandal, philosophy's response to 85–6
Schelling, F.W.J. 130, 147, 148, 150, 159, 161, 168
scholasticism 20
Schopenhauer, Athur 41, 67n.15
science
    astrophysics 89
    cognitive sciences 198
    General Science 34
    Heidegger and 91, 95
    knowledge and 105
    natural sciences 152–3, 167
    normal science 95
    philosophy and 114
    quantum physics 200, 202–8
    speculative realism and 131
    unlocking the power of 29, 34
Science of Logic 150, 151
Searle, John 182–4, 193n.11
secondary subjectivity 59
secondness 78, 79, 80
Sein 104, 109
self-awareness, post-Kantian 42
self-determination 43, 167–8
Seminar II 56
signification 20
signifiers 199
signs 27–8

Simondon, Gilbert 154, 157–65
Simoniti, Jure 16n.4, 212 (*see also* chapter 3; preface)
snuff 6, 7, 11–12
social facts 183, 192
social objects 78, 79–80, 182
social ontology, modelled on anti-realism 183–4
Socrates 7–8, 105
Sojourns 53
souls
    entering other bodies 12
    leaving and returning to bodies 6, 7, 9, 11
    post-mortem fate of 14
Sources of the Self: The Making of the Modern Identity 16n.4
space, time and 203–4, 207, 208
space travellers, Cartesian 7, 8, 9–11
speaking, thinking and 28–9
speculation, philosophical 149
speculative idealism 134
speculative materialism 108, 131
speculative philosophy 116, 149, 153–4
speculative realism 1, 131, 153 (*see also* chapter 7)
Speculative Realism Workshop at Goldsmiths, University of London (2007) 107–8
SPIELRAUM 191–2
Spinozism controversy 133
spiritual subjects, natural substances and 145–53
Spiritual Words 11
spontaneity
    concepts and 63, 64
    as a mark of the modern man having lost the certitude of predestination 61–2
    of the modern subject 62–4
    suppression of 64
    of truth 64
Strawson *et al.* 146
structuralism, French 55, 137n.3, 201
stupidity, individuation and 158
subjectivist metaphysics 118, 119, 126, 134
subjectivity
    of cognition 140n.22
    correlationism and 106–8, 118

human 101, 155–6, 157
secondary 59
transcendental 101, 142n.46, 173
subject(s)
correlationism and 87
as an ideality without reality 65–6
individuals qualifying as 158
objects and 41, 49, 51–2, 53–5, 118
reality and the 201
self-determining 167–8
truth and 62
Submission 187
substance 161
substantial-in-itself 148
supernatural phenomena 3
Swift, Jonathan 17n.16, 17n.17
Symbolic of inscription 206
symbolic realization 206
symbols
expressivity of 28, 29
of a language 27
mathematical 28
universal symbolism 29
synthetic judgments, *a priori* 81–2, 117

Talking About Nothing: Numbers, Hallucinations and Fictions 181
Taylor, Charles 16n.4
technology 73, 80
"Theses on Feuerbach" 147, 149
things
ideas and 60
language and 27
nominal definition of a thing 26
signs and 27–8
thing-in-itself 58–9, 71n.76, 102, 103, 104–6, 108–9, 115
things–ideas–language triangle 23–7, 30, 31
thinking
the call to 95
correlationism the thinking subject 19
minds as a thinking thing 6
speaking and 28–9
thinkability 82–8
thinking-as-knowing 164
as thoughtless 94
without speaking 22

thirdness 80
Thomasson, Amie 189
thought(s)
the ability to read the thoughts of others 2, 4
absolutization/relativization of 128–9
being and 96
blind thought 28–9
language and 21, 22
subjective forms of 114–15
thinking as thoughtless 94
thought experiments 1, 16n.4
Thus Spoke Zarathustra 49
time
ancestral thesis and 115–17
ancestral time 106
being and 93–4
space and 203–4, 207, 208
tool-analysis 102
Topology and Time 161
total flight simulator, metaphor of 199
totality 204
totalization 60, 61, 62, 66
Tournier, Michel 57, 58–9
transcendentalism
biology and 166
epigenetics and 168–9
Hegel and 146
human beings and 110
hyper- and a hypo-normative 169
L'individuation psychique et collective and 164
Kantian transcendental idealism 89, 146, 147, 174
Malabou and 165–71
meta-transcendentalism 173
positive features of modified transcendentalism 172–3
Post-Kantian 201
realism and 100
the status of being and 173
the transcendental condition 133
Transcendental Deduction 138n.11
transcendental extinction 1
transcendental materialism as critical-dialectical naturalism 145–53, 154, 172
transcendental phenomenology 101, 109

transcendental philosophy 19, 101
transcendental subjectivity 101,
    142n.46, 173
transcendentals 173
    what it is not 171–2
transgressive philosophers and
    philosophizing 93–7
transgressive realism 88–90, 93
Tristes tropiques 55
truth
    as *aletheia* 156
    authentic scene of 1
    demonstration of a 30
    Descartes and 127–8
    as event 55
    hypertruth 74, 75, 78–9, 82
    hypotruth 73–4, 79, 82
    ideas, things and 22
    as immediate correspondence 60
    language and 27–8, 31, 34
    legitimizing its place in the world 60
    mesotruth 74–5, 82
    in modernity 63
    new concept of 61
    ontology and 79
    reality and 64, 65, 66, 77, 79, 80
    secondness and 79
    spontaneity of 64
    the subject and 62
    surplus of 66
    three theories of 73–6
    truth bearers 75–7
    truth-events 174
    truth-in-itself 42–3, 65
    truth makers 75–6, 80–1
    truth tellers 75–6, 78–80
    two modes of 50–1
Tyssot de Patot, Simon 13–15

Uexküll, Jakob von 156
unamendability 76, 77
universal symbolism 29
*The Untruth of Reality: The
    Unacknowledged Realism of Modern
    Philosophy* 16n.4
Ur-errancy 156, 157

verification, positive theory of 75
*La Vie, les avantures et le Voyage de
    Groenland du Révérend Père
    Cordelier Pierre de Mésange* 13
Voiage du Monde de Descartes (*The Voyage
    to the World of Descartes*) 5–11
volunteering 197
Vorstellung 133, 136
vortex theory 17n.16
*Voyages et avantures de Jacques
    Massé* 14
La vraie méthode 28

wave function 206, 207
"Whither the Transcendental?: Hegel,
    Analytic Philosophy, and the
    Prospects of a Realist
    Transcendentalism Today" 145,
    146, 153, 154–5, 157, 164, 167,
    171, 173
wisdom, philosophy and 105
wonder 86
words and ideas, things and 23–7, 31
Workmanship of the Understanding 25
The World 6, 9, 10
world, practical totalization of the 62–4

Žižek, Slavoj 161–2, 212 (*see also* chapter
    10)
Zollikon Seminars 156

www.ingramcontent.com/pod-product-compliance
Lightning Source LLC
Chambersburg PA
CBHW072230290426

44111CB00012B/2036